Foundation ActionScript Animation

Making Things Move!

Keith Peters

Foundation ActionScript Animation: Making Things Move!

ISBN-13 (pbk): 978-1-59059-518-3
ISBN-10 (pbk): 1-59059-518-1

Printed and bound in the United States of America 9 8 7 6 5 4

Distributed to the book trade worldwide by Springer-Verlag New York, Inc., 233 Spring Street, 6th Floor, New York, NY 10013. Phone 1-800-SPRINGER, fax 201-348-4505, e-mail orders-ny@springer-sbm.com, or visit www.springeronline.com.

For information on translations, please contact Apress directly at 2560 Ninth Street, Suite 219, Berkeley, CA 94710. Phone 510-549-5930, fax 510-549-5939, e-mail info@apress.com, or visit www.apress.com.

The source code for this book is freely available to readers at www.friendsofed.com in the Downloads section.

Credits

Lead Editor
Chris Mills

Technical Reviewer
Todd Yard

Editorial Board
Steve Anglin, Dan Appleman, Ewan Buckingham, Gary Cornell, Tony Davis, Jason Gilmore, Jonathan Hassell, Chris Mills, Dominic Shakeshaft, Jim Sumser

Project Managers
Laura Cheu and Richard Dal Porto

Copy Edit Manager
Nicole LeClerc

Copy Editors
Marilyn Smith, Ami Knox, and Nicole LeClerc

Assistant Production Director
Kari Brooks-Copony

Production Editor
Kelly Winquist

Compositor
Dina Quan

Proofreader
Elizabeth Berry

Indexer
John Collin

Cover Image Designer
Corné van Dooren

Interior and Cover Designer
Kurt Krames

Manufacturing Director
Tom Debolski

To Kazumi and Kristine, who saw way too much of the back of my head silhouetted by a computer monitor while I was writing this. OK, now we are going to the park.

CONTENTS

FOREWORD

There is a magical line that separates artist from artisan—a line conceived by a spark of creativity but carved, laboriously, by boundless passion, energy, and dedication. The artist exudes an envious ability to simultaneously inspire awe, impart experience, and evoke emotion in others. Whereas once the title was reserved for the master painter, sculptor, or architect, we now have a wider appreciation of what comprises art and thus what comprises the artist.

A mere century ago, we saw films as absolute, objective slices of reality—as documents devoid of artistry. Today, we can appreciate their subjective nature and the many intricacies that separate a master work from a home movie. This was not always so. When Louis and Auguste Lumiere first showed their film of the arrival of an express train at Lyons station, the audience fled the theater in terror, afraid for their lives at the sight of the oncoming train. Today, we know better. We know how to "read" film. We are film-literate. But we cannot yet say the same thing about programming.

Today, we look upon programming as a purely technical pursuit. We talk of a divide between the creative and the technical, and lump programmers in the latter. The programmer is today as the filmmaker was early last century: an artist toiling in relative obscurity, awaiting a code-literate society to appreciate the nuances of her art. Will it take a century for this happen? I don't think so.

Thanks to programmer-artists like Keith Peters, we are seeing bridges being built between the realms of programming and the visual arts, leading to a growing social understanding and appreciation for the art behind programming. Keith's code is visual, alive, pulsing, breathing, growing, changing—many times in wholly unpredictable, unique, and wonderful ways. Variables, statements, loops, methods, and classes combine to create emotive, moving experiences that take us beyond our everyday experience to discover new worlds made entirely of light and sound.

This is not a book about programming; it's about magic. Within its covers you will find the potions and spells that will hopefully lead you on your own artistic journey of programming. Welcome artist, programmer, magician. Get ready for an amazing adventure!

Aral Balkan
September 12, 2005
Brighton, England

ABOUT THE AUTHOR

Keith Peters is a Flash developer in the Boston area. He has been working with Flash since 1999 and is currently the senior flash architect at Flash Composer (www.flashcomposer.com). Keith has been a contributing author to eight other friends of ED books. But probably his biggest claim to fame is his personal website, www.bit-101.com, where he strives to create a new and unique Flash experiment each day. This has resulted in over 700 open source Flash examples—probably the largest single author repository of open source Flash material on the Web.

ABOUT THE TECHNICAL REVIEWER

Todd Yard is a lead Flash developer at Brightcove (`www.brightcove.com`) in Cambridge, Massachusetts, and has contributed as an author or technical editor on 11 other friends of ED Flash books, including *Flash 8 Essentials* and *Extending Flash MX 2004*.

ABOUT THE COVER IMAGE DESIGNER

Corné van Dooren designed the front cover image for this book. Having been given a brief by friends of ED to create a new design for the Foundation series, he was inspired to create this new setup combining technology and organic forms.

With a colorful background as an avid cartoonist, Corné discovered the infinite world of multimedia at the age of 17—a journey of discovery that hasn't stopped since. His mantra has always been "The only limit to multimedia is the imagination," a mantra that is keeping him moving forward constantly.

After enjoying success after success over the past years—working for many international clients, as well as featuring in multimedia magazines, testing software, and working on many other friends of ED books—Corné decided it was time to take another step in his career by launching his own company, *Project 79*, in March 2005.

You can see more of Corné's work and contact him through the websites `www.cornevandooren.com` or `www.project79.com`.

If you like his work, be sure to check out his chapter in *New Masters of Photoshop: Volume 2*, also by friends of ED (ISBN 1590593154).

ACKNOWLEDGMENTS

Todd Yard, this book's technical reviewer, for excellent technical reviewing, keeping me honest, and lending me large portions of Chapter 17.

Steve Rycroft, my editor at friends of ED for several years, for keeping me busy cranking out other chapters while this book fermented in my head.

Chris Mills, this book's editor, for taking my concept of the book and finally making it a reality.

Marilyn Smith, this book's copy editor, for making me sound much more intelligent than I actually am.

All the people in the ActionScript, Math, and Physics forums at Flashkit and Were-Here, from 1999 through 2003. You put most of these ActionScript weapons in my hands; I insist you take some responsibility for what I've done with them.

INTRODUCTION

This is a great book!

Now that's a pretty conceited opening line, so let me clarify. The book's greatness has nothing to do with my writing ability, personality, or anything else about *me*. I consider it great because of the subjects it covers. This is the book I've been looking for since 1999. If someone else had written it back then, I would have bought it, read it, called it a great book, and that would be the end of the story. But since nobody seemed to be stepping up to the task, I decided to do it myself.

Even the list of contents isn't my brilliant idea. It's the list of things I struggled to learn over the years, and the questions constantly asked on various Flash forums, in mailing lists, and in feedback from my personal site. In short, this is the stuff that *I* wanted to learn, and I'm betting it's the stuff *you* want to learn as well.

Let me also admit that very few of the techniques here are things I invented. They are the result of years of researching not only established formulas and methods, but also efficient ways of implementing these methods in Flash, given its special limitations and strengths. I can't even say that I had all of these answers when I started the book. A fair amount of research was done while writing, and I am a much wiser man than I was when I started.

You should keep a few things in mind as you read through this book. First, know that I try to avoid saying that any technique is "*the* way" or even "the best way" to do something. I've found that as soon as you label something the "coolest, best, fastest, and easiest" way of doing something in Flash, someone is going to come out of the woodwork with a cooler, better, faster, and easier way. So, I'll just say that the techniques in the book will work, look good, and be relatively efficient in terms of CPU and memory use. But feel free to improve on them, and let me know when you do!

Second, you won't find a lot of start-to-finish, polished project tutorials here. I'm not going to walk you through building a full-featured game with a splash screen, sound effects, and high-score table. I might show you how to move a spaceship around, like in the game Asteroids, and how to tell when it's hit something. The rest is up to you. Publishers of books and magazines often seem to think that readers want a step-by-step description of how to build some specific project, down to the last detail. That's great if you happen to want to build that exact project. But chances are you already have a pretty cool game, application, or other project in mind, and you just need to know how to build the various pieces and put them together. That is the knowledge that I strive to bring to you.

Finally—and I'll be repeating this one endlessly throughout the book—a lot of the math and physics I present will have serious departures from a standard text on the same subject. I take a lot of shortcuts and a few out-and-out cheats, all in the name of a smooth-running movie. While you could, in theory, create a Flash movie that has almost perfectly accurate physics, you might wind up measuring its speed in *seconds per frame* rather than *frames per second*! So, there are sacrifices and tradeoffs.

In most cases I'll point out these departures. And in every case, a lot of effort and testing has gone into making sure that if it isn't exactly accurate, it at least *looks* like it's accurate.

But enough warnings and disclaimers. This is a great book! Have fun with it. Make stuff you never dreamed you could make in Flash. Above all, use this book as a jumping-off point. Experiment, learn other subjects, and add the knowledge you gain to the examples given. I look forward to seeing what you come up with!

Part One

ACTIONSCRIPTED ANIMATION BASICS

this._height += (this.targetHeight - this._height)/speed;
};shape.targetHeight = shape._height;
shape.onEnterFrame = function() {
var speed = 5;
this._width += (this.targetWidth - this._width)/speed;
this._height += (this.targetHeight - this._height)/speed;
};

Chapter 1

BASIC ANIMATION CONCEPTS

What we'll cover in this chapter:

- What is animation?
- Frames and motion
- Dynamic vs. static animation

Flash, at its core, is an animation machine. From the very earliest versions, Flash has supported animation through tweens—where you create a couple of keyframes that are different and let Flash fill in what is in between. However, this book is not about tweens. This book is about the powerful language built into Flash, called ActionScript. This book covers programming, math, and physics techniques used to make things move with ActionScript. As you'll see, this gives you levels of power, control, and interactivity that you could never hope to match with tweening.

But before we dive into specific techniques and formulas for moving things around with ActionScript, let's take a quick look at exactly what animation is, some of the basic techniques behind it, and some concepts that you can use to make your Flash animations more dynamic and interesting.

Sure, you can skip this chapter if you are just dying to write some code. But I strongly suggest you come back to it at some point. If nothing else, you'll find some interesting insights into the subject.

What is animation?

First, the question of all questions: What is animation? Well, per the *American Heritage Dictionary of the English Language, Fourth Edition* (Houghton Mifflin Company, 2000), it means the following:

1. To give life to; fill with life.
2. To impart interest or zest to; enliven.
3. To fill with spirit, courage, or resolution; encourage.
4. To inspire to action; prompt.
5. To impart motion or activity to.
6. To make, design, or produce (a cartoon, for example) so as to create the illusion of motion.

While I could get philosophical with the first four definitions, what we are really talking about here are the fifth and sixth definitions. Animation means motion. I like to broaden that a bit and say that animation is change over time, specifically some type of visual change. Motion is basically the change in something's position over time. One minute it is over here; the next minute it is over there. Theoretically, it was also in the space between those two points, but I won't get metaphysical about it (not just yet anyway). It moved, and some time elapsed between the time it was at the first point and the time it was at the next one.

But an object doesn't necessarily need to change its location in order to be considered animated. It could just be changing its shape. Remember those photo-morphing programs that were all the rage in the late 1990s? You start with one picture of a girl and one picture of a tiger, and the program creates an animation between them. Or the object could be changing its size or orientation, such as a plant growing or a top spinning. Or it could even simply be changing its color. If you've been around long enough, you might remember some of the earliest animations on home PCs consisted of just cycling colors. You make a picture of a waterfall with a bunch of shapes in various shades of blue. You then cycle the colors of those shapes. If done right, the result gives the impression of falling water, even though, technically, nothing is moving at all.

The connection of animation to time is an important one. Without any motion or change, there is no animation, of course, but also there is no sense of time. Sometimes you might see a web cam image of an empty room or a city skyline, where nothing seems to be happening. It's impossible to tell if you are looking at a still image or a live video stream. Finally, you might notice some subtle change—a flickering light or a moving shadow. Just that slight flicker has reassured you that time is present, and maybe if you keep watching, something else will change. If you don't see any change after a while, you become convinced that it is a still image. There is no time, and you know nothing else will be happening in the picture.

That brings up another point: Animation keeps us interested in things. While the *Mona Lisa* is a wonderful piece of work and one of the most famous paintings of all time, I bet the average person gets bored after looking at it for 15 minutes, tops, and then wanders off to see what else he can brag about having seen. But stick him in front of the latest high-budget Hollywood action film, and he won't budge for a good two and a half hours. And if he does need to go to the restroom or to get a snack, he will wait for a "slow" part—one without so much animation. That's the power of animation.

Frames and motion

Now, let's go back for a minute to that last definition of animate:

To make, design, or produce (a cartoon, for example) so as to create the **illusion** of motion.

Interesting that the definition writers should choose to throw that word *illusion* in there, yet entirely accurate. It happens that with just about every form of motion media, only an illusion of motion exists. Here's where we get to the concept of frames.

Virtually all visual animation media uses *frames*—a series of still images shown very rapidly to simulate motion or change. Anything you see on a computer, television, or movie screen is based on frames. This goes back to the earliest days of cartoon animation, where the individual pictures were drawn on sheets of cellophane and became known as *cels*, and the earliest motion pictures, where a similar technique was used with multiple photographs.

The concept is simple: You show a bunch of images that vary slightly from one to another, and the mind blurs them together as a single, moving image. But why do we insist on calling it an *illusion of motion*? If you see a man walk across the room on a movie screen, is that not motion? Of course, it's only an image of a man, not the real thing, but that's not why we don't consider it to be real motion.

Remember when I talked about an object being over here and then later over there, and I said it moved through the intervening space? Well, that is real motion. Objects move through space smoothly, not in several jumps. (You quantum physicists in the audience, just be quiet.) But any and all frame-based motion does just that. It doesn't move from spot to spot; it disappears and reappears in another location in the next frame. The faster it's moving, the bigger jumps it takes.

If I showed you a picture of a man on the left side of a room, and then a few seconds later another picture of the same man on the right side of the room, you'd say I showed you two pictures, not an animation. If I showed you half a dozen pictures of him in the process of crossing the room, you'd still say it was a series of individual photos. (See Figure 1-1 for an example of a series of still photographs.) If I presented enough photos fast enough, that wouldn't change the fact that they are still just a whole bunch of still photos, but you would no longer see it that way. Your mind would just take it in as a man moving across the room. It is no more real motion than the original two photos were, but at *some point*, the mind gives up and buys into the illusion. As a matter of fact, that point has been well researched by the film industry.

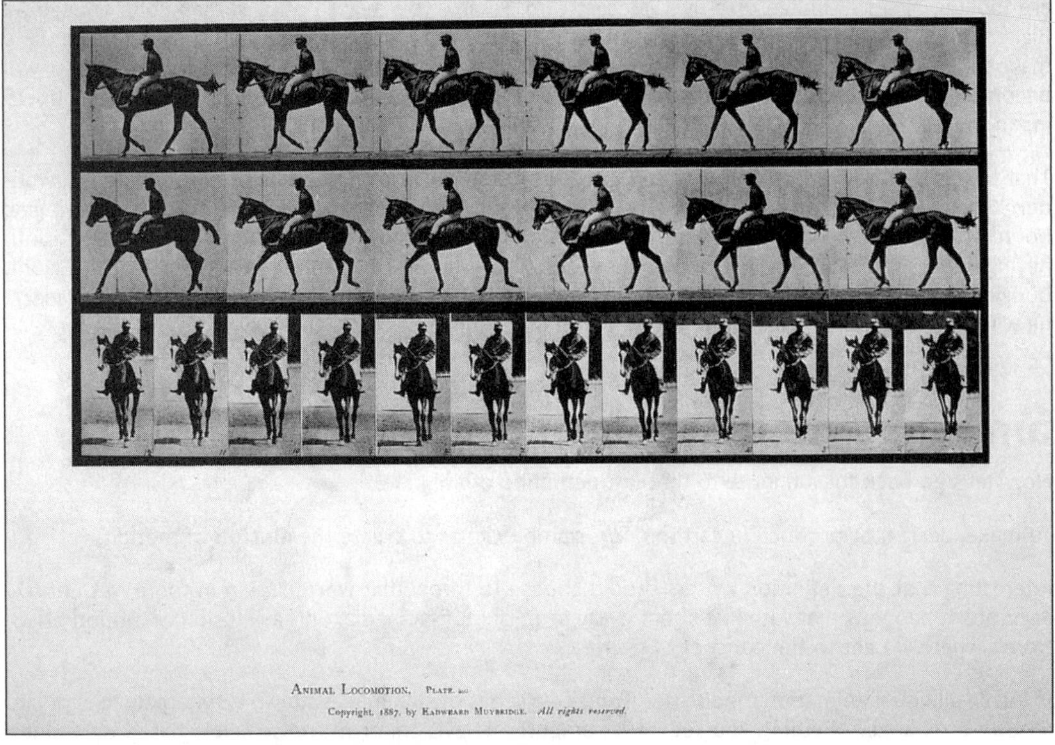

Figure 1-1. A series of still photographs by Eadweard Muybridge

Researchers have found that at a rate of 24 frames per second, people are perfectly happy to accept those frames as a single moving image. Go too much slower than that, and the jumpiness gets annoying and starts to break the illusion. And it seems that the human eye can't distinguish frame rates very much higher than that, so going 100 frames per second isn't going to make your movie seem any more realistic (although higher frame rates in programmed animation can result in more responsiveness in interaction).

Frames as records

The whole concept of frames makes three things possible: storage, transmission, and display. You can't really store, transmit, and display a man walking across a room. But you can store a picture, or many. And you can transmit them and display them. Thus you can show that animation almost anywhere, at any time, as long as you have or can receive the stored images and have a way to display them.

Now, let's get a little more general definition of what a frame is. So far, I've been referring to a frame as a still image or a drawing. Let's call it a record of a system at a specific point in time. That "system" could be your two-year-old daughter caught mid-grin, and the record would be that image. On the other hand, that system could be a collection of virtual objects, and the record could be their shapes, sizes, colors, positions, and so on at that particular moment in time. Thus, your movie would become not a series of still images, but rather a series of descriptions of images. Instead of just displaying the image, the computer would take that description, create the image from it, and then display it. You can even go a step further by using programmed frames.

Programmed frames

Since you have a computer that can calculate things on the fly, you don't really need a long list of descriptions for your frames. You can cut down to a description of the first frame and some rules on how to build the subsequent frames. So, now the computer is not merely creating an image from a description. It's creating the description first, and then creating and displaying the image.

Consider how much file space you could save using this approach. Images take up a lot of hard disk space and bandwidth. And 24 images per second add up fast. If you can boil that down to one description and a set of rules, you've possibly reduced the file size by a factor of hundreds. Even a very complex set of rules for how the objects should move and react takes up less space than a single medium-sized image. Indeed, one of the first things people notice about scripted animation is just how small it winds up being.

Naturally, there is a trade-off. As your system gets larger and your rules get more complex, the computer must work furiously to calculate the next scene description, and then work overtime to render it. If you're trying to maintain a particular frame rate, that gives the CPU a limited amount of time (milliseconds) to think about it. If it can't calculate the scene in time, your frame rate will suffer. On the other hand, image-based animation doesn't care so much about what's in the scene or how complex it is. It just shows the next picture, generally right on time.

> *I've used prerendered animation to my advantage at least once. I was putting together a presentation of a number of complex Flash ActionScripted animations. File size was not a problem, since the animations were going to be played from a local machine. But timing was critical, and I had no idea how smoothly the ActionScript would render the images on this unknown, untested computer. So I brought the Flash movies into Director and exported the whole thing as a giant QuickTime movie. Since the movie was now just a series of prerendered images, it didn't really matter anymore how complex they were. As long as the computer was capable of displaying a QuickTime movie, I knew it would do so smoothly. The presentation went off without a hitch.*

Dynamic vs. static animation

Another advantage to using coded animation goes far beyond simple file size. It's the fact that a coded animation becomes dynamic. Have you ever watched the movie *Titanic*? I hope I'm not giving away too much, but the boat sinks—every time. It sank in the theaters, it sinks on VHS, and it even sinks on DVD. Short of pressing the stop or pause button, you can't stop it from sinking. That's because a movie is a series of still images. The images near the end of this particular series show the boat sinking, and that's that.

Now let's move from the *Titanic* movie to a Flash website. Remember the late 1990s, when Flash was originally taking off? Everyone had to have a Flash website intro. Some shapes would slide in and grow or fade out. A cheap audio loop would play. Some trendy buzzwords would fade or slide in or out. Maybe a beam of light or some shadows would appear. Wow!

OK, I won't be too harsh. At least two or three I remember really were "wow" material—real works of art. The intros for the Gabocorp and Ray of Light sites, shown in Figures 1-2 and 1-3, were legendary. But when I think back on it, I recall actually sitting through them only a couple of times. They were a minute or two long, and I watched them two or three times. Was that because they weren't good? No, it was because after you saw them a couple of times, there wasn't much more to see. Just like the *Titanic* movie, the website intros did the same thing each time. I call that *static animation* (my own personal oxymoron!), because the animation never changes. Each frame, from start to finish, is predefined.

Now, a coded animation isn't necessarily dynamic. I could take an object and, using code, put it in a certain position and have it move across the screen. Each time you play the movie, the same code runs and causes the same movement. That's hardly dynamic.

But what if I take an object, and again using code, determine a random point to place it and a random direction and speed to move it? Now each time you play the movie, something different will happen.

Figure 1-2. The legendary gabocorp.com intro

Figure 1-3. Intro for rayoflight.com

Or what if, when the movie starts, I find out the time of day and month of the year, and use that data to create a scene—say a winter morning, a summer afternoon, or an evening in April?

Or how about if I have some factors in my movie that can be changed while the movie is running, via the keyboard and mouse? That would allow the user to interact with the objects on the screen. That's about as far from static as you can get. You could even save the Titanic!

Perhaps the most interesting aspect of dynamic animation, and what this book is mainly about, is the application of real-world mathematics and physics principles to the objects in the movie. You don't merely have some object move off in some random direction; you also give it some gravity, so that as it moves, it starts to fall down. When it hits the "ground," it bounces, but not as high as it started out. Then it eventually settles down and just sits there. Now you add some user interaction to that, allowing the user to "pick it up" with the mouse or move it around with the keyboard. As the user throws the object around, she starts getting the feeling that she is really handing a physical object.

With this type of animation, the user is no longer just sitting there watching some frames play out. She has entered into the environment you have created. How long is she going to stay there? She will remain as long as the environment keeps her interested. The more she can interact with the environment, the longer she will be interested. Make it interesting enough, and she will stay there a lot longer than she would sit through your intro (and sadly, probably longer than she would sit in front of the *Mona Lisa*). I have many e-mail messages from people telling me they spent their entire morning or afternoon playing with the experiments on `www.bit-101.com`. And not only will people stay longer, but they will also come back for more.

Summary

So, where is all this leading? In this opening chapter, I've gone over some of the basics of animation. But what do you actually do with this? Well, that's up to you.

In the following chapters, I'm going to put some tools in your hands and give you a quick lesson in how to use each one. What you build with these tools is entirely your decision. The most obvious use for much of what's in this book would be for game creation. Games are essentially interactive animations with some goals for players to achieve. But I really want to avoid this becoming simply a games book. I have used almost all of the techniques here in some kind of professional work other than games—from horrendous 3D menus and other not-so-bad navigation systems, to advertisements and educational applications.

A word of warning: Pick up any web design book, and you'll find a chapter telling you all about how too much animation is bad. I won't disagree, but I'm not going to say another word about it. If you want to hang yourself with animation, I'm going to spend the next few hundred pages giving you all the rope you need!

shape.targetHeight = shape._height;
shape.onEnterFrame = function() {
var speed = 5;
this._width += (this.targetWidth - this._width)/speed;
this._height += (this.targetHeight - this._height)/speed;

Chapter 2

BASICS OF ACTIONSCRIPT FOR ANIMATION

What we'll cover in this chapter:

- Basic animation
- Movie clips
- Classes and OOP
- User interaction

If the first chapter was a somewhat philosophical overview of animation, this one is a sort of technical overview of what it takes to animate with ActionScript. This chapter covers the essentials of loops for animation, movie clips, classes, and user interaction. It gives you the majority of the information you need to understand the ActionScript techniques used in the rest of the book.

Basic animation

To start off, let's quickly review what Chapter 1 covered.

- Animation is made with frames, with each frame slightly different to present the illusion of motion.
- Frame-by-frame or tweened animation contains an image or description of an image for each frame.
- Dynamic animation contains an initial description of an image and rules that are applied to alter the description on each frame.

Most of the rest of this book will focus on the rules for dynamic animation, providing a catalog of techniques to change the image description, resulting in realistic motion. In this chapter, you'll see how to structure the initial description, how to apply those rules on each frame, and how to put the whole thing together. You'll be creating some working examples as you go, and most of these will be based on the same basic file.

A note on versions

The examples in this book were written in ActionScript 2. Most of them will also work in ActionScript 1 with a few minor adjustments. Probably the major one will be data typing. In ActionScript 1, you cannot specify which type of data a variable is supposed to hold. Starting with ActionScript 2, you can add a colon and a data type after declaring a variable with the key word `var`, like so:

```
var name:String = "Keith";
```

In ActionScript 1, this causes an error. So, if for some reason you are still using ActionScript 1, you can just drop the data type, like this:

```
var name = "Keith";
```

Of course, if you want to use classes, or any of the new expressiveness features (filters, blend modes, and so on) introduced in Flash 8, you'll need to upgrade to ActionScript 2, since these features are not supported in ActionScript 1.

Setup

To get started, create the basic file you'll be working with in this chapter. Fire up your copy of Flash and follow these steps:

1. Create a new document and save it as `chapter2base.fla`.
2. Use the oval tool to make a circle 50 pixels across.

3. Select the circle and press *F8* to convert it to a movie clip. Give it the name `ball` and make sure the registration point is set to be in the center, as shown in Figure 2-1.

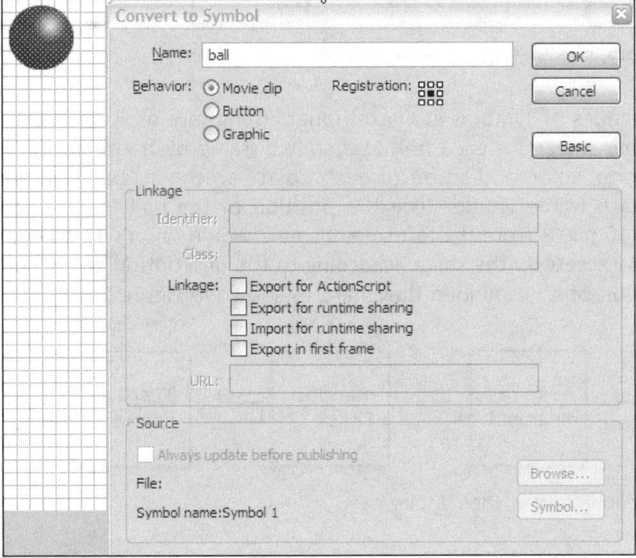

Figure 2-1. Converting to a movie clip

4. Click OK, and you should have an instance of the new ball movie clip on stage and selected.
5. Use the Property inspector to name this instance `ball`, as shown in Figure 2-2.
6. In the timeline, click the Insert Layer icon, or choose Insert ➤ Timeline ➤ Layer from the menu.
7. Double-click the new layer's name and change it to `code` or `actions`, or whatever name you prefer to use to signify that this layer is for ActionScript only. (I'll refer to this as the *code layer*.)
8. With frame 1 of the code layer selected, open the Actions panel by pressing *F9* or by choosing Window ➤ Development Panels ➤ Actions from the menu.

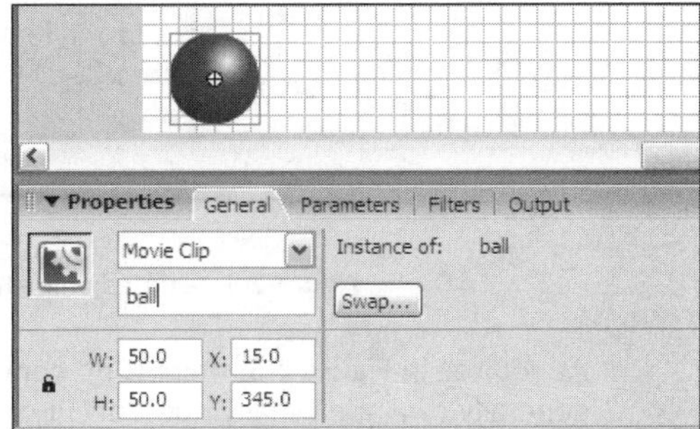

Figure 2-2. Naming the instance

You are now ready to write code. Keep this file open, as you'll be jumping right into it after a quick background discussion of what you'll be doing.

Looping

Almost all coded animation contains some kind of loop. If you think about a frame-by-frame animation, you might come up with a flowchart that would be something like a series of bitmaps, where each frame is already an image and just needs to be shown, as shown in Figure 2-3.

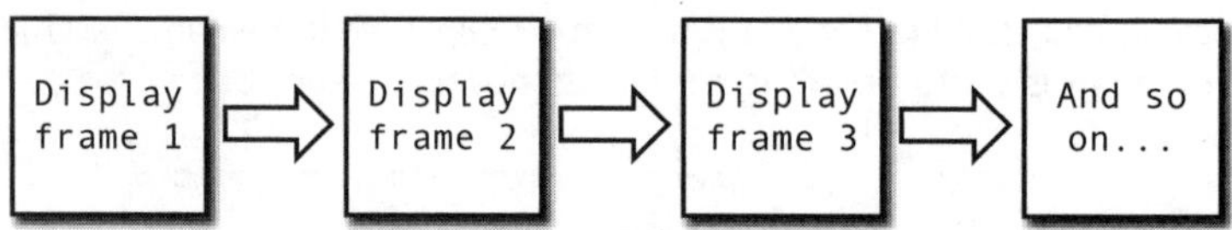

Figure 2-3. Frame-by-frame animation

When you get into shapes or symbols in Flash though, things are a bit different. Flash doesn't create and store a new bitmap image for each frame, even in a frame-by-frame movie. For each frame, Flash stores the position, size, color, and so on of each object on the stage. So, if you had a ball moving across the screen, each frame would store the position of the ball on that frame. Maybe frame 1 would say the ball is 10 pixels from the left side, frame 2 would say it's 15 pixels, and so on. The Flash player reads in this data, sets up the stage according to the description given, and displays that frame. From that, you get a bit of an expanded flowchart, as shown in Figure 2-4.

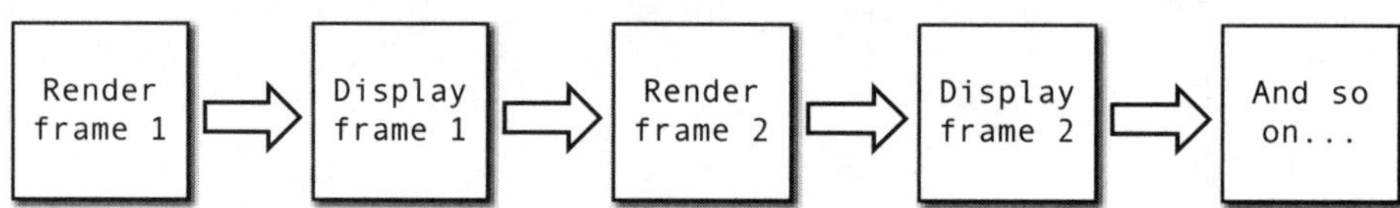

Figure 2-4. Rendering frames, then displaying

But when you consider how I described a dynamic, coded animation, the flowchart looks more like Figure 2-5.

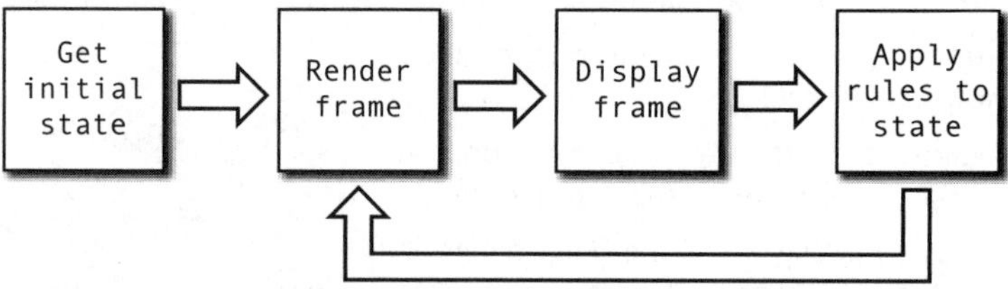

Figure 2-5. Scripted animation

As you see in Figure 2-5, there is no concept of frame 1, frame 2, and so on. ActionScripted animation generally can, and usually does, occur all in just one frame. And here you can start to see what I mean by a loop.

First, you set up an initial state. You can do this by dragging movie clips onto the stage, just as if you were creating a tweened animation. Or you can describe the entire scene in code alone. Either way, you then render and display the frame.

Next, you apply your rules. The rules can be as simple as, "The ball will move 5 pixels to the right," or they can be made up of dozens of lines of complex trigonometry. The examples in the book will cover most of that spectrum.

Applying the rules will result in a new state—a new description that is then rendered and displayed. Then you apply the same rules all over again.

Note that it is the same set of rules being applied over and over. You don't have one set of rules for the first frame, and then another set for the next, and so on. So, your challenge is to come up with a set of rules that will handle every possible situation that can arise in your scene. What happens when your ball moves so far to the right that it's off the stage? Your set of rules needs to account for this. Do you want to allow the user to interact with the ball with his mouse? Your rules will need to take that into account as well.

It sounds daunting, but it's really not that complex. Basically, you start off with some very simple behavior by creating a rule or two, and when that works, add another rule.

These "rules," as I keep calling them, are actually ActionScript statements. Each rule can be a single statement or composed of several or even many statements. In the example of moving the ball 5 pixels to the right, the rule would look something like this:

```
ball._x = ball._x + 5;
```

You're just saying take whatever the ball's x position (horizontal axis) is, add 5 to it, and make that its new x position. You can even simplify that by saying this:

```
ball._x += 5;
```

The += operator just says add the value on the right to the value of the variable on the right, and assign the result back to that variable.

Here's a more advanced set of rules that you'll see later in the book:

```
var dx:Number = ball._x - _xmouse;
var dy:Number = ball._y - _ymouse;
var angle:Number = Math.atan2(dy, dx);
var targetX:Number = _xmouse + Math.cos(angle) * springLength;
var targetY:Number = _ymouse + Math.sin(angle) * springLength;
vx += (targetX - ball._x) * spring;
vy += (targetY - ball._y) * spring;
vx *= friction;
vy *= friction;
ball._x += vx;
ball._y += vy;
clear();
lineStyle(1, 0, 100);
moveTo(ball._x, ball._y);
lineTo(_xmouse, _ymouse);
```

Don't worry about what it all means just yet. Just know that Flash is going to need to run this code over and over to generate each new frame.

So, how do you get these loops to run? I'll show you my first attempt to do this, which reflects the error that many beginning ActionScripters make. It's based on the loop structures that exist in almost every programming language, such as `for` and `while`. You set up a loop with one of those structures, which will cause the code within it to execute repeatedly. Here's what I did:

```
for(i = 0; i < 500; i++){
    ball._x = i;
}
```

It seems pretty simple. The variable `i` starts out as 0, so the `ball` movie clip is placed at zero on the x axis—the far left of the stage. The `i++` causes the value of `i` to be increased by one each time through the loop, from 0 to 1 to 2, 3, 4, and so on, and each time, that value is assigned to `ball._x`, moving it across the stage left to right. When it hits the value of 500, the statement `i < 500` will be false, and the loop will end.

Go ahead and put that code into the Actions panel of the `chapter2base.fla` file. Run it and see what happens.

You'll find that the ball doesn't move across the stage; it simply appears on the right side. Why didn't it move to all the points in between? Well, actually it did! You just didn't see it, because you never let Flash update the screen. Figure 2-6 is another flowchart that shows essentially what happened.

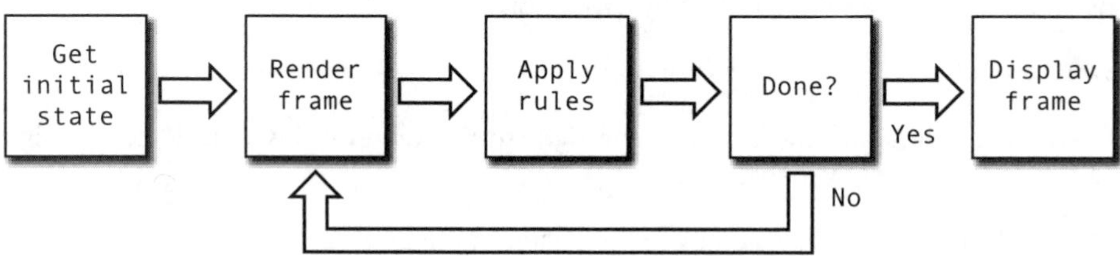

Figure 2-6. Why you can't animate with a for loop

You actually applied the rules and moved the ball into position, creating a new scene 500 times. But it didn't get displayed until after the loop was done. This is because Flash updates the screen only at the end of a frame. This is a very important point.

Here is the sequence of actions Flash takes on each frame:

1. Position all objects that are currently on the stage, in any level, layer, loaded movie clip, and so on.
2. Execute all ActionScript that needs to be called on that frame, on any layer or level on any movie clip or button, or nested within any movie clip, no matter how deep.
3. Check if it is time to display the frame yet. If you set your frame rate to 20 frames per second, Flash will check if at least 50 milliseconds have gone by since the last time it displayed a frame. If so, it will display the frame it just rendered, and move to the next frame. If not, it will wait until the right amount of time has passed.

You should note a couple of things about this timing factor. First, frame rates are notoriously inaccurate. Never rely on them for strict timing. Second, it is possible that the amount of rendering and ActionScript execution will take longer than the allotted time for a frame. You don't have to worry about your script getting chopped off, though. Flash will finish executing the script (step 2) before it moves onto step 3, even if it slows down the frame rate. Flash will actually wait up to 15 seconds for your script to finish on any particular frame. It will then display the infamous, "A script is causing the player to run slowly. . ." message.

So, in the preceding example, Flash waited for the `for` loop to finish before going to the next frame, and it updated the screen only just before it went to the next frame. That's why you saw the jump rather than the movement.

So, what you need to do is break up the loop across frames, so that you get back to the sequence of events shown in Figure 2-5.

Frame loops

Starting again with `chapter2base.fla`, let's get the animation to work.

1. Delete any existing code you previously placed in the Actions panel for frame 1 of the code layer, and replace it with the following:

```
ball._x++;
```

The ++ means "add one to the value of the variable." If you test the movie now, nothing much happens. Actually, what does happen is that Flash adds one to the x position of the ball, and then displays the result. When you have a movie consisting of only one frame, Flash executes the code on that frame, renders and displays the result, and that's pretty much the end of that. What you need to do is to run that one line over and over. One of the simplest ways to do that is to add another frame to the timeline.

2. Select the layer with the ball graphic in it and press *F5* or choose Insert ➤ Timeline ➤ Frame from the menu. This adds another frame identical to the existing frame 1. Your timeline should look like Figure 2-7.

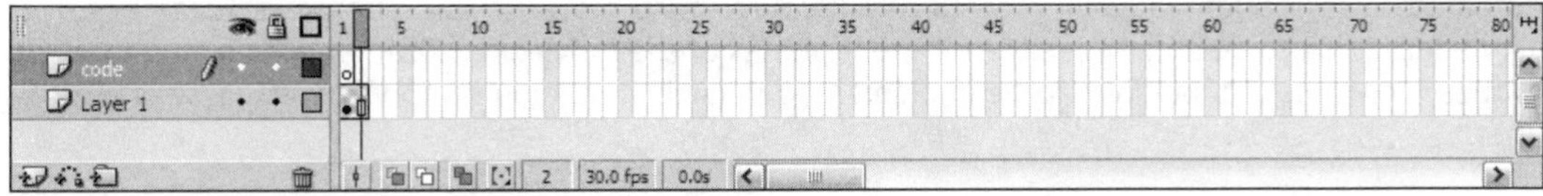

Figure 2-7. Timeline for a frame loop

Now, Flash executes and displays frame 1, and then moves to frame 2. There is no new code to execute there, and nothing has changed on stage, so it just displays the same thing again. The magic is that, by default, Flash will loop back to frame 1 of a timeline after it has hit the final frame. When it does that, it sees the code you've placed there—as if for the first time—executes it, and displays the result. Then it moves on to frame 2 and back again to 1, over and over, ad infinitum.

Now, the ball slowly crawls across the stage. Nothing earth shattering, but if you are brand new to this, congratulations, you've just created your first ActionScripted animation!

Let's take this a step further and create an initialization frame. This is just a place to set things up. Here, you put any code that you want to run only a single time, rather than loop.

3. Delete any existing code from the Actions panel and add two new frames to both layers by pressing *F5* twice on each one.

4. Click frame 2 of the code layer and press *F6*, or choose Modify ➤ Timeline ➤ Convert to Keyframes from the menu, to change that frame to a new keyframe. Then do the same thing on frame 3 to make that a keyframe as well. The result is shown in Figure 2-8.

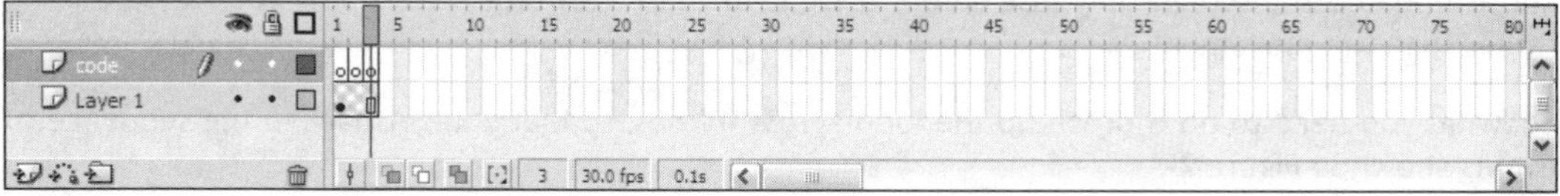

Figure 2-8. Frame loop with initialization frame

5. Place the following code on frame 1 on the code layer:

```
ball._x = 100;
ball._y = 100;
```

6. Place this code on frame 2:

```
ball._x += 5;
```

7. Place this code on frame 3:

```
gotoAndPlay(2);
```

Now, frame 1 is the initialization frame. As soon as the movie starts, it executes what it finds there and displays the results. So, no matter where you place the ball on the stage to begin with, your initialization code will make sure it starts at location 100, 100. Then it moves on to frame 2, which is your main action code. This moves the ball 5 pixels to the right. Finally, frame 3, rather than just allowing a default loop back to frame 1, sends the movie back to frame 2, to reexecute the action code.

This is the exact setup used extensively in Flash 5 and earlier, and it is still perfectly workable, if a bit outdated. Even though you will very shortly discover much more flexible and powerful setups, it is very educational to be able to see the different phases of the movie: initialization, action, and looping, as these concepts will continue to be implemented in each animation setup you will investigate hereafter.

Clip events

Hang in there, because we're taking one more trip down memory lane. Clip events were the main alternative to frame loops back in the old Flash 5 days. Although now heavily frowned upon, they deserve a quick look, if only to compare their architecture to what you just did and where you'll soon be going.

Clip events refer to code that is placed, not on the timeline, but directly on a movie clip itself. This is done by selecting a movie clip that is on stage and then opening the Actions panel. You'll notice that the Actions panel has a few different modes, depending on what is selected. Up to now, you have been putting code on frames, by selecting a frame before writing code. You might have noticed that the title bar of the Actions panel shows Actions – Frame in that case. When a movie clip is selected, it should show Actions – Movie Clip. Figure 2-9 shows both of these modes. The Actions panel may also tell you that you have a button selected.

Personally, I find the indication of what is selected and where the code is going to be far too subtle, and one of the mistakes I still make constantly is to write a bunch of code in the Actions panel, only to have my program fail to compile because I had some movie clip selected rather than the timeline. So keep an eye out for that one.

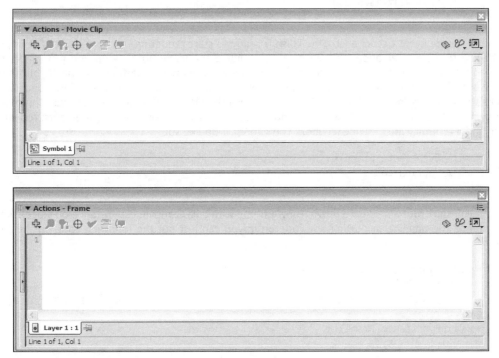

Figure 2-9. The Actions panel shows where the code is going

When you select a movie clip and then put some code in the Actions panel, that code is assigned directly to that clip. We usually say that the code is "on" the clip. Any and all code that appears on a clip must be within a clip event block. This looks something like this:

```
onClipEvent(eventName){
   // code goes here
}
```

In addition to `onClipEvent(eventName)`, there is `on(eventName)`. The "*on*" events have to do with mouse and keyboard actions, such as `press` and `release`.

The event name refers to one of the many events that may occur in a Flash movie. An event is simply that: something happening in the movie. Events fall into two main categories: system events and user events. A system event is when something happens within the computer, Flash, or your movie, such as data loading, content loading, or a new frame starting. User events refer to something the user has done, and generally have to do with keyboard or mouse activity.

The two main events you'll be looking at here are load and enterFrame. The load event occurs when the movie clip instance first occurs on stage. In other words, the movie clip has loaded into the player and is ready to be displayed. The important thing is that the load event occurs only once for any particular instance. Thus, you can use it for your initialization code. You simply place your code between the two curly brackets:

```
onClipEvent(load){
   // initialization code
}
```

The enterFrame event occurs each time Flash is ready to start rendering the next frame. The important thing to remember about this event is that, unlike the frame loop setup you just made, the enterFrame event still continues to fire on a regular basis, even on a single-frame movie. If your frame rate is set to 20 frames per second, enterFrame will fire approximately every 50 milliseconds. And, unlike the initial for loop experiment, Flash will refresh the display after each enterFrame. This makes it a perfect place to put your "rules," or action code, as you have your two requirements: repeating code and a redisplay after each execution. You can set it up like so:

```
onClipEvent(enterFrame){
    // action code
}
```

Thus, if you start with a new base movie (single frame with a ball movie clip instance on stage), without altering the timeline or putting any code on it, you can just put the following code on the ball instance:

```
onClipEvent(load){
  this._x = 100;
  this._y = 100;
}
onClipEvent(enterFrame){
   this._x += 5;
}
```

Note the use of the keyword this. Since the code is on the movie clip, any code refers directly to the movie clip itself and the timeline internal to that clip. If you said ball._x += 5, it would look inside itself for an object named ball, and not finding one, nothing would happen. It would not look on the main timeline for an object of that name. This has to do with the subject of *scope*, which refers to where some piece of code is and affects what it has access to from that location. You'll run into the issue of scope many times throughout the book. Here, you can use the keyword this to refer to the current object—the ball movie clip. You could also just leave it off altogether and say _x += 5, as this would be implicitly added by the compiler. Either way, the result is exactly the same effect you had before of the ball moving across the stage to the right.

Earlier, I mentioned that clip events were frowned upon with the release of Flash MX. Probably the biggest reason for this has to do with *code centralization*. Suppose someone else made the movie you just completed, and you need to make some changes to it. You open it and see a ball sitting on stage. You can see instantly by looking at the timeline that there is no code on the timeline, by the absence of the little a symbol on any of the frames, and the movie is only one frame long, so there is no tweening going on. Yet, when you test the movie, the ball moves across the stage.

To find the clip-event code, you need to do a little poking around: click the ball to select it, and then open the Actions panel. This is not such a bad scenario for this small example. But take a complex movie with dozens of buttons and movie clips on stage, and movie clips within movie clips (within movie clips within movie clips, and so on), maybe all with their own clip events, and try to find that one line of code that is causing that one effect you want to change. I swear nothing makes you want to kill your fellow Flash developer more than that situation.

Modern *best practices* dictate that all code within a movie be on the main timeline, preferably on frame 1 of a layer set aside for just code. Alternatively, the code can be in external ActionScript files that are *included* in the file. In this case, you create your ActionScript in any text or code editor and save it as a text file in the same directory as your FLA file. You can name it something like `game_code.as`. Then in the FLA file, on the timeline, you can type this:

```
#include "game_code.as"
```

Note the leading # and lack of semicolon at the end of the line. When Flash encounters this line, it will read in the text file and interpret it, just as if you had typed all that code right on the timeline itself. This basically achieves the same goal, which is to have all of the code for the movie centralized in one location, rather than forcing some later developer (possibly yourself) to go on a hunting expedition to find it all.

ActionScript 2 class files are a different way of organizing code. They usually wind up being multiple files rather than a single file for all the code in a movie. These class files are a highly structured way of organizing large amounts of complex code. I'll talk about classes in the "Classes and OOP" section later in this chapter.

One other issue with frame loops and clip events is that the code is not very flexible. Once you write some code on a frame or on a movie clip, there's no way to change it at runtime. Say you had a game with a spaceship that just kind of wandered around the screen until it saw an enemy, and then went into attack mode. The code for wandering would probably be very different from the code for attacking. But there's no direct way to say, "On each frame, execute this code. OK, now you're in attack mode, now on each frame, execute this other code." There are indirect ways of doing this, but they can get a bit more complex than would be ideal.

So, how do you get all of your code into a single frame, and still have a loop that allows for updating the display after each loop, and make it flexible? Up through Flash 5, you couldn't do this. But then comes Flash MX to the rescue. . .

Flash MX events and event handlers

Flash MX introduced many important changes in ActionScript—changes and improvements that were largely responsible for catapulting Flash into the serious Rich Internet Application forefront. One of the biggest changes was the new event architecture that made programming very complex behaviors far easier than was possible in earlier versions.

I've already talked a little about events. These are things that occur when something happens in the system or the user does something with the keyboard or mouse. Prior to Flash MX, the only real way to capture these events was with an `onClipEvent(`*eventName*`)` or `on(`*eventName*`)` block on a movie clip or button. This meant that you had to place a movie clip on stage at author time and write the code on it. There was no way, for example, to attach a movie clip to the stage at runtime and assign some enterFrame behavior to it. Naturally, developers came up with various workarounds, but they usually resulted in very complex structures with code hidden throughout the movie and library.

With Flash MX and MX 2004, events are accessible from anywhere and can be handled by assigning a function to the event. Each time that event occurs, the function assigned to it will be executed. At any time while the movie is running, you can remove the handler function or change it to a new one. You can do this for any movie clip or button anywhere in the movie, right from the main timeline.

To understand events, you should understand a couple of additional concepts: *listeners* and *handlers*. Listeners and handlers are actually well-named entities, because that's exactly what they do. A listener is an object that *listens* for events. A handler is a function that *handles* the event when it occurs.

Listeners

A listener takes the form of an object or a movie clip or a button. An *object* here means an ActionScript object created by saying something like myObj = new Object(). That would be a generic object. Actually, in ActionScript, pretty much everything is an object. Even a movie clip is an object with some specialized features.

Certain types of objects can listen for only certain types of events. For example, a movie clip can listen for an enterFrame event because it has frames. A button or generic object does not have frames, so it would not make sense for it to listen for an enterFrame event. A generic object does not have any graphics that could be "pressed" with the mouse, so it cannot listen for a press event, as a button or movie clip can.

Some types of objects are automatically listeners for some types of events. For instance, a movie clip is always a listener for the enterFrame or press event. In other cases, you need to tell an object to listen for a certain event. In other words, you make it a listener for that event. Generally, you do this by calling the addListener method of the object that generates that event. OK, that's probably as clear as mud, so let's see an example. Say you wanted a generic object to listen for mouseDown events. First, you make the object:

```
var myObj:Object = new Object();
```

A quick note on basic syntax: The keyword var here just tells Flash you are now defining a variable. The variable's name is myObj. The colon and Object is the ActionScript 2 syntax for telling Flash what type of data this variable will hold. It's going to hold a generic object. Then you use the new operator to create the new instance. Again, if you are still using ActionScript 1, this syntax will cause an error, as ActionScript 1 does not support data typing. Simply lose the colon and object type:

```
var myObj = new Object();
```

The Mouse object is responsible for generating any and all mouse events. So, you can use the Mouse.addListener method to make myObj a listener for any events having to do with the mouse:

```
Mouse.addListener(myObj);
```

Now myObj will listen for mouse events. Perhaps a more accurate way of describing it is that the listener is *notified* of events. Note that, in this case, you are *adding* a listener to the Mouse object. Internally, Mouse keeps a list of all objects that want to be informed of mouse events. This would include all buttons and movie clips, by default, and any other objects that have registered with it by using its addListener method. Whenever a mouse event occurs, Mouse runs through this list and lets each object on it know what event has occurred.

Yet another way of describing it is to say that the object that becomes a listener is *subscribing* to the event or set of events. And the object that generates the event is *broadcasting* the event to all its subscribers.

Additionally, if you no longer want an object to listen to events, you can tell it to stop listening, or *unsubscribe*, by calling the removeListener method:

```
Mouse.removeListener(myObj);
```

This tells Mouse to remove the object from its internal list of listeners so it will not receive further notifications.

Handlers

When a listener receives notification that an event has occurred, it probably wants to act on that information. It does that by executing a function specially named to correspond to that particular event. The function name usually starts with on, followed by the name of the event, such as onEnterFrame, onMouseMove, onLoad, and so on. This function is known as that object's *event handler* for that event. You simply give the listener object a function with that special name, in the following format: *object.onEventName = function*. You can create a function right there, or assign the name of a function that already exists. Here are a couple of examples, continuing from the earlier mouse listener code:

```
var myObj:Object = new Object();
Mouse.addListener(myObj);

myObj.onMouseDown = function(){
   trace("mouse down");
}

myObj.onMouseUp = mouseUpHandler;

function mouseUpHandler(){
   trace("mouse up");
}
```

Go ahead and type the preceding code into a new movie and test it (using the same procedure as you did for this chapter's first example, in the "Setup" section). You'll see that, as expected, Flash traces a message each time the mouse is pressed or released. If you are just a beginner in ActionScript, and understand and can apply this code, congratulations! You have just moved up to "intermediate" status.

The first handler example creates an anonymous function right then and there, assigning it to myObj's onMouseDown handler. The second example assigns its onMouseUp handler the variable mouseUpHandler.

This happens to be the name of a function created right below the assignment. Now, that might look a little backwards to you, because the function isn't created until after it is assigned. It works though, because when Flash enters a frame with code in it, it first looks for any defined functions and parses them, and then executes the rest of the code on the frame. Thus, even if the function is defined at the very bottom of the code listing for a particular frame, it will be available to the very first line of code in that frame. However, that works only when you define your function this way:

```
function myFunc(){
   // do something
}
```

Another way to define a function is as follows:

```
myFunc = function(){
   // do something
}
```

Only functions defined the first way will be immediately parsed by Flash. If you create your functions using the second syntax, they must be defined prior to the point where they are called in the code.

OK, now that you know a little bit more about handlers, you can get a better understanding of listeners. Earlier, I said that an object that generates events *broadcasts* that event, or *notifies its listeners* of the event. How does it do that exactly? Well, all it really does is call the function on that object that has the correct handler name. For example, say a movie has two buttons, and in addition, you have added an object named myObj as a mouse listener. Mouse now contains a list of listeners something like this:

```
button1
button2
myObj
```

When the user presses the mouse button, Mouse says, "Whoa! Mouse down! Must notify listeners!" (or something like that). It then goes through its list and calls the onMouseDown function of each listener, like so:

```
button1.onMouseDown();
button2.onMouseDown();
myObj.onMouseDown();
```

This example creates a function and assigns it to myObj.onMouseDown. As you can see, this function is now called, and the trace occurs. What if you had not created a function for onMouseDown? Mouse would still attempt to call the function, but Flash would see myObj.onMouseDown as undefined and not do anything. In some languages, to assign an object as a listener, that object must conform to a certain interface. In other words, it would need to actually have a function assigned to onMouseDown, even if that function did nothing. ActionScript 2, however, is far more lenient. It allows just about anything to be a listener and deals with any missing handlers at runtime.

Those are the basics of events and handlers through the ages. I'll be introducing many other events as we move along. For now, let's get back to animation.

Events for animation

So where does all this talk about events bring us? We were looking for a way to apply code to animate an object and allow for a screen refresh after each iteration. Earlier, you saw an example of using the enterFrame clip event for animation. Let's come up to present time with this technique.

In Flash MX or MX 2004, you simply add an onEnterFrame handler to the movie clip, like so:

```
ball.onEnterFrame = function()
{
    this._x += 5;
}
```

One point that is sometimes confusing to people is that you are getting an enterFrame event, even though the movie has only one frame. The playhead is not actually entering a new frame; it's just stuck on frame 1. Just realize that it isn't the act of the playhead moving to a new frame that generates the enterFrame event, but more the other way around—the event tells Flash when to move the playhead. Think of it more as a timer, albeit a pretty inaccurate one. Flash takes the frame rate set for the movie and determines how often it *should* enter a new frame. It then fires the event repeatedly at that interval. If there is another frame to go to, it goes there. But regardless, you can count on the event firing.

The earlier examples had initialization code, either on an initialization frame or in an onClipEvent(load) block. You can simply put any initialization code outside the onEnterFrame function. Since your movie is only one frame, that code will run only once.

Open your master copy of chapter2base.fla, or create a new FLA file per the instructions at the beginning of the chapter, and put the following code on frame 1:

```
ball._x = 100;
ball._y = 100;

function onEnterFrame():Void
{
    ball._x += 5;
}
```

It's a beautiful thing, isn't it? All the code right there for anyone to see, understand, and change when the time comes. And most important, it works like a charm. The ball moves across the stage just as expected. You can tidy it up a bit more though.

One principle of Flash best practices is that there shouldn't be any stray code on the timeline. The timeline should have only functions and a single call to one of those functions to start everything moving. You can move the first couple of lines of code into a function called init, and the sole action on the timeline will be a call to that function:

```
init();

function init(){
    ball._x = 100;
    ball._y = 100;
}
```

```
function onEnterFrame():Void
{
    ball._x += 5;
}
```

This code couldn't be easier to understand. Everything is contained in two functions whose names describe exactly what they do. Compare this setup to a series of frames with lists of statements and gotoAndPlay calls, or code hidden on various movie clips on the stage or within other movie clips, or code hidden away on clips in the library.

Note that not every example in this book will be quite so organized. In cases where I am showing a quick example of a principle, I'll just provide the bare minimum of code necessary to demonstrate that principle. In a full application though, structure and organization are key.

Well, that covers most of the basics on how to structure animation with ActionScript. I've explained how to get rules to run over and over, and how to update the screen after each application of those rules, causing the illusion of motion. But what do you move? So far, you have been moving around a movie clip. But are movie clips the only option, or just the best one?

Movie clips

Let's look at the types of things that exist in Flash. I'll call them *elements*. These are the different types of elements Flash has:

- Bitmaps
- Compiled clips and components
- Videos
- Buttons
- Graphics
- Movie clips
- BitmapData objects
- Text (static, dynamic, and input)
- Shapes (lines and fills)

By far, the most useful of these elements, from an animation viewpoint, is the movie clip.

Movie clips can contain any other type of element and can listen for mouse and keyboard events. Movie clips can also be preassembled in the library and put on stage at runtime.

You've already used movie clips in just about every example so far. Now, let's take a look at how the movie clips come to be and some of their more important features.

Movie clip symbols and instances

The first thing to know is that when you talk about movie clips, you are potentially talking about two different things:

- A movie clip in the library
- A movie clip on stage in the movie

The movie clip in the library is technically called a movie clip *symbol*, and the movie clip on the stage is called a movie clip *instance*. The library symbol is like a template. Only one symbol exists for any given movie clip. The on-stage instances are copies of the symbol, and you can have any number of copies of any one symbol. Despite this specific terminology, most people refer to both objects simply as *movie clips*. You'll probably catch me doing the same in places where what I am referring to is obvious. If there is any question though, I will use their proper names: symbol and instance.

Movie clip creation

Movie clip symbols are created in two basic ways. You've already seen one of these ways twice in this chapter: select some stage element and "convert" it to a movie clip symbol. The other way is to simply create a new symbol.

You can create a new symbol by pressing *CTRL-F8* (*⌘-F8* on a Mac), by choosing Insert ➤ New Symbol from the menu, or by choosing New Symbol from the Library panel menu. The dialog box that comes up is identical to the Convert to Symbol dialog box (shown earlier in Figure 2-1), but the movie clip it creates will be empty. It will also immediately be opened for editing, allowing you to add content if you wish. Make sure that you specify Movie Clip and not Graphic or Button when creating the symbol.

Next, you need to know how to get a movie clip instance on the stage. You can do this in four main ways: manually, copying an existing instance, attaching a new movie clip, or creating an empty movie clip. Manually means to simply drag the symbol onto the stage in the authoring environment. Not much needs to be said about that. The other methods require a bit more explanation.

Duplicating movie clips

Once you have a movie clip on stage, you can make additional instances of it by copying that instance, using the `duplicateMovieClip` command. When you duplicate a movie clip, it inherits all properties of the instance you are copying, including any properties that you have changed with ActionScript during runtime. It also inherits any code that was placed on it in an `onClipEvent` block. Because of this last characteristic, duplicating was heavily used in Flash 5, where clip events were rampant. However, with the new event model and ActionScript 2 classes, duplication has largely fallen out of use.

Attaching movie clips

Far more common now is creating instances by attaching them, using `attachMovie`. This command is used to create a brand-new movie clip instance on stage at runtime. By attaching, you can leave your stage completely blank and dynamically attach all the content as your program sees fit. Designers might have a harder time with this method, as they can't really see what is going where until the movie is run. But most programmers embrace it, as it gives far more control over each element—where and when it appears, what it does, and when it goes away.

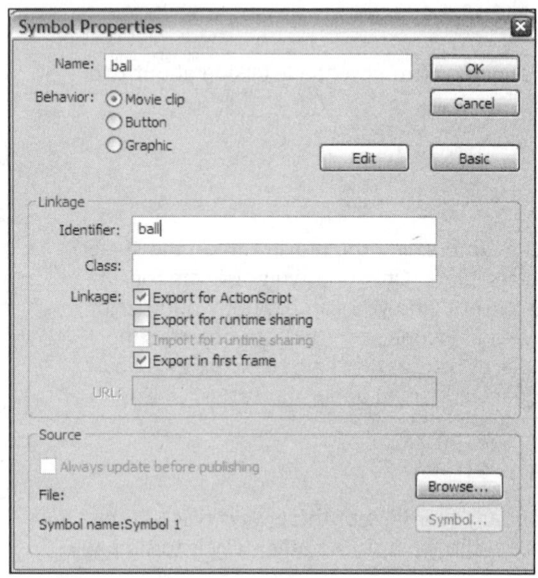

Figure 2-10. Setting export properties

To attach a movie clip, you need to do one important piece of setup work: *export it from the library*. To export a movie clip from the library, right-click (⌘-click on a Mac) the library symbol and choose either Properties or Linkage. You can also do it while creating or converting the movie clip in that dialog box. Whichever method you use, you will see a check box option labeled Export for ActionScript. When you select that, you will see the Identifier field become active and filled with the name of the symbol. You will also see the Export in first frame check box become active and selected, as shown in Figure 2-10. For now, those defaults are fine, and you can click OK.

Exporting the symbol forces Flash to include that symbol in the final SWF file. If a symbol is never placed on stage in the authoring environment, and is not exported with the Export in first frame option checked, that data will not be included when the SWF is published. If the symbol is not in the SWF, then obviously it will be impossible to create an instance of it.

Let's try it out. Open `chapter2base.fla` again. Delete the instance of `ball` from the stage, select `ball`'s symbol in the library, and export it with the default settings, as just described. Now add this code to frame 1:

```
attachMovie("ball", "ball", 0);
ball._x = 100;
ball._y = 100;
```

Test the movie, and you'll see an instance of the ball on stage at 100, 100. The parameters of the `attachMovie` call are as follows:

- `"ball"`: The linkage identifier of the symbol. This is the name in the identifier field when you set it to export, and it is generally the same as the name of the symbol.
- `"ball"`: The name of the instance you are creating. This is the same as when you used the Property inspector to manually name the instance on stage. For this example, it is fine if the instance name is the same as the linkage name. If you are attaching multiple clips though, you need to ensure that each one has a unique name, as you'll see in moment.
- `0`: The depth at which to place the new instance. Instances with higher depths will appear in front of instances with lower depths.

Most important, you should know that every dynamically created instance must have a unique name and depth. If you create a new instance with the same name or same depth as an existing one, the older one will disappear.

Let's see a quick example of just how powerful attachMovie is. Replace the preceding code with the following:

```
for(var i:Number = 0; i < 100; i++){
   var ball:MovieClip = attachMovie("ball", "ball" + i, i);
   ball._x = Math.random() * Stage.width;
   ball._y = Math.random() * Stage.height;
   ball._xscale = ball._yscale =
      Math.random() * 100 + 50;
}
```

When you play the movie, you should see something like Figure 2-11.

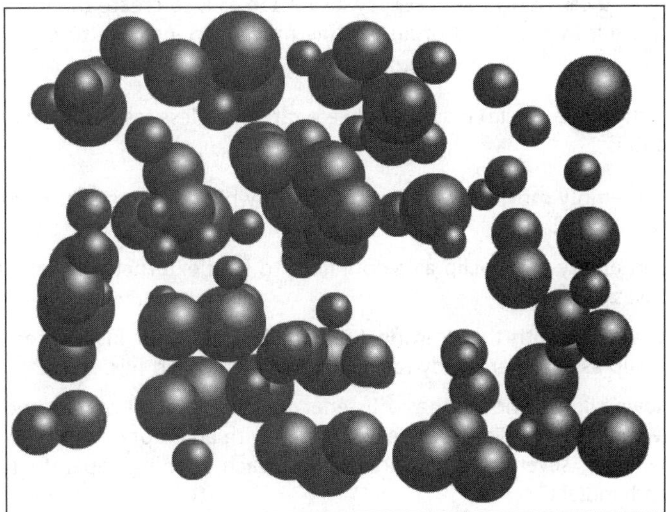

Figure 2-11. Randomly attached particles

This example uses a for loop to attach 100 instances of the ball symbol, giving each one a random size and position. The important thing to note is that the example uses the loop index, the variable i, to give each one a unique name and depth. The statement "ball" + i becomes "ball0" for the first instance, "ball1" for the second, and so on. Thus, none of the instances are overwritten. You'll be using very similar loops many times throughout this book.

Another important thing to realize about the attachMovie command is that it's actually a method of a movie clip. In the previous case, you're really saying _root.attachMovie. But suppose you had an existing movie clip instance named dog and a movie clip symbol in the library named collar. You could say this:

```
dog.attachMovie("collar", "spikesCollar", 0);
```

This would attach an instance of the collar symbol inside the dog instance, with the specified name and depth. You could continue to nest the movie clips:

```
dog.spikesCollar.attachMovie("leash", "spikesLeash", 0);
```

Note that there is no depth conflict, as spikesLeash is at depth 0 within spikesCollar, which is at depth 0 within dog.

Creating empty movie clips

The final method for creating movie clip instances doesn't even require a symbol. As such, they are not really instances of a particular symbol in the library, but I'll still refer to them as instances. To create an empty movie clip, use the createEmptyMovieClip method. The command is almost exactly the same as attachMovie, but it leaves off the linkage identifier. You just need to specify the instance name and depth:

```
createEmptyMovieClip("holder", 0);
```

As with attachMovie, you can apply createEmptyMovieClip as is to create the instance on the current timeline, or you can use it as a method of an existing movie clip instance to create a new movie clip inside that.

At first, creating an empty movie clip may seem like a rather useless task. But empty movie clips actually have many functions:

- You can use an empty movie clip as a container in which to attach other movie clips, keeping them together as a unit.
- You can use an empty movie clip as a container to load external content such as JPEG images or external SWFs.
- When you're working with the drawing API (which I will cover in Chapter 4), you can use an empty movie clip as a holder for dynamically drawn lines and fills.
- An empty movie clip can be used as a listener for almost any event. Some developers find it tidier to have their onEnterFrame code associated with an empty movie clip rather than _root. Or you could have several empty movie clips, each running separate tasks on their own onEnterFrame handlers.

Classes and OOP

In this book, I concentrate on the various principles and formulas involved in creating ActionScripted animation, rather than on teaching object-oriented programming (OOP) or specific coding methodologies. Thus, I won't get too involved in the creation of large class libraries and building complex inheritance structures and frameworks. Rather, I'm going to keep things as simple as possible.

The animation concepts you'll learn here can definitely be incorporated into more advanced ActionScript classes. However, my goal is not to hand you a prebuilt set of animation classes to copy and paste, but to pass on some understanding of the principles.

All that being said, let's take a ten-minute, drive-by course on classes.

If you think you do not have any familiarity with classes, you may be wrong. If you've written any code in Flash, chances are you used several classes. A *class* simply refers to a type of object. MovieClip is a class referring to, you guessed it, movie clips. Text fields, movie clips, buttons, strings, and numbers all have classes.

A class basically has two things associated with it: properties (data or information) and behaviors (actions, or things it can do). Properties are essentially variables that hold information relating to the class, and behaviors are just functions, though when a function is part of a class, we usually refer to it as a *method*.

A basic class

Similar to the relationship between symbols and instances, classes are templates, and objects (also known as instances) are individual manifestations of a particular class. You can make a simple class like this:

```
class MyClass {
   public var myProperty:Number = 100;

   public function myMethod() {
      trace("I am here");
   }
}
```

You'll see that within the class are only two things: a variable named `myProperty` and a function named `myMethod`. These will become properties and methods of any instance of this class you create. The word `public` means that any code outside the object will be able to access that property or call that method. If you create properties or methods that are meant only for use internal to the class, you can label them `private`, which prevents them from being messed with by outside code.

This class code must be in an external text file named the same as the class, with the suffix `.as`, as in `MyClass.as`. You can create the file by using the ActionScript editor in Flash (creating a new ActionScript file) or by using your favorite code editor or any other text-editing program. This file must be in the same directory as your FLA file or in your class path.

The *class path* is simply a list of directories. When you specify a class name in your code, Flash will search those directories for a class with that name. You can set an overall class path, which will apply to any and all FLA files, in the ActionScript 2.0 Settings panel, accessed by pressing the "ActionScript 2.0 Settings" button in the Preferences panel, as shown in Figure 2-12, and an additional class path for a specific FLA file in the Publish Settings dialog box. By default, the current directory of the FLA file, and the classes directory in the Flash configuration directory, are what compose your class path. If you wind up with a bunch of other classes that you want to use across several projects, you can put them in their own directory and add that directory to the class path.

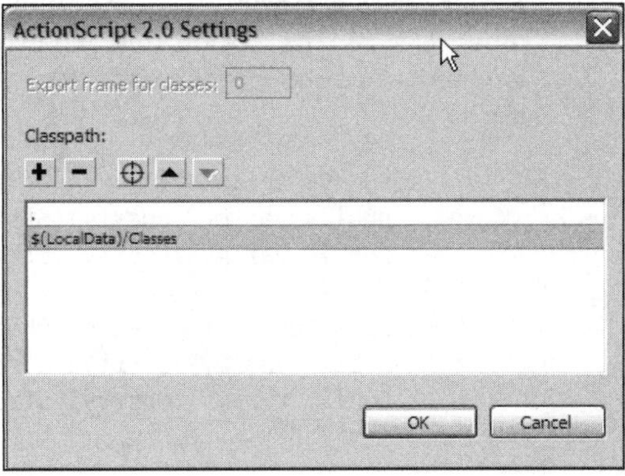

Figure 2-12. Specifying your class path

Back in Flash, create a new FLA file and save it in the same directory where you just created the class file. On the timeline, you can make a new instance of the class like this:

```
var myInstance:MyClass = new MyClass();
```

Flash will search the class path for the specified class. When it finds it in the current directory, it will use that code to create a new instance of the class. This instance will have all the properties and methods defined in the class. You can test it by running the following:

```
trace(myInstance.myProperty);   // traces 100
myInstance.myMethod();   // traces "I am here"
```

Constructors

You can set a *constructor* for the class, which is a method that has the same name as the class and is automatically called when a new instance is created. You can pass arguments to the constructor as follows.

First, create the class:

```
class MyClass {
   public function MyClass(arg) {
      trace("constructed");
      trace("you passed " + arg);
   }
}
```

Then, back on the timeline in Flash, create the instance:

```
var myInstance:MyClass = new MyClass("hello");
```

This should trace "constructed" and then "you passed hello".

Inheritance

A class can *inherit* from, or extend, another class. This means that it gets all the same things that the other class has. The *subclass* (the one that is inheriting) can then add additional properties and behaviors, or change some of the ones from the *superclass* (the one that is being extended). This is done like so:

```
class MyBaseClass {
   public var myProperty1:String = "A";
   public var myProperty2:String = "B";
}
class MySubClass extends MyBaseClass {
   public var myProperty2:String = "C";
   public var myProperty3:String = "D";
}
```

Remember that each class must be in its own file named after the class name, with the `.as` extension, so you will have a `MyBaseClass.as` file and a `MySubClass.as` file in the same directory as your FLA file. Now, you can make a couple of instances and see what happens:

```
var myBaseInstance:MyBaseClass = new MyBaseClass();
trace(myBaseInstance.myProperty1); // traces "A"
trace(myBaseInstance.myProperty2); // traces "B"
```

```
var mySubInstance:MySubClass = new MySubClass();
trace(mySubInstance.myProperty1); // traces "A"
trace(mySubInstance.myProperty2); // traces "C"
trace(mySubInstance.myProperty3); // traces "D"
```

The first instance has no surprises. But notice that the second one has a value of "A" for myProperty1, even though MySubClass does not define myProperty1. The class inherited it from MyBaseClass. Next, notice that myProperty2 traces "C", not "B". We say that the subclass has *overridden* the property. Finally, the subclass adds a new property, myProperty3, which the base class does not have.

A MovieClip subclass

You may or may not write a class, and then write another class that extends that. But chances are that, if you do much with ActionScript 2, you will eventually wind up extending the MovieClip class. The class MovieClip is the template for all the ActionScript properties and methods that are part of a movie clip object. It contains properties such as _x, _y, _xscale, _alpha, _currentframe, and so on, and methods like gotoAndPlay, attachMovie, lineTo, and so on.

If you write a class that extends MovieClip, it will automatically inherit all the properties and methods inherent to a movie clip. Then you can add specific behaviors or properties that apply only to the type of object you are creating. For example, say you wanted to make a spaceship object for a game. You might want it to contain some graphics, have a position on the screen, move around, rotate, change its appearance over time, contain some sounds, listen for enterFrame events for animation, and listen for keyboard and mouse events for interaction. These are all things that movie clips can do, so it makes sense to extend MovieClip. You could then add custom properties such as speed, fuel, and damage and custom behaviors such as takeOff, crash, shoot, and selfDestruct. The class might start out something like the following:

```
class SpaceShip extends MovieClip {
   var speed = 0;
   var damage = 0;
   var fuel = 1000;

   function takeOff() {
      // . . .
   }
   function crash() {
      // . . .
   }
   function shoot() {
      // . . .
   }
   function selfDestruct() {
      // . . .
   }
}
```

Let's make an actual class that extends MovieClip and see it in action.

1. Start again with chapter2base.fla. Right-click the ball symbol in the library and choose Linkage from the pop-up menu.
2. Select Export for ActionScript and leave Export on first frame checked. In the AS 2.0 Class field, enter Ball. This links the ball symbol to the Ball class, which you are about to create.
3. Create an ActionScript file named Ball.as in the same directory as the movie, and type the following in it:

```
class Ball extends MovieClip {
    function onEnterFrame():Void
    {
        this._x += 5;
    }
}
```

This class adds only one thing to the base MovieClip class: defining the onEnterFrame function to handle that event.

You can see how powerful this could be for animation, especially when you are creating more than one of the same thing with some complex behavior. Rather than creating or assigning the code each time you create a new instance, it becomes a native part of the new object as soon as it's born.

User interaction

Finally, we come to user interaction, one of the key points of what you are doing here. After all, if it weren't for interaction or some sort of dynamic input going into the movie, you might as well just use tweens.

Actually, there is not a whole lot left to discuss here that I haven't already touched on earlier in the chapter. User interaction is based on user events, and these generally come down to mouse events and keyboard events. Let's quickly go through the various user events and their handlers.

Mouse events

A movie clip or button is automatically a listener for any of these events. You just need to create an event handler function for that event. The name of that event is always on plus the capitalized name of the event. For example, if you had a clip named square, you could handle the press event as follows:

```
square.onPress = function():Void
{
   // actions
}
```

The following are the mouse events:

- dragOut: Occurs when the user presses a mouse button while over graphical content and, while still pressing the mouse button, moves the mouse off of that content.
- dragOver: Occurs after dragOut if the user, still holding down that mouse button, drags back over the graphical content. I'm not sure I could come up with a useful example of this one if I tried, but if you ever find yourself needing such a thing, it's available.

- mouseDown: Occurs whenever a mouse button is pressed, regardless of mouse location, visibility, or any other factors. This is often a source of confusion for programmers who think of mouseDown as press. In fact, when a mouse button is pressed, every single movie clip in the movie will receive a mouseDown event.
- mouseMove: Occurs whenever the mouse is moved. You should be careful about using this event, as it can generate hundreds of calls per second and really slow down a movie. Use it only when necessary, turn it off when you are done with it, and keep the code it executes to a minimum.
- mouseUp: Occurs whenever a mouse button is released. All the same rules for mouseDown apply.
- mouseWheel: Occurs when the user scrolls the mouse wheel, if it exists. Note that even though a movie clip is a listener for mouse events by default, for some reason, it will not automatically listen for the mouseWheel event. If you want a movie clip to handle this event, you must explicitly call Mouse.addListener(*yourMovieClip*) to add it as a mouse listener.
- press: Occurs when the user presses a mouse button while the cursor is over any visible graphical elements in the movie clip. If the movie clip's _visible property is set to false, it will not receive press events. Any portion of graphical content that is invisible due to masking will not generate press events if clicked on. However, setting the _alpha property to zero will effectively make the content invisible while still allowing it to receive press events.
- release: Occurs after press when the user releases the mouse button while still over any visible graphical content in a movie clip. All the same rules for press apply. The release event occurs only after a press event, and press events are always followed by either release or releaseOutside.
- releaseOutside: Occurs after press when the user has moved the mouse off the graphical content and then releases the mouse button. User interface buttons almost always listen for release and ignore releaseOutside. This allows the user to cancel the button press by moving off the button before releasing.
- rollout: Occurs when the mouse is over visible graphical content and moves off, while no mouse buttons are being pushed.
- rollover: Occurs when the user moves the mouse pointer over the graphical content in a movie. As with press, the content must be visible and not hidden by a mask, though the _alpha property can be set to zero.

As you can see, most of these events deal with the graphical content in a movie clip. As such, they really apply only to movie clips or buttons, which can also contain graphics. You cannot listen for, say, a press event on a generic object or a custom class that does not subclass MovieClip, as these would have no visible graphical content. The only mouse events such an object can listen for are mouseDown, mouseUp, mouseMove, and mouseWheel.

Keyboard events

Movie clips are technically listeners for keyboard events. But there's a catch—a serious one. The movie clip must have *keyboard focus*, which is usually acquired only by using the *Tab* key to tab between objects. This means that you need to set focusEnabled = true and tabEnabled = true, and then tab to the movie clip. Then the movie clip can receive keyboard events. Oh, but if you move the mouse at all—even 1 pixel—your movie clip will lose focus and won't respond to keyboard events.

Given the fleeting nature of the automatic keyboard listening, it is usually best to just force the issue by saying Key.addListener(*yourMovieClip*). This allows the movie clip to receive all key events, regardless of focus.

The following are the keyboard events:

- keyDown: Supposedly occurs whenever a key is pressed. This is a bit misleading though, because in most cases, you will get a continuous series of keyDown events as long as the key is being held down.
- keyUp: Occurs whenever a key that has been pressed is released. If you want to ensure that you get only one event per key press, this is the one to use.

Mouse position

In addition to mouse events, two very important properties are always available to determine the current location of the mouse pointer: _xmouse and _ymouse. Note that these are properties of a movie clip, and the values returned are the mouse's position in relation to the registration point of that clip. For example, if you had a movie clip instance named clip sitting at 100, 100 on the stage, and the mouse pointer were at 150, 250, you would get the following results:

- _root._xmouse would be 150.
- _root._ymouse would be 250.
- clip._xmouse would be 50.
- clip._ymouse would be 150.

Notice how the movie clip is taking the mouse position in relation to its own position.

Key codes

Often, you want to know not just that a key has been pressed, but which key has been pressed, or if a particular key is currently being pressed. ActionScript provides a couple of functions to handle such things.

First is Key.getCode. This returns a number responding to the code of the key that was last pressed. Now, if you know all the key codes by heart, you're all set. But more likely, you'll want to use the key enumerations, which allow you to use a human-readable word describing the key—such as Key.SPACE, Key.UP, or Key.DOWN—rather than numbers. You just compare the result from Key.getCode() to the key you want to handle, as follows:

```
if(Key.getCode() == Key.UP){
   // move object up
}
```

or

```
if(Key.getCode() == Key.SPACE){
   // pause game
}
```

You can find a full list of the key enumerations in the Flash help files.

If you want to find out if a specific key is currently being pressed, use the Key.isDown function, passing it the code of the key you want to check:

```
if(Key.isDown(Key.UP)){
   // move object up
}
```

Whereas Key.getCode() will always return the code of the last key pressed, even if that key was pressed six hours ago, Key.isDown() returns true only if the specified key is down at the time you check it.

One thing you should know about key handling is that when you are testing a movie in the Flash authoring environment, the IDE intercepts some keys to control the IDE itself. *Tab*, all function keys, and any keys assigned as shortcuts to menu items will not be received by your movie while testing. You can disable this by choosing Control ➤ Disable Keyboard Shortcuts from the menu while the movie is running. This allows you to test your movie as it will actually work in a browser.

Summary

This chapter covered just about all the basics of ActionScript needed for animation. You now know about frame loops, events, listeners, handlers, and movie clips. I've touched on classes, objects, and basic user interaction. That's a lot of material! Don't worry if some of these areas are still a little vague. I'll be covering most of them in much more detail as I get into specific techniques, and you can always come back here to brush up on any concepts. At the very least, now you are familiar with the terms and concepts, and you're ready to move forward.

};shape.targetHeight = shape._height;
shape.onEnterFrame = function() {
var speed = 5;
this._width += (this.targetWidth - this._width)/speed;
this._height += (this.targetHeight - this._height)/speed;

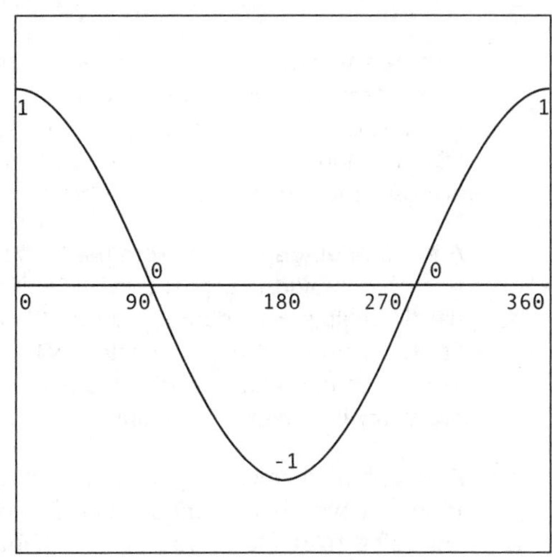

Chapter 3

TRIGONOMETRY FOR ANIMATION

What we'll cover in this chapter:

- What is trigonometry?
- Angles
- Trig functions
- Rotation
- Waves
- Circles and ellipses
- Pythagorean Theorem
- Distance between two points
- Important formulas in this chapter

I wanted to put this chapter near the beginning of the book, as you'll be using trigonometry extensively for animation techniques, starting with the examples in Chapter 5. In fact, I'll even touch on it in the next chapter on rendering techniques. However, feel free to jump ahead if you already know basic trig or are just anxious to get into animating things. You can always come back here when you come across something you don't understand.

A lot of people shy away from math and trigonometry, saying things like, "I'm not good with numbers. I can barely add two plus two." The funny thing is that in programming with trigonometry, you are hardly dealing with numbers at all. It's far more in the realm of visualizing shapes and relationships. For the most part, you are dealing with variables containing positions, distances, and angles. You never see the actual numbers. It's mostly a matter of memorizing various relationships. In fact, 90% of the trig you will need for basic animation will come down to two functions: `Math.sin` and `Math.cos`.

And, as a disclaimer, and possibly a bit of encouragement, I have to admit that I have no formal math training beyond high school algebra and geometry, most of which I have long forgotten. All of what I am going to relate to you in this chapter is stuff I have learned from various books, websites, and other online resources. The disclaimer part is that it's possible that some of what I might say might not hold up in front of a trigonometry professor, and if you are programming some mission-critical rocket launch (something not likely to be done in Flash anyway), you'd better pick up a real book on trig. The good news is that I can pretty much guarantee that what I tell you here will work for basic Flash animation. The other good news is that if I can learn this stuff, so can you.

What is trigonometry?

Trigonometry is basically the study of triangles and the relationship of their sides and angles. If you look at any triangle, you'll see that it has three sides and three angles (hence the name *tri-angle*). It happens that these sides and angles have very specific relationships. For example, if you take any triangle and make one of the angles larger, the side opposite of that angle will get longer (assuming the other two sides stay the same length). Also, the other two angles will get smaller. Exactly how much each of these things changes takes a bit of calculation, but the ratios have all been figured out and codified.

A very specific type of triangle has one of its angles exactly equal to 90 degrees. This is called a *right triangle* and is indicated by a little square in the corner of that angle. It happens that in a right triangle, the various relationships are far simpler and quite easy to figure out with some basic formulas. This makes a right triangle a very useful construct. Almost all of the trig you will see in this chapter and the rest of the book deals with right triangles.

Angles

As trigonometry is mostly about angles, let's tackle that subject first. An *angle* is simply the shape formed by two intersecting lines, or the space in between those lines. The more space, the higher the measurement of the angle. Actually, two intersecting lines will form four angles, as you can see in Figure 3-1.

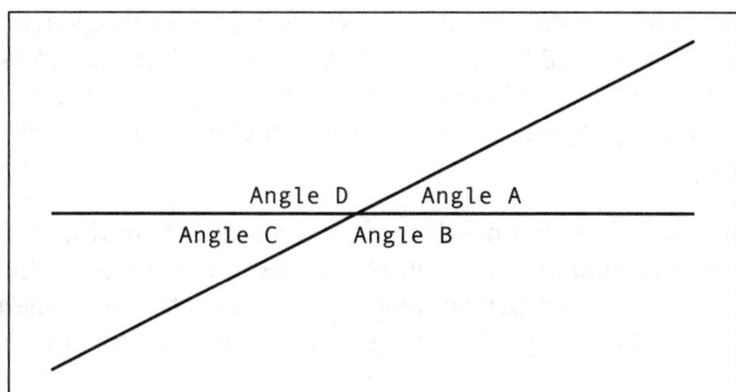

Figure 3-1. Two lines form four angles

Radians and degrees

The two major systems for measuring angles are degrees and radians. You are probably very familiar with degrees, and no doubt you could draw a 45- or 90-degree angle in your sleep. The system of 360 degrees in a circle has become a part of our culture. We talk about "doing a 180," meaning "going in the opposite direction," even when we are not talking about physical direction, but referring to taking an opposite viewpoint. But it turns out that computers have a lot more affinity for radians when it comes to talking about angles. So, like it or not, you need to know about radians.

A *radian* is equal to approximately 57.2958 degrees. Now, you're probably rolling your eyes and saying, "Well, isn't that logical?" But there is some actual logic to it. A full circle, or 360 degrees, works out to 6.2832 radians. Still not making any sense? Well, remember pi—that symbol, π? That is equal to about 3.1416, meaning that a circle (6.2832 radians) measures exactly 2 pi. It still may not seem too logical now, but work with it enough, and you'll get used to thinking of a 360 degrees as 2 pi, 180 degrees as pi, 90 degrees as pi/2, and so on. Figure 3-2 illustrates some common radian measurements.

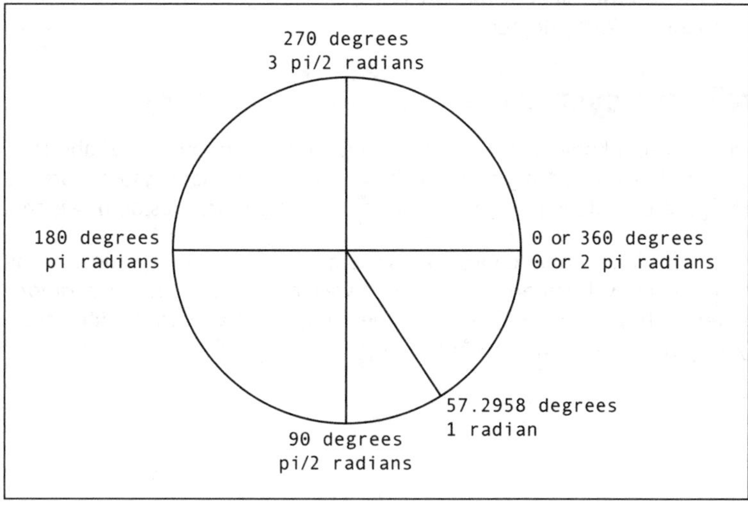

Figure 3-2. Radians and degrees

Now, I could pretty much leave the discussion there and just tell you that you'll be using radians from here on out. You might sigh a bit, and then get used to it and live happily ever after. But you're going to encounter many situations where you'll need to use degrees along with radians. For example, it just so happens that the `_rotation` property of a movie clip is measured in degrees, and you'll often need to use or set that property.

For example, say you have a vehicle that needs to turn in the direction of its motion. If you figure out the motion using trig, the angle you get will be in radians, but to rotate the vehicle, you need degrees. Or, conversely, suppose you want to move something in the direction it happens to be pointing. You can check its `_rotation` to get the angle, but that's going to be degrees, and to use it in any trig formula, you need radians.

Why the heck are they using two completely different systems in the same program? Well, it's kind of indicative of Flash's dual nature. On one hand, it's a designer tool. You have all your drawing and transformation tools to make pretty graphics. I'm sure most designers would look at you cross-eyed if you told them to enter a radian value to rotate the text for the logo they are creating. On the other hand, Flash is a developer tool, and like most programming languages, ActionScript uses radians. So, like it or not, you'll be working with both, and you'll need to know how to convert degrees to radians and vice versa. Here are the formulas:

```
radians = degrees * Math.PI / 180
degrees = radians * 180 / Math.PI
```

As you go through this book, you'll be running into a lot of formulas. Here and there, I will point out a formula as one that you should memorize—burn into the backs of your eyelids. These are the first ones. If you need to look up this formula every time you want to use it, you'll never get any code written. It should just roll off your fingers onto the keyboard whenever you need it. I even wrote it in ActionScript for you, with `Math.PI` rather than just pi or its funny symbol, because that's how you'll be typing it over and over.

From this, you can easily see that 180 degrees is about 3.14. . . radians. In other words, half a circle is pi radians, which makes sense, since a full circle is 2 pi. Going the other way, you can see that one radian is indeed roughly 57.29. . . degrees.

Flash's coordinate system

While we're on the subject of angles, this would be a good time to say a word about how space is laid out in Flash, numerically speaking. If you've dealt with any coordinate systems prior to Flash, you're probably going to get a little dizzy here, as everything is pretty much upside down and backwards.

The most common two-dimensional coordinate systems signify horizontal measurements with x and vertical measurements with y. Flash does this, too. However, the zero x, zero y position (0, 0) is usually shown in the center, with positive x going off to the right, negative x to the left, positive y going up, and negative y going down, as shown in Figure 3-3.

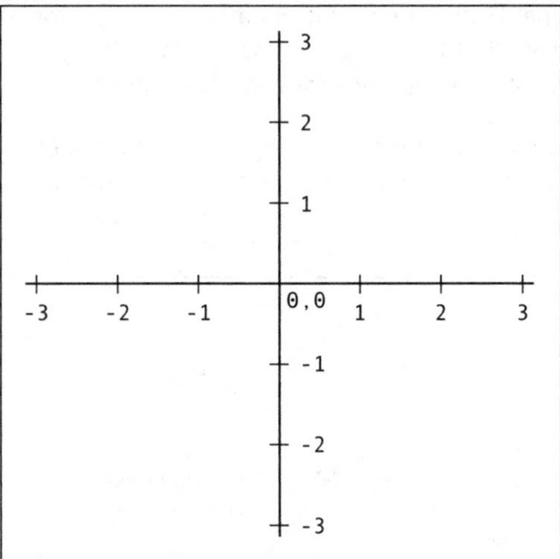

Figure 3-3. Standard coordinate system

Flash, however, is based on a video screen coordinate system, where 0, 0 is at the top left, as shown in Figure 3-4. The x values still increase from left to right, but the y axis is reversed, with positive values going down and negative values going up. I believe this system has its historical roots in the way the electron gun scans the screen to build the picture—left to right, top to bottom—but it doesn't really matter. That's the way it works, and it's probably not going to change very soon.

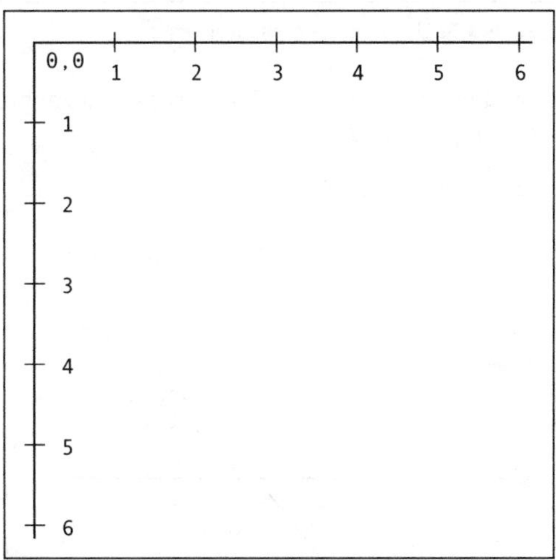

Figure 3-4. Flash's coordinate system

It is possible to build a system where you can work with numbers in a standard coordinate system, and convert them to Flash's coordinates just before rendering. Basically, you would flip the y values, and offset everything half a screen to move the center to the top-left corner. However, the problem is that all those calculations take time. Flash already suffers a bit in the performance department compared with other languages, so personally, I trade my brainpower for CPU cycles. Learn to live with the backward coordinates, and reserve the calculations for the cool effects.

But wait, there's more! Let's talk about measuring angles. In most systems, angles are measured counterclockwise, with 0 degrees being shown as a line extending into the positive x axis, as shown in Figure 3-5.

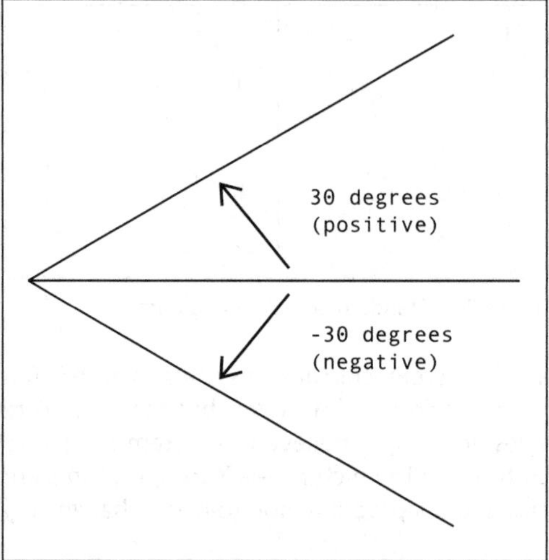

Figure 3-5. Usual angle measurements

Again, Flash has it backwards, as illustrated in Figure 3-6. It rotates its angles clockwise as they go positive. Counterclockwise means a negative angle.

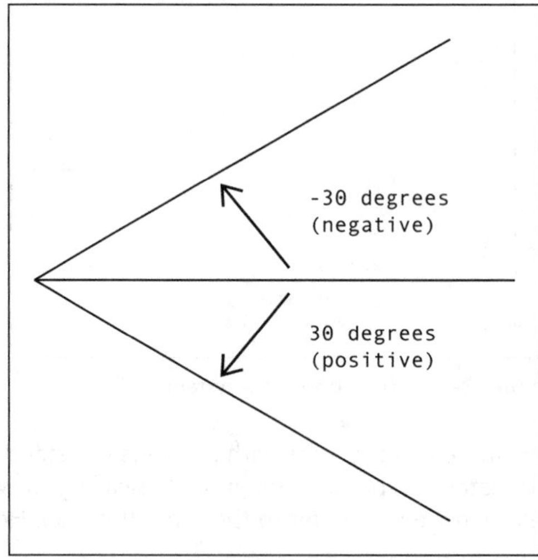

Figure 3-6. Flash's angle measurements

And again, you can work out a system to reverse the angles before rendering, or conserve the computation and learn to live with it. I suggest the latter, and this is the tactic I will use for all the code in this book.

Triangle sides

There's not too much to say about the sides of a triangle by themselves, but there are some specific terms to cover. Until further notice, I will be talking about right triangles, where one of the angles is 90 degrees. In this case, the sides have special names, as shown in Figure 3-7. The two sides that touch the 90-degree angle are called *legs*, and the opposite side is called the *hypotenuse*. The hypotenuse is always the longest side.

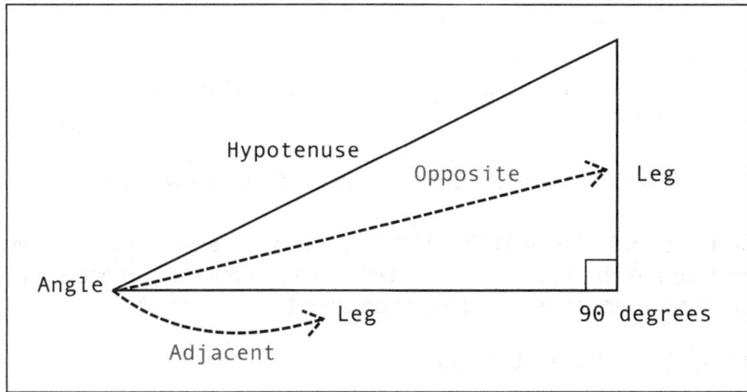

Figure 3-7. The parts of a right triangle

When we refer to the side *opposite* an angle, we are talking about the side that does not touch that angle. When we refer to an *adjacent* side, we mean one of the sides that does touch the angle. Mostly, we will deal with one of the two non-90 degree angles. In this case, when we say *adjacent*, we mean the adjacent leg, not the hypotenuse.

The interesting thing about triangles is the relationships between the measurements of the sides and the measurements of the angles. These relationships become useful for animation, so let's take a look at them next.

Trig functions

ActionScript has trig functions for calculating the various triangle relationships: sine, cosine, tangent, arcsine, arccosine, and arctangent. Here, I'll define these and the ActionScript functions for accessing them. Then I'll get to some real-life uses for these functions.

Sine

Here is your first bit of real-life trigonometry. The *sine* of an angle is the ratio of the angle's opposite leg to the hypotenuse. (When referring to sine, we are always referring to the sine of an angle.) In ActionScript, you can use the function `Math.sin(angle)`.

Figure 3-8 shows the sine of an angle that is 30 degrees. The opposite leg has a measurement of 1, and the hypotenuse has a measurement of 2. The ratio is thus one to two, or mathematically speaking, 1/2 or 0.5. Thus, we can say that the sine of a 30-degree angle is 0.5. You can test this in Flash like so:

```
trace(Math.sin(30));
```

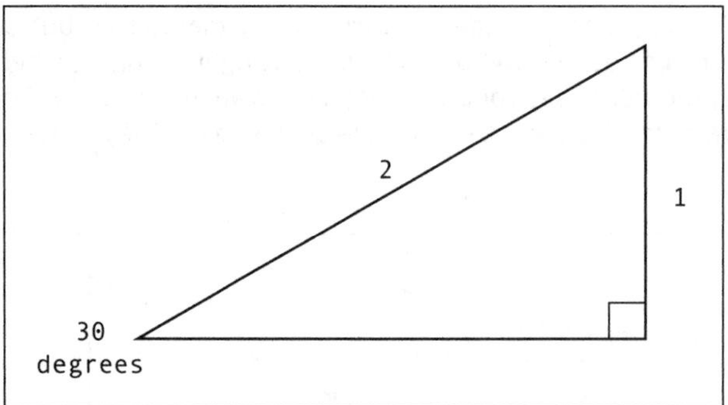

Figure 3-8. The sine of an angle is the opposite leg/hypotenuse

Now, hold on, that traces out –0.988031624092862, which is not even close. Can you spot the error? We forgot to convert to radians. I guarantee you will make this mistake on occasion (I still do), so get used to looking out for it. Here's the corrected code, with the conversion.

```
trace(Math.sin(30 * Math.PI / 180));
```

Success! That traces 0.5.

Now, it's fine for an abstract triangle like that to say that the angle is 30 degrees, and the measurements of the sides are 1 and 2. But let's move it into the real world, or at least the world of the Flash coordinate system. Remember that in Flash, positive vertical measurements go down, and positive angle measurements go clockwise. So, in this case, the opposite side and the angle are both negative, as you can see in Figure 3-9.

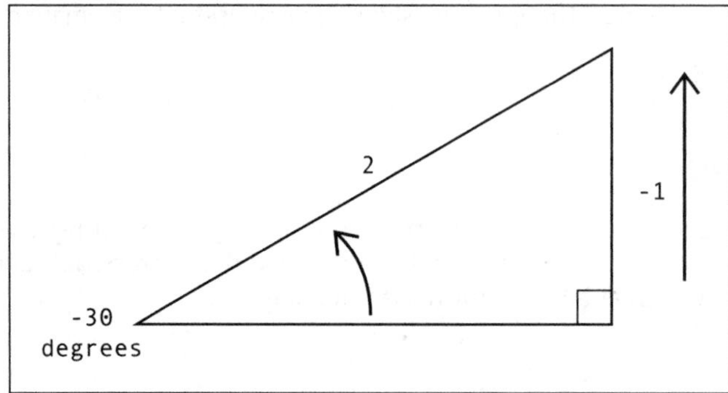

Figure 3-9. The same triangle in Flash coordinate space

So, the ratio becomes –1/2, and we are talking about the sine of –30. So, we say that the sine of –30 degrees is –0.5. Go ahead and alter the Flash trace statement to verify that.

```
trace(Math.sin(-30 * Math.PI / 180));
```

OK, that wasn't too painful, was it? Let's take a look at another trig function: cosine.

Cosine

You can access cosine in Flash with `Math.cos(angle)`. Cosine is defined as the ratio of the adjacent leg of an angle to the hypotenuse. Figure 3-10 shows that relationship.

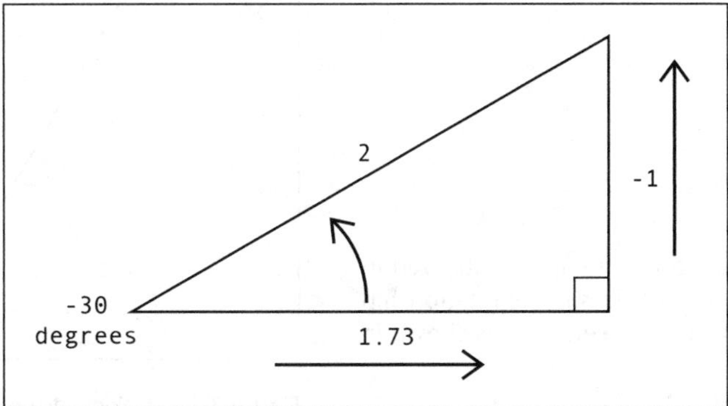

Figure 3-10. The cosine of an angle is the adjacent leg/hypotenuse.

Figure 3-10 shows the same angle as Figure 3-9, but now I've added the approximate measurement of the adjacent leg: 1.73. Notice that it goes to the right, so as an x measurement, it's positive. The cosine of the angle is thus 1.73/2, or 0.865. So we can say that the cosine of –30 degrees is 0.865. Test it as follows:

```
trace(Math.cos(-30 * Math.PI / 180));
```

This is the same as the last trace, but with the call to `Math.cos`, rather than to `Math.sin`. This traces to 0.866025403784439, which is pretty close to 0.865. The difference is due to the fact that I rounded off the length of the adjacent leg. For the triangle shown, the actual length would be closer to 1.73205080756888. You'll find that if you divide that by 2, you'll get pretty darned close to the actual cosine of –30 degrees.

So far, everything has been taken from the lower-left angle. What if you looked at things from the viewpoint of the top-right angle? Well, first you'd need to re-orient the triangle so that the angle in question aligns with the coordinate system, as you can see in Figure 3-11. That angle is equal to 60 degrees, and as it's going clockwise, it's positive. The vertical measurement now goes down from that angle, so it's positive, and the horizontal measurement goes to the right, so it's positive too. (I added plus signs in the figure to point out the difference, but in general, this is not necessary; values will be positive unless specifically indicated as being negative.)

Now, the sine of that angle is its opposite leg over the hypotenuse, or 1.73/2 (0.865). And the cosine is the adjacent over the hypotenuse, 1/2 or 0.5. So, basically, the cosine of one angle is the sine of the other angle, and the sine of one is the cosine of the other. I'm not sure how useful that will ever be in Flash, but it's important to note that these are just relationships and ratios, and everything is connected.

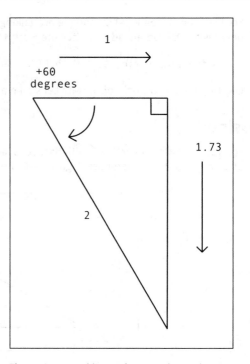

Figure 3-11. Looking at the opposite angle

Tangent

Another major trig function is tangent, retrieved in Flash with `Math.tan(angle)`. This is the relationship of the opposite leg to the adjacent leg, as shown in Figure 3-12.

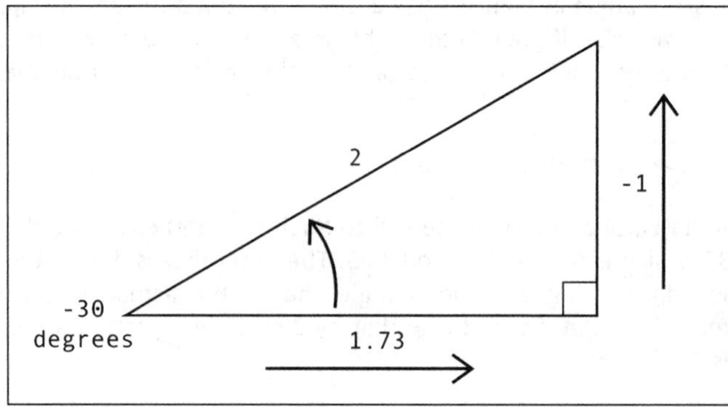

Figure 3-12. The tangent of an angle is the opposite leg/adjacent leg.

Here, the ratio works out to –1/1.73, or –0.578. For more accuracy, check it directly in Flash:

```
trace(Math.tan(-30 * Math.PI / 180));
```

You'll get –0.577350269189626.

Truth be told, you won't use tangent too much by itself in your day-to-day ActionScript animation code. You'll find yourself using sine and cosine a *lot* more, though tangent can be used to create some interesting effects now and then.

On the other hand, arctangent can be extremely useful, as you'll see shortly, so keep that tangent ratio in your head.

Arcsine and arccosine

Similar to tangent, arcsine and arccosine are not that useful in your normal Flash animation endeavors. However, it's important to know that they are there and how to use them. Basically, all these do is the reverse of sine and cosine. In other words, you feed in a ratio, and you get back an angle (in radians). The ActionScript functions are `Math.asin(ratio)` and `Math.acos(ratio)`. Let's just give them a quick test to make sure they work.

OK, you learned that the sine of 30 degrees is 0.5. Thus, it follows that the arcsine of 0.5 should be 30 degrees. Check it out:

```
trace(Math.asin(0.5) * 180 / Math.PI);
```

Remember to convert back to degrees in order to see 30, not 0.523, which is the equivalent value in radians.

And you know that the cosine of 30 degrees is roughly 0.865. Remember that if you test this value, which is rounded off, you aren't going to get exactly 30, but it will be close enough to prove the point. Here's the test:

```
trace(Math.acos(0.865) * 180 / Math.PI);
```

You should get 30.1172947473221 as the result. If you want to go back and plug in the actual cosine of 30 degrees, you should get a more accurate result.

See this stuff isn't so hard, is it? And you're almost finished learning the basic functions. You just have one more to go, and then you'll start looking at what you can actually do with trig.

Arctangent

As you no doubt have already guessed, arctangent is simply the opposite of tangent. You feed it the ratio of the opposite and adjacent sides, and it gives you back the angle. In Flash, you actually have two functions to check arctangent. The first is named and works just as you'd expect from the previous examples. It's `Math.atan(ratio)`, and you supply it the fraction you got by dividing the opposite and adjacent sides.

For example, you know from the earlier discussion that the tangent of 30 degrees is 0.577 (rounded off). You can try this:

```
trace(Math.atan(0.577) * 180 / Math.PI);
```

You'll get back something pretty close to 30. Now, that seems so basic and straightforward, why would you ever need another function to do the same thing? Well, to answer that, look at the diagram shown in Figure 3-13.

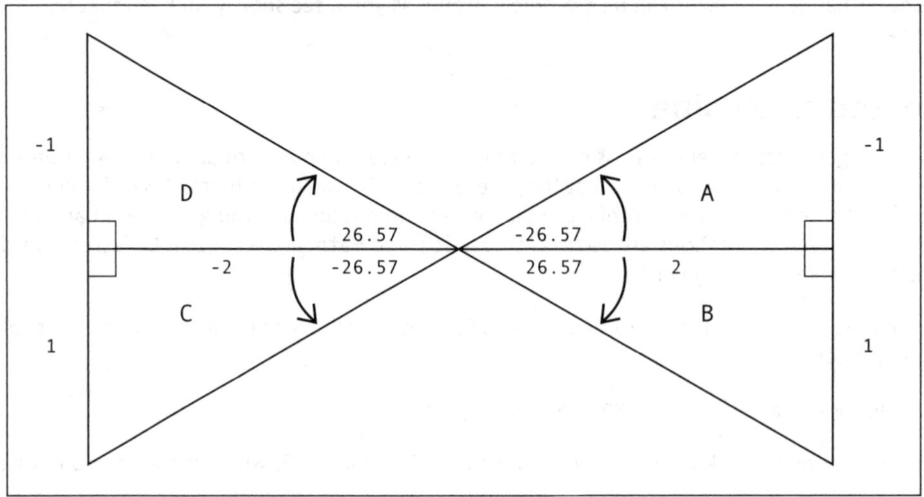

Figure 3-13. Angles in four quadrants

Figure 3-13 shows four different triangles: A, B, C, and D. Triangles A and B have a positive x value, and triangles C and D extend into negative x dimensions. Likewise, triangles A and D are in the negative y space, while triangles B and C have positive y measurements. So, for the ratios of the four inner angles, you get this:

- A: –1/2 or –0.5
- B: 1/2 or 0.5
- C: 1/ –2 or –0.5
- D: –1/ –2 or 0.5

So, say you divide your opposite leg by your adjacent leg and come up with a ratio of 0.5. You feed in that with `Math.atan(0.5)`, convert it to degrees, and you get approximately 26.57. But which triangle are you talking about now: B or D? There is really no way of knowing, since they both have a ratio of 0.5. This may seem like a minor point, but as you will see in some real-life examples coming up shortly, it becomes quite important.

Welcome `Math.atan2(y, x)`. This is the other arctangent function in Flash, and it is quite a bit more useful than `Math.atan(ratio)`. In fact, I would go so far to say you will probably wind up using this one exclusively. This function takes two values: the measurement of the opposite side and the measurement of the adjacent side. For most purposes in Flash, this means the y measurement and the x measurement. A common mistake is to enter them as x, y, rather than y, x, as specified. For the example given, you'd enter `Math.atan2(1, 2)`. Go ahead and try it out, remembering to convert to degrees:

```
trace(Math.atan2(1, 2) * 180 / Math.PI);
```

This should give you the angle, 26.565051177078, which is correct for triangle B as shown earlier. Now, knowing that –1/ –2 (triangle D) gave us some confusion, let's try that out.

```
trace(Math.atan2(-1, -2) * 180 / Math.PI);
```

This gives you the possibly unexpected result of –153.434948822922. What is that all about? Perhaps the diagram in Figure 3-14 will explain.

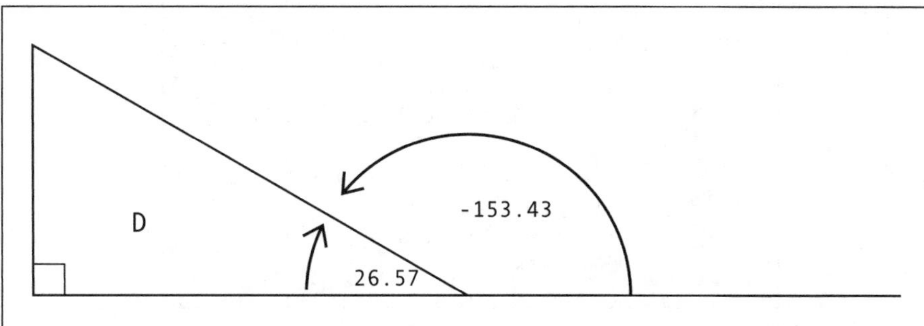

Figure 3-14. Two ways of measuring an angle

While the inner angle of triangle D is indeed +26.57, as taken from its own bottom leg, remember that in Flash, angles are measured clockwise from the positive x axis. Thus, from Flash's viewpoint of screen measurements, the angle you are looking at is –153.43.

How is this useful? Well, let's get to your first practical application of trigonometry in Flash.

Rotation

Here is the challenge: You want to rotate a movie clip so that it always points to the mouse. This is a very useful tool to add to your toolbox. It can be used in games, mouse trailers, those eyes that follow the mouse around the screen, interface elements, and so on. In fact, rotation is not just limited to the mouse. Since the mouse coordinates are just x and y values, you can extend this technique to force a movie clip to point to any particular point, such as another movie clip or the center or corner of the screen.

Let's work through an example. You can follow along with the steps or just open `rotate_to_mouse.fla` (which you can download from `www.friendsofed.com`, along with all of the other code for this book), to have all the work done for you.

First, you need a movie clip. Make an arrow and convert it to a movie clip symbol with the name `arrow`, as shown in Figure 3-15. Keep the registration point in the center, as this is the point it will rotate around. The most important thing to remember when drawing your symbol is to make sure that it is "pointing" to the right, or positive x axis, because this is how it will look when rotated to 0 degrees.

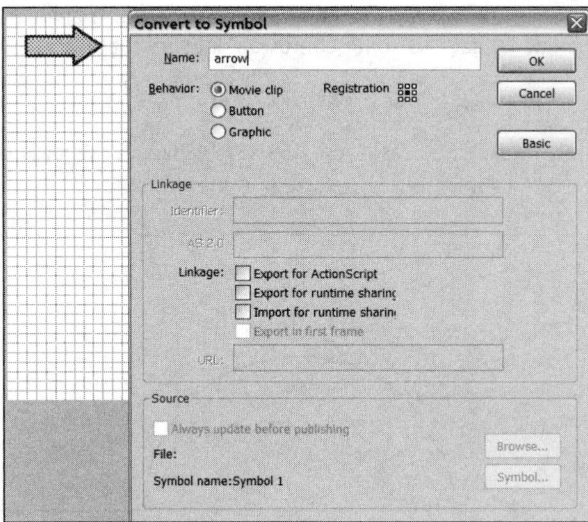

Figure 3-15. Making the arrow symbol

Keep an instance of this movie clip in the center of the stage and name it `arrow`. Then deselect it or click frame 1 on the timeline and open the Actions panel. You don't want to put code on the symbol itself, which would require clip events; you want the code to go on the timeline. Figure 3-16 shows what you will be doing.

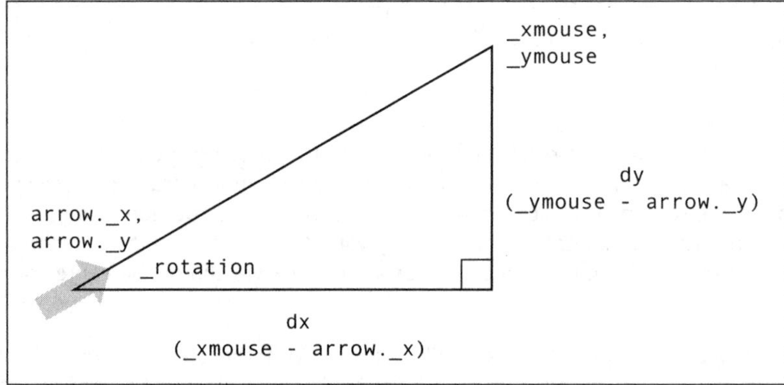

Figure 3-16. Computing the rotation

Look familiar? It's the same triangle you've been dealing with for a while now, just mapped to the mouse and arrow coordinates. The mouse position can always be read with the _xmouse and _ymouse properties. You can get the location of the arrow with its _x and _y properties. Subtracting these, you get the length of the two triangle legs. Now, you simply need to use `Math.atan2(dy, dx)` to find the angle. Then convert it to degrees and set the arrow's _rotation property to the result. It will look like this:

```
var dx = _xmouse - arrow._x;
var dy = _ymouse - arrow._y;
var radians = Math.atan2(dy, dx);
arrow._rotation = radians * 180 / Math.PI;
```

Of course, to get animation, you need to set up a loop. As discussed in detail in the previous chapter, event handlers are your best bet. You have two choices: onEnterFrame or onMouseMove. Either one will work. Let's go with onEnterFrame:

```
onEnterFrame = function(){
   var dx = _xmouse - arrow._x;
   var dy = _ymouse - arrow._y;
   var radians = Math.atan2(dy, dx);
   arrow._rotation = radians * 180 / Math.PI;
}
```

Test it. What do you know? It works like a charm!

Now, suppose that you didn't have Math.atan2. You could get the ratio of opposite to adjacent by dividing dy by dx and pass that in to Math.atan. All you need to do is change the fourth line in the preceding code as follows:

```
var radians = Math.atan(dy / dx);
```

Try that one, and you'll see the problem pretty quickly. If the mouse is to the left of the arrow, the arrow will not point to it, but directly away from it. Can you figure out what is going on? Going back to the diagram showing triangles A, B, C, and D (Figure 3-13), remember that triangles A and C share the same ratio, as do triangles B and D. There is no way for Flash to know which angle you are referring to, so it simply gives you A or B. So, if your mouse is in the D quadrant, Flash is going to return the angle for the B quadrant and rotate the mouse into that area.

You can no doubt see the benefits of Math.atan2 now. You'll be using it many times throughout the book.

Waves

Let's get into some more concrete uses of trig in Flash. Surely you've heard the term *sine wave* before, and surely you've seen the shape shown in Figure 3-17, which is a graphical representation of a sine wave.

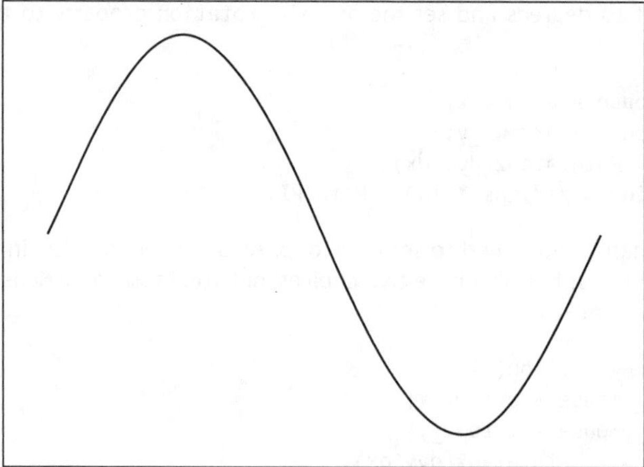

Figure 3-17. A sine wave

But what exactly does that shape have to do with the sine function? It is the graph of the results of the sine function, when fed in all the angles from 0 to 360 (or 0 to 2 pi in radians). From left to right is the value of the angle used, and the y value of the graph is the sine of that particular angle. In Figure 3-18, I've indicated some specific values.

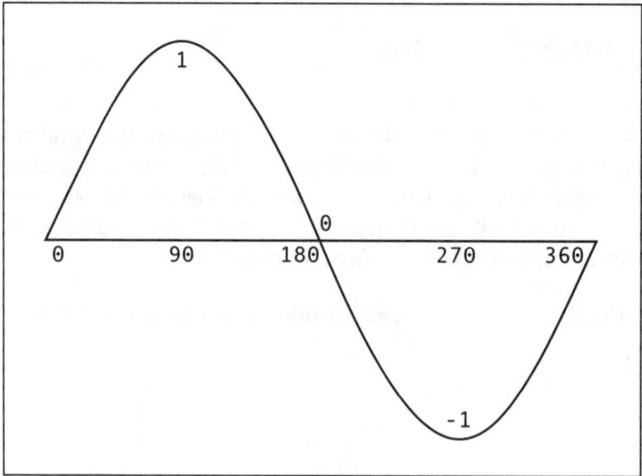

Figure 3-18. Values of sine

Now you can see that the sine of 0 is 0. The sine of 90 degrees or pi/2 radians is 1. The sine of 180 degrees, or pi radians, is 0 again. The sine of 270 degrees, or 3/2 pi, is –1. The sine of 360 degrees, or 2 pi, is back to 0 once again. Let's play with this sine wave a bit in Flash. Type in the following code:

```
for(angle = 0;angle < Math.PI * 2; angle += .1){
     trace(Math.sin(angle));
}
```

From here on out, you should start getting used to radians alone. You'll be leaving degrees behind, except when you actually need them for rotation or some other purpose.

In this example, the variable angle starts out as 0 and increments by 0.1 until it's greater than Math.PI * 2. It then traces the sine of that angle. If you look at the long list of results, you'll see it starts out at 0, goes up to almost 1, then down to almost –1, and back to around 0. You'll never hit exactly 1 or 0 because, using an increment of 0.1, you'll never get an exact multiple of pi or pi/2.

Smooth up and down motion

So what can you use Math.sin(angle) for? Have you ever needed to move something up and down or back and forth smoothly? This is your function. Consider this: Instead of just going from 0 to 1 and –1 and back to 0, and stopping there, keep adding on to the angle. You'll keep getting the wave over and over again. And instead of just taking the 1 and –1, multiply those values by some higher value, say 100, and you have a stream of values that goes from 100 to –100, back and forth, continuously.

In the file bobbing.fla, I've created a movie clip named ball, placed it on stage, named the instance ball as well, and then added the following code:

```
angle = 0;
onEnterFrame = function(){
      ball._y = 200 + Math.sin(angle) * 50;
      angle += .1;
}
```

First, you need to set angle to 0; otherwise, it will start as undefined. In ActionScript 1, if you added a value to undefined, the undefined would be converted to zero, and the math would work fine. With ActionScript 2, adding a value to undefined will give you NaN (not a number), which isn't useful at all for calculating positions of movie clips.

In the onEnterFrame handler, you take the sine of that angle and multiply it by 50. This will give you a range of values from 50 to –50. If you add that to 200, your values will be from 250 to 150. Make that the _y position of the ball, and then add 0.1 to the angle for the next time around. You get a nice smooth up and down motion.

Play around with the various values. You'll notice that changing the .1 to another value changes the speed of the motion. This makes sense, because the faster or slower the angle is increasing, the faster or slower the return values from Math.sin will go from 1 to –1. Obviously, changing the 50 changes how far the ball moves, and changing the 200 changes the point that it oscillates around. From this, you could abstract the values into variables like so:

```
angle = 0;
centerY = 200;
range = 50;
speed = .1;

onEnterFrame = function(){
      ball._y = centerY + Math.sin(angle) * range;
      angle += speed;
}
```

Keeping actual numbers out of your motion code is a very good practice, and you should strive to do it as much as possible. In this case, it's all pretty much in the same place anyway. But what happens when you get a couple of pages worth of code, and those values are used in several places throughout? Every time you want to change the speed, you need to hunt down every instance of that .1 value and change it. You could do a search and replace, but if something else in the file has .1 in it, that would get replaced as well. By keeping the numbers out of the code, preferably up at the top of the listing, you know exactly where all your variables are.

Linear vertical motion

In the wave1.fla file, I added linear vertical motion, just to give you some inspiration for your own animation. Here's the code for that file:

```
angle = 0;
centerY = 200;
range = 50;
xspeed = 1;
yspeed = .05;

onEnterFrame = function(){
      ball._x += xspeed;
      ball._y = centerY + Math.sin(angle) * range;
      angle += yspeed;
}
```

Pulsing motion

One very important thing to keep in mind is that you can apply sine values to items other than physical locations. In the pulse.fla file, I used the values to affect the scale of the ball instead. This gives it a pulsating appearance. Here's the code:

```
angle = 0;
centerScale = 100;
range = 50;
speed = .1;

onEnterFrame = function(){
      ball._xscale = ball._yscale =
                     centerScale + Math.sin(angle) * range;
      angle += speed;
}
```

The principles are the same. You have a center point (which is 100% scale in this case), a range, and a speed. Don't stop there. Apply some sine waves to _alpha, _rotation, or any other interesting property.

Waves with two angles

Here's another idea to get you started: Rather than just a single angle, set up two sets of values, angle1 and angle2, along with separate centers and speeds for both. Apply one sine wave to one property and the other sine wave to another property, such as position and scale. I can't guarantee you'll come up with anything useful, but playing around like this, you will really get a feel for how these functions work.

I've included one example in the random.fla file to get you started. This takes two angles, speeds, and centers, and applies one of the angles to the ball's x position and the other angle to the y position. The result is something like a bug flying around a room. Although it is all very mathematically predetermined, it looks pretty random. Here's the code:

```
angleX = 0;
angleY = 0;
centerX = 270;
centerY = 200;
range = 100;
xspeed = .07;
yspeed = .11;

onEnterFrame = function(){
      ball._x = centerX + Math.sin(angleX) * range;
      ball._y = centerY + Math.sin(angleY) * range;
      angleX += xspeed;
      angleY += yspeed;
}
```

Waves with the drawing API

Finally, in wave2.fla, I took out the ball and used the drawing API to draw the sine wave.

```
angle = 0;
centerY = 200;
range = 50;
xspeed = 1;
yspeed = .05;

moveTo(0, 200);
lineStyle(1,0, 100);
x = 0;

onEnterFrame = function(){
      x += xspeed;
      y = centerY + Math.sin(angle) * range;
      lineTo(x, y);
      angle += yspeed;
}
```

I'll cover the drawing API in detail in the next chapter, but you should have fun playing with this file and seeing the various waves you can draw with it. Note that the sine wave comes out a bit "upside down," again due to the y axis being reversed in Flash.

Circles and ellipses

Now that you've mastered sine waves, let's move on to their lesser-known cousins, cosine waves. These are formed in the same way as sine waves, but use the cosine function instead of sine. If you recall from the earlier discussion about how sine and cosine basically end up being the inverse of each other, you won't be surprised to learn that the two waves form the same shape, but in a different position. Figure 3-19 shows a cosine wave.

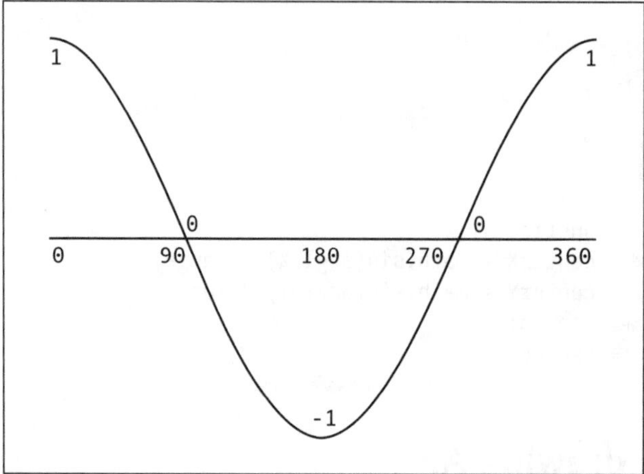

Figure 3-19. A cosine wave

This shows that the cosine of 0 is 1, and as it moves through to 2 pi radians or 360 degrees, it goes to 0, –1, 0, and then back to 1. So, it's essentially the same curve as produced by the sine wave, just shifted over a bit.

Circular movement

It goes without saying that you can use cosine in place of sine in just about any situation where all you need is an oscillating motion. But cosine actually has a much more common and useful function in coordination with sine: moving an object in a circle. Figure 3-20 shows an object at several points as it moves around a circle.

If you were to take the circle in Figure 3-20 and turn it so you were looking straight at its edge from the right, you would just see the object going up and down. Its center would be the center of the circle, and its range would be the radius of the circle. You would calculate its position just as you did in the first sine experiment: by taking the sine of the angle times the range. In this case, sine would be the appropriate function to use, because if you look at the triangle formed, you are calculating the length of y—the leg opposite the angle.

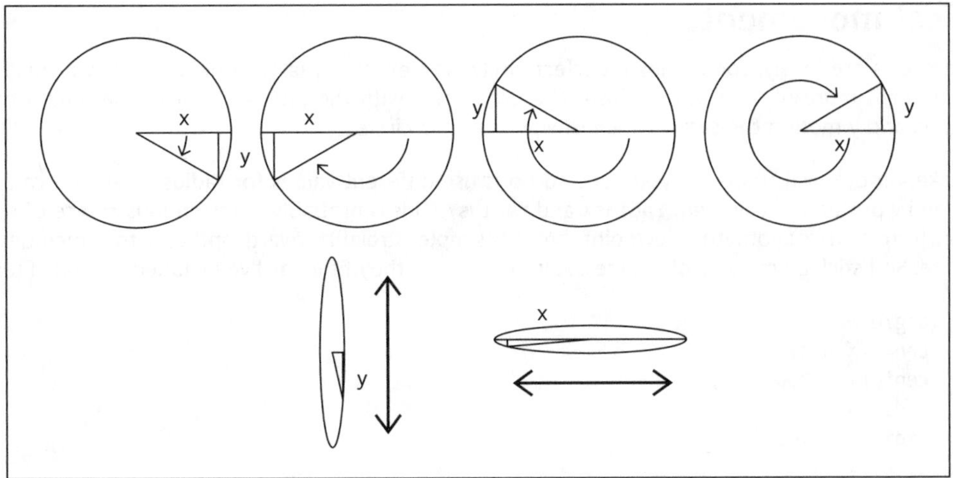

Figure 3-20. Positions of an object as it moves around a circle

Now, imagine that you are looking at the circle from its bottom edge instead. In this view, you see the object moving back and forth, left to right. This time, you are calculating the length of x—the leg adjacent to the angle—so you should be using cosine.

The important thing to realize is that these calculations are operating off the same angle, unlike the `random.fla` example you saw earlier, which used two different angles to compute the x and y positions. You just use sine to calculate y and cosine to calculate x. Here's how it looks in ActionScript:

```
angle = 0;
centerX = 270;
centerY = 200;
radius = 100;
speed = .1;

onEnterFrame = function(){
      ball._x = centerX + Math.cos(angle) * radius;
      ball._y = centerY + Math.sin(angle) * radius;
      angle += speed;
}
```

You can create this example yourself, or open `circle.fla`, which has all the work done for you. Test it and verify that you do indeed have a perfect circle.

Notice that the range in both cases is the hypotenuse of the triangle, and it's equal to the radius of the circle. Thus, I changed `range` to `radius`, to reflect that fact.

All the code is doing is using cosine to get the x position and sine to get the y position. You should get very used to those relationships. In Flash, almost any time you are talking about x, you should immediately think cosine, and you should almost always connect y with sine. In fact, spend as much time as you need to fully understand that last bit of code. It is going to be one of the most useful tools in your ActionScript animation toolbox.

Elliptical movement

While circles are lovely, sometimes a perfect circle isn't exactly what you need. What you might be looking for is more of an oval or ellipse. The problem is with the radius. It makes the ranges of the x motion and y motion the same, which is why you get a circle.

To make a more oval shape, all you need to do is use different values for radius when you calculate the x and y positions. I call them radiusX and radiusY. This is probably a horrendous choice of terminology from a strict geometric viewpoint, but it is simple, straightforward, and easy to remember and visualize. So I stick by my variable names. And here's how they fit in, as I've included in oval.fla:

```
angle = 0;
centerX = 270;
centerY = 200;
radiusX = 200;
radiusY = 100;
speed = .1;

onEnterFrame = function(){
      ball._x = centerX + Math.cos(angle) * radiusX;
      ball._y = centerY + Math.sin(angle) * radiusY;
      angle += speed;
}
```

Here, radiusX is 200, which means that ball is going to go back and forth 200 pixels from centerX as it circles around. radiusY is 100, which means it will go up and down only 100 pixels each way. So, now you have an uneven circle, which is not a circle at all anymore, but an ellipse.

Pythagorean Theorem

Finally, we come to the Pythagorean Theorem. I'm not sure how officially this is a part of trigonometry, but it's pretty interwoven with the subject and is another formula that you will use a lot. So, this is the best place to put it.

Pythagorus was a Greek guy who lived a long time ago. That's your history lesson. Simply stated, his theorem says A squared + B squared = C squared. Now, if you know what the theorem is all about beforehand, that communicates it perfectly. Otherwise, it sounds like some kind of bizarre nursery rhyme. So let's explore it in more depth.

A more descriptive statement of the theorem is the sum of the squares of the two legs of a right triangle is equal to the square of the hypotenuse. That's a mouthful. Say you have the triangle shown in Figure 3-21.

The two legs, A and B, have measurements of 3 and 4. The hypotenuse, C, measures 5. Mr. Pythagorus tells us that $A^2 + B^2 = C^2$. Let's test it. Plug in the numbers, and you have $3^2 + 4^2 = 5^2$, which works out to 9 + 16 = 25. Yup, that works out pretty well.

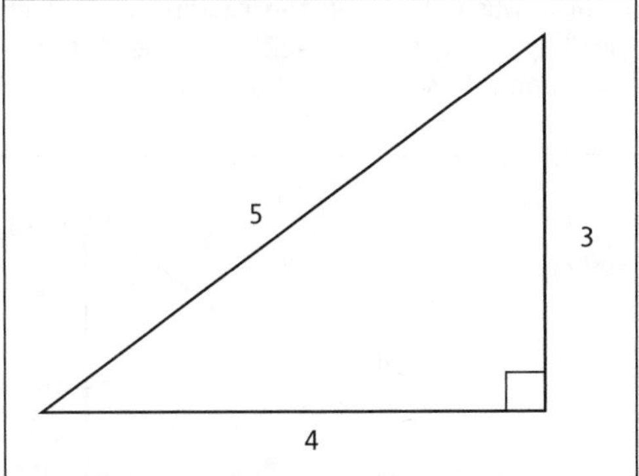

Figure 3-21. A right triangle

Now, if you happen to know all three measurements like that, the Pythagorean Theorem is nothing more than an interesting relationship. But, if you know only two of the measurements, it becomes a powerful tool to quickly find the third. In Flash, the most common situation is where you know the lengths of the two legs and you want to know the hypotenuse. Specifically, you want to find the distance between two points.

Distance between two points

Say you have two movie clip instances on stage and you want to find out how far apart they are. This is the most common use of the Pythagorean Theorem in Flash.

What do you have to work with? You have the x and y positions of each of movie clip. Let's call the position of one x1, y1, and the other x2, y2. So, you have a situation like the one illustrated in Figure 3-22.

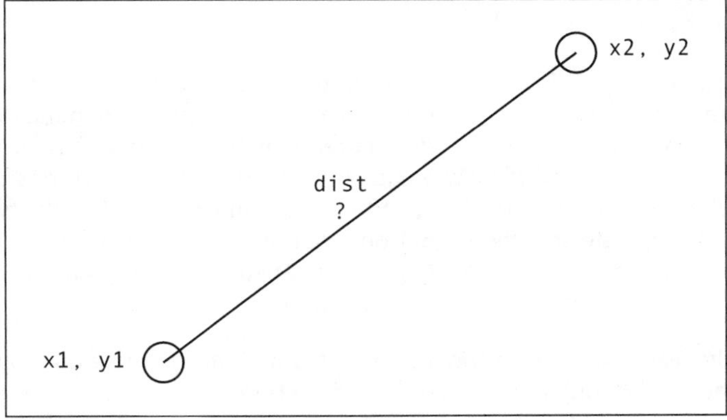

Figure 3-22. What is the distance between the two objects?

If you have been particularly brainwashed during the reading of this chapter, you will already see a right triangle forming in the diagram in Figure 3-22, with the distance line as the hypotenuse. In Figure 3-23, I finish it off for you and add some actual numbers.

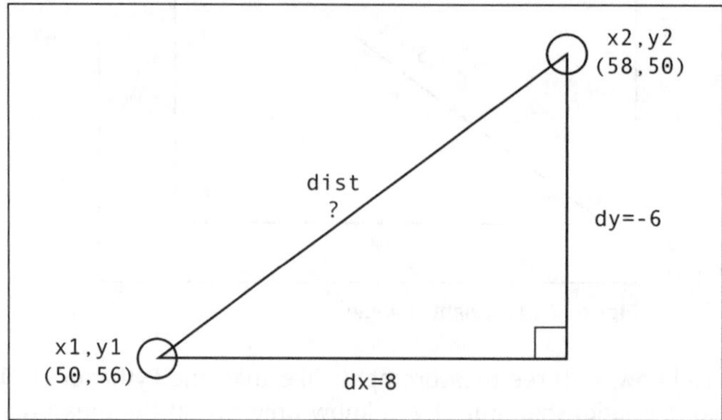

Figure 3-23. Turn it into a right triangle.

Here, dx is the distance between the two movie clips on the x axis, and dy is the distance on the y axis. You can now easily find dx by subtracting x1 from x2: 58 – 50 = 8. Similarly, you subtract y1 from y2 to get dy, which is 6. Now, per Pythagorus, if you square both of these and add them together, you'll get the square of the distance. In other words $-6^2 + 8^2 = dist^2$. Breaking that down, you get 36 + 64, or $100 = dist^2$. Basic algebra says that you can reduce that to $\sqrt{100} = dist$. And from that, you can easily figure out that the distance between the two clips is 10.

Now, let's abstract that a bit so you can have a formula that you can use in any situation. Given two points, x1, y1 and x2, y2, you figure the x distance and y distance, square them, sum them, and take the square root. Here it is in ActionScript:

```
dx = x2 - x1;
dy = y2 - y1;
dist = Math.sqrt(dx*dx + dy*dy);
```

Pay particular attention to these lines. They make up the next big tool in your toolbox. The first two lines just get the distances on each axis. Note that if you are just interested in the distance, and won't be using dx and dy to calculate any angles, it doesn't really matter whether you subtract `x1` from `x2` or vice versa. The final result for `dist` will always be positive. The last line performs three steps in one shot: It squares each of the values, adds them, and finds the square root. For clarity, you could break down those steps into separate statements. But once you are familiar with that single line, it will be crystal clear to you. You'll see it and think "Pythagorean Theorem." And then, you'll really know you are brainwashed.

Now, let's try it in the real world. Create two movie clips, put them anywhere on stage, and name them `mca` and `mcb`. (Or you can just open the `mc_dist.fla` file.) Here's the code:

```
dx = mca._x - mcb._x;
dy = mca._y - mcb._y;
dist = Math.sqrt(dx*dx + dy*dy);
trace(dist);
```

Test the movie, and you'll get the distance between the two clips. Try moving them around and testing a few times. It shouldn't matter if one is to the right, left, top, or bottom of the other. You'll always get a positive value for the distance.

OK, that's interesting, but not very dynamic. Just to show you that you can do this in real time, and that it isn't limited to movie clips, delete mcb, add in a text field with the instance name dist_txt, and change the code to the following (or open mouse_dist.fla):

```
onMouseMove = function(){
      dx = mca._x - _xmouse;
      dy = mca._y - _ymouse;
      dist = Math.sqrt(dx*dx + dy*dy);
      dist_txt.text = dist;

      clear();
      lineStyle(1,0,100);
      moveTo(mca._x, mca._y);
      lineTo(_xmouse, _ymouse);
}
```

Here, dx and dy are calculated by subtracting the current mouse position from mca's position. The dist value is thrown into the text field, and a line is drawn from the movie clip to the mouse location (you'll find more on the drawing API in the next chapter). Finally, the whole thing is put in an onMouseMove handler, to update it each time the mouse moves.

Test the file and move your mouse around. A line will connect it to the movie clip, and you'll get a constant readout of the length of that line.

In later chapters, when I talk about collision detection, you'll find out about some weaknesses with the built-in hitTest method, and see how you can use the "Pythagorean Theorem" formula to create a distance-based method of collision detection. It is also very useful in calculating forces like gravity or springs, where the force between two objects is proportional to the distance between them.

Important formulas in this chapter

Look at this. You have a brand-new shiny toolbox, and already you have more than a half dozen tools to put in it. The full set of tools will also appear Chapter 19, but let's look at what you've added so far.

Calculate basic trigonometric functions:

```
sine of angle = opposite / hypotenuse
cosine of angle = adjacent / hypotenuse
tangent of angle = opposite / adjacent
```

Convert radians to degrees and degrees to radians:

```
radians = degrees * Math.PI / 180
degrees = radians * 180 / Math.PI
```

Rotate to the mouse (or any point):

```
// substitute _xmouse, _ymouse with the x, y point to rotate to
var dx = _xmouse - movieclip._x;
var dy = _ymouse - movieclip._y;
movieclip._rotation = Math.atan2(dy, dx) * 180 / Math.PI;
```

Create waves:

```
// assign value to _x, _y or other property of movie clip,
// use as drawing coordinates, etc.
// note: angle does not have to be zero,
// but must be defined as something prior to adding speed
angle = 0;
onEnterFrame = function(){
   value = center + Math.sin(angle) * range;
   angle += speed;
}
```

Create circles:

```
// assign position to _x and _y of movie clip,
// use as drawing coordinates, etc.
onEnterFrame = function(){
   xposition = centerX + Math.cos(angle) * radius;
   yposition = centerY + Math.sin(angle) * radius;
   angle += speed;
}
```

Create ovals:

```
// assign position to _x and _y of movie clip,
// use as drawing coordinates, etc.
onEnterFrame = function(){
   xposition = centerX + Math.cos(angle) * radiusX;
   yposition = centerY + Math.sin(angle) * radiusY;
   angle += speed;
}
```

Get the distance between two points:

```
// points are x1,y1 and x2,y2
// can be movie clip positions, mouse coordinates, etc.
dx = x2 - x1;
dy = y2 - y1;
dist = Math.sqrt(dx*dx + dy*dy);
```

Of course, if I just wanted to publish a list of formulas, I could have saved myself a lot of time and done just that. So look these over and make sure you fully understand how each one works. If you have any questions, go back to the point in the chapter where it was introduced, experiment with it, and research it more if you need to, until you can really think with the concept.

Summary

This chapter covered nearly all the trigonometry you will need for animating in ActionScript. There is one principle, called The Law of Cosines, that I left out for now, as it is a lot more complex and deals with triangles that are not right triangles (they have no angle measuring 90 degrees). If you are now addicted to trig and just can't get enough, you can jump ahead to Chapter 14, which covers inverse kinematics, where trig really comes in handy.

But, for now, you know about sine, cosine, and tangent and their opposites: arcsine, arccosine, and arctangent, as well as the ActionScript methods to calculate each one.

Best of all, you got some hands-on experience using most of them in ActionScript, with some of the most common real-life uses of them. As you move through the book, you'll see many more ways in which these techniques become useful. But you now have a solid footing with the concepts, and when you come across those examples, you should have no problem understanding them or how they work.

The next chapter covers some of the more common rendering techniques for getting graphics on the screen, including the all-important drawing API. As you go through that chapter, see if you can find ways to use the rendering methods to visualize some of the trig functions you've learned here. I'm sure you'll have no trouble creating some beautiful pictures or animations with trigonometry.

};shape.targetHeight = shape._height;
shape.onEnterFrame = function() {
var speed = 5;
this._width += (this.targetWidth - this._width)/speed;
this._height += (this.targetHeight - this._height)/speed;

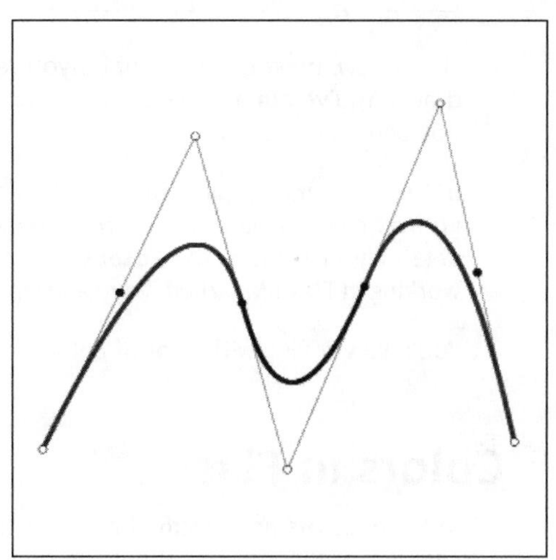

Chapter 4

RENDERING TECHNIQUES

What we'll cover in this chapter:

- Colors in Flash
- The Drawing API
- Color transforms
- Filters
- Bitmap control
- Important formulas in this chapter

Up to now, most of the graphics you've added to the sample programs in the book have been predrawn. You've put a circle, an arrow, or another shape on the stage, converted it to a movie clip symbol, and that was that.

In this chapter, I'm going to dive into visual content creation in ActionScript. Specifically, I'm going to go over color in Flash, the drawing API, and the `Color` object. Additionally, I'll cover three items available only in Flash 8: the `ColorTransform` object, filters, and the `BitmapData` object. So, if you are working in Flash MX 2004, you can skip those three sections.

You'll be working with a lot of colors in this chapter, so let's cover that subject first.

Colors in Flash

In Flash, colors are specified as numbers. A color number can be anything from 0 to 16,777,215. In case you are wondering about the significance of that number, it comes from the fact that there are 16,777,216 possible color values, which is 256 × 256 × 256. Flash uses RGB color, meaning that every color is made up of a red, a green, and a blue component. Each of these component colors can have a value from 0 to 255. So, there are 256 possible shades each of red, green, and blue, resulting in the nearly 16.8 million colors.

This system is also known as 24-bit color. It takes eight bits—ones or zeros—to represent the number 256. Eight bits times three (red, green, blue) means it takes 24 bits to represent the 16.8 million possible colors. Additionally, there is a 32-bit color system, which also has an 8-bit number set aside for alpha, or transparency.

Now, since it's pretty tough to visualize what color 11,273,634 might look like, we often tend to resort to another system of representing such numbers: hexadecimal. If you've used color values in HTML, this is nothing new to you, but let's cover the basics anyway.

Using hexadecimal color values

Hexadecimal, or hex for short, is a base 16 system. In other words, each digit can be from 0 to 15, rather than 0 to 9 as in the usual base 10 system. We don't have any single digits to represent the numbers 10 to 15, so we borrow the first six letters of the alphabet, A to F. So, each digit in a hex number can be from 0 to F. (In Flash, hex values are not case-sensitive, so you can use A through F or a through f.) To signal that we are using a hex number in HTML, you prefix it with #. In ActionScript, as with many other languages, you use the prefix 0x. For example, the number 0xA is equal to decimal 10, 0xF is equal to 15, and 0x10 is equal to 16.

In decimal, each digit is worth ten times the digit to its right. In other words, the number 243 means two times 100, four times 10, and three times 1. In hex, each digit is worth 16 times its right-hand neighbor. For example, 0x2B3 means two times 256, B (or eleven) times 16, and three times 1.

For 24-bit colors, this goes all the way up to 0xFFFFFF, which, if you do the math, is magically equal to 16,777,215. Furthermore, those six hex digits can be broken down into three pairs. The first pair represents the red component, the second pair represents the green, and the last two digits represent blue. This is often symbolized as 0xRRGGBB. 32-bit colors are likewise often seen as 0xAARRGGBB, with the AA being the alpha channel. (You would never put R, G, or B into an actual hex number; this is merely a symbolic way of telling you what color channel each digit controls.) You'll see where 32-bit colors come in when you look at the BitmapData object in the "Bitmap control" section later in this chapter.

Remember that each component color can have a value anywhere from 0 to 255, or in hex, 0x00 to 0xFF. Thus, the color red can be represented as 0xFF0000, which denotes full red, zero green, and zero blue. Likewise, 0x0000FF is completely blue.

If you took the earlier mentioned value of 11,273,634, and converted it to hex (I'll show you an easy way to do that in a minute), you'd get 0xAC05A2. You can easily break this down into red = AC, green = 05, blue = A2. Seeing that red and blue are rather high, and green is almost nothing, you can guess that this color is rather purplish, something you'd never be able to tell from the decimal value.

Note that it doesn't matter which number format you use in ActionScript. For any function that takes a color value, you can use either decimal or hex. The numbers 11273634 and 0xAC05A2 are exactly the same thing to Flash. It's just that one is more readable to us poor humans.

You might be wondering how to convert between the two formats. Well, converting from hex to decimal is pretty easy. Just trace the value. The trace function will convert to decimal for you.

```
trace(0xAC05A2);
```

One way to get hex is to use the toString(16) method, like so:

```
trace((11273634).toString(16));
```

This will trace ac05a2. If you are going to use that value somewhere, don't forget to add the 0x.

Combining colors

Another common question is how to combine three red, green, and blue values to form a valid overall color value. Say you have three variables, red, green, and blue. Each of them holds a value from 0 to 255, and you want to create a valid color value. Here's the formula to do just that:

```
color24 = red << 16 | green << 8 | blue;
```

This makes use of two bitwise operators you may not have seen before. *Bitwise operators* work on numbers on a binary level—on ones and zeros.

As I mentioned, RGB colors are 24-bit colors. If you were to list those 24 bits, you would have a string of 24 ones and zeros. Breaking up the hex 0xRRGGBB into binary, you have this:

```
RRRRRRRRGGGGGGGGBBBBBBBB
```

You see eight bits for red, eight for green, and eight for blue. This makes sense, because eight bits are equal to 256.

In the color combination formula, the first bitwise operator is <<, which is the bitwise left shift operator. This shifts the binary representation of the value a number of places to the left. Say you have a red value of 0xFF or 255. This can be represented in binary as follows:

```
11111111
```

Shifting it 16 places to the left gives you this:

```
111111110000000000000000
```

As a 24-bit color number, this is red. Seen in hex, this is 0xFF0000—again, full red.

Now, say you have a green value of 0x55 (85 decimal). In binary, it looks like this:

```
01010101
```

Shift this eight places, and you get this:

```
000000000101010100000000
```

So, the original eight bits now fall completely in the green range.

Finally, you have a blue value of 0xF3 (243 decimal), which is this in binary:

```
11110011
```

Since this already all falls into the blue range, you don't need to touch it.

Now, you have three values for red, green, and blue:

```
111111110000000000000000
000000000101010100000000
000000000000000011110011
```

You could simply add them together to get a single 24-bit number, but there's a quicker and cooler way: use bitwise OR, the | symbol. This compares the digits of two numbers on a binary level and says if either digit is equal to one, the result will be one. If both digits are zero, the result is zero. You can OR the red, green, and blue values together, and it will say, "If this OR this OR this is one, the result is one." And you get this result:

```
111111110101010111110011
```

If you convert that to hex, you get 0xFF55F3. Of course, you never see the bits or deal with the ones or zeros at all. You'd just type this:

```
var color24:Number = 0xFF << 16 | 0x55 << 8 | 0xF3;
```

Or, if you are working with decimal values, you could use this form:

```
var color24:Number = 255 << 16 | 85 << 8 | 243;
```

Again, Flash doesn't care whether you use hex or decimal.

You could do something similar by converting each of the red, green, and blue values to a hex string, concatenating them into one long string, and converting that back to a number. But if you've ever tried it, you'll know that you get into some complicated and slow string logic. Conversely, bitwise operators are probably the fastest operators in ActionScript, since they work on such a low level.

Extracting component colors

Finally, you might also need to take a color value and extract the various component values from it. Let's go the opposite way and take the value 0xFF55F3 and try to get the red, green, and blue values from it. Here's the next formula for your toolbox:

```
red = color24 >> 16;
green = color24 >> 8 & 0xFF;
blue = color24 & 0xFF;
```

Let's take the lines one at a time. First, you've probably guessed that >> is the bitwise right shift operator, which shifts the bits so many places to the right. You can't have fractional bits, so any bits that are shifted too far right are just discarded. So, begin with red:

```
111111110101010111110011
```

When you shift the color value 16 places to the right, it becomes this:

```
11111111
```

Or it's simply 0xFF, or 255.

For green, shift it 8 places, and you get this:

```
1111111101010101
```

Here, you've knocked the blue values out, but you still have the red ones hanging around. This is where you use another bitwise operator, &, also called AND. Like OR, this compares two values, but says, "If this digit AND this digit are both one, then the result is one. If either one is zero, the result is zero." You compare it to 0xFF, so you are comparing these two numbers:

```
1111111101010101
0000000011111111
```

Since all the red digits are being compared with zero, they will all result in zero. Only the digits that are both one will fall through, so you get this:

```
0000000001010101
```

With blue, you don't need to shift anything, just AND it with 0xFF, which will preserve the blue and knock out the red and green.

Now that you know more than you ever hoped to know about colors in Flash, let's start using them.

The Drawing API

Just so I don't lose anyone, let me tell you right off the bat what an API is. It stands for application programming interface. Generally, API refers to a set of methods and properties that you can use in your program to access a certain set of related behaviors and properties. The drawing API refers to the properties and methods that allow you to draw lines, curves, fills, gradient fills, and so on with ActionScript. This API has surprisingly few methods, but there is a lot to know about them and a lot of neat tricks you can do with them.

The drawing API was introduced in Flash MX. Prior to that, all graphical content had to be drawn in the authoring environment. With the drawing API, a lot more became possible.

> *Because of the drawing limitations in earlier versions of Flash, people thought up ingenious ways to do dynamic drawing. One of the best examples was the 45-degree line movie clip. This consisted of a single movie clip in the library, set to export so that it could be attached at runtime or placed on stage somewhere so it could be duplicated. It contained a simple line drawn from 0, 0 to 100, 100. At runtime, to draw a line between any two points, you would create a new instance of this line clip, position it on the first point, and scale it so it that it fit between the first and second points. While this technique had some drawbacks, such as not allowing for fills or different widths of lines, it was surprisingly efficient, and was the way that almost all dynamic drawing was done prior to Flash MX.*

Beginning with Flash MX, you got the following methods:

- `clear()`
- `lineStyle(width, color, alpha)`
- `moveTo(x, y)`
- `lineTo(x, y)`
- `curveTo(x1, y1, x2, y2)`
- `beginFill(color, alpha)`
- `endFill()`
- `beginGradientFill(fillType, colors, alphas, ratio, matrix)`

In Flash 8, several enhancements were added to the `lineStyle` and `beginGradientFill` methods. It also introduced the `beginBitmapFill` and `lineGradientStyle` methods. As this is just a quick overview, I'm not going to go into the newer methods and syntax. But be assured that what you see here will work just fine in Flash 6, 7, and 8.

The drawing API methods are methods of every movie clip object, so a method can be called like this:

```
myMovieClip.lineTo(100, 100);
```

Let's look at each of these methods and see some examples of their basic use.

Removing drawing with clear

`clear` is the simplest method of them all. It simply removes any previously drawn lines, curves, or fills from the movie clip. Note that it will affect *only* graphics that were created using other drawing API methods. In other words, if you drew a shape on stage in the authoring environment, calling `clear()` at runtime would not affect that shape.

Use of the `clear` method has an important and somewhat unexpected effect on drawing efficiency. In the drawing API, it happens that the more you draw in a particular movie clip, the slower it goes. For a few dozen shapes, the slowdown is not noticeable, but little by little, each new shape takes longer and longer to draw. Even if the new shape completely covers and obliterates everything else, the vector information for those older shapes is still there and will be completely redrawn each time. This can be important in animation, where you are redrawing almost the same thing over and over. Using `clear` handles this by completely removing all prior vector information from the clip.

Setting line appearance with lineStyle

With the `lineStyle(width, color, alpha)` method, you set up the appearance of all subsequently drawn lines. This command has no effect on previously drawn lines. In fact, other than clearing them, or drawing something else on top of them, there is no way of affecting or changing lines or fills that have been drawn. Once they are there, that's that.

The parameters for this method are pretty self-explanatory, but let's review them quickly:

- `width`: The width of the line in pixels. The only valid values are zero or positive integers. Although you can pass in decimal values, they will be rounded off to the nearest positive integer. If you pass in zero or a negative value, Flash will draw a 1-pixel thick line.
- `color`: The color you want the line to be. This is in a decimal or hex format, as described earlier in this chapter.
- `alpha`: The transparency of the lines. This can be from 0 to 100, representing a percent of opacity. A setting of 100 is obviously fully opaque, and 0 is fully transparent or invisible.

Depending on which Flash version you are using, some of these parameters are optional. You can say `lineStyle(1)` and get a 1-pixel thick, black line, with all the other default parameters. But it's become my habit to always specify the first three parameters, even if I'm using the default values. So, in this book, you'll often see `lineStyle(1, 0, 100)`. Actually, even the first parameter is optional. If you leave off the width, just calling `lineStyle()`, the line style will be cleared, and you'll get an invisible line. This is the same as if you had started issuing drawing commands without setting the line style: You won't see any lines.

Another little fact that often trips people up is that the `clear` method clears not only the current drawing, but the current line style settings as well. If you set up a custom style, draw some lines into a movie clip, and then clear them, you'll need to reset your line style before drawing anything else. Otherwise, you'll be back to drawing zero-width (invisible) lines again.

Drawing lines with lineTo and moveTo

There are a couple of different ways to implement line drawing in a graphics language. One is to have a `line` command that takes a starting point and an ending point, and draws a line between them. The other way is to have a `lineTo` command that takes a single point: the ending point of the line. This is how ActionScript works. So, if you're drawing a line *to* some point, where are you drawing it *from*? Well, if you haven't drawn anything yet, you'll be drawing from the point 0, 0 of whatever graphics object you are drawing into. Say you just type this line in a movie:

```
lineTo(100, 100);
```

You'll see a line going from the top-left corner (0, 0), to 100, 100 (assuming you've set a line style). After you've drawn at least one line, the ending point for that line will be the starting point for the next line. Finally, you can use the moveTo method to specify a new starting point for the next line.

Think of the drawing API as a robot holding a pen on a piece of paper. When you start, the pen is at 0, 0. When you tell it to draw a line to a point, it just moves the pen across the paper to that new point. For each new line, it just moves from wherever it left off, to the next new point. The moveTo method is like saying, "OK, now lift up the pen and move it to this next point." Although issuing a moveTo command does not result in any new graphic content, it will affect how the next graphics command is carried out. Unless you specifically want to draw your first line from 0, 0, you will generally call moveTo as your first drawing command to place the drawing API "pen" where you want to begin.

You now have enough commands under your belt to do something serious. Let's create a simple drawing application. This program will rely completely on the drawing API for its content, so you don't need to create any movie clip symbols beforehand. In fact, all you need to do is type the following code in the Actions panel for frame 1 of a new movie:

```
init();
function init()
{
      lineStyle(1, 0, 100);
}
function onMouseDown():Void
{
      moveTo(_xmouse, _ymouse);
      onMouseMove = draw;
}
function onMouseUp():Void
{
      delete onMouseMove
}
function draw():Void
{
      lineTo(_xmouse, _ymouse);
}
```

You can find this file among the book's downloadable files (available from www.friendsofed.com) as ch04_01.fla. I'll go through it line by line. In addition to the drawing functions, this program makes pretty good use of event handlers (discussed in Chapter 2).

First, the code calls init, where the line style is set to a 1-pixel black line—simple enough.

Then there's the onMouseDown method. This gets called whenever the user presses a mouse button. Generally, this means the user wants to start drawing a line at the current mouse cursor position. Well, that's exactly what this function does. It puts the virtual pen down at the mouse location by calling moveTo and passing in the mouse coordinates. It then assigns a handler function for onMouseMove.

At this point, every time the user moves the mouse, the draw function is called. And what does that do? Not too much, although it's the meat of the program. It just draws a line to the current mouse location.

Finally, there's the onMouseUp handler. This removes the onMouseMove handler so that no more drawing will happen.

OK, you have a neat little drawing program there. You could probably set up some simple controls to make it a full-featured drawing application without too much effort. Just create some variables for color and width, and create some buttons or other controls to change them, and call the lineStyle method again with the new values. Oh, and throw in a button that calls the clear method. I'm going to leave that as an exercise for you to do on your own, if you are interested. Meanwhile, I'm going to dive back into the rest of the drawing API.

Drawing curves with curveTo

The next drawing function, curveTo(x1, y1, x2, y2), starts off the same as lineTo, in that it begins its drawing at the point where the last drawing ended, at the point where the last moveTo command moved the pen to, or at 0, 0 if no drawing has been done yet. It also makes use of lineStyle in exactly the same way as moveTo. The only difference is the shape of the line drawn.

As you can see, curveTo takes two points. The first one is a control point that affects the shape of the curve. The second point is the ending point of the curve. The formula used is a standard formula for what is called a quadratic Bezier curve. This formula calculates a curve from one point to another, which curves towards the control point. Note that the curve will not *touch* the control point. It's more like the curve is attracted to it.

Let's see it in action. Start a new FLA document and enter the following code in frame 1 (you can find this file listed as ch04_02.fla):

```
var x0:Number = 100;
var y0:Number = 200;
var x2:Number = 300;
var y2:Number = 200;

function onEnterFrame(Void):Void {
      var x1:Number = _xmouse;
      var y1:Number = _ymouse;
      clear();
      lineStyle(1, 0, 100);
      moveTo(x0, y0);
      curveTo(x1, y1, x2, y2);
      lineStyle(1, 0, 40);
      lineTo(_xmouse, _ymouse);
      lineTo(x0, y0);
}
```

Test the file and move your mouse around. The file uses two preset points for the beginning and ending points, and uses the mouse position for the control point. Notice that the curve never actually reaches the control point, but gets about halfway there.

Curving through the control point

Now, say you actually wanted to have the curve hit the control point. Well, here's another toolbox tip. You can use the following formula to calculate the actual control point so that the curve will go through the point you specify. Again, you'll be starting out with x0, y0 and x2, y2 as the end points, and x1, y1 as the control point. I'll call the point you want the curve to go through, xt, yt (t for target). In other words, if you want the curve to be drawn through xt, yt, what x1, y1 do you need to use? Here's the formula:

```
x1 = xt * 2 - (x0 + x2) / 2;
y1 = yt * 2 - (y0 + y2) / 2;
```

Basically, you just multiply the target by two, and subtract the average of the starting and ending point. If you want, you can graph it all out and see exactly how it works. Or, you can just test it, see that it works, and have faith that it always will.

Let's look at the formula in action, using the mouse coordinates as xt, yt. Here's the code for frame 1, which you can find in ch04_03.fla.

```
var x0:Number = 100;
var y0:Number = 200;
var x2:Number = 300;
var y2:Number = 200;
function onEnterFrame(Void):Void
{
	var x1 = _xmouse * 2 - (x0 + x2) / 2;
	var y1 = _ymouse * 2 - (y0 + y2) / 2;
	clear();
	lineStyle(1, 0, 100);
	moveTo(x0, y0);
	curveTo(x1, y1, x2, y2);
}
```

Only the lines that find x1 and y1 change.

Creating multiple curves

The next direction you're probably looking at going is creating multiple curves, where instead of a single curve, you have a long line that curves smoothly in several directions. First, I'll show you the wrong way of going about it, which is the way I originally tried it. Basically, you start out with a number of points, draw a curve from the first through the second to the third, then through the fourth to the fifth, then through the sixth to the seventh, and so on. Here it is in code (in ch04_04.fla):

```
init();
function init()
{
	// first set up an array of random points
	var points:Array = new Array();
	for (var i = 0; i < 9; i++)
	{
		points[i] = new Object();
```

```
            points[i].x = Math.random() * Stage.width;
            points[i].y = Math.random() * Stage.height;
        }
        lineStyle(1, 0, 100);

        // now move to the first point
        moveTo(points[0].x, points[0].y);

        // and loop through each next successive pair
        for (i = 1; i < points.length; i += 2)
        {
            curveTo(points[i].x, points[i].y,
                    points[i + 1].x, points[i + 1].y);
        }
    }
```

The first for loop in the init method just sets up an array of nine points. Each point is an object with an x and y property, and they are randomly thrown around the stage. Of course, in a real program, your points might not be random. I just used that method for quick setup.

Then the line style is set, and the pen is moved to the first point. The next for loop starts at one and increments by two each time, so it draws a curve through point one to two, then through three to four, then through five to six, and then through point seven to point eight. The loop will stop there, which is perfect because point eight is the last one. You also might notice that there must be a minimum of three points, and the number of points must be odd.

It all seems fine until you test it. As shown in Figure 4-1, it doesn't look very curvy at all. In fact, it often looks a bit spiky. The problem is that there is no coordination between one curve and the next, except that they share a point.

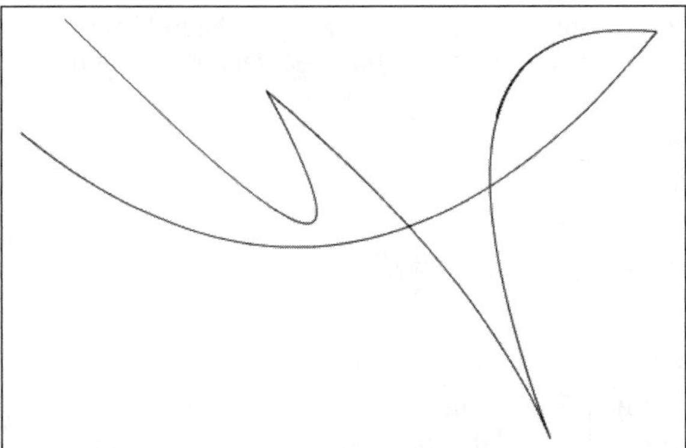

Figure 4-1. Multiple curves, the wrong way. You can plainly see where one curve ends and the next begins.

You're going to have to plug in a few more points to make it work right. Here's the strategy: Between each set of two points, you need a new point that sits exactly in the middle. You then use these as the starting and ending points for each curve, and use the original points as the control points.

Figure 4-2 illustrates the solution. In the figure, the white dots are the original points, and the black dots are the in-between points. There are three curveTo methods here, which I've given different colors so you can see where they start and end. (Figure 4-2 is actually a screenshot from a file called multicurvedemo.fla, which you can download from this book's page on www.friendsofed.com.)

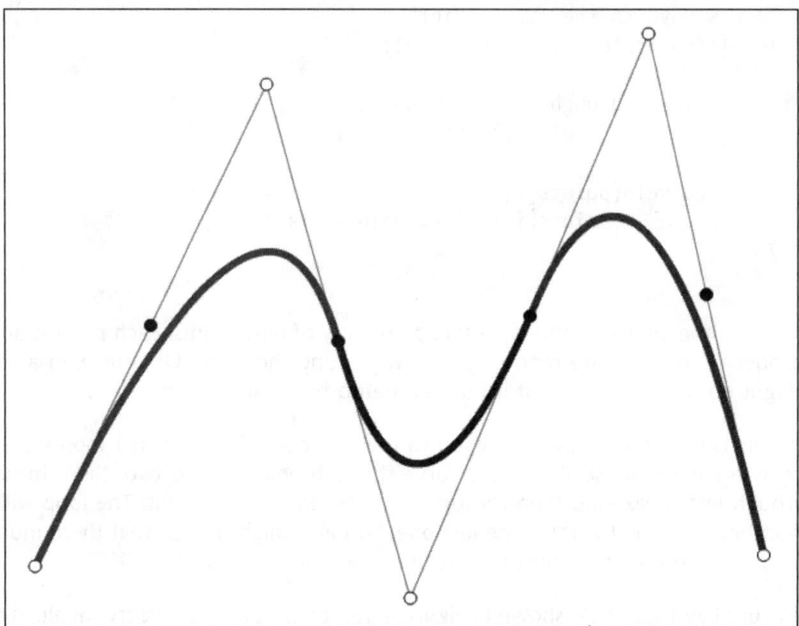

Figure 4-2. Multiple curves with midpoints

Notice in Figure 4-2 that the first and last midpoints are not used, and the first and last original points remain terminal points for the curves. You really need to make in-between points only for the second point up to the second-to-last point. Here's an updated version of the previous example for the random curves (found in ch04_05.fla):

```
init():
function init()
{
      var points:Array = new Array();
      for (var i = 0; i < 9; i++)
      {
            points[i] = new Object();
            points[i].x = Math.random() * Stage.width;
            points[i].y = Math.random() * Stage.height;
      }
      lineStyle(1, 0, 100);
      moveTo(points[0].x, points[0].y);
      for (i = 1; i < points.length - 2; i++)
      {
            var xc:Number = (points[i].x + points[i + 1].x) / 2;
```

```
                var yc:Number = (points[i].y + points[i + 1].y) / 2;
                curveTo(points[i].x, points[i].y, xc, yc);
        }
        curveTo(points[i].x, points[i].y, points[i+1].x, points[i+1].y);
}
```

Note that in the new code, the `for` loop starts at 1 and ends at `points.length - 2`. This prevents it from processing the first and last pairs of points. What it does is create a new x, y point, which is the average of the next two points in the array. Then it draws a curve through the next array point, to the new average point. When the loop ends, the index, `i`, will still be pointing to the second-to-last element. Thus, you can draw a curve through that to the last point.

This time, you will come up with a nice smooth shape, rather than those spikes, as shown in Figure 4-3. Also note that you are not limited to an odd number of original points any more. As long as you start with at least three points, you'll be fine.

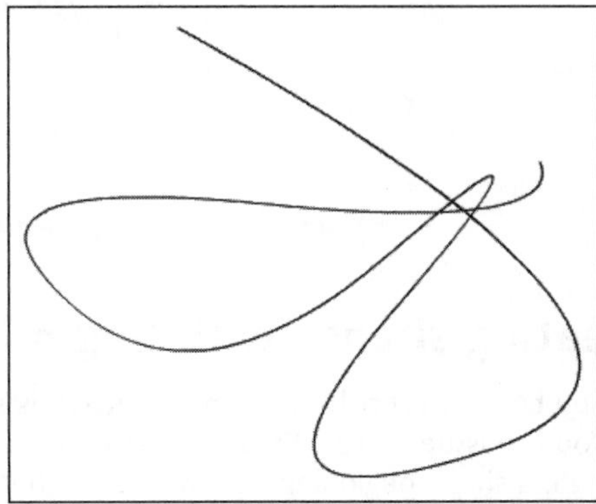

Figure 4-3. Smooth multiple curves

As a bit of a variation on a theme, the following code (found in `ch04_06.fla`) creates a closed curve using the same technique. Basically, it computes an initial midpoint, which is the average of the first and last points, and moves to that. Then it loops through all the rest, figuring midpoints for each one, finally drawing its last curve back to the initial midpoint.

```
init();
function init()
{
        var points:Array = new Array();
        for (var i = 0; i < 9; i++)
        {
                points[i] = new Object();
                points[i].x = Math.random() * Stage.width;
                points[i].y = Math.random() * Stage.height;
        }
        var xc1:Number = (points[0].x + points[points.length - 1].x) / 2;
        var yc1:Number = (points[0].y + points[points.length - 1].y) / 2;
        lineStyle(1, 0, 100);
        moveTo(xc1, yc1);
        for (i = 0; i < points.length - 1; i++)
        {
                var xc:Number = (points[i].x + points[i + 1].x) / 2;
                var yc:Number = (points[i].y + points[i + 1].y) / 2;
                curveTo(points[i].x, points[i].y, xc, yc);
        }
        curveTo(points[i].x, points[i].y, xc1, yc1);
}
```

Figure 4-4 shows the result.

Figure 4-4. Multiple closed curves

Creating shapes with beginFill and endFill

The `beginFill(color, alpha)` method is so simple that there's not really too much to say about it. You can issue a `beginFill` command almost any time during the process of drawing. Flash will compute a shape beginning with wherever the drawing location happens to be and ending wherever the drawing location is when the `endFill` command is issued or, if it never is, wherever the location is when the code completes for that frame and the frame is rendered. Generally, though, the sequence is as follows:

- `moveTo`
- `lineStyle` (if any)
- `beginFill`
- A series of `lineTo` and `curveTo` methods, ending at the original point moved to
- `endFill`

Actually, you can use the first three methods in just about any order without affecting what is drawn. You don't need to specify a line style. Remember that if you do not specify a line style, you get an invisible line, which is perfectly valid for drawing fills. It's also fine to draw both at the same time.

If you do not draw a line back to the original point from which you started, Flash will draw it for you in order to close the shape as soon as you call `endFill`. This final line will be drawn with whatever line style is present at the time you call `endFill`. However, it is definitely a good practice to get into the habit of finishing your own shapes. Not only are you guaranteed that the last line will be drawn even if Macromedia decides to change that particular behavior, but another person who looks at your code later will know that you actually did intend to draw the shape.

Go ahead and play around with drawing fills. You can even use the closed curve example from the previous section (`ch04_06.fla`), as that is already generating a closed shape. Just throw in a `beginFill` statement anywhere before the first `curveTo`—say, `beginFill(0xff00ff, 100);`, which will create a bright purple fill—and finish off the code with `endFill();`.

If you did this, I'm sure you noticed that, where sections of the curve cross over itself, the fill kind of disappears. There's not much you can do about that, but for the most part, you'll probably be drawing shapes that don't intersect like that anyway. On the other hand, once you get used to how it works, you can use that behavior to create some interesting shapes.

Creating gradient fills with beginGradientFill

Now we come to the monster function of the drawing API: `beginGradientFill(fillType, colors, alphas, ratio, matrix)`. In many senses, this works in the same way as `beginFill`; it has the same quirks and behaviors, and you always end it with the same old `endFill`. The big difference is in how the fill looks. I feel like I shouldn't have to say that `beginGradientFill` creates a gradient fill, but then again, I feel like I'd be leaving something out if I *didn't* say it. So there you go.

A gradient fill is basically a fill of at least two colors. One part of the shape starts out with one color, and it slowly blends into another color, perhaps moving through one or several other predefined colors on its way.

Specifying the fill type

You can create two kinds of gradient fills: linear and radial. In a linear fill, the gradient of colors lies along a line from one point to another. By default, that line goes left to right, but you can make it go up and down or at any other angle. Figure 4-5 shows a few examples of linear fills.

Figure 4-5. Linear fills

In order to see a linear fill, you need at least two different colors. If that's all you specify, the fill will blend from the first to the second. If you specify more colors, the fill will blend smoothly from the first, to the second, to the third, and so on until it hits the last one.

A radial fill works with pretty much all the same parameters that a linear fill uses, but interprets them a bit differently, creating a gradient that starts in the center of the space you define and radiates outward in all directions, creating a circle or oval. The first color you specify will be used as the center of the circle, and the final color will be the outline of the circle. The only item that is not needed is the angle. Figure 4-6 shows an example of a radial fill.

Figure 4-6. A radial fill

So, for the `beginGradientFill(fillType, colors, alphas, ratios, matrix)` method, the first parameter is `fillType`. That's pretty simple. It's a string that can contain one of two values: `"linear"` or `"radial"`. You get what you ask for.

Setting the colors, alphas, and ratios

Along with the `colors` parameter—to specify the colors, of course—you can also specify the position of each color in the fill by assigning it a number from 0 to 255, where 0 is the start of the fill and 255 is the end. These numbers, one for each color, are known as the `ratios` of the fill. Thus, if you wanted to make a two-color fill, you'd probably specify 0 and 255 as the `ratios`. To make an even blend of three colors, you could say 0, 128, 255. This would put the second color exactly in the middle of the other two. If you did something like 0, 20, 255, the first color would almost immediately blend into the second, and then very slowly blend into the third. Remember that these are not pixel values, but fractions of 255.

You can also specify the transparency of each color in the blend. This is known as alpha and can be from 0 to 100. If you don't want any transparency, you can make each alpha 100. If you set the first alpha to 100 and the last to 0, the gradient will not only blend the colors, but will smoothly fade out. This can be useful for creating soft shadows.

Each one of these arguments is an array. This makes sense, because you are probably going to be passing in at least two colors, alphas, and ratios, and possibly many more. You could create a new array and populate it with your values for each parameter, like so:

```
var colors:Array = new Array();
colors[0] = 0xffffff;
colors[1] = 0x000000;
```

But there's a much easier way to do it. You can create and populate an array on the fly by listing the elements you want in it between square brackets, separated by commas:

```
var colors:Array = [0xffffff, 0x000000];
```

In fact, you don't even need to make a `colors` variable. You can plug that array right into the `beginGradientFill` statement as an argument. Thus, you can get something like this:

```
beginGradientFill("linear",
                  [0xffffff, 0x000000],
                  [100, 100],
                  [0, 255],
                  matrix);
```

This defines two colors, two alpha values (both 100%), and start and end ratio values, so the gradient will start as white and blend into black at the end. Of course, you can create variables for each parameter if you want, and if you are defining a lot of colors, it will be clearer that way. The one caveat here is that these three arrays *must* all contain the same amount of elements. If you define three colors, you *must* have three alphas and three ratios. If any one contains more or less than the others, it's going to fail silently—no gradient, no fill, no error message.

All you need now is the start and end position and the angle of the fill. As you might have guessed, that's what the mysterious `matrix` parameter is for.

Creating the matrix

A *matrix* is usually a two-dimensional grid of values used for calculating various values. Matrices are used extensively in graphics for rotating, scaling, and moving things. That's exactly what you're doing here with the gradient. You need to position it, size it, and possibly rotate it. To use the matrix, you need to create a matrix object. This is a generic object with nine properties: a through `i`. These create a three-by-three matrix, which Flash can use to position, size, and rotate your gradient.

Fortunately, Macromedia gives you a much easier way to use the matrix. Again, you create an object and give it some properties. But rather than completely nondescriptive names like a, b, and c, the property names are: matrixType, x, y, w, h, and r. The matrixType is simply a string, which must be set to "box"; x and y are the start position of the gradient; w and h are the width and height; and r is the rotation (in radians). You generally want to set the x and y values to the top-left position of your fill, and the w and h values to the size of your fill. Similar to the way you can create an array with square brackets, you can create an object with curly brackets. So, you can do something like this:

```
var matrix:Object = {matrixType:"box",
                     x:0,
                     y:0,
                     w:100,
                     h:100,
                     r:Math.PI/2};
```

Again, you could plug this right into the beginGradientFill function call, but it's already kind of long, so I usually like to create the matrix as a separate variable and pass it in that way.

Let's see it in action. Here's some code, which you can find in ch04_07.fla:

```
init();
function init()
{
      lineStyle(1, 0, 100);
      var colors:Array = [0xffffff, 0xff0000];
      var alphas:Array = [100, 100];
      var ratios:Array = [0, 255];
      var matrix:Object = {matrixType:"box",
                           w:100, h:100, x:0, y:0, r:0};
      beginGradientFill("linear", colors, alphas, ratios, matrix);
      moveTo(0, 0);
      lineTo(100, 0);
      lineTo(100, 100);
      lineTo(0, 100);
      lineTo(0, 0);
      endFill();
}
```

When you test this, you'll see a nice white-to-red gradient square. Now let's draw the square in a different location, by changing the drawing code so you have the following code (in gradient2.fla):

```
moveTo(100, 100);
lineTo(200, 100);
lineTo(200, 200);
lineTo(100, 200);
lineTo(100, 100);
```

Now your square is all red. What happened? Well, the gradient starts at 0 on the x axis, and it's only 100 pixels wide, so at the point your square begins, the gradient has already reached full red, and it's red from there on out. So again, you are going to want the x, y of the matrix to be at the top-left point of your shape, like so (in the ch04_08.fla file):

```
var matrix:Object = {matrixType:"box",
                     w:100,
                     h:100,
                     x:100,
                     y:100,
                     r:0};
```

Here, the x, y is the same as the start of the square. Using the same square. You can now play around with the matrix and gradient fill setting to see what kind of effects you can create. First, try three colors:

```
var colors:Array = [0xffffff, 0x0000ff, 0xff0000];
var alphas:Array = [100, 100, 100];
var ratios:Array = [0, 128, 255];
```

Don't forget the alphas and ratios. Move the middle ratio around to see how that affects the gradient. Instead of 128, try 64 or 220.

The next example is a straight alpha blend. The colors are the same; only the alpha changes:

```
var colors:Array = [0x000000, 0x000000];
var alphas:Array = [100, 0];
var ratios:Array = [0, 255];
```

Try changing the angle now. Here's a 45-degree angle:

```
var matrix:Object = {matrixType:"box",
                     w:100,
                     h:100,
                     x:100,
                     y:100,
                     r:Math.PI/4};
```

Using Math.PI/2 will make a vertical gradient by rotating it 90 degrees. -Math.PI/2 will make it go up, and Math.PI will make it go from right to left, rather than from left to right.

Finally, switch over to a radial gradient type:

```
beginGradientFill("radial", colors, alphas, ratios, matrix);
```

And now try all the same tricks that you used on the linear gradient fill on the radial version.

If you are using Flash 8, you should definitely check out the additional material on beginGradientFill in the help files. In particular, the Flash 8 method of creating a matrix is quite nice. You can also read more about matrices in Chapter 18.

Color transforms

Next up in your rendering arsenal is the Color object and its methods, as well as the ColorTransform object, available in Flash 8. Unlike the drawing API, these don't allow you to create graphics, but merely change the color of an existing graphic contained in a movie clip or other display object instance. Actually, it is more accurate to say that you are altering the color of the movie clip. Let's dive in and see how it all works.

Changing color with the Color object

Note that although the Color object has been deprecated in Flash 8, it still works. It has been included here for use in Flash 7 movies.

To change the color of a movie clip, you first create a new Color object, passing it the name of an existing movie clip instance in the constructor, like so:

```
var myColor:Color = new Color(myMovieClip);
```

Then you call a method of that Color object, which affects the color of the movie clip. Note that you don't need to do anything to the movie clip itself. The Color object is kind of a wrapper that goes around the clip, and whatever you do to the object changes the clip.

Two methods of Color allow you to change the color of a movie clip: setRGB and setTransform. These methods work quite differently.

Setting a single color with setRGB

The setRGB method takes in a single color value. It changes the entire movie clip to the given color. If you had a movie clip that contained an imported bitmap, and you created a Color object, and on that object you said setRGB(0xff0000), you wouldn't have a reddish picture; instead, you'd have a solid red rectangle. setRGB obliterates any existing color in a movie clip. It doesn't respect lines or fills either. They will all be changed equally. Anything in the clip that is visible gets its color changed to whatever color setRGB tells it.

Knowing this, you should understand then that setRGB is best for blocks of colors and simple shapes. It's senseless to create some fancy, multicolored graphic, only to slap a coat of single-colored paint over the whole thing.

Let's try out setRGB to get a feel for it. Create any shape and convert it to a movie. Put an instance of that clip on stage and give it a name. As usual, I've already done this for you in ch04_09.fla, naming the instance star. The star instance has a yellow fill and a thick blue border. Now for the code:

```
var starColor:Color = new Color(star);
starColor.setRGB(0xff00ff);
```

Test that out. Voila! No more yellow fill. No more blue border. Just a solid mass of purple star, as shown in Figure 4-7.

Figure 4-7. Before and after setRGB (trust me, this is purple)

That's about it for `setRGB`. Try it out with different movie clips and different colors. You'll get the hang of it pretty quickly.

> `setRGB` *has a companion method called* `getRGB`. *This simply returns the color that you last set. If you haven't yet set a color, it will return zero.*

Transforming colors with setTransform

The `setTransform` method is the powerhouse of color manipulation in Flash. With it, you don't merely slap on a layer of color, but actually intelligently shift the color values, tint, or alpha of a movie clip. Thus, if you have an imported bitmap photo embedded in a movie clip, you can do some rudimentary image processing on it. Let's take a look at how this one works.

First, you need to create an object to pass into the `setTransform` method. This object contains all the information it needs to alter the color. It has eight properties: two each for red, green, blue, and alpha. The names of the properties are `ra`, ga, ba, aa, `rb`, gb, ab, and bb. The "a" values are a percentage and can range from 100 to –100. The "b" values are an addition and can range from 255 to –255. Now, what do I mean by a percentage or addition? Basically, Flash evaluates each pixel of the movie clip and gets the original value for each color channel (`r`, g, b, or a). It multiplies that by the percentages specified in the "a" properties, and then adds on the values from the "b" properties. Here is the actual formula, using red as an example:

```
newRed = oldRed * ra / 100 + rb;
```

The same goes for green, blue, and alpha. Let's say the red value for a particular pixel is 128, `ra` is 60, and `rb` is 20. You get a new red value for that pixel of 128 × 60 / 100 + 20, or 96.8. It's roughly three quarters as bright as it was.

The `ch04_10.fla` file has a nice example of using `setTransform`. I've included a commemorative picture of myself, along with a free slider component you can use in your own projects if you want. The picture is contained in a movie clip named `pic`. The sliders call the change function when they change.

This function creates a new object and assigns the values of all the sliders to it, and then calls setTransform on pic, using that object. Here's the code in full:

```
var myColor:Color = new Color(pic);
ra.changeHandler = change;
ga.changeHandler = change;
ba.changeHandler = change;
aa.changeHandler = change;
rb.changeHandler = change;
gb.changeHandler = change;
bb.changeHandler = change;
ab.changeHandler = change;

function change()
{
      var transformObject:Object = new Object();
      transformObject.ra = ra.value;
      transformObject.ga = ga.value;
      transformObject.ba = ba.value;
      transformObject.aa = aa.value;
      transformObject.rb = rb.value;
      transformObject.gb = gb.value;
      transformObject.bb = bb.value;
      transformObject.ab = ab.value;
      myColor.setTransform(transformObject);
}
```

A cool trick is to create a negative image. You can do this by setting the percentage sliders for r, g, and b to the bottom (–100), and the additive sliders for the same to the top (255). In effect, this completely reverses the values of each color.

Changing colors with the ColorTransform object

If you are using Flash 8, the correct way to do color transforms is via the ColorTransform object. All the stuff you just learned about offsets and percentages still applies, but the syntax is a little different.

First, you should know that a movie clip now has a new property, which is an object called transform. This object itself contains various properties that you can use to scale, rotate, position, and colorize the movie clip. The property of interest here is colorTransform. Realize that this is a property of a property of a movie clip, so it's accessed like this:

```
myMC.transform.colorTransform
```

To change a movie clip's coloring, you assign a new ColorTransform object to this property. And just what, you might ask, is a ColorTransform object? This is really pretty much the same kind of object as the transformObject object created in the previous example, but rather than leaving it as a generic object, in Flash 8, it has been formalized into its own official class. Instead of saying this:

```
myTransform = new Object()
```

And then assigning all those `ra`, `rb`, and so on properties, you can say something like this:

```
myTransform = new ColorTransform(0.5, 1.0, 0.5, 0.5, 10, 10, 10, 0);
```

Also, you might notice that the percent values are now decimals in the range of –1 to 1, rather than –100 to 100. The offsets still go from –255 to 255. The actual constructor for the `ColorTransform` object looks like this:

```
ColorTransform(redMultiplier,
               greenMultiplier,
               blueMultiplier,
               alphaMultiplier,
               redOffset,
               greenOffset,
               blueOffset,
               alphaOffset)
```

For the `Color` object, the formula for transforming a particular channel is like so:

```
newRed = oldRed * ra / 100 + rb;
```

For the `ColorTransform` object, it winds up being like this:

```
newRed = oldRed * redMultiplier + redOffset;
```

One more thing you need to know is that `ColorTransform` is actually part of the `flash.geom` package. In ActionScript 2, *packages* are just a way of organizing code. You access a package with dot notation, using syntax that is similar to the way you access properties of an object. So, to create a `ColorTransform` object, you actually need to say this:

```
new flash.geom.ColorTransform(. . .)
```

Another way to do it, if you know you're going to be using `ColorTransform` a lot and don't want to type `flash.geom` over and over, is to *import* the class. Just place the following line at the start of your file:

```
import flash.geom.ColorTransform;
```

Now the class will be available for you to create instances directly, without prefixing the package name every time.

Just to give you an example of how this might make things a little easier, I modified the file for the previous example, `ch04_10.fla`, to a Flash 8 file named `ch04_10a.fla`. I changed the top sliders to have a range of –1 to 1, instead of –100 to 100, and replaced the code with this:

```
import flash.geom.ColorTransform;

ra.changeHandler = change;
ga.changeHandler = change;
ba.changeHandler = change;
aa.changeHandler = change;
rb.changeHandler = change;
```

```
gb.changeHandler = change;
bb.changeHandler = change;
ab.changeHandler = change;

function change()
{
        pic.transform.colorTransform =
                new ColorTransform(ra.value,
                                   ga.value,
                                   ba.value,
                                   aa.value,
                                   rb.value,
                                   gb.value,
                                   bb.value,
                                   ab.value);
}
```

Make sure your publish settings are set to a Flash 8 file if you create this one yourself. I think you'll agree this approach makes things a little easier.

Filters

Filters are bitmapped effects that can be applied to any display object. They can be applied in the Flash IDE via the Filters panel or via ActionScript. Since this book is about ActionScript, I'll limit the discussion to the scripted methods of applying filters. The following filters are included in Flash 8:

- Drop shadow
- Blur
- Glow
- Bevel
- Gradient bevel
- Gradient glow
- Color matrix
- Convolution
- Displacement map

The convolution and displacement map filters can be applied only by ActionScript; there is no way to access those filters in the IDE.

I'm not going to go into the details of each and every filter. They are documented in the Flash 8 help files, and an entire chapter (if not a whole book) could be devoted to them. But since I have enough material to cover in this book as it is, I'm just going to give you an overview of their use and a couple of examples.

Creating a filter

Filters are created by using the new operator and the name of the filter, passing in the required parameters. For example, to make a blur filter, one of the simplest, you would say this:

```
var blur:BlurFilter = new BlurFilter(5, 5, 3);
```

In this case, the parameters are xBlur, yBlur, and quality. This example will blur an object 5 pixels on both axes, with a medium-quality blur.

Another thing to realize is that filters are in their own package, called flash.filters. So, you can put this at the beginning of the file:

```
import flash.filters.BlurFilter;
```

Alternatively, you can create your filter like this:

```
new flash.filters.BlurFilter(5, 5, 3);
```

If you want to import *all* the filters in the package, you can use this shortcut:

```
import flash.filters.*;
```

Now, you can create any type of filter directly.

So now you have a blur filter, but how do you make it blur a particular object?

Any movie clip has a property called filters. This is an array containing all the filters that have been applied to that object (whether they were applied by code or in the IDE), since any object can have multiple filters applied. You just need to get your blur filter into that array. Ideally, this would be as simple as applying a basic array operation, push, and saying myMC.filters.push(blur);. But alas, it's not that easy. If no filters have been applied to an object, the filter property will be undefined, so there will be no array to push anything onto. And even if there is already an array there, Flash does not listen for changes to the filters array and won't take note of the change until a whole new array is assigned to filters.

If you know that the object doesn't have any filters applied, or you are willing to overwrite them, you can just make a brand-new array, stick your blur filter in it, and assign that new array to the filters property. Let's try that. Create a new document, and then create a movie clip with some graphics in it. I made another star this time, with the instance name star. (You can find my example in ch04_11.fla.) Now put the following code on the timeline:

```
import flash.filters.BlurFilter;
var blur:BlurFilter = new BlurFilter(5, 5, 3);
var myFilters:Array = new Array();
myFilters.push(blur);
star.filters = myFilters;
```

Voila! You have a blurry star. You can shortcut this a little:

```
import flash.filters.BlurFilter;
var blur:BlurFilter = new BlurFilter(5, 5, 3);
var myFilters:Array = [blur]; // makes new array with blur as element 0
star.filters = myFilters;
```

Or shortcut it a lot:

```
star.filters = [new flash.filters.BlurFilter(5, 5, 3)];
```

As long as you are creating a new array, putting your filter in it, and applying it to the `filters` property, Flash will be happy.

But what if you already have a filter applied and want to keep it, or worse yet, you aren't sure if there are any filters? Here's the logic: First check if `filters` is undefined. If so, create a new array. If not, just grab the existing array, which will contain any existing filters. Then push your filter onto it and assign it back to `filters`. Here's how that looks:

```
import flash.filters.BlurFilter;
var blur:BlurFilter = new BlurFilter(5, 5, 3);
if(star.filters == undefined)
{
   star.filters = new Array();
}
var oldFilters:Array = star.filters;
oldFilters.push(blur);
star.filters = oldFilters;
```

Try applying a filter to the star in the IDE. You'll see that both filters are applied.

Animating filters

Now that you know the basics of how to use filters with ActionScript, let's apply what you've already learned to make a really cool effect: an animated drop shadow. For this effect, use the following code (which you can find in `ch04_12.fla`):

```
import flash.filters.DropShadowFilter;
var star:MovieClip;
var starFilter:DropShadowFilter;
init();
function init() {
      starFilter = new DropShadowFilter();
      starFilter.blurX = 20;
      starFilter.blurY = 20;
}
function onEnterFrame(Void):Void {
      var dx:Number = star._x - _xmouse;
```

```
        var dy:Number = star._y - _ymouse;
        starFilter.angle = Math.atan2(dy, dx) * 180 / Math.PI;
        starFilter.distance = Math.sqrt(dx*dx + dy*dy) * .1;
        star.filters = [starFilter];
    }
```

The class first stores a reference to the star symbol and the main filter. The init function creates the filter and sets some of its properties. The onEnterFrame function calculates the angle and distance from the mouse to the star, using trig that was covered in Chapter 3 (make sure the registration point of your object is centered for this one). It uses these to set the angle and distance properties of the drop shadow filter, and applies that filter to star. This turns out to be pretty simple. In fact, when I finished writing the code for this effect, I was surprised at just how short it turned out to be.

Bitmap control

For me, the BitmapData object is one of the most exciting improvements in Flash 8. Although Flash has always had varying abilities to import, load, and use bitmap images, it has never offered this level of ActionScripted control over them. With the new BitmapData object, you now have pixel-level control of bitmap images and the ability to create bitmaps at runtime, so you can do some very complex image manipulation.

As with filters, I could fill an entire book telling you everything about BitmapData. That would be fun, but it's not the purpose of *this* book. So I'm going to run through some of the basics with a couple of examples.

First, you need to create a new BitmapData object. You do this by calling new BitmapData () with the following parameters:

```
new BitmapData (width:Number,
                height:Number,
                transparent:Boolean,
                fillColor:Number)
```

As you might have guessed by now, BitmapData is also in its own package, called flash.display.BitmapData. So, you need to either import that package or use the full package name when creating a BitmapData object. As for the parameters, width and height are pretty obvious. Transparent means that the image you create can contain an alpha channel for transparency, so choose true or false for this. fillColor is the initial color with which the image will be created. This brings us to the subject of 32-bit colors.

At the start of the chapter, I talked about colors and said you could create colors as 24-bit hexadecimal numbers in the format 0xRRGGBB. Since BitmapData objects support an alpha channel as well as three color channels, colors are expressed as 32-bit hexadecimal numbers in the format 0xAARRGGBB, where AA stands for alpha or transparency. Thus, 0xFFFFFFFF creates an opaque white color, 0x00FFFFFF creates a completely transparent white color, and 0x80FFFFFF creates an approximately 50% transparent white color.

When you create a BitmapData object, you probably want some way to make it visible. By now, you are familiar with the movie clip method, attachMovie, and perhaps even attachSound. Well, Flash 8 adds a new method to movie clips: attachBitmap. Here's how it looks:

```
mc.attachBitmap(bitmapData, depth, pixelSnapping, smoothing)
```

The first parameter, bitmapData, is the BitmapData object you just created. That and depth, which is obvious, are the only two required parameters. You can also specify a string for pixelSnapping, which determines whether or not the bitmap will snap to whole pixel values. Valid pixelSnapping values are "auto" (default), "always", or "none". The smoothing parameter determines if smoothing will be applied when the image is scaled or otherwise transformed. It's either true (default) or false.

So, let's try out a BitmapData object. Type this code into frame 1 of a new Flash 8 movie:

```
import flash.display.BitmapData;
var bitmap:BitmapData = new BitmapData(100, 100, false, 0xffff0000);
_root.attachBitmap(bitmap, 0);
```

Test it, and you should see a red square. At first glance, this doesn't seem any more interesting than if you had just done the same thing with the drawing API. But realize that this is not a vector drawing of a square with a red fill. This is a bitmap image, in which each pixel is separately defined and alterable.

In fact, the value of each and every pixel can be read or changed with getPixel, getPixel32, setPixel, and setPixel32. The difference between the two versions is that getPixel and setPixel use 24-bit numbers and ignore the alpha channel, and the "32" versions use 32-bit numbers to include transparency information. Let's play with that a bit and make a rudimentary spray paint tool like one you'd find in any bitmap paint program.

Create a new Flash 8 document and put the following code right on the first frame:

```
import flash.display.BitmapData;
var density:Number = 100;
var radius:Number = 50;

var bitmap:BitmapData = new BitmapData(Stage.width,
                                       Stage.height,
                                       false,
                                       0xffffffff);
_root.attachBitmap(bitmap,0);

function onMouseDown():Void {
      sprayColor = Math.random() * 0xffffff;
      onEnterFrame = spray;
}

function onMouseUp():Void {
      delete onEnterFrame;
}
```

```
function spray():Void {
      for (var i:Number = 0; i<density; i++) {
            var angle:Number = Math.random() * Math.PI * 2;
            var randRadius:Number = Math.random() * radius;
            var randX:Number = Math.cos(angle) * randRadius;
            var randY:Number = Math.sin(angle) * randRadius;
            bitmap.setPixel32(_xmouse + randX,
                              _ymouse + randY,
                              sprayColor);
      }
}
```

This is probably the most complex code I've given you so far, but other than the BitmapData stuff, it's all stuff that I've already covered. I'm just using more of it all at once. Let's step through it though.

First, some variables are defined to hold references to the various objects and values that are used throughout the program. The BitmapData object is created and attached right to _root.

The mouse event handlers just add and remove a handler for the enterFrame event, which is the spray function. That handler is where all the action takes place. Here, we get back into a bit of trigonometry. First, you calculate a random angle from 0 to 2 * Math.PI, which you'll remember is in radians and is equal to 360 degrees. Next, you calculate a random radius based on the radius property set earlier, and use a bit of trig to convert the radius and angle into x, y values. Then use setPixel32 to set the pixel at the mouse location plus the random x, y value to the spray color, which is randomly determined each time you start to draw.

Actually, you'll see there's a for loop there, so this happens a whole bunch of times on each frame. How many times is determined by the density value.

Go ahead and test it, and play with the density and radius values to see the different effects they create. You're probably already thinking how you could throw in some controls to let the user change these parameters.

At first glance, you might think, "Big deal. I could do the same thing with the drawing API or by attaching small movie clips and coloring them." True, you could do just that, but if you've tried drawing hundreds and hundreds of individual shapes with the drawing API, you'll notice that the more you draw, the slower it goes. After several hundred shapes are drawn, the lag becomes very noticeable and the program becomes unusable. The same goes for attaching movie clips. A bitmap is quite different, though. You could spray new layers of paint on with this program all day, with no change in its speed or efficiency.

If you want to begin to see some even cooler effects, throw the following line into the file, somewhere up at the top:

```
_root.filters = [new flash.filters.BlurFilter(2, 2, 3)];
```

This adds a blur to the content and really makes it obvious that you are dealing with bitmaps, not vectors.

Of course, setting pixels is one of the simplest operations you can do to a BitmapData object. In addition to getting and setting pixels, you can apply about another two dozen methods to a BitmapData object. Using these, you can copy pixels, set thresholds, dissolve, merge, scroll, and more. One of my personal favorites is the Perlin noise function, which allows you to create random, organic patterns. These are useful for anything from smoke and clouds to landscapes and water ripples. Experiment with the methods that interest you.

Important formulas in this chapter

You've added a few more valuable tools to your collection in this chapter, mostly relating to handling color.

Convert hex to decimal:

```
trace(hexValue);
```

Convert decimal to hex:

```
trace(decimalValue.toString(16));
```

Combine component colors:

```
color24 = red << 16 | green << 8 | blue;
```

Extract component colors:

```
red = color24 >> 16;
green = color24 >> 8 & 0xFF;
blue = color24 & 0xFF;
```

Draw a curve through a point:

```
// xt, yt is the point you want to draw through
// x0, y0 and x2, y2 are the end points of the curve
x1 = xt * 2 - (x0 + x2) / 2;
y1 = yt * 2 - (y0 + y2) / 2;
moveTo(x0, y0);
curveTo(x1, y1, x2, y2);
```

Summary

This chapter didn't cover too much about making anything move, but it did show you a number of ways to create visual content, which you'll learn how to animate in future chapters. Specifically, the chapter covered the following topics:

- Color, 24-bit and 32-bit
- The drawing API
- Filters
- The `BitmapData` object

These subjects will give you the tools you need to make dynamic, expressive content for your animation, and since everything covered here is based on ActionScript, you can animate directly using all of these methods. Just use some code to create content, change the variables used in the code, and render it again.

You'll be using many of the techniques introduced in this chapter throughout the book, so it will be useful for you to know and understand them well now. In fact, you'll get your first hands-on experience using several of these techniques in the next chapter, which covers velocity and acceleration.

Part Two

BASIC MOTION

};shape.targetHeight = shape._height;
shape.onEnterFrame = function() {
var speed = 5;
this._height += (this.targetHeight - this._height)/speed;

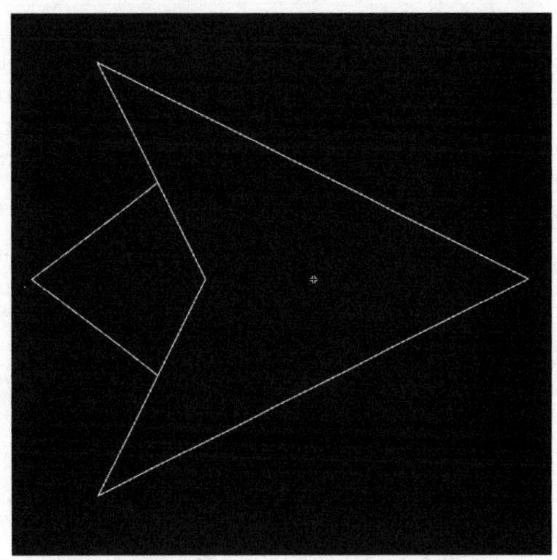

Chapter 5

VELOCITY AND ACCELERATION

What we'll cover in this chapter:

- Velocity
- Acceleration
- Important formulas in this chapter

Well, congratulations! You've made it to the point in the book where the action really starts. This means that: (a) you've persevered through all the chapters so far, (b) you skimmed over the previous chapters and felt like you knew enough of it to get by, or (c) you got bored and jumped ahead. However it happened, here you are. Just remember, if you start having trouble, you can probably find help in an earlier chapter.

This chapter gets you started with basic motion: velocity, vectors, and acceleration. These concepts will be used for almost every bit of ActionScripted animation you do from here on out.

Velocity

The most basic property of something that is moving is velocity. Many people equate the term *velocity* with speed. That's part of it, but only part. The concept of velocity contains a very important second factor: *direction*. And that is pretty much our layman's definition for velocity: *speed in a particular direction*. Let's take a look at exactly how this definition differs from simple speed.

If I tell you that I got in my car at point X and drove 30 miles per hour for one hour, you'd have a pretty hard time finding me. On the other hand, if I said I drove due north for one hour at the same speed, you'd know precisely where I was. This is pretty important in animation, because you need to know where to put movie clips. It's fine to say a movie clip is moving at a certain speed, but you're going to need some specific x, y coordinates to assign to it on each frame to give it the illusion of motion. This is where velocity comes in. If you know where something is at the start of a particular frame, how fast it is moving, and in what direction, you know where to put it at the start of the next frame.

The speed part of it is usually defined in terms of pixels per frame (ppf). In other words, if a movie clip is at a certain point as it enters a frame, it's going to be so many pixels away from that point at the end of the frame.

In most cases, using pixels per frame works fine, and it is definitely the simplest to program. However, due to the unstable nature of frame rates in Flash, using pixels per frame may make your animation slow down at certain points when too much is happening, there is too much to compute, or the CPU is busy doing something else. If you are programming some kind of game or simulation in which it is crucial that the animation proceeds at a very uniform rate, you might want to use an interval-based animation instead. I've included an example of that approach in Chapter 19.

Before getting into coding velocity, I want to talk a little bit about vectors, as that's how velocity is generally depicted.

Vectors and velocity

A *vector* is something that has magnitude and direction. In the case of velocity, the magnitude is the speed. Vectors are drawn as arrows. The length of the arrow is its magnitude, and the direction the arrow is pointing in is, naturally, the direction of the vector. Figure 5-1 shows some vectors.

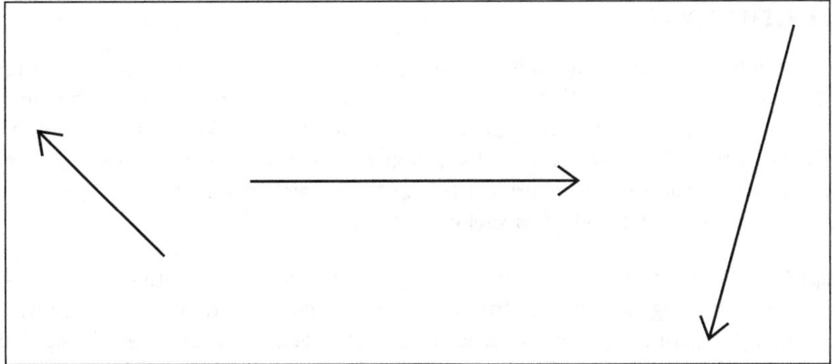

Figure 5-1. A few vectors

One thing to note is that the magnitude is always positive. A vector with a negative magnitude would simply be a vector going in the opposite direction, as illustrated in Figure 5-2.

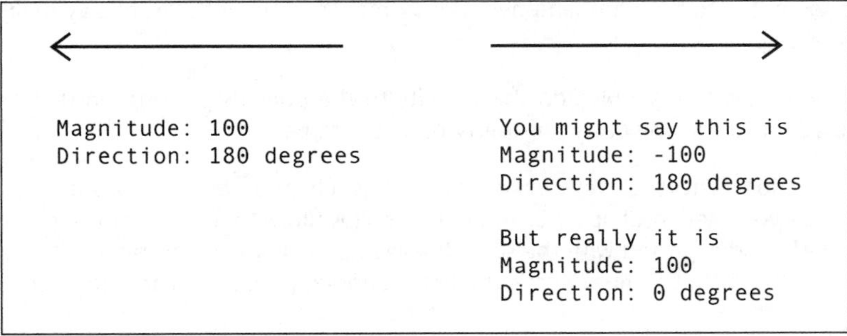

Figure 5-2. Negative velocity is really velocity in the opposite direction.

Another thing to note is that vectors don't really have any set position. Even in the case of velocity, the vector doesn't state where something is starting or where it ends up; it just indicates how fast and in which direction the object is moving. Thus, two vectors can be equal if they have the same direction and magnitude, even if they are describing two different objects in two different locations, as shown in Figure 5-3.

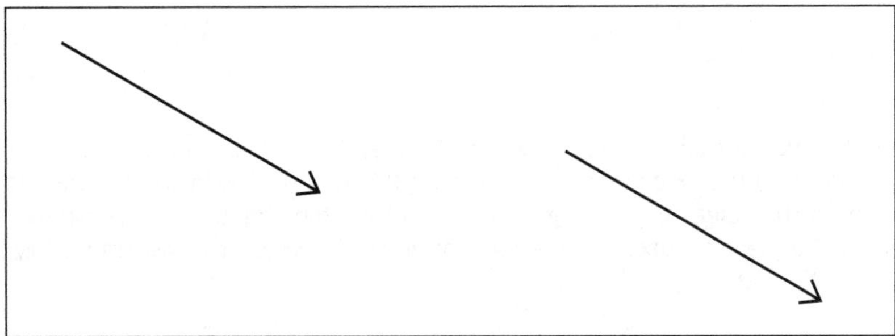

Figure 5-3. If vectors have the same magnitude and direction, they are the same. Position doesn't matter.

Velocity on one axis

I'm going to simplify things at first, by limiting velocity to a single axis: the x axis, or horizontal motion. This is basically saying that the direction is zero degrees, due east, or from the left side of the screen to the right side of the screen—however you want to look at it. The speed is just how many pixels it moves in that direction each frame. Thus, if I say that the velocity on the x axis is 5, I mean that the object will move 5 pixels each frame from left to right. This also means that if I say the velocity is –5 on the x axis, it will move right to left, 5 pixels each frame.

Now, you caught me there, didn't you? Already I'm talking about a negative magnitude when I just told you there's no such thing. Technically speaking, the velocity would actually be 5 and the direction 180 degrees. Similarly, a positive y velocity would be that speed at 90 degrees (straight down), and a negative y velocity would be 270, or –90 degrees (straight up). In practice, though, when you are calculating component x, y velocities, they always come through as positive and negative numbers, and you are often going to see me writing things like, "the x velocity is –5." So, if it helps you, think of the minus sign as indicating "to the left" for x velocity or "up" for y velocity, rather than meaning negative.

Throughout the book, I will use vx to stand for velocity on the x axis, and vy to mean velocity on the y axis. Positive vx means to the right, and negative vx means to the left. Positive vy means down, and negative vy means up.

For velocity on one axis, you simply add the velocity to the object's position on that axis. Whatever your vx is, you add it to the object's _x property on each frame.

Let's see it in action. The first few examples in this chapter will use a similar setup as the `chapter2base.fla` you used in Chapter 2. You'll use an FLA file with a single movie clip symbol in the library, named `ball` and exported with the same linkage name. For each example, I'll give you code to put on frame 1 of the main timeline. Here's the first example, which you can find in `ch05_01.fla`:

```
init();
function init():Void
{
	vx = 5;
	ball = attachMovie("ball", "ball", 0);
	ball._x = 0;
	ball._y = Stage.height / 2;
}
function onEnterFrame():Void
{
	ball._x += vx;
}
```

In this example, first you set an x velocity (vx) of 5. Remember that is 5 pixels per frame, so on each frame, the vx is added to the _x property. Then it goes through the business of getting the ball out of the library and onto the stage, and setting up the event handler for the `enterFrame` event. On each frame, the ball will be placed 5 pixels to the right of where it was on the last frame. Try it out. Pretty good illusion of motion, eh?

Play around with it. Give it higher values or lower values for vx. Try some negative values and watch it move in the other direction. See if you can make it move on the y axis instead.

Velocity on two axes

Moving along two axes is pretty simple. You just define a vx and a vy, and then add the vx to the _x property and the vy to the _y property on each frame. So, what you are saying is that for each frame, the object is going to move so many pixels on the x axis and so many pixels on the y axis.

The next example (ch05_02.fla) demonstrates this, and here it is:

```
init();
function init():Void
{
	vx = 5;
	vy = 5;
	ball = attachMovie("ball", "ball", 0);
	ball._x = 0;
	ball._y = Stage.height / 2;
}
function onEnterFrame():Void
{
	ball._x += vx;
	ball._y += vy;
}
```

Again, play around with the velocity variables until you get a good feel for them. Don't forget to try out some negative values.

Angular velocity

OK, so far, so good. You have some real animation going on, using velocity on two axes. But in many cases—maybe most cases—x and y velocity won't be the initial data you have.

The fact is I'm kind of cheating with the definition of velocity here. I said it's speed in a direction, but now I've given you two different speeds in two different directions. The reason I did that is because, in Flash, you position objects by placing them on x, y coordinates. So you need to end up with a velocity and position on both axes, but that's not necessarily what you start out with.

What if you just have a value for speed and an angle for direction, per the definition. Say you want something to move at an angle of 45 degrees and a speed of 3 pixels per frame. I don't see any vx or vy, or anything even similar in that description.

Fortunately, you've already been introduced to the tools you need to derive vx and vy from that description. Think back to the discussion of trigonometry in Chapter 3. Now, look at Figure 5-4, which shows what you want the ball to do on each frame: move 3 pixels at an angle of 45 degrees.

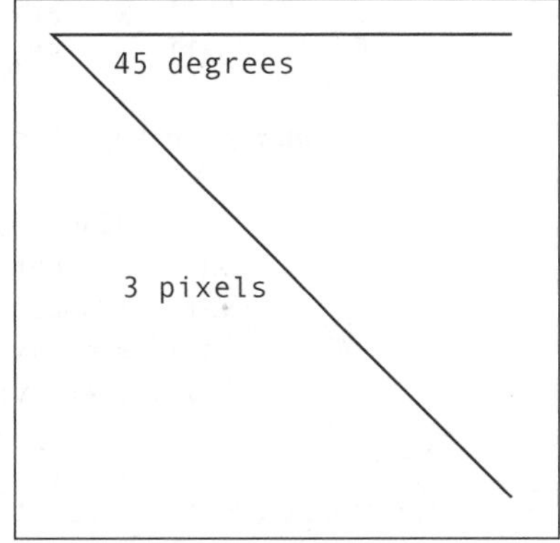

Figure 5-4. A magnitude and a direction

Does this diagram look familiar? How about if I add another line, as shown in Figure 5-5? What do you know? You have a right triangle, with one angle and the hypotenuse defined!

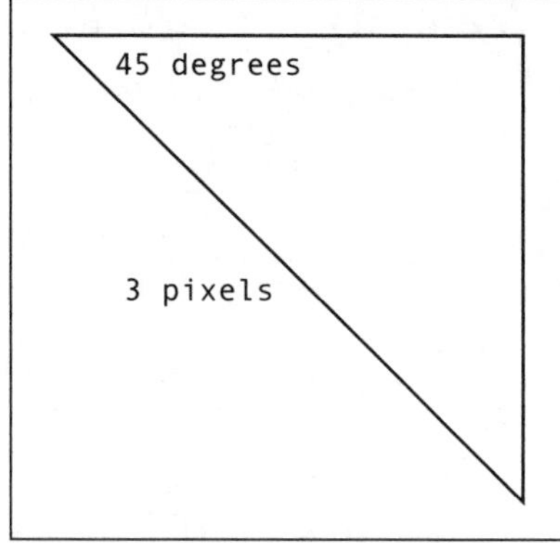

Figure 5-5. Magnitude and direction mapping becomes a right triangle.

Notice that the two legs of that triangle lie on the x and y axes. In fact, the leg that lies on the x axis is equal to the distance the ball is going to move on the x axis. The same goes for the leg on the y axis. Remember that in a right triangle, if you have one side and one angle, you can find all the rest. So, given the 45 degrees and the hypotenuse of 3 pixels, you should be able to use `Math.cos` and `Math.sin` to find the lengths of vx and vy.

The side adjacent to the angle is vx. The cosine of an angle is the adjacent/hypotenuse. Or, stated another way, the adjacent side is the cosine of the angle times the hypotenuse. Similarly, the opposite side is vy. Sine is opposite/hypotenuse, or the opposite is the sine times hypotenuse.

Here's the exact code you would use:

```
vx = Math.cos(angle) * speed;
vy = Math.sin(angle) * speed;
```

Now don't you dare forget to convert the 45 degrees to radians before passing it into the `Math` functions! Once you have the vx and the vy, you can easily add these to the x, y position of the object you are animating.

The next example (`ch05_03.fla`) has the following code on frame 1:

```
init();
function init():Void
{
	angle = 45;
	speed = 3;
	ball = attachMovie("ball", "ball", 0);
	ball._x = Stage.width / 2;
	ball._y = Stage.height / 2;
}
function onEnterFrame():Void
{
	var radians:Number = angle * Math.PI / 180;
	var vx:Number = Math.cos(radians) * speed;
	var vy:Number = Math.sin(radians) * speed;
	ball._x += vx;
	ball._y += vy;
}
```

The main difference here is that you're starting off with angle and speed rather than vx and vy. The velocities are calculated as local variables, used, and discarded. Of course, in a simple case like this, where the angle and speed are never changing, it would make more sense to calculate the velocities once and save them as timeline variables. But in most advanced motion, both the direction and speed of motion will be constantly changing, so the vx and vy will not remain static.

To experiment with this example, change the angle around. See for yourself that you can make the ball travel at any speed and any angle by simply changing those two numbers.

Now, let's take another look at this example in terms of vectors.

Vector addition

Vector addition is when you have two vectors working in a system and you want to find the resultant overall vector. Here, you have a vector on the x axis, another vector on the y axis, and an overall velocity vector. You add vectors by simply placing them together head to tail. The resultant vector is the line you can draw from the starting point of the first vector on the chain to the ending point of the last one. In Figure 5-6, you can see three vectors being added together and their resultant vector.

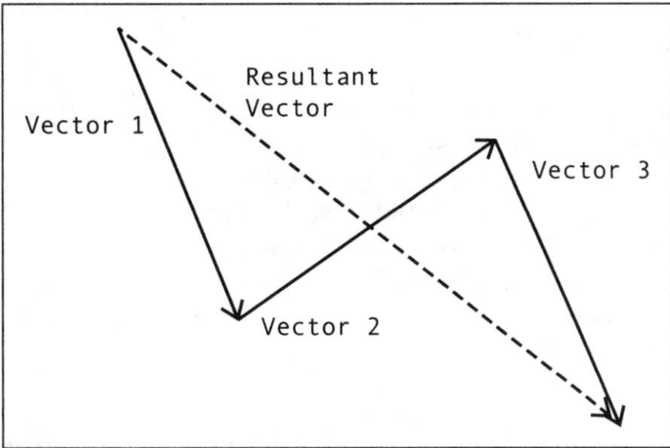

Figure 5-6. Vector addition

It doesn't matter in what order you place the vectors; the result will always be the same. And time has no part in it. You could say an object moved this way, then it moved that way, and then it moved the other way, in any order. Or you could say that it moved in all three ways at once. The result is that it wound up moving at a certain speed in a certain direction when all was said and done.

Let's go back to our example. If you lay down the x-axis velocity vector, and then put the y-axis velocity vector on the end of that, the resulting line is the overall velocity. Figure 5-7 illustrates the velocities as vectors.

What do you know? It's the same picture! Take that as a sign that you are doing something right.

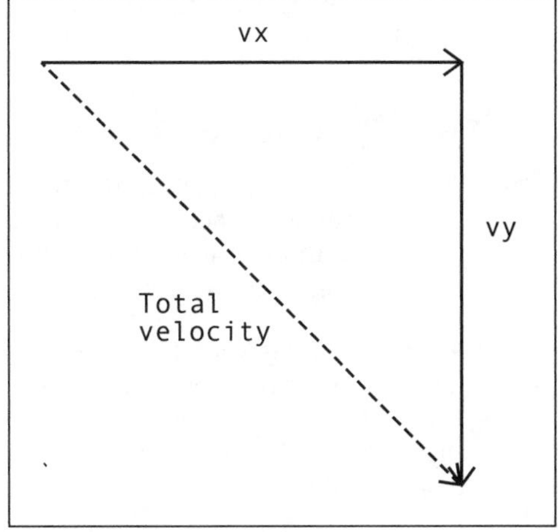

Figure 5-7. Velocities as vectors

A mouse follower

Let's use the velocity concepts to expand on an earlier concept. Back in Chapter 3, you built an example with an arrow that always pointed to the mouse. That example used Math.atan2 to compute the angle between the mouse and the arrow movie clip, and then rotated it so it lined up with that angle. With what you just learned, you can now throw some speed into the mix and get a velocity based on the current angle. This example uses the same arrow movie clip, rather than the ball. Here is the code for it (ch05_04):

```
init();
function init():Void
{
	speed = 5;
	arrow = attachMovie("arrow", "arrow", 0);
	arrow._x = Stage.width / 2;
	arrow._y = Stage.height / 2;
}
function onEnterFrame():Void
{
	var dx:Number = _xmouse - arrow._x;
	var dy:Number = _ymouse - arrow._y;
	var angle:Number = Math.atan2(dy, dx);
	arrow._rotation = angle * 180 / Math.PI;
	var vx:Number = Math.cos(angle) * speed;
	var vy:Number = Math.sin(angle) * speed;
	arrow._x += vx;
	arrow._y += vy;
}
```

While this is a pretty complex effect, there shouldn't be anything in here that you don't fully understand by now. You're getting the x distance and y distance to the mouse, and from that using Math.atan2 to get the angle that forms. You're then using that angle to rotate the arrow, and using Math.cos and Math.sin along with the speed to find the x and y velocities. Finally, you're adding the velocities to the position.

Velocity extended

I'm entering into dangerous territory here, but I'm going to start taking the definition of velocity into places it was never meant to go. While, in a strict sense, velocity refers to change of position and physical motion through space, there's no need to limit the concepts you've just learned to just the _x and _y properties of movie clips.

A movie clip has a lot of properties you can tinker with, and almost all of them can accept a wide range of values that you can change over time to produce animation. Perhaps *velocity* isn't the correct word for it, but the concept is similar, and this is the ideal place to talk about these other properties. Due to the similarities, I often continue to use the word *velocity* in my variable names far more often than I should.

An example would be having a movie clip spin around. In this case, you are changing the object's _rotation property on each frame by adding a value to it. You can make it spin quickly by adding a high value to the _rotation property on each frame, or have it spin more slowly by adding a smaller value. Correct or not, I usually refer to the variable that holds the spinning speed as vr, for rotational velocity.

Using the familiar arrow movie clip, you can come up with something like this (ch05_05.fla):

```
init();
function init():Void
{
        vr = 5;
        arrow = attachMovie("arrow", "arrow", 0);
        arrow._x = Stage.width / 2;
        arrow._y = Stage.height / 2;
}
function onEnterFrame():Void
{
        arrow._rotation += vr;
}
```

In terms of velocity here, the speed is 5 and the direction is clockwise. I might even get away with that one, as there's still some motion going on, but when I start using terms like "alpha velocity" (how fast something is fading in or out), I'm sure I'll ruffle some feathers. Still, I find it useful to think of such properties in these same terms. I want to change the alpha at a certain rate by adding or subtracting to its value on each frame. As I often find myself changing several properties over time, each at certain rates, it's nice to relate them all by calling them velocities. Thus, I might wind up with something like this:

```
function onEnterFrame():Void
{
    arrow._x += vx;
    arrow._y += vy;
    arrow._alpha += vAlpha;
    arrow._rotation += vr;
    arrow._xscale = arrow._yscale += vScale;
    // etc.
}
```

You'll see a lot of examples like this later in the book, so I hope you'll forgive my occasional v.

That about does it for velocity and its "cousins." Now, let's move on to acceleration.

Acceleration

It's common to think of acceleration as speeding up and deceleration as slowing down. And while this is not incorrect, for this book, I use a slightly more technical definition for acceleration.

Many similarities exist between velocity and acceleration in terms of how they are described. They are both vectors. Like velocity, acceleration is described as a value and a direction. However, whereas velocity changes the position of an object, acceleration changes its velocity.

Think of it this way. You get in your car, start it up, and put it in gear. What is your velocity? It's zero. By stepping on the gas pedal (also known as the *accelerator*, hmmm . . .), your velocity begins to change (at least the speed portion of it; the direction is changed with the steering wheel). After a second or two, you're going 4 or 5 miles per hour (mph). Then your speed increases to 10 mph, 20 mph, 30 mph, and so on. The engine is applying force to the car to change its velocity.

Thus, you have the layman's Flash definition for acceleration: *A force that changes the velocity of an object.*

In purely ActionScript terms, you can say that acceleration is a value that you add to a velocity property.

Here's another example. Say you have a spaceship that needs to go from planet A to planet B. Its direction will be whatever direction planet B happens to be in relation to planet A. It points in that direction and fires its rockets. As long as those rockets are firing, force is being applied to the ship, and its velocity is going to change. In other words, the spaceship will continue to go faster and faster.

At some point, the captain decides the ship is going fast enough, and he might as well conserve fuel, so he shuts down the rockets. Assuming there is no friction in space, the ship is going to continue along at the same velocity. As the rockets are no longer firing, no more force is being applied to the ship. Since there is no more acceleration, the velocity does not change.

Then the ship approaches its goal. It needs to slow down or it's going to fly right past planet B (or if the navigator was accurate enough, the ship is going to become a *part* of planet B). So what does the captain do? You don't have brakes in space—there's nothing for them to grab a hold of. Instead, the captain turns the ship around so it faces the opposite direction, and fires up the rockets again. This applies negative acceleration, or acceleration in the opposite direction. Really, this is the same thing I covered while discussing vectors. The force is again changing the velocity, but this time it is reducing the velocity. The velocity will get less and less, and eventually arrive at zero. Ideally, that will coincide with the point when the ship is a couple of inches above the surface of the planet. At that point, the captain can kill the rockets and let gravity finish the job. (I'll talk about gravity in the "Gravity as acceleration" section, coming up soon.)

Acceleration on one axis

Let's put it into practice in Flash. Like the first velocity example, this first acceleration example stays on one axis. We'll jump back to the ball movie clip for the next few examples.

Here's the code for the first example (`ch05_06.fla`):

```
init();
function init():Void
{
	vx = 0;
	ax = 0.2;
	attachMovie("ball", "ball", 0);
	ball._x = 0;
	ball._y = Stage.height / 2;
}
function onEnterFrame():Void
```

```
{
        vx += ax;
        ball._x += vx;
}
```

Here, you start out with velocity (vx) being zero. The acceleration (ax) is 0.2. This is added to the velocity on each frame, and then the velocity is added to the ball's position.

Test this example. You'll see that the ball starts out moving very slowly, but by the time it leaves the stage, it's zipping right along.

Now, let's get closer to the spaceship example, and allow the ball to turn the acceleration off and on, and even reverse it. You can use the cursor keys for this. You can easily check if a particular key is currently being pressed with the `Key.isDown()` method, passing in the constant name for the key you want to check. (All the constants are listed in the Flash help files.) For now, we just care about the left and right cursor keys, which are `Key.LEFT` and `Key.RIGHT`. Here's the code (`ch05_07.fla`):

```
init();
function init():Void
{
        vx = 0;
        ax = 0.2;
        attachMovie("ball", "ball", 0);
        ball._x = Stage.width / 2;
        ball._y = Stage.height / 2;
}
function onEnterFrame():Void
{
        if (Key.isDown(Key.LEFT))
        {
                vx -= ax;
        }
        else if (Key.isDown(Key.RIGHT))
        {
                vx += ax;
        }
        ball._x += vx;
}
```

In this example, you're simply checking if either the left or right cursor key is down. If the left cursor key is down, you subtract the ax value from the velocity. If the right cursor key is down, you add it. If neither is down, the velocity stays the same. Finally, the velocity is added to position.

Test the example. You'll see that you don't have complete control over the speed of the object. You can't stop it on a dime, so to speak. You can only slow it down to the point it stops. And if you slow it down too much, it starts going in the opposite direction. See if you can stop it just before it hits the edge of the stage.

I'm sure some game ideas are already popping into your head. Hold onto them, You're about to expand your mastery of this technique many times over.

Acceleration on two axes

As with velocity, you can have acceleration on the x axis and y axis at the same time. You just set up an acceleration value for each axis (I usually use the variable names ax and ay), add those to vx and vy, and finally add vx and vy to the _x and _y properties.

It's pretty easy to adapt the previous example to work with the y axis as well. You just need to add the following:

- The ay and vy variables
- Checks for the up and down cursor keys
- The right acceleration to the right velocity
- Velocity to the corresponding axis position

Here's the code (ch05_08.fla):

```
init();
function init():Void
{
	vx = 0;
	vy = 0;
	ax = 0.2;
	ay = 0.2;
	attachMovie("ball", "ball", 0);
	ball._x = Stage.width / 2;
	ball._y = Stage.height / 2;
}
function onEnterFrame():Void
{
	if (Key.isDown(Key.LEFT))
	{
		vx -= ax;
	}
	else if (Key.isDown(Key.RIGHT))
	{
		vx += ax;
	}
	if (Key.isDown(Key.UP))
	{
		vy -= ay;
	}
	else if (Key.isDown(Key.DOWN))
	{
		vy += ay;
	}
	ball._x += vx;
	ball._y += vy;
}
```

Notice that I put the left/right checks and up/down checks in separate if statements. You could put the check for each key in its own separate if statement, but if the left key is down, you don't really need to check for the right key. The else statement shortcuts this: If the first if statement is true, it won't evaluate the else part. Similarly, you could continue with up and down checks as additional else statements. But by splitting them up, you can have, for example, the up and left cursor keys pressed at the same time and respond to them both, allowing for diagonal motion.

Play around with this one for a while. You'll see that you can now navigate all over the screen. Try to get the object moving say, left to right, and then press the up key. Note that the x velocity is not affected at all. The object keeps moving on the x axis at the same rate. You've just added some y velocity into the picture. This is equivalent to the spaceship turning 90 degrees and firing the rockets.

Gravity as acceleration

So far, I've been talking about acceleration in terms of a force being applied to an object by the object itself, such as a car engine or a rocket. That's certainly valid, but there's another aspect to acceleration. It happens that any force that acts to change the velocity of an object uses the principle of acceleration. This includes such things as gravity, magnetism, springs, rubber bands, and so on.

You can look at gravity in a couple of ways. From the wide-angle perspective of the solar system, gravity is an attraction between two bodies. The distance and angle between those two bodies must be taken into account to figure the actual acceleration on each body.

The other way to look at gravity is from a close-up viewpoint, here on earth, or very near it. In our everyday existence, gravity does not noticeably change depending on our distance from the earth. Although technically speaking, the force of gravity is slightly less when you are flying in a plane or up on a mountain, it's nothing you would notice. So, when simulating gravity on this level, you can pretty much define it as a set value, as you saw in the earlier examples with the acceleration variables.

Also, because the earth is so large and we are so small, it's easy to ignore any actual direction of acceleration and just say that the direction is "down." In other words, no matter where your object is, you can safely define gravity as acceleration on the y axis alone.

To put it into ActionScript, all you need to do is define a value for the force of gravity and add it to the vy on each frame. Generally speaking, a fraction works well, something like 0.5 or below. Much more than that, and things will "feel" too heavy. With smaller values, things seem to float like feathers. Of course, you can always use these effects to your advantage; for example, to create simulations of different planets with varying gravities.

This next example adds gravity. Here's the code (ch05_09.fla):

```
init();
function init():Void
{
	vx = 0;
	vy = 0;
	ax = 0.2;
	ay = 0.2;
	grav = 0.1;
	attachMovie("ball", "ball", 0);
```

```
        ball._x = Stage.width / 2;
        ball._y = Stage.height / 2;
    }
    function onEnterFrame():Void
    {
        if (Key.isDown(Key.LEFT))
        {
            vx -= ax;
        }
        else if (Key.isDown(Key.RIGHT))
        {
            vx += ax;
        }
        if (Key.isDown(Key.UP))
        {
            vy -= ay;
        }
        else if (Key.isDown(Key.DOWN))
        {
            vy += ay;
        }
        vy += grav;
        ball._x += vx;
        ball._y += vy;
    }
```

Here, I made the gravity value pretty low so the ball doesn't go off the screen too quickly, and you can still control it with the keys.

Notice that first you add the acceleration from the key presses to the vx and vy, then you add the gravity to the vy. Dealing with complex systems of multiple forces winds up not being that complex. You just calculate the acceleration of each force and tack it onto the velocity. No complex averaging or factoring is going on. Each force just gets added on. When you've gone through and handled all the forces, you add the velocity to the position. Here, you are using only a couple of forces, but later in the book, you will be calculating many different forces acting on a single object.

This goes right back to vector addition. If you start off with the original velocity as a vector, each acceleration, gravity, or force is an additional vector tacked on to that velocity. When you've added all of them on, you just draw a line from the beginning to the end, and you have your resulting velocity. You'll find it's the same as if you had added on the x and y components of each force.

Now imagine that your movie clip is a hot air balloon. You probably want to add a force called *lift*. This is another acceleration on the y axis. This time, however, it's negative, or in the "up" direction. Now, you have three forces acting on the object: the key force, gravity, and lift. If you think about it, or try it out, you'll see that the lift force needs to be slightly stronger than the gravity force in order for the balloon to rise. This is pretty logical—if they were exactly equal, they would cancel each other out, and you'd be back to square one, with only the key force having any effect.

Another one to try is creating some wind. Obviously, this is a force on the x axis. Depending on which direction the wind is blowing, it could be a positive or negative force, or as you now know, a 0 or 180 degree direction.

Angular acceleration

As I mentioned, acceleration has a value—the force—and a direction, just like velocity. And like velocity, if you are starting with those two factors, you need to break them down into the component x and y forces. Now, If you've been paying attention, you know that the way to do that is by using `Math.cos` and `Math.sin`. Here's how that looks:

```
var force:Number = 10;
var angle:Number = 45; // degrees
var ax:Number = Math.cos(angle * Math.PI / 180) * force;
var ay:Number = Math.sin(angle * Math.PI / 180) * force;
```

Now that you have acceleration for each axis, you can update the velocity on each axis, and from that, update the object's position.

Let's resurrect the mouse follower from earlier in the chapter and make it work with acceleration instead of just plain velocity. Remember that in the earlier incarnation, you took the angle from the arrow to the mouse and used that to determine vx and vy. This time, you'll use the same calculations, but employ them to determine ax and ay instead. Then you'll add the acceleration values to the velocity values and the velocity values to the _x and _y properties. Here's the code (`ch05_10.fla`):

```
init();
function init():Void
{
	force = 0.5;
	vx = 0;
	vy = 0;
	arrow = attachMovie("arrow", "arrow", 0);
	arrow._x = Stage.width / 2;
	arrow._y = Stage.height / 2;
}
function onEnterFrame():Void
{
	var dx:Number = _xmouse - arrow._x;
	var dy:Number = _ymouse - arrow._y;
	var angle:Number = Math.atan2(dy, dx);
	arrow._rotation = angle * 180 / Math.PI;
	var ax:Number = Math.cos(angle) * force;
	var ay:Number = Math.sin(angle) * force;
	vx += ax;
	vy += ay;
	arrow._x += vx;
	arrow._y += vy;
}
```

Notice that I also turned speed into `force` and made it much smaller. Since acceleration is additive, you want to start with small amounts. It builds up quickly. Also note that now vx and vy are declared without `var`, making them timeline variables, which will be accessible from any function. Earlier, they were calculated newly on each frame, but now you need to keep track of them and add or subtract from their value each time. Of course, you could do away with the ax and ay variables here altogether, and just add the result of the sine and cosine lines directly to the velocities. I kept them separated for clarity.

Now, that code isn't *too* complex is it? But look back to the first motion example you did at the beginning of the chapter, and see just how far you've come. The first one was so flat, it might as well have been a tween. By learning just a couple of basic principles, you've now created something a million times more fluid and dynamic—something that almost feels alive. And you're not even at the end of the chapter yet!

OK, let's pull everything together and see how much farther you can go with it.

A spaceship

I've been talking a lot about spaceships traveling from here to there. Well, with the ground you've covered so far, you should be able to put together a reasonable spaceship simulation.

Here's the plan. The spaceship will be a movie clip. You can use the left and right keys to rotate it left and right. The up key will act to fire the rocket. Of course, the rocket is in the back of the ship and fires straight back. Thus, the force that the rocket applies will cause acceleration in the direction the ship is facing at that time. Actually, what you're going to make is a lot like the ship in the old game, *Asteroids*, minus the actual asteroids.

First, you need a ship. I made a pretty basic one out of four short, white lines, as a homage to the original that I'm copying. If you have more artistic talent than I seem to have, go right ahead and whip something up in PhotoShop or Swift 3D. It will work the same when you get to the code. At any rate, Figure 5-8 shows what I came up with (`ch05_11.fla`).

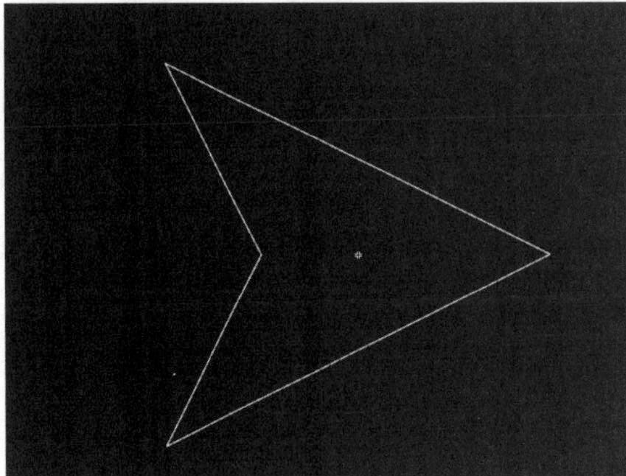

Figure 5-8. Behold the future of space travel.

This graphic is built in a movie clip symbol in the library called `ship`. It is set to export with the linkage name `ship`, so I can create an instance of it at runtime. Note also that the registration point is in the center of the ship, to allow for smooth rotation.

I also wanted to have some way of indicating visibly that the rocket was being fired. So inside the `ship` movie clip, I created a new keyframe and drew in a stylized flame—very stylized, as you can see in Figure 5-9.

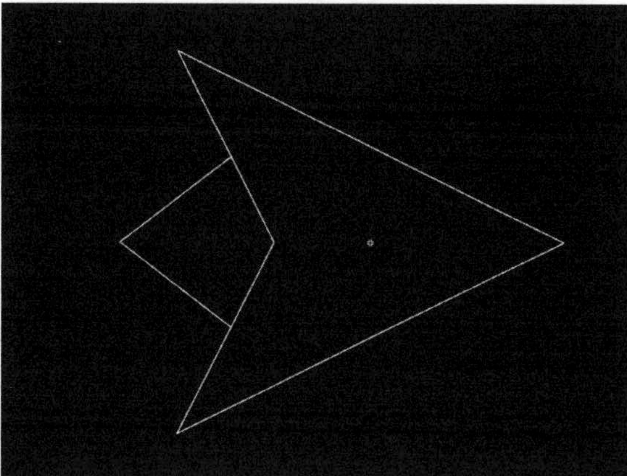

Figure 5-9. Beware of flame.

Now that the ship has two frames, it's going to play them one after the other, creating a flickering flame. While you might want to build that into some kind of cool effect, that wasn't what I was looking for. I just wanted the flame to be on or off, so I added another layer to the timeline, clicked frame 1 of this new layer, and added the following code to it:

```
stop();
```

Now, you're ready to call me out on this, aren't you? I told you that you should avoid putting code anywhere but frame 1 of the main timeline, and here, only a few chapters into the book, I'm putting code on the timeline of a movie clip. What gives? Well, every rule has its exceptions. This is one of those.

Many times, it is useful to use the frames in Flash to hold various visual states of an object; in this case, the states of the ship firing and the ship not firing. Of course, I could do this another way. I could make two ship symbols, export them from the library, and attach one or the other dynamically, depending on the state of the ship. Or, I could make a flame movie clip and attach that when the ship is firing, and remove it when it's not. I could even use the drawing API to draw the ship and the flame, which would be completely dynamic. However, for a simple case like this, most of those solutions would be pure overkill. All I want to do is swap images, and frames offer a very efficient, built-in way for me to do that. So I use it.

OK, you're cool with that, but what about the code? Well, it's hardly code. It's a single statement, and it needs to run only one time to stop the movie clip from automatically playing. It's not affecting the logic of the ship program, the ship's motion, or anything else. It's just controlling a display factor.

No future developer is going to be pulling his hair out trying to figure out why this ship movie clip isn't playing, because it's obvious from the start that it isn't an animation, but a set of states. The alternative would be to tell the ship movie clip to stop somewhere in the code on the main timeline. This mixes in this one line for stopping the clip with all the motion code, and might actually be more confusing. "Why is he stopping the ship before it even starts?" Furthermore, this exact scenario has been used often enough by enough developers that it has become an accepted practice. A single `stop` action on the timeline of a movie clip is not a sin.

Ship controls

OK, now that you have built your ship, let's get its controls working. As I just mentioned, it has three controls: turn left, turn right, and fire rocket, mapped to the left, right, and up keys, respectively. You can use `Key.isDown` within the `onEnterFrame` handler function to test for these keys and update the display of the ship. Let's start out with just the code for that and nothing else. As usual, this will go right on the main timeline, frame 1, Actions panel (`ch05_11.fla`):

```
init();
function init():Void
{
	vr = 5;
	ship = attachMovie("ship", "ship", 0);
	ship._x = Stage.width / 2;
	ship._y = Stage.height / 2;
}
function onEnterFrame():Void
{
	if (Key.isDown(Key.LEFT))
	{
		ship._rotation -= vr;
	}
	else if (Key.isDown(Key.RIGHT))
	{
		ship._rotation += vr;
	}
	if (Key.isDown(Key.UP))
	{
		ship.gotoAndStop(2);
	}
	else
	{
		ship.gotoAndStop(1);
	}
}
```

First you define `vr`, rotational velocity, or how fast the ship is going to turn when you tell it to turn. Remember, it's best to keep hard-coded numbers out of your functions. Define them as variables somewhere at the top of your code and use the variables in your calculations. If you find that the ship rotates too quickly or slowly, you can change this value.

In the onEnterFrame handler function, you check for the left or right keys, and if either of them is down, you either add or subtract vr to the ship's current rotation. Finally, check if the up key is being pressed. If so, send the ship to frame 2, If not, send it to frame 1. Now, here you see some numbers in the code. For this simple two-state ship, I stuck with frame numbers. A better solution, especially if you may have additional frames or multiple-frame animations as states, would be to use frame labels. For example, frame 1 could be labeled "rocketoff" and frame 2 could be labeled "rocketon". Then your goto statements would be something like this.gotoAndStop("rocketon");. This is not only clearer, but if you move your frames around, you don't have to worry about your goto statements suddenly referring to the wrong frames. Again though, for such a simple example, I'm going to leave them as numbers.

Go ahead and test this example. You should be able to use the keyboard to rotate the ship and fire the rocket. It doesn't do anything yet, but it's starting to look good. Let's make it move.

Thrust

OK, you've got your spaceship there, you've aimed it where you want it to go—3, 2, 1, blastoff! So, how do you get this thing to go somewhere? Well, it's pretty much just the opposite of what you just did in the revised mouse follower example. In that example, you calculated an angle and then figured out rotation and acceleration based on that. Here, you'll start with the rotation and work backward to find the angle and then the force on x and y.

Obviously, acceleration is going to happen only if the rocket is being fired, so this code will go in the if statement that checks for the up key. You'll know the rotation, which is in degrees. Convert that to radians and use sine and cosine, along with the force variable, to find out the acceleration on each axis. I've renamed force to thrust here. Here's the final code for the example, with the new parts shown in bold (ch05_11.fla):

```
init();
function init():Void
{
	vr = 5;
	thrust = 0.2;
	vx  = 0;
	vy = 0;
	ship = attachMovie("ship", "ship", 0);
	ship._x = Stage.width / 2;
	ship._y = Stage.height / 2;
}
function onEnterFrame():Void
{
	if (Key.isDown(Key.LEFT))
	{
		ship._rotation -= vr;
	}
	else if (Key.isDown(Key.RIGHT))
	{
		ship._rotation += vr;
```

```
        }
        if (Key.isDown(Key.UP))
        {
            var radians:Number = ship._rotation * Math.PI / 180;
            var ax:Number = Math.cos(radians) * thrust;
            var ay:Number = Math.sin(radians) * thrust;
            vx += ax;
            vy += ay;
            ship.gotoAndStop(2);
        }
        else
        {
            ship.gotoAndStop(1);
        }
        ship._x += vx;
        ship._y += vy;
    }
```

Test it and fly your ship around. It's pretty amazing just how easily you can make some complex motion like that.

Important formulas in this chapter

So, now you have a few more tools for your toolbox. Here they are.

Convert angular velocity to x, y velocity:

```
vx = speed * Math.cos(angle);
vy = speed * Math.sin(angle);
```

Convert angular acceleration (any force acting on an object) to x, y acceleration:

```
ax = force * Math.cos(angle);
ay = force * Math.sin(angle);
```

Add acceleration to velocity:

```
vx += ax;
vy += ay;
```

Add velocity to position:

```
movieclip._x += vx;
movieclip._y += vy;
```

Summary

This chapter covered basic velocity and acceleration, the two factors that will make up the vast majority of your scripted animations. You've learned about vectors and vector addition. You've seen how to accomplish velocity on a single axis, two axes, and on an angle by converting it to its x and y components. And you've learned about acceleration—how it relates to velocity and how to apply it to a single axis, two axes, or an angle.

The biggest thing to take from this chapter is a basic understanding of the application of acceleration and velocity, as described in the following steps:

- Convert existing angular velocity to component x, y velocities.
- Convert angular acceleration to component x, y acceleration.
- Add the acceleration on each axis to the velocity on that axis.
- Add the velocity on each axis to the position on that axis.

In the next chapter, you'll build on these concepts, adding some environmental interaction with bouncing and friction.

};shape.targetHeight = shape._height;
shape.onEnterFrame = function() {
var speed = 5;
this._width += (this.targetWidth - this._width)/speed;
this._height += (this.targetHeight - this._height)/speed;

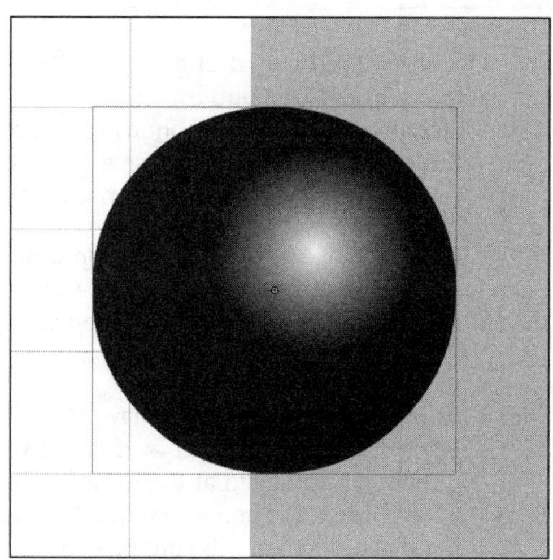

Chapter 6

BOUNDARIES AND FRICTION

What we'll cover in this chapter:

- Environmental boundaries
- Friction
- Important formulas in this chapter

You've covered a lot of ground in the preceding chapters, so that you can now take any graphic, wrap it in a movie clip, and use all kinds of forces to move it around the screen. However, you've probably already run into a small annoyance with many of the examples you've created so far: When you move the object off the screen, bang—it's gone. Sometimes, if it's moving fast at some angle, you have no way of knowing how to get it back. Your only option is to restart the movie.

In most real-world scenarios, some *boundaries* exist—sometimes walls and a ceiling, but at the very least, almost always the ground. Unless you're making a space simulator, you want to have some kind of environmental barriers to keep your objects in view. If you are doing the space thing, you need at least some way to keep your main objects in view.

Another thing you may or may not have noticed is how this environment, or lack thereof, fails to have any effect on the object as it moves. You start an object moving, and it just keeps on going in the direction it's headed at the same speed, until you apply some other force. Actually, this isn't a bug at all, but the way the universe works. The term *inertia* is used to describe the fact that an object traveling through space will continue to travel at the direction and speed at which it is moving until some other force is applied. Or, to state it differently, its velocity won't change unless something changes it. In common experience, one of the things that changes an object's velocity is some sort of *friction*—even if only the friction of air. So, while you've successfully simulated an object moving in a vacuum, you are probably itching to make it a little more like something in your everyday environment.

This chapter will cover both of these issues. First you'll learn how to work with boundaries, and then how to mimic friction. Let's go.

Environmental boundaries

We'll start by setting some boundaries, literally. With any activity you're involved in—whether it's playing a sport, working at your job, building a house, and so on—there's usually some concept of the space for that activity. You're saying, "I'm only interested in things that happen in this area. If something is happening somewhere outside this area, I don't really care about it at this moment. If something is happening inside this space though, I need to pay attention to it."

If one of the objects in your zone of interest moves outside that space, then you have a choice to make. You can move it back into the zone somehow, or you can cross it off the list of things that you're paying attention to. Another option is to follow it. In other words, you move the space so that it continues to enclose the object, even though the object is moving. It's not so much different in Flash.

In your movie, you set up a space for your objects. Generally, this is the whole stage, but the area can be some portion of the stage, or even a space that is larger than the stage. Since the objects are moving, there's a good chance that they will eventually leave that space. When they leave, you can forget about them, move them back into the area, or follow them. I'll cover strategies for all of these approaches. First, though, let's just figure out where the boundaries are and how to specify them.

Setting boundaries

In most cases, a simple rectangle works as a boundary. Let's start with the simplest example, with the boundaries based on the size of the stage. In this case, the top and left boundaries are zero, and the right and bottom boundaries are Stage.width and Stage.height. You can store these in variables if you want, like so:

```
var left:Number = 0;
var top:Number = 0;
var right:Number = Stage.width;
var bottom:Number = Stage.height;
```

Or you can simply use the stage properties directly in your code. As I mentioned earlier, it is best to set variables like this early in the code, and not refer to actual numbers in the midst of your animation code. In this case, though, there is one small side effect of hard-coding these values. If the stage size changes, do you want to continue using the old values, or change things so that the area of interest still encompasses the entire stage?

As is, the values for right and bottom won't change when the movie is resized. You need to change them yourself. To accomplish this, you need to know when the stage is changing size. Luckily, the Stage object broadcasts a resize event whenever this happens. By listening for this event, you can know when to update your boundary values. You listen for this event as follows:

```
Stage.addListener(this);
onResize = function() {
   right = Stage.width;
   bottom = Stage.height;
}
```

First, you set up the current timeline as a listener for Stage events. Then you define an event handler called onResize, which is the default name of the event-handling function for the resize event. When that is called, it updates the right and bottom variables. The top and left variables don't need to change, as they will continue to be zero.

OK, now that you have your boundaries in place, what do you do with them? Well, you check all the movable objects you are paying attention to at the moment, and see if they are still within this space. You can do this with a couple of if statements. Here is a simplified version of what they look like:

```
if(ball._x > right) {
   // do something
} else if(ball._x < left) {
   // do something
}

if(ball._y > bottom) {
   // do something
} else if(ball._y < top) {
   // do something
}
```

Here again, I've used if statement shortcutting for efficiency. If the ball's x position is greater than the right edge, then it is way over there on the right. There's no way it could also be way over by the left edge, so you don't need to check that in a separate if statement. You need to check the left variable only in the case that the first if fails. Do the same for the top and bottom. However, it is possible for the object to be out of bounds on the x and y axis at the same time, so keep those two checks separate.

But what is this "something" you're supposed to do when the object goes out of bounds? You have four main options:

- Remove it
- Bring it back into play as if it were a brand-new object (regeneration)
- Wrap it back onto the screen, as if it were the same object reappearing at a different location
- Have it bounce back into the area

Let's start with simple removal.

Removing objects

Simply removing the object once it goes out of bounds is especially useful if you have objects being continually generated. The ones you remove will be replaced by new ones coming in, so you won't end up with an empty stage. Also, you won't wind up with too many objects being moved around, which would eventually slow down the Flash player.

To remove a movie clip, simply call `movieClipName.removeMovieClip()`. This will remove the instance from the stage. You'll also want to make sure that the code doesn't continue to try to move the movie clip. If the handler is attached directly to the clip itself, such as `movieClipName.onEnterFrame = . . .`, you are all set, as this function will be removed along with the clip. But if you are moving the clip from an external `enterFrame` handler, you'll need to do this manually.

If the instance is the only thing being moved, and that motion is the only thing being done by the `onEnterFrame` function, you can simply say `delete onEnterFrame;` to stop running that code altogether. On the other hand, if a number of objects are being moved around, you should have references to them stored in an array, and you loop through the array to move each object. If so, you can simply use the `Array.splice` method to remove that particular reference from the array. You'll see that in action shortly.

So, if you want to remove a movie clip, knowing what the boundaries are, you can come up with something like this for your `if` statement:

```
if(ball._x > right) {
   ball.removeMovieClip();
} else if(ball._x < left) {
   ball.removeMovieClip();
}

if(ball._y > bottom) {
   ball.removeMovieClip();
} else if(ball._y < top) {
   ball.removeMovieClip();
}
```

Per Flash documentation, removeMovieClip *is only for movie clips that have been dynamically generated via* createEmptyMovieClip, attachMovie, *or* duplicateMovieClip. *A movie clip instance placed on stage in the authoring environment will not be removed using this method. The full story is a little more complicated, though. It all has to do with depths.*

Whenever you dynamically create a movie clip, you must specify a depth for it. Normally, you choose zero or some positive whole number. If you ever want to know at what depth you've placed a movie clip, you can check it with the movie clip's getDepth *method. But if you try it out on a movie clip instance created at author time, you'll see it's a negative number, starting at –16,383. That's the real reason these types of movie clips can't be removed. Flash can't remove an instance at a negative depth.*

The good news is that this brings up a workaround. You can use swapDepths *to move the movie clip up to a positive depth, and then remove it. You can use it in accordance with* getNextHighestDepth *to automatically choose a safe depth. The code would look something like this for a movie clip named* ball *on* _root*:*

```
ball.swapDepths(_root.getNextHighestDepth());
ball.removeMovieClip();
```

You should be aware of one caveat, however: Movie clips above a depth of 1,048,575 cannot be removed either. If you know that you haven't used any depths close to that, you can be relatively safe using getNextHighestDepth. *But beware—Flash MX 2004 components sometimes place elements at that depth, even if the component is just in your library and never placed on stage! So, if you have any of these components in your movie, you should check to make sure that the return value of* getNextHighestDepth *is less than 1,048,575 before using it, and if so, swap to a lower number.*

All seems well and good. But there is one small problem. Now, you might not even notice this problem in many cases, but sometimes, it could wind up making things look wrong. To see what I mean, take a look at the picture in Figure 6-1.

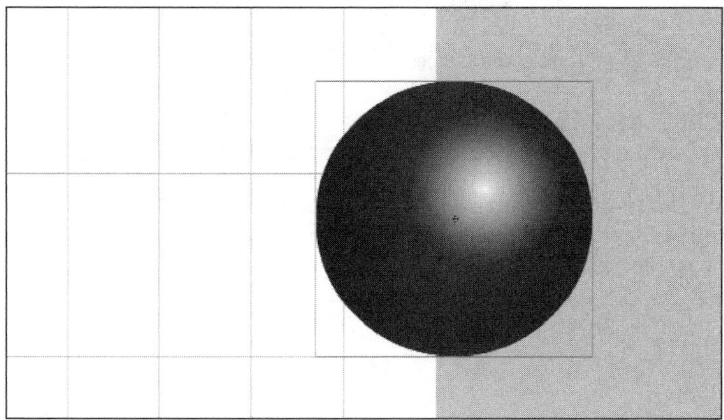

Figure 6-1. This ball isn't fully off stage, but it will be removed.

In Figure 6-1, you can see that the ball's position, as determined by its registration point in the center, is indeed past the right edge of the screen. It will be removed. If the ball is moving fast enough, that will probably look OK. But what if it's moving very slowly, just a pixel per frame or less? You're watching it ease off the edge of the screen, it gets halfway, and POP! It's gone. It's kind of like an actor removing his costume when he is only halfway off stage. It kind of ruins the illusion.

So, instead, you want to let the ball get all the way out of the picture. Then, when it's out of sight and out of mind, you can quietly execute it.

To do this, you need to take into account the movie clip's width. Actually, since the registration point is in the center, you just need to worry about half of its width. You can do that right in the if statement, like so:

```
if(ball._x - ball._width / 2 > right) {
   ball.removeMovieClip();
} else if(ball._x + ball._width / 2 < left) {
   ball.removeMovieClip();
}
```

You do the same on the y axis with the ball's height. This gives you the picture shown in Figure 6-2.

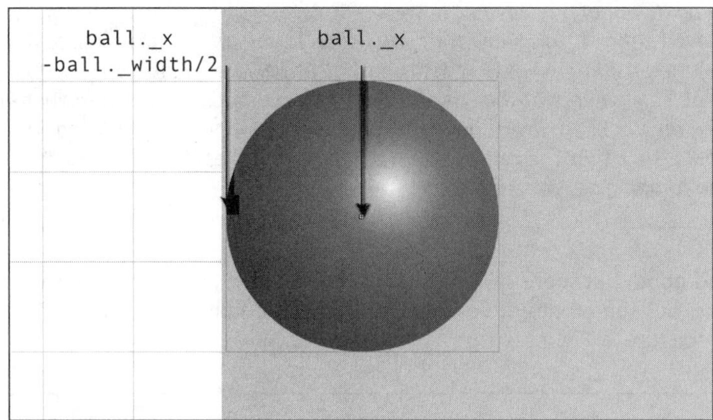

Figure 6-2. This ball is completely off stage and can be safely removed.

Note that although this particular example uses a ball, or round object, the same code should work for an object of any shape, as long as the registration point of the movie clip is in the center.

Let's try it out. Using an FLA file with a movie clip symbol named ball, exported from the library with the same linkage name, here is the code to put on frame 1 (in the ch06_01.fla file, available from the book's download page at www.friendsofed.com, along with the rest of the code for this book):

```
init();
function init()
{
      count = 20;
      top = 0;
```

```
        left = 0;
        bottom = Stage.height;
        right = Stage.width;
        balls = new Array();
        for (var i = 0; i < count; i++)
        {
            var ball = attachMovie("ball", "ball" + i, i);
            ball._x = Math.random() * Stage.width;
            ball._y = Math.random() * Stage.height;
            ball.vx = Math.random() * 2 - 1;
            ball.vy = Math.random() * 2 - 1;
            balls.push(ball);
        }
    }
    function onEnterFrame(Void):Void
    {
        for (var i:Number=balls.length - 1;i>=0;i--)
        {
            var ball = balls[i];
            ball._x += ball.vx;
            ball._y += ball.vy;
            if (ball._x - ball._width / 2 > right)
            {
                ball.removeMovieClip();
                balls.splice(i, 1);
            }
            else if (ball._x + ball._width / 2 < left)
            {
                ball.removeMovieClip();
                balls.splice(i, 1);
            }
            if (ball._y - ball._height / 2 > bottom)
            {
                ball.removeMovieClip();
                balls.splice(i, 1);
            }
            else if (ball._y + ball._height / 2 < top)
            {
                ball.removeMovieClip();
                balls.splice(i, 1);
            }
        }
    }
```

This should be pretty simple for you to follow. First, you create the boundaries based on the stage size. Then attach 20 instances, randomly placing them on the stage and giving them random x and y velocities, and push them into the array.

The onEnterFrame function simply uses a flat velocity to move the balls around, checks the boundaries, and removes any balls that are out of bounds. Note that it not only removes the ball from the display list, but uses the Array.splice function to remove the reference from the array. Array.splice takes the index at which you want to start removing elements and how many elements you want to remove. In this case, you are removing only one element: the one at the current index. When you test this, you won't even be aware of them being removed, which is a good thing, but you can rest assured that they are not hanging around off stage, consuming valuable memory and CPU cycles.

You might notice that the for statement in this example is a little different from those in other examples:

```
for (var i:Number=balls.length - 1;i>=0;i--)
```

This causes the for statement to go backwards through the array instead of forwards. This is necessary because, if you use splice on the array, the indexing for the array will change, and when you increment i, you will wind up skipping over one of the elements. Going backwards handles this.

Note that in a simple case like this, the result of the if statement is exactly the same in every instance. If that is the case, you can combine all the statements into a single if statement, like so:

```
if(ball._x - ball._width / 2 > right ||
   ball._x + ball._width / 2 < left ||
   ball._y - ball._height / 2 > bottom ||
   ball._y + ball._height / 2 < top)
{
   ball.removeMovieClip();
   balls.splice(i, 1);
}
```

The || symbol means "or." So, you're essentially saying, "If the object is off to the right, OR the object is off to the left, OR it is off to the top OR the bottom, remove it." This technique is probably fine for most cases of removal, as it doesn't really matter *where* the object went out of bounds, just that it did. In other cases, though, you might want to respond differently if the object hit a particular boundary, such as the left wall as opposed to the right wall. In those instances, you will need to use separate if statements. You'll see that in the example of screen wrapping, coming up shortly.

Regenerating objects

The next strategy is to regenerate the object that has gone off stage. Actually, it's not really so much regeneration as repositioning and revelocitizing (yeah, I just made up that word). The idea is that when an object has gone off stage and is no longer necessary, you can bring it back into play as if it were a brand-new object. This gives you a steady stream of objects without ever having to worry about having too many objects on stage, as there will always be a set amount.

This technique is very useful for things like fountain effects, where you have a stream of particles spraying constantly. The particles go off stage and are reintroduced at the source point of the stream.

The mechanics of regeneration are pretty similar to removal. You need to wait until the object is out of bounds, but instead of removing it, you just move it.

Let's dive right in by making a fountain. For the fountain particles, I used the same ball from the last experiment, but resized the graphic to be just 4 pixels across. The source of the fountain will be the bottom center of the stage. All particles will originate there, and when they go off stage, they will be replaced there. Also, all particles will start out with a random negative y velocity and a smaller random x velocity. This means they will shoot upwards and also move slightly either to the left or right. When particles regenerate, their velocities will be reset the same way. Particles will also react to gravity. Here's the code (`ch06_02.fla`):

```
init();
function init()
{
      count = 50;
      top = 0;
      left = 0;
      bottom = Stage.height;
      right = Stage.width;
      gravity = 0.5;
      balls = new Array();
}
function onEnterFrame(Void):Void
{
      var ball:MovieClip;
      var index:Number = balls.length;
      if (index < count)
      {
            ball = attachMovie("ball", "ball" + index, index);
            ball._x = Stage.width / 2;
            ball._y = Stage.height;
            ball.vx = Math.random() * 2 - 1;
            ball.vy = Math.random() * -10 - 10;
            balls.push(ball);
      }
      for (var i = 0; i < balls.length; i++)
      {
            ball = balls[i];
            ball.vy += gravity;
            ball._x += ball.vx;
            ball._y += ball.vy;
            if (ball._x - ball._width / 2 > right ||
                ball._x + ball._width / 2 < left ||
                ball._y - ball._height / 2 > bottom ||
                ball._y + ball._height / 2 < top)
            {
                ball._x = Stage.width / 2;
                ball._y = Stage.height;
                ball.vx = Math.random() * 2 - 1;
                ball.vy = Math.random() * -10 - 10;
            }
      }
}
```

You start off in the init function by defining the number of particles, an array to hold them, the boundary definitions, and a value for gravity.

The first section of the onEnterFrame function creates a new ball on each frame, until enough have been created, as determined by the count variable. It positions them at the bottom of the stage, gives them a random velocity, and pushes them onto the array.

The next section just loops through all the elements of the balls array. For each one, it adds gravity to its vy, adds the velocity to the position, and then checks to see if it has crossed any boundaries. If it has, it gets sent back to the starting position and "reborn" with a new velocity. It will act the same as a newly created particle. Thus, your fountain will flow forever.

You should definitely play around with this one. Have the fountain shoot off in different directions. Make it shoot out of a wall, or even the ceiling. Change the random factors to make a wider or narrower fountain, or one that shoots higher or lower. Try adding some wind into the mix (hint: make a wind variable and add it to vx).

Screen wrapping

The next common way to handle objects going out of bounds is what I call *screen wrapping*. The concept is simple: If an object goes off the left side of the screen, it reappears on the right. If it goes off the right, it comes back on the left. If it goes off the top, it comes back on the bottom. You get the idea.

Screen wrapping is pretty similar to regeneration, in that you put the object back on the screen at a different location. But in regeneration, you generally return all objects to the same location, making them look like brand-new objects. In wrapping, you are usually trying to maintain the idea that this is the same object; that it has just gone out the back door and in the front, so to speak. Thus, you generally don't change velocity during a screen wrap.

This again hearkens back to one of my old favorite games, *Asteroids*. As you remember from Chapter 5, this was one of the problems with the spaceship movie: The ship would fly off stage, and it was sometimes impossible to figure out where it was and how to get it back. With screen wrapping, your movie clip is never more than a pixel from the edge of the screen.

Let's rebuild that spaceship example and add this behavior. Here's the code you'll want to use (ch06_03.fla), with the new stuff in bold:

```
init();
function init()
{
	vr = 5;
	thrust = 0.2;
	vx = 0;
	vy = 0;
	left = 0;
	right = Stage.width;
	top = 0;
	bottom = Stage.height;
	ship = attachMovie("ship", "ship", 0);
```

```
        ship._x = Stage.width / 2;
        ship._y = Stage.height / 2;
    }
    function onEnterFrame(Void):Void
    {
        if (Key.isDown(Key.LEFT))
        {
            ship._rotation -= vr;
        }
        else if (Key.isDown(Key.RIGHT))
        {
            ship._rotation += vr;
        }
        if (Key.isDown(Key.UP))
        {
            var radians:Number = ship._rotation * Math.PI / 180;
            var ax:Number = Math.cos(radians) * thrust;
            var ay:Number = Math.sin(radians) * thrust;
            vx += ax;
            vy += ay;
            ship.gotoAndStop(2);
        }
        else
        {
            ship.gotoAndStop(1);
        }
        ship._x += vx;
        ship._y += vy;
        if (ship._x - ship._width / 2 > right)
        {
            ship._x = left - ship._width / 2;
        }
        else if (ship._x + ship._width / 2 < left)
        {
            ship._x = right + ship._width / 2;
        }
        if (ship._y - ship._height / 2 > bottom)
        {
            ship._y = top - ship._height / 2;
        }
        else if (ship._y < top - ship._height / 2)
        {
            ship._y = bottom + ship._height / 2;
        }
    }
```

As you can see, you've just added boundary definitions and the checks for them. Note that you are back to separate if and else statements, as the actions are different for each circumstance.

Bouncing

And now we arrive at probably the most common and possibly the most complex of bounds handling methods. But it's really not much more complicated than wrapping, so don't get scared.

The strategy with bouncing is to detect when the object has gone off screen, only this time, you leave it pretty much where it is and just change its velocity. The rules are simple: If it went off the left or right edge, you reverse its x velocity. If it went off the top or bottom, you reverse its y velocity. Reversing an axis velocity is pretty simple. Just multiply the value by –1. If the velocity is 5, it becomes –5. If it's –13, it becomes 13. The code is even simpler: `vx *= -1` or `vy *= -1`.

There are a couple more changes from wrapping. First, in wrapping, you let the object go completely off stage before you reposition it. You do that by taking its position and adding or subtracting half its width. For bouncing, you want to do almost exactly the opposite. You don't want to wait until the object is totally off stage before you make it bounce. In fact, you don't want it to be even part way out of the picture. If you were to throw a real ball against a real wall, you wouldn't expect to see it go part-way into the wall before bouncing back. It would hit the wall, stop right there, and then bounce back. So, the first thing you want to know is the instant that *any part* of the object has gone over the edge. All you need to do is reverse the way you are adding the half width/height. So, for example, instead of saying this:

```
if(ball._x - ball._width / 2 > right) . . .
```

you say this:

```
if(ball._x + ball._width / 2 > right) . . .
```

The difference between these two can be seen in Figure 6-3.

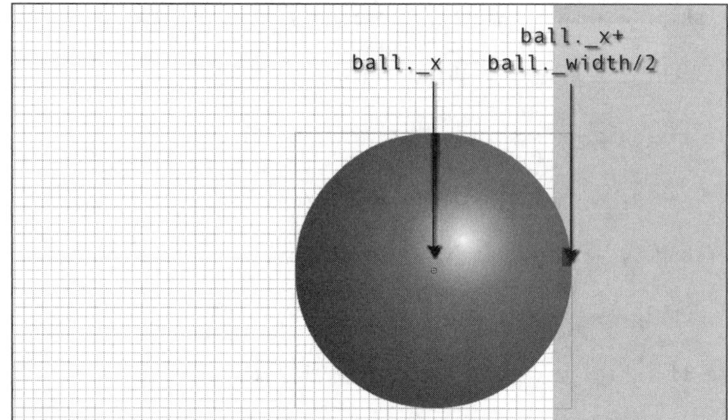

Figure 6-3. This ball is just slightly off stage, but it needs to bounce.

So, you've now determined that the object has crossed the least bit of one of the boundaries. I said before that you now reverse the velocity on that axis. But there's a little more to it than that. You also need to reposition the object so that it is sitting right on the edge of the boundary. This has the obvious cosmetic effect of making the object look more like it's hitting and bouncing, rather than sinking into the wall. But it is also a necessary step for other reasons. You'll find that if you don't adjust the object's position, then on the next frame, it may still be past that boundary, even after it moves. If this happens, the object will again reverse its velocity and head back *into* the wall! Then you get this situation where the movie clip seems to be stuck halfway in and out of the wall, just sitting there and vibrating. It's not pretty.

The point where you need to place the object to have it sitting right on the boundary is actually the same point you are checking in the `if` statement. You just need to restate it a bit with a little basic algebra. Here's the full `if` statement for the x axis:

```
if(ball._x + ball._width / 2 > right)
{
   ball._x = right - ball._width / 2;
   vx *= -1;
}
else if(ball._x - ball._width / 2 < left)
{
   ball._x = left + ball._width / 2;
   vx *= -1;
}
```

Figure 6-4 shows what the ball would look like after being repositioned.

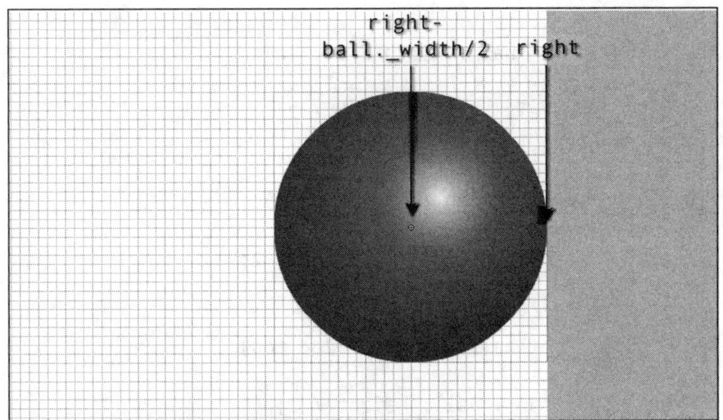

Figure 6-4. The ball has been repositioned to be exactly against the boundary.

So, the steps for bouncing are as follows:

- Check if the object went past any boundary.
- If so, place it on the edge of that boundary.
- Then reverse the velocity.

That's all there is to it. I guess it's time to stop talking and show you some action. This next example uses the same ball movie clip once again, but scaled back up to a decent size. Here's the code (ch06_04.fla):

```
init();
function init()
{
	top = 0;
	left = 0;
	bottom = Stage.height;
	right = Stage.width;
	ball = attachMovie("ball", "ball", 0);
	ball._x = Stage.width / 2;
	ball._y = Stage.height / 2;
	vx = Math.random() * 10 - 5;
	vy = Math.random() * 10 - 5;
}
function onEnterFrame(Void):Void
{
	ball._x += vx;
	ball._y += vy;
	if (ball._x + ball._width / 2 > right)
	{
		ball._x = right - ball._width / 2;
		vx *= -1;
	}
	else if (ball._x - ball._width / 2 < left)
	{
		ball._x = left + ball._width / 2;
		vx *= -1;
	}
	if (ball._y + ball._height / 2 > bottom)
	{
		ball._y = bottom - ball._height / 2;
		vy *= -1;
	}
	else if (ball._y - ball._height / 2 < top)
	{
		ball._y = top + ball._height / 2;
		vy *= -1;
	}
}
```

Test this a few times to see the ball moving at different angles. Try making the velocity higher or lower.

I have to admit that this is one of those many areas in the book where the math and calculations are not exactly in accordance with real-world physics. If you look at Figure 6-5, you'll see where the ball should actually hit the wall, and also where this simulation places it.

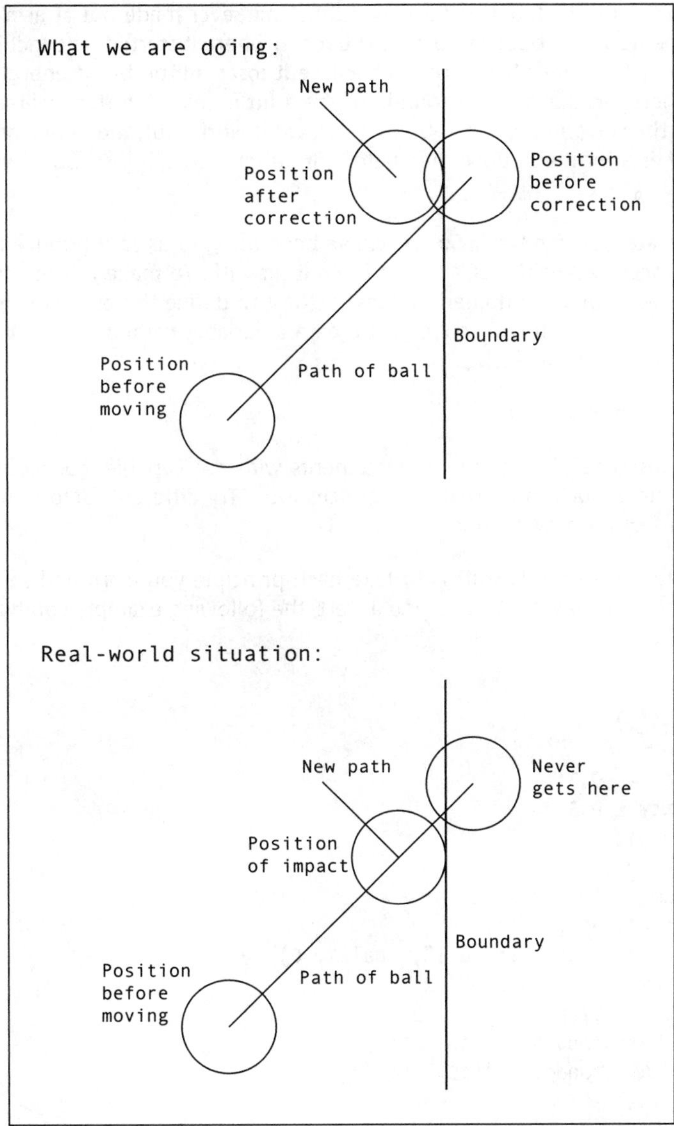

Figure 6-5. This technique isn't perfect, but is quick, easy, and close enough for most situations.

Determining the correct position takes more complex calculations. Although you are free to figure out how to do this (using the trigonometry covered in Chapter 3), I guarantee you that you wouldn't really notice much of a difference in most situations. Again, if you're doing some kind of simulation where exact calculations and positions are vital, you'll really need to find another book, and probably reconsider your choice of software. But for almost any game or visual effect you'll be creating with Flash, this method will serve you just fine. However, you can add one more thing to take the realism just one notch higher.

If you were to hold the most rubbery, bounciest rubber ball ever made out at arm's length and drop it, it would fall to the floor and bounce up *almost* back to where it started. The fact is that it will never make it all the way back to your hand. This is because it loses a little bit of energy in the bounce. It might lose some energy in the form of sound; maybe a little heat. The floor will absorb some of its energy, and maybe the surrounding air will, too. However it works out, the important point is that the ball is traveling slower after the bounce than before. In other words, it loses some velocity on the axis of the bounce.

You can easily re-create this with Flash. So far, you've been using `-1` as your bounce factor. That means that the object bounces back with 100% of the force it hit with. To make it lose some energy, simply use a fraction of `-1`. As with other numeric values, it's best to define this as a variable up at the top of your file and use the variable in your code. Just create a variable named bounce and set it to something like –0.7 at the top of your file:

```
var bounce:Number = -0.7;
```

Then replace each instance of `-1` in the `if` statements with the variable, bounce. Go ahead and try that, and you'll see how much more real the bounces look. Try different factors for the bounce variable until you get a feel for how it works.

One of the best ways to learn this stuff is to take each principle you learn and see how many other principles you can combine it with. To give you a start, the following example combines bouncing with gravity (`ch06_05.fla`):

```
init();
function init()
{
	bounce = -0.7;
	gravity = 0.5;
	top = 0;
	left = 0;
	bottom = Stage.height;
	right = Stage.width;
	ball = attachMovie("ball", "ball", 0);
	ball._x = Stage.width / 2;
	ball._y = Stage.height / 2;
	vx = Math.random() * 10 - 5;
	vy = Math.random() * 10 - 5;
}
function onEnterFrame(Void):Void
{
	vy += gravity;
	ball._x += vx;
	ball._y += vy;
	if (ball._x + ball._width / 2 > right)
	{
		ball._x = right - ball._width / 2;
		vx *= bounce;
	}
	else if (ball._x - ball._width / 2 < left)
```

```
        {
            ball._x = left + ball._width / 2;
            vx *= bounce;
        }
        if (ball._y + ball._height / 2 > bottom)
        {
            ball._y = bottom - ball._height / 2;
            vy *= bounce;
        }
        else if (ball._y - ball._height / 2 < top)
        {
            ball._y = top + ball._height / 2;
            vy *= bounce;
        }
}
```

This gives you quite a realistic simulation of a ball bouncing around and finally coming to rest. Perhaps you want to try to use the keyboard to add some acceleration to the ball, or apply something else you've already learned.

Now, let's leave behind the discussion of boundaries and talk about what happens in between the boundaries—what happens while your movie clip is moving through space.

Friction

So far, you've seen two scenarios:

- The object is simply moving with whatever velocity it has until it hits a boundary.
- Either the object itself or some external force is applying some acceleration to the object, changing its velocity.

With either setup, unless the object is being pushed or pulled, or it hits something, it will keep going in the same direction at the exact same speed. But in the real world, it doesn't happen just like that.

Here's an example. Grab a piece of paper, crumple it up very loosely, and throw it as hard as you can. There's a good chance it didn't even make it across the room. Sure, gravity was pulling it down (y axis), but when it left your hand, it was moving pretty fast on the x axis. Yet, very quickly, it had almost zero x velocity.

Obviously, no "negative acceleration" was pulling the paper back towards your hand, yet, its velocity was changed. This is known as *friction*, *drag*, *resistance*, or *damping*. Although it's not technically a force, it does kind of act that way, in that it changes an object's velocity. The rule is that friction reduces only the magnitude of the velocity. Whichever direction the object is headed in, this will not be changed by friction. In other words, friction can reduce velocity to zero, but it will never make an object turn around and go in the other direction.

So, how do you implement friction in code? It turns out there are two ways. Like most things in life, you have the right way and the easy way. But unlike your parents, I'm going to recommend the easy way. Even so, I'm going to show you both ways, starting with the "right" one, and let you make up your own mind.

Friction, the right way

Friction is actually subtractive of velocity, which is to say you have a certain value for friction, and you subtract that from your velocity. Actually, you need to subtract it from the magnitude, or speed, of the velocity. You can't just subtract the friction from the x axis and y axis separately. If you do that for an object traveling at an angle, one of the component velocities will reach zero before the other, and the object will continue on for a while either vertically or horizontally, which will look pretty strange.

So, what you need to do is find the angular velocity in terms of speed and direction (if you don't have it already). To find the speed, you take the square root of vx squared plus vy squared (yes, that's the Pythagorean Theorem, which you should recognize from Chapter 3). To find the angle, you calculate `Math.atan2(vy, vx)`, which looks like this in code:

```
var speed:Number = Math.sqrt(vx * vx + vy * vy);
var angle:Number = Math.atan2(vy, vx);
```

Then you can subtract the friction from the speed. But you want to make sure you don't send the speed into negative values, which would reverse the velocity. So, if your friction is greater than your speed, the speed just becomes zero. Here is the code for that calculation:

```
if(speed > friction)
{
   speed -= friction;
}
else
{
   speed = 0;
}
```

At that point, you need to convert the angular velocity back into vx and vy, sine and cosine, like so:

```
vx = Math.cos(angle) * speed;
vy = Math.sin(angle) * speed;
```

Quite a bit of work, eh? Here's how it looks all together (ch06_06.fla):

```
init();
function init()
{
      friction = 0.1;
      ball = attachMovie("ball", "ball", 0);
      ball._x = Stage.width / 2;
      ball._y = Stage.height / 2;
      vx = Math.random() * 10 - 5;
      vy = Math.random() * 10 - 5;
}
function onEnterFrame(Void):Void
{
      var speed:Number = Math.sqrt(vx * vx + vy * vy);
      var angle:Number = Math.atan2(vy, vx);
      if (speed > friction)
```

```
        {
              speed -= friction;
        }
        else
        {
              speed = 0;
        }
        vx = Math.cos(angle) * speed;
        vy = Math.sin(angle) * speed;
        ball._x += vx;
        ball._y += vy;
  }
```

Here, I've given you a scaled-back velocity code. The friction is set to 0.1, and the ball is given a random velocity on the x and y axes. In the onEnterFrame method, speed and angle are calculated as I just described. If speed is less than friction, subtract; otherwise, speed equals zero. Finally, vx and vy are recalculated and added to the position.

Go ahead and test this example several times to see it at different speeds and angles. That's how friction looks. It took a dozen lines of code and four trig functions to accomplish. You could probably come up with a more optimized version, but all those calculations will be in there, one way or the other. I think you'll agree that it's time to look at the easy way.

Friction, the easy way

As you would expect, the easy way to do friction is not as accurate as the technique I just described, but I bet nobody will ever notice. It consists of two lines of simple multiplication. All you need to do is multiply the x and y velocities by some fraction of 1. A number like 0.9 or 0.8 usually works quite well. So, on each frame, the vx and vy become 80% or 90% of what they were last time. In theory, the velocity will approach zero, but never actually reach it. In practice, the computer can calculate such minute numbers only so far, and eventually it's going to round down to zero velocity. But long before that, the motion will be so small it will be indiscernible.

The good news is that the velocity is never going to go negative with this method, so you don't have to worry about checking for that. Also, the x and y velocities will approach zero at the same rate, so there's no need to convert axis velocities to angular and back.

Here's the easy method in code (ch06_07.fla):

```
init();
function init()
{
      friction = 0.9;
      ball = attachMovie("ball", "ball", 0);
      ball._x = Stage.width / 2;
      ball._y = Stage.height / 2;
      vx = Math.random() * 10 - 5;
      vy = Math.random() * 10 - 5;
}
function onEnterFrame(Void):Void
```

```
{
        vx *= friction;
        vy *= friction;
        ball._x += vx;
        ball._y += vy;
}
```

Now, that's certainly easier! Test this version a number of times and get a feel for it. Can you see the difference in motion between this and the correct method? Probably you can, because you've just seen them side by side. To the average viewer though, this one will look pretty realistic.

Friction applied

Now, let's return to our familiar spaceship and apply some friction to that universe. It's quite a different feel for just three additional lines of code. Here's the code (`ch06_08.fla`):

```
init();
function init()
{
        friction = 0.97;
        vr = 5;
        thrust = 0.2;
        vx = 0;
        vy = 0;
        left = 0;
        right = Stage.width;
        top = 0;
        bottom = Stage.height;
        ship = attachMovie("ship", "ship", 0);
        ship._x = Stage.width / 2;
        ship._y = Stage.height / 2;
}
function onEnterFrame(Void):Void
{
        if (Key.isDown(Key.LEFT))
        {
                ship._rotation -= vr;
        }
        else if (Key.isDown(Key.RIGHT))
        {
                ship._rotation += vr;
        }
        if (Key.isDown(Key.UP))
        {
                var radians:Number = ship._rotation * Math.PI / 180;
                var ax:Number = Math.cos(radians) * thrust;
                var ay:Number = Math.sin(radians) * thrust;
                vx += ax;
```

```
            vy += ay;
            ship.gotoAndStop(2);
        }
        else
        {
            ship.gotoAndStop(1);
        }
        vx *= friction;
        vy *= friction;
        ship._x += vx;
        ship._y += vy;
        if (ship._x - ship._width / 2 > right)
        {
            ship._x = left - ship._width / 2;
        }
        else if (ship._x + ship._width / 2 < left)
        {
            ship._x = right + ship._width / 2;
        }
        if (ship._y - ship._height / 2 > bottom)
        {
            ship._y = top - ship._height / 2;
        }
        else if (ship._y < top - ship._height / 2)
        {
            ship._y = bottom + ship._height / 2;
        }
    }
```

Don't forget to think outside the x, y box. Friction can be applied anywhere you have any type of velocity. Say you have something rotating (with a vr). Applying friction to that will eventually cause it to slow down and stop spinning. Here's a quick example of applying friction to a spinning arrow movie clip (ch06_09.fla):

```
var vr:Number = Math.random() * 100 - 50;
var friction:Number = 0.95;

function onEnterFrame():Void
{
    vr *= friction;
    arrow._rotation += vr;
}
```

This is a very simple file, with the movie clip placed on stage manually and the code right on the timeline.

You can see how you could use this approach for all types of objects, such as a roulette wheel, an electric fan, or a propeller.

Important formulas in this chapter

Let's review the important formulas introduced in this chapter.

Remove an out-of-bounds object:

```
if(mc._x - mc._width / 2 > right ||
   mc._x + mc._width / 2 < left ||
   mc._y - mc._height / 2 > bottom ||
   mc._y + mc._height / 2 < top)
{
      mc.removeMovieClip();
}
```

Regenerate an out-of-bounds object:

```
if(mc._x - mc._width / 2 > right ||
   mc._x + mc._width / 2 < left ||
   mc._y - mc._height / 2 > bottom ||
   mc._y + mc._height / 2 < top)
{
      // reset mc position and velocity.
}
```

Screen wrapping for an out-of-bounds object:

```
if(mc._x - mc._width / 2 > right)
{
   mc._x = left - mc._width / 2;
}
else if(mc._x + mc._width / 2 < left)
{
   mc._x = right + mc._width / 2;
}
if(mc._y - mc._height / 2 > bottom)
{
   mc._y = top - mc._height / 2;
}
else if(mc._y + mc._height / 2 < top)
{
   mc._y = bottom + mc._height / 2;
}
```

Apply friction (the correct way):

```
speed = Math.sqrt(vx * vx + vy * vy);
angle = Math.atan2(vy, vx);
if(speed > friction)
{
   speed -= friction;
}
else
{
   speed = 0;
}
vx = Math.cos(angle) * speed;
vy = Math.sin(angle) * speed;
```

Apply friction (the easy way):

```
vx *= friction;
vy *= friction;
```

Summary

This chapter covered an object's interaction with its own environment. Specifically, an object's interaction with the edges of its universe and the universe itself. You learned the possible ways to deal with an object that has gone off the edge of the world, including removing, regenerating, wrapping, and bouncing. And, you now know more about friction than you probably ever wanted to know. But with these simple techniques, you can make the objects in your movies move with a great deal of realism. In the next chapter, you'll delve into allowing the user to interact with the objects.

};shape.targetHeight = shape._height;
shape.onEnterFrame = function() {
var speed = 5;
this._width += (this.targetWidth - this._width)/speed;
this._height += (this.targetHeight - this._height)/speed;
}

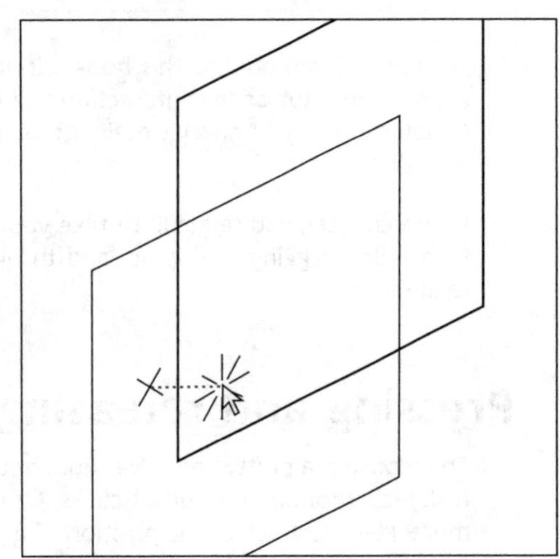

Chapter 7

USER INTERACTION: MOVING OBJECTS AROUND

What we'll cover in this chapter:

- Pressing and releasing a movie clip
- Dragging a movie clip
- Throwing

For most of you reading this book, a primary goal with your animation is to allow smooth user interaction, and a lot of this interaction will be through the mouse. I talked about mouse events back in Chapter 2, but you haven't really done much with them yet. Now, you'll get some hands-on practice with them.

In this chapter, you're going to take your first steps into the field of user interaction. You'll learn how to handle dragging, dropping, and throwing. But first, let's get started with the basics of press and release.

Pressing and releasing a movie clip

The mouse is a pretty cool invention, but in essence, it's a simple device. It really does only two things: It detects motion and button clicks. Of course, the computer then uses that information to do a lot more: keeping track of the position of a mouse cursor, determining where the cursor is when the click occurs, determining how fast the mouse is moving, and figuring out when a double-click occurs. But really, when you look at it in terms of events, it all comes down to clicks and movement.

You can also break clicks down into two parts: the event that occurs when the mouse button goes down and the next event when it comes up. Sometimes, those events occur almost instantaneously. Other times, the events are separated by time and motion, which is usually interpreted as a *drag*—click, move, and then release. In this chapter, you'll concentrate on those three things: the mouse going down, the mouse going up, and any motion that occurs in between the two.

A movie clip can respond to most mouse events at any time, regardless of the position of the mouse and the movie clip. Even if the mouse cursor is nowhere near the clip, or the clip is empty of any graphical content, or the clip is invisible, it can still get mouse events. But of course, it's very valuable to know when the mouse is clicked *on* a movie clip. Thus, you need some way of differentiating between when the mouse button is being pressed or released *over* the movie clip's graphics and when it is being pressed anywhere else in the movie. This is why ActionScript has five separate events for mouse clicks: `onMouseDown`, `onMouseUp`, `onPress`, `onRelease`, and `onReleaseOutside`.

The `onMouseDown` and `onMouseUp` event handlers are called for every movie clip in the movie, whenever the mouse button is pressed or released, regardless of mouse position in relationship to the movie clip. If the movie clip is in existence in the movie at the time of the mouse event, it will get the event.

The `onPress` event handler is called only when the mouse button is pressed while the mouse cursor is over some graphical portion of a movie clip. I guess the idea is to simulate your finger touching an actual button and pressing it down. Furthermore, only one movie clip will receive the `onPress` event when it is fired. That is the topmost movie clip with graphical content that has any defined `onPress`, `onRelease`, or `onReleaseOutside` event handlers. In other words, if two overlapping movie clips both have some kind of mouse-click-handling functions assigned, only the top clip will receive any of the mouse events, as illustrated in Figure 7-1. A clip without any of these event handlers assigned will allow these events to pass through to any movie clip below it that is interested in handling them.

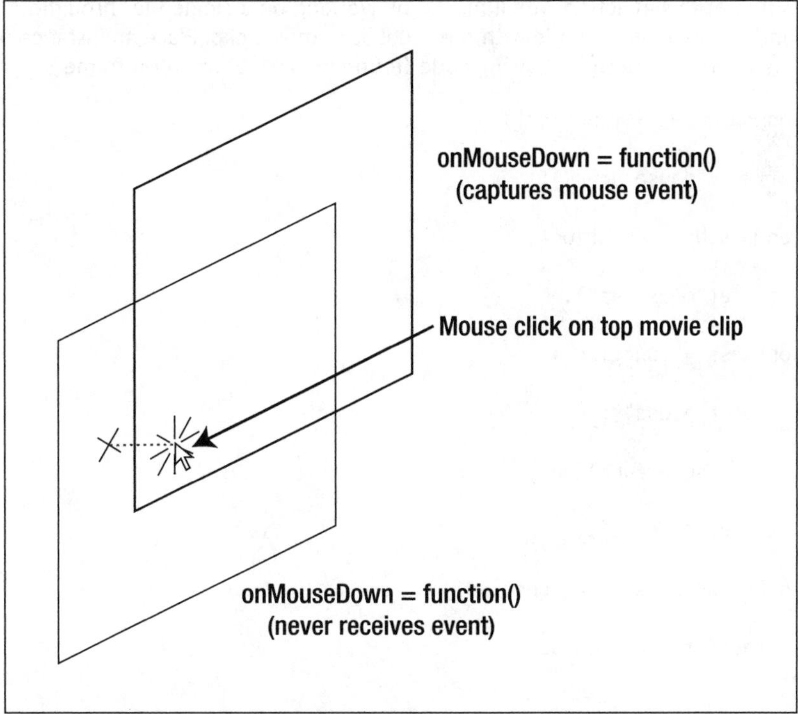

Figure 7-1. Two overlapping movie clips with mouse event handlers. Only the top one receives the event.

Another tricky aspect of this is a movie clip that contains other movie clips. If you define `onPress`, `onRelease`, or `onReleaseOutside` on the outer clip, it will capture all of these events, and the inner movie clips will not be able to respond to them.

The `onRelease` handler is called only after an `onPress` event occurs, when the mouse button is released while the mouse cursor is still over the movie clip. In other words, for an `onRelease` event to occur, the mouse cursor must be over the movie clip's graphics when the mouse is clicked *and* when it is released. For an `onReleaseOutside` to occur, first an `onPress` must occur, then the mouse cursor is moved off the graphics, and then the mouse button is released. Thus, you can see that an `onPress` event must always be followed by either an `onRelease` event or an `onReleaseOutside` event (unless, of course, you've spilled a beverage of some sort onto your mouse and the buttons get permanently stuck in a down state).

The next important feature about mouse events is that, like `onEnterFrame`, all of them are automatically listened for by every movie clip in the movie. All you need to do is create a function with the appropriate name, and it will be called as soon as that event occurs for that movie clip.

OK, let's see some of this in action. You'll mostly be working on a single file throughout this chapter, so go ahead and set up a new FLA file with the usual ball movie clip. Place an instance of the ball on stage and name it ball. Place the following code (found in ch07_01.fla) on frame 1:

```
ball.onMouseDown = function()
{
	trace("mouse down");
}
ball.onMouseUp = function()
{
	trace("mouse up");
}
ball.onPress = function()
{
	trace("press");
}
ball.onRelease = function()
{
	trace("release");
}
ball.onReleaseOutside = function()
{
	trace("release outside");
}
```

This just sets up handlers for the five mouse button events and lets you know when they occur. You can build this file and play around with it to see exactly when and where particular mouse events occur, until it is all clear. Here are some things to notice:

- Mouse down and mouse up events occur no matter where you click.
- If you click on the ball, you get a mouse down event *and* a press event.
- When you then release the mouse, you get a mouse up event and then either a release or release outside event.
- It's impossible to get a release or release outside event without first getting a press event.

Now that you know how to press and release a movie clip, we'll move on to the dragging part.

Dragging a movie clip

You can handle dragging a movie clip using two different techniques: with the mouseMove event or with the startDrag/stopDrag methods. Although you'll be using the latter for the examples in this chapter, let's look at how to use the mouseMove event for dragging first. It will give you some experience in handling the mouseMove event and a deeper understanding of how events work.

Dragging with mouseMove

By manually handling the mouseMove event, you can update the movie clip's position to match the mouse cursor's each time the mouse moves. It's worth noting that this is the only way to drag more than one object at a time. You sometimes run into this when making a custom cursor out of a movie clip. The cursor needs to follow the mouse position around, but what if you want to drag something, too? One solution is to use mouseMove for the cursor, and leave the usual drag methods (startDrag/stopDrag) free for normal dragging. So it's a nice little technique to have under your belt, even if you don't use it on regular basis.

The strategy is this: On the mouseDown event, you want to set up a mouseMove handler. This handler will just set the ball's x and y positions to equal the current mouse position. On the mouseUp event, you remove that handler.

You can use the file you just created for mouse events, and change the code on frame 1 to this (ch07_02.fla):

```
ball.onPress = function()
{
	ball.onMouseMove = drag;
}
ball.onRelease = function()
{
	delete ball.onMouseMove;
}
function drag()
{
	ball._x = _xmouse;
	ball._y = _ymouse;
}
```

The onPress method causes the drag method to be called every time the mouse moves, and the onRelease method deletes that as a handler.

If you test this example, you'll notice several problems. One is that the ball sometimes gets "stuck" to the mouse, even after you release the mouse. This is because the mouse refreshes its position at a much faster rate than the movie clip, which can move only once per frame. Thus the mouse can "get ahead" of the movie clip, and sometimes when the mouse button is released, the mouse cursor is outside the graphical area of the clip. If this is the case, onRelease will not register. Fixing this is as simple as adding the following method:

```
ball.onReleaseOutside = function()
{
	delete ball.onMouseMove;
}
```

This causes the ball to be released when the mouse button is released, no matter where the mouse cursor is.

You might have also noticed one other problem with this setup. If you click on the edge of the ball and start dragging it, you'll see that it suddenly jumps and centers itself on the mouse cursor. This is because you're setting the ball's x and y positions to exactly equal to the mouse position. You could do some fancy footwork to get around that, finding the offset of the mouse to the ball when the mouse is pressed, and adding that to the ball's position as you drag. I'll leave that as a project for you, if you're interested in pursuing it. But I'm going to move on to the usual method of dragging a movie clip.

Dragging with startDrag/stopDrag

All movie clips have built-in methods called `startDrag` and `stopDrag`, which handle all of the functionality of the method I just described (in what was an educational detour, I hope), and then some. About the only drawback is that it allows for dragging only a single movie clip at a time.

The concept is pretty simple. In your press handler, you call `startDrag`. In the release handler, you call `stopDrag`. You still need to make an `onReleaseOutside` method.

`startDrag` can be called without any parameters. You can take the file you've been using for this chapter's examples and change the code on frame 1 to this (in `ch07_03.fla`):

```
ball.onPress = function()
{
	ball.startDrag();
}
ball.onRelease = function()
{
	ball.stopDrag();
}
ball.onReleaseOutside = function()
{
	ball.stopDrag();
}
```

Pretty simple, eh? Test this, and you'll also notice that the "snapping" problem is gone. The ball will drag from whatever position you clicked on it. If you actually *want* it to snap to the center though, you can do so by passing `true` to the first parameter of `startDrag`:

```
ball.startDrag(true);
```

You can also limit the dragging to a rectangular area by passing in coordinates for the left, top, right, and bottom of the area you want to be able to drag in. Here is the full syntax for `startDrag`:

```
startDrag(lockCenter, left, top, right, bottom)
```

Combining dragging with motion code

At this point, you know pretty much everything about simple dragging and dropping in Flash. Unfortunately, in the process, you've reverted back to a static object that just kind of sits there unless you're dragging it. Let's add some velocity and maybe even some acceleration and bouncing.

You already have a nice setup for velocity, gravity, and bouncing in the ch06_05.fla file from the previous chapter. That's a good starting point. It would seem logical to simply add your drag-and-drop code to that code. Let's try it. You should end up with something like this (ch07_04.fla):

```
init();
function init()
{
	bounce = -0.7;
	gravity = 0.5;
	top = 0;
	left = 0;
	bottom = Stage.height;
	right = Stage.width;
	ball = attachMovie("ball", "ball", 0);
	ball._x = Stage.width / 2;
	ball._y = Stage.height / 2;
	vx = Math.random() * 10 - 5;
	vy = Math.random() * 10 - 5;
}
ball.onPress = function()
{
	ball.startDrag();
}
ball.onRelease = function()
{
	ball.stopDrag();
}
ball.onReleaseOutside = function()
{
	ball.stopDrag();
}
function onEnterFrame(Void):Void
{
	vy += gravity;
	ball._x += vx;
	ball._y += vy;
	if (ball._x + ball._width / 2 > right)
	{
		ball._x = right - ball._width / 2;
		vx *= bounce;
	}
	else if (ball._x - ball._width / 2 < left)
	{
		ball._x = left + ball._width / 2;
		vx *= bounce;
	}
	if (ball._y + ball._height / 2 > bottom)
	{
		ball._y = bottom - ball._height / 2;
```

```
            vy *= bounce;
        }
        else if (ball._y - ball._height / 2 < top)
        {
            ball._y = top + ball._height / 2;
            vy *= bounce;
        }
    }
```

As you can see, all that you've added to the original code is the handlers for onPress, onRelease, and onReleaseOutside.

If you test this now, you'll see the problem immediately when you start to drag. Yes, the dragging works, but the motion code is working at the same time. The result is the feeling that the ball is slipping out of your hand. You need some way of switching on or off the motion code, so that it doesn't happen while you're dragging. The simplest way to do this is to set a variable called dragging to true or false when you start or stop dragging. First, of course, you need to declare the variable in the init function:

```
dragging = false;
```

Then you set it in your onPress, onRelease, and onReleaseOutside handlers:

```
ball.onPress = function()
{
    dragging = true;
    ball.startDrag();
}
ball.onRelease = function()
{
    dragging = false;
    ball.stopDrag();
}
ball.onReleaseOutside = function()
{
    dragging = false;
    ball.stopDrag();
}
```

Now, in your onEnterFrame method, you simply check the dragging variable. If it's false, you can do all your normal stuff. You could phrase this something like this:

```
if(dragging == false)
```

But there is an even more concise way. The !, or NOT operator, converts true to false and false to true. Thus, you can say:

```
if(!dragging)
```

This is read, "If not dragging. . .," which means pretty much what it sounds like as an English phrase. (It's always great when your code becomes that readable!) So, your onEnterFrame function becomes this:

```
function onEnterFrame(Void):Void
{
        if(!dragging)
        {
                vy += gravity;
                ball._x += vx;
                ball._y += vy;
                if (ball._x + ball._width / 2 > right)
                {
                        ball._x = right - ball._width / 2;
                        vx *= bounce;
                }
                else if (ball._x - ball._width / 2 < left)
                {
                        ball._x = left + ball._width / 2;
                        vx *= bounce;
                }
                if (ball._y + ball._height / 2 > bottom)
                {
                        ball._y = bottom - ball._height / 2;
                        vy *= bounce;
                }
                else if (ball._y - ball._height / 2 < top)
                {
                        ball._y = top + ball._height / 2;
                        vy *= bounce;
                }
        }
}
```

When you test this, you'll see that you're getting closer, but you're not quite there yet.

When you start dragging, all you're doing is dragging. When you drop the ball, the motion code resumes where it left off. The main problem now is that the velocity also resumes where it left off. This sometimes results in the ball flying off in some direction when you release it, which is pretty unnatural. You can easily fix that by just setting vx and vy to zero, either when you start dragging or when you stop. Either one works, as long as it is done before the motion code resumes. Let's put it in the start drag section:

```
ball.onPress = function()
{
        vx = 0;
        vy = 0;
        dragging = true;
        ball.startDrag();
}
```

That takes care of the problem and leaves you with a fully functional drag-and-drop, with integrated velocity, acceleration, and bouncing. You can see the full code listing in ch07_05.fla.

Just one issue remains: When you drop the ball, it falls straight down—no more x-axis motion. Although this is the correct behavior, it's a bit boring. If you could actually throw the ball and have it fly off in whatever direction you threw it, that would be some heavy-duty interactivity. Well, that's exactly what you're going to do next.

Throwing

What do we mean by *throwing* when it comes to a Flash movie? It means you click on an object to start dragging it, move it in a particular direction, and when you release it, it keeps moving in the direction you were dragging it.

For the velocity, you need to determine what velocity the object has while it is being dragged, and then set the object's velocity to that value when it is dropped. In other words, if you were dragging a movie clip 10 pixels per frame to the left, then when you release it, its velocity should be vx = -10.

Setting the new velocity should be no problem for you; just assign new values to vx and vy, as shown in Figure 7-2. But determining what those values are might be a little tricky. Actually, calculating dragging velocity turns out to be almost exactly the opposite of applying velocity in your motion code. In applying velocity, you add velocity to the object's old position to come up with the object's new position. So, the formula would be old + velocity = new. To determine the velocity of an object while it's being dragged, you simply rearrange the equation to get velocity = new - old.

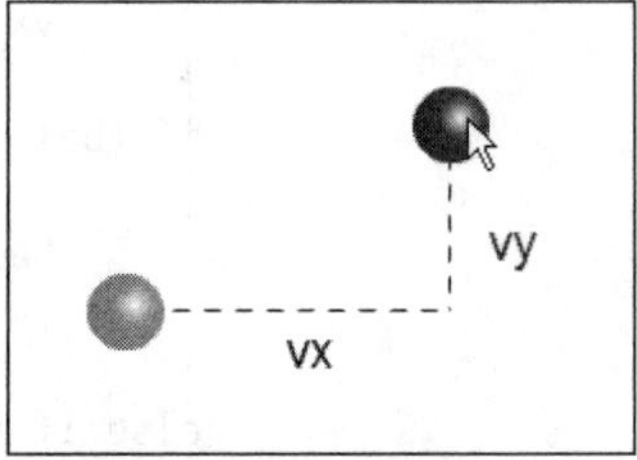

Figure 7-2. The ball has been dragged to a new position. The velocity is the distance from its last position to this new position.

As you are dragging the movie clip, it's going to have a new position on each frame. If you take that and subtract the position it was in on the previous frame, you'll know how far it moved in one frame. That's your pixels-per-frame velocity!

Let's take an example, simplifying it to a single axis. A movie clip is being dragged. On a particular frame, you note that its x position is 150. On the next frame, you see that its x position is 170. Thus, in one frame, it was dragged 20 pixels on the x axis, and its x velocity at that point is +20. If you were to release it just then, you would expect it to continue moving at an x velocity of 20. So, of course, you would set vx = 20.

The major thing this requires is a couple of variables to hold the old x and y position values. You can call those oldX and oldY, and declare them as timeline variables. Now, as soon as you start dragging, you want to note the ball's position and store it in oldX and oldY. This can be done in the mouseDown handler, as follows:

```
oldX = ball._x;
oldY = ball._y;
```

Then, in your enterFrame handler, you just subtract the current x position from oldX, and current y from oldY. This gives you the current velocity, so you can store these values directly in vx and vy:

```
vx = ball._x - oldX;
vy = ball._y - oldY;
```

Do this in an else block after the if(!dragging) block. So, the ball is either moving on its own or it's being dragged. That's your if and else. It will become clearer when you see it in code very shortly.

Once you determine the velocity, you're finished with the old values, and you can now use those variables to store the position of the ball on the current frame:

```
oldX = ball._x;
oldY = ball._y;
```

Now, when you release the ball, you don't need to do anything at all. The velocity has been kept track of all through the drag, and the latest velocity is already stored in vx and vy. As soon as you reenable the motion code, the ball will move at whatever velocity it was just being dragged with. The result: You threw the ball!

Here is the final throwing code (ch07_06.fla):

```
init();
function init()
{
      dragging = false;
      friction = 0.98;
      bounce = -0.7;
      gravity = 0.5;
      top = 0;
      left = 0;
      bottom = Stage.height;
      right = Stage.width;
      ball = attachMovie("ball", "ball", 0);
      ball._x = Stage.width / 2;
      ball._y = Stage.height / 2;
      vx = Math.random() * 10 - 5;
      vy = Math.random() * 10 - 5;
}
ball.onPress = function()
{
      oldX = ball._x;
      oldY = ball._y;
      dragging = true;
      ball.startDrag();
};
ball.onRelease = function()
{
```

```
        dragging = false;
        ball.stopDrag();
};
ball.onReleaseOutside = function()
{
        dragging = false;
        ball.stopDrag();
};
function onEnterFrame(Void):Void
{
        if (!dragging)
        {
                vy += gravity;
                vx *= friction;
                vy *= friction;
                ball._x += vx;
                ball._y += vy;
                if (ball._x + ball._width / 2 > right)
                {
                        ball._x = right - ball._width / 2;
                        vx *= bounce;
                }
                else if (ball._x - ball._width / 2 < left)
                {
                        ball._x = left + ball._width / 2;
                        vx *= bounce;
                }
                if (ball._y + ball._height / 2 > bottom)
                {
                        ball._y = bottom - ball._height / 2;
                        vy *= bounce;
                }
                else if (ball._y - ball._height / 2 < top)
                {
                        ball._y = top + ball._height / 2;
                        vy *= bounce;
                }
        }
        else
        {
                vx = ball._x - oldX;
                vy = ball._y - oldY;
                oldX = ball._x;
                oldY = ball._y;
        }
}
```

Now that's pretty darned interactive, and a good representation of real-world physics re-created in Flash. It really feels like you're throwing something around. You can even play catch with yourself. In this example, I also added in a bit of friction to simulate some atmosphere. Play around with all the variables for gravity, bounce, and so on. This is a great sample file to get a feel for how all of these things work, because you can experiment in real time and see how all the parameters affect the motion.

As a note, you could easily switch around the `if` and `else` statements, and do something like this:

```
if(dragging)
{
	// dragging code
}
else
{
	// motion code
}
```

You just need to change the `if(!dragging)` to `if(dragging)`. Use whichever approach makes more sense to you.

Summary

While this was not a long chapter, it covered some extremely valuable ground, and made some great headway in interactivity. By now, you should be able to drag any object, drop it, and throw it.

Most important, you've worked with a lot of the small details that go into doing a really professional job with interactivity. In future chapters, you'll be looking at many other ways of allowing the user to interact with objects in your movies. The complexity is going to start building up fast, but if you have these basics down, you'll do great.

Part Three

ADVANCED MOTION

};shape.targetHeight = shape._height;
shape.onEnterFrame = function() {
var speed = 5;
this._width += (this.targetWidth - this._width)/speed;
this._height += (this.targetHeight - this._height)/speed;
};

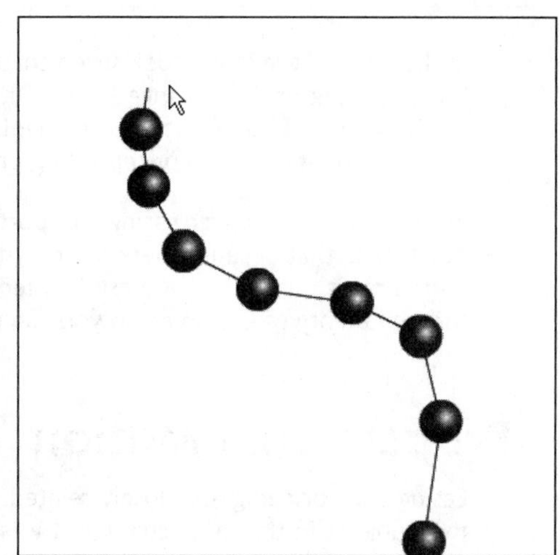

Chapter 8

EASING AND SPRINGING

What we'll cover in this chapter:

- Proportional Motion
- Easing
- Springing
- Important formulas in this chapter

It's hard to believe that it took seven chapters to get through "the basics," but here you are at Chapter 8, the beginning of the advanced stuff. Or, as I prefer to think of it, the point where things start to get *really* interesting. Up to now, each chapter covered more general techniques and concepts. Beginning with this chapter, I'll be concentrating on one or two specialized types of motion per chapter.

In this chapter, I'll cover easing (proportional velocity) and springing (proportional acceleration). But don't think that because there are only two items, this is a chapter you can skim through quickly. I've gotten more mileage from these two techniques than just about any others. And I'm going to run you through plenty of examples, so you can get an idea of just how powerful these techniques are.

Proportional Motion

Easing and springing are closely related. Even though I had planned from the beginning to put these two subjects in the same chapter, it wasn't until I sat down to plan this chapter in more detail that I realized just *how* similar they are to each other.

Both techniques involve moving a movie clip from an existing position to a target position. In easing, the clip kind of slides into the target and stops. In springing, the clip bounces around back and forth for a bit, and then finally settles down at the target. The two techniques have the following in common:

- You set a target.
- You determine the distance to that target.
- Your motion is proportional to that distance—the bigger the distance, the more the motion.

The difference between easing and springing is in what aspect of the motion is proportional. In easing, *velocity* is proportional to the distance; the further away from the target, the faster the object moves. As it gets very, very close to the object, it's hardly moving at all.

In springing, *acceleration* is proportional to the distance. If the object is far away from the target, a whole lot of acceleration is applied, increasing the velocity quickly. As the object gets closer to its target, less acceleration is applied, but it's still accelerating! It flies right past the target, and then acceleration pulls it back. Eventually, friction causes it to settle down.

Let's dive in to each technique separately, starting with easing.

Easing

One thing I want to clear up right off the bat is that there is more than one type of easing. Even in the Flash IDE, while you're making a motion tween, you have the ability to "ease in" or "ease out." The type of easing I will be discussing here is the same as the "ease in" of a motion tween. A bit later in this chapter, in the "Advanced easing" section, I'll provide you with a link where you can find out how to do all kinds of easing.

Simple easing

Simple easing is a very basic concept. You have something over here and you want to move it over there. Since you're creating the "illusion of motion," you want to move it there gradually, over several frames. You could simply find the angle between the two, set a speed, use some trigonometry to work out the vx and vy, and set it in motion. Then you could check the distance to the target on each frame (using the Pythagorean Theorem, as described in Chapter 3), and when it was there, stop it. That approach might actually be adequate in some situations, but if you're trying to make something look like it's moving naturally, it won't do.

The problem is that your object would move along at a fixed velocity, reach its target, and stop dead. If you're talking about some object moving along and hitting a brick wall, yes, it might be sort of like that. But when you're moving an object to a *target*, this generally implies that someone or something knows where this target is, and is moving something into place there deliberately. In such a case, the motion will start out fairly fast, and then slow down as it gets closer to the target. In other words, its velocity is going to be proportional to the distance to the target.

Let's take an example. You're driving home. When you are a few miles away, you're going to be traveling as fast as the speed limit allows you (OK, maybe even faster—maybe even fast enough to earn yourself a ticket). When you pull off the highway and into your neighborhood, you'll be going a bit slower. Once you're on your own street, a block or two away, you'll be going far slower. As you approach your driveway, you're down to a few miles per hour. When you reach the last few feet of the driveway, you're moving a lot slower than when you pulled into the driveway. And inches before you stop, you're moving at a fraction of that speed.

If you take the time to look, you'll see this behavior manifests itself even in small things like closing a drawer or door. You start out fast and gradually slow down. The next time you go to close a door, make an effort to follow through with the same speed you started with. Just be prepared to explain to anyone nearby why you're slamming doors.

So, when you use easing to move an object into position, it automatically takes on a very natural appearance. One of the coolest things is that simple easing is actually very easy to do. In fact, it's probably easier than figuring out the angle, the vx, and the vy, and moving at a fixed speed.

Here is the strategy for easing:

1. Decide on a number for your proportional motion. This will be a fraction of 1.
2. Determine your target.
3. Calculate the distance from the object to the target.
4. Multiply the distance by the fraction. This is your velocity.
5. Add the velocity value to the current position.
6. Repeat steps 3 through 5 until the object is at the target.

Figure 8-1 illustrates the concept.

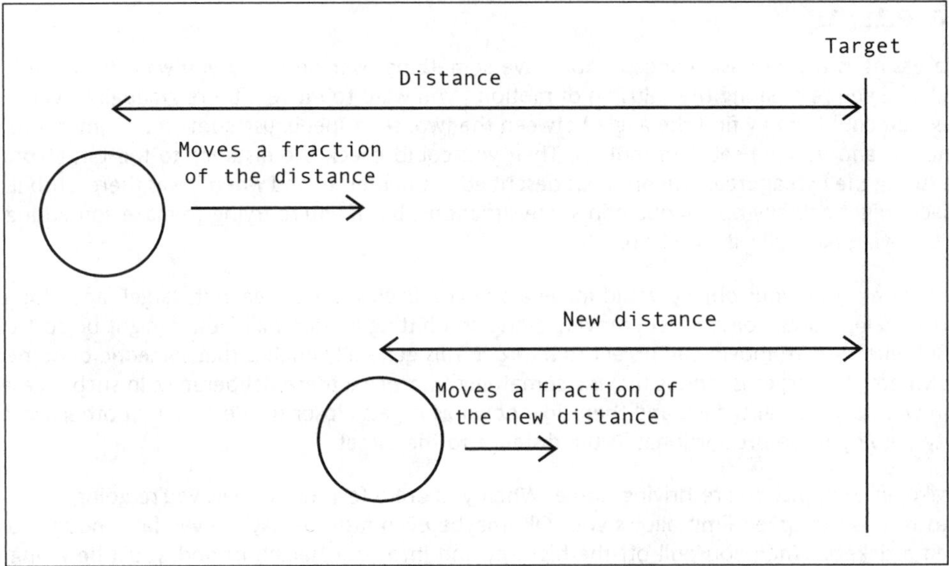

Figure 8-1. Basic easing

Let's go through these steps one at a time, and see how each looks in ActionScript. Don't worry about where to put the code yet. I'm just showing you what the code looks like and what it means.

First, decide on a fraction to represent the proportion. As I said, the velocity will be proportional to the motion. Specifically, this means that the velocity will be a fraction of the distance, something between 0 and 1. The closer it is to 1, the quicker the object will move. The closer it is to 0, the slower it will move, but be careful, because too low a value will prevent the object from reaching the target at all. For starters, choose something like 0.2. I'm going to call this variable `easing`. So you can start off with the following code:

```
var easing:Number = 0.2;
```

Next, determine your target. This is a simple x, y position. You can make it center stage for lack of anything better.

```
var targetX:Number = Stage.width / 2;
var targetY:Number = Stage.height / 2;
```

Then calculate the distance to the target. Assuming you have a movie clip named ball, you just subtract the ball's x and y from the target x and y.

```
var dx:Number = targetX - ball._x;
var dy:Number = targetY - ball._y;
```

Your velocity is then the distance times the fraction:

```
vx = dx * easing;
vy = dy * easing;
```

And you know what to do from there:

```
ball._x += vx;
ball._y += vy;
```

Steps 3 to 5 need to be repeated, so those will go in your `enterFrame` function. Let's take a closer look at those three steps, as they can be largely simplified.

```
var dx:Number = targetX - ball._x;
var dy:Number = targetY - ball._y;
vx = dx * easing;
vy = dy * easing;
ball._x += vx;
ball._y += vy;
```

You can condense the first two lines into the second two pretty easily:

```
vx = (targetX - ball._x) * easing;
vy = (targetY - ball._y) * easing;
ball._x += vx;
ball._y += vy;
```

Or, if you're into the whole brevity thing, you can shrink it even further:

```
ball._x += (targetX - ball._x) * easing;
ball._y += (targetY - ball._y) * easing;
```

The first few times you do easing, you might want to go with one of the more verbose syntaxes to make it clearer. But once you've done it a few hundred times, the third version communicates perfectly. I'll stick with the second version here, just to reinforce the idea that you're dealing with velocity.

Now, let's see it in action. You can start out with the same base file you've been using throughout the book. It just needs to contain a movie clip symbol named ball. Place an instance of the ball on stage, and then add the following code on frame 1 (found in `ch08_01.fla`):

```
var easing:Number = 0.2;
var targetX:Number = Stage.width / 2;
var targetY:Number = Stage.height / 2;
onEnterFrame = function () {
	var vx:Number = (targetX - ball._x) * easing;
	var vy:Number = (targetY - ball._y) * easing;
	ball._x += vx;
	ball._y += vy;
};
```

Make sure that the ball is originally placed far from the center, so you can see it moving. Play around with the easing variable to see how it affects the resulting motion.

The next thing you might want to do is make the ball draggable so you can move it around and see how it always goes back to its target. This is pretty similar to the drag-and-drop technique you set up in Chapter 7. Here's the code (ch08_02.fla):

```
var easing:Number = 0.2;
var targetX:Number = Stage.width / 2;
var targetY:Number = Stage.height / 2;
var dragging:Boolean = false;
ball.onPress = function()
{
	dragging = true;
	this.startDrag();
}
ball.onRelease = ball.onReleaseOutside = function()
{
	dragging = false;
	this.stopDrag();
}
onEnterFrame = function ()
{
	if(!dragging)
	{
		var vx:Number = (targetX - ball._x) * easing;
		var vy:Number = (targetY - ball._y) * easing;
		ball._x += vx;
		ball._y += vy;
	}
};
```

When to stop easing

If you are doing simple easing to a single target, eventually you'll get to the point where the object is at the target and the purpose of the easing has been achieved. But, in the examples so far, the easing code continues to execute, even though the object isn't visibly moving anymore. This is a waste of CPU resources. If you've reached your goal, you might as well stop trying. At first glance, this would be as simple as checking if the object is at its target and turning off the enterFrame code, like so:

```
if(ball._x == targetX && ball._y == targetY)
{
    // code to stop the easing
}
```

But it winds up being a little more tricky.

The type of easing we are discussing involves something known as Xeno's Paradox. Xeno was yet another Greek guy who liked to measure things. Xeno tried to break down motion as follows: In order for something to move from point A to point B, it first must move to a point halfway between the two. Then it needs to travel from that point to a point halfway between there and point B. And then halfway again. Since you always need to move halfway to the target, you can never actually reach the target.

The paradox is that this sounds logical, but obviously, we do move from one point to another every day, so there's something wrong there. Let's take a look at it in Flash. On the x axis, a movie clip is at position 0. Say you want to move it to 100 on the x axis. To fit into the paradox, make the `easing` variable 0.5, so it always moves half the distance to the target. It progresses like this:

- Starting at 0, after frame 1, it will be at 50.
- Frame 2 will bring it to 75.
- Now the distance is 25. Half of that is 12.5, so the new position will be 87.5.
- Following the sequence, the position will be 93.75, 96.875, 98.4375, and so on. After 20 frames, it will be 99.999809265.

As you can see, it gets closer and closer, but never actually reaches the target, theoretically. However, things are a bit different when you examine what the code does. It comes down to the question, "How small can you slice a pixel?" The answer is 20. In fact, there's a name for a twentieth of a pixel: a *twip*. Internally, Flash calculates anything that uses pixels with twips. This includes positions of movie clips. Thus, if you trace the position of a movie clip, you might notice that it is always in multiples of 0.05.

In the example here, the closest a movie clip can get to 100 without actually getting there is 99.95. When you try to split the difference at that point, you're trying to add on (100 – 99.95) / 2. This comes out to 0.025, or a fortieth of a pixel. But a twip is as low as you can go. You can't add "half a twip," so you wind up adding 0. If you don't believe me, try the following code with a movie clip instance named `ball` on stage:

```
var targ:Number = 100;
ball._x = 0;
for(var i:Number=0;i<20;i++)
{
      trace(i + ": " + ball._x);
      ball._x += (targ - ball._x) * .5;
}
```

This just loops through 20 times, moving the ball half the distance to the target. It's basic easing code. I threw it in a `for` loop because I was only interested in tracing the positions, not actually seeing the motion. What you'll find is that by the eleventh iteration, the ball has reached 99.95, and that's as far as it gets.

> *In tracing positions, you might also notice that occasionally you get a number like 96.85000000000001. This has to do with the way fractions are stored in a binary format, and has nothing to do with pixels, twips, or Flash itself. For more information, do a web search for "binary round-off errors."*

To make a long story short, no, your movie clip object is not going to get closer and closer, but yes, your movie clip might never reach its target. So, if you're doing a simple comparison, as in the previous example, your easing code will never get shut off. What you need to do is answer the question, "When is it close enough?" This comes down to determining if the distance to the target is less than a certain amount. For many applications, I've found that if an object is within a pixel of its target, it's safe to say it has arrived, and I can shut off easing.

If you are dealing with two dimensions, you can calculate the distance using the formula I introduced in Chapter 3:

```
distance = Math.sqrt(dx * dx + dy * dy).
```

If you are dealing with a single value for distance, as when you are moving an object on a single axis, you need to use the absolute value of that distance, as it may be negative. You can do this by using the Math.abs method.

OK, I've done way too much talking. Let's see it in some code. Here's a simple program to demonstrate turning off easing (ch08_03.fla):

```
var easing:Number = 0.2;
var targ:Number = Stage.width / 2;
onEnterFrame = ease;
function ease() {
	var dx:Number = targ - ball._x;
	if(Math.abs(dx) < 1)
	{
		ball._x = targ;
		delete onEnterFrame;
		trace("done");
	}
	else
	{
		var vx:Number = dx * easing;
		ball._x += vx;
	}
};
```

As you can see, this example expands the easing formula a bit to first calculate the distance, since you'll need this to see if easing should be stopped. Perhaps now you can see why you need to use the absolute value of dx. If the ball were to the right of the target, dx would wind up as a negative number, the statement if(dx < 1) would evaluate as true, and that would be the end of things. By using Math.abs, you make sure that the actual distance is less than 1. You then place the ball where it is trying to go and disable the motion code.

Remember that if you are doing something like a drag-and-drop with easing, you'll want to reenable the motion code when the ball is dropped. Why don't you go ahead and see if you can figure out that one for yourself. I'll give you a small hint: You want to reset onEnterFrame to equal move.

A moving target

In the examples so far, the target point has been a single, fixed location, but that's not a requirement. The distance is calculated on each frame, and the velocity is then calculated based on that. Flash doesn't care whether or not it reaches the target, or if the target keeps moving. It just happily goes on saying, "Where's my target? What's the distance? What's my velocity?" on each and every frame.

You can easily make the mouse an easing target. Just plug the mouse coordinates in where you had targetX and targetY before. Here's a simpler version that does just that (ch08_04.fla):

```
var easing:Number = 0.1;
onEnterFrame = function () {
      var dx:Number = _xmouse - ball._x;
      var dy:Number = _ymouse - ball._y;
      ball._x += dx * easing;
      ball._y += dy * easing;
};
```

Move the mouse around and see how the ball follows, and how it goes faster when you get further away.

Think of what other moving targets you could have. Maybe a movie clip could ease to another movie clip. Back in the early days of Flash, mouse trailers—a trail of movie clips that followed the mouse around—were all the rage. Easing was one way of doing this. The first clip eased to the mouse, the second clip eased to the first, the third to the second, and so on. Go ahead and try it out (but if you put it on a live website, I'll deny any responsibility).

Easing isn't just for motion

If there is one point I want to get across in this book, it's that the examples I give are simply that: examples. In each case, I'm mainly just manipulating numbers that are used for various movie clip properties. For the most part, I'm using the _x and _y properties to control positions of movie clips. Just remember that movie clips have a bunch of other properties that you can manipulate, and most of them are represented by numbers. So when you read a particular example, definitely try it out, but don't leave it at that. Try the same example on other properties. Here, I'll give you a few ideas to get you started.

Transparency

Apply easing to the _alpha property of a clip. Start out by setting it to 0, and making the target 100:

```
ball._alpha = 0;
var targetAlpha:Number = 100;
```

Then you can fade it in with easing in an enterFrame handler:

```
ball._alpha += (targetAlpha - ball._alpha) * easing;
```

Or reverse the 0 and 100 to make it fade out.

Rotation

Set the _rotation property and a target rotation. Of course, you need something that can be visibly rotated, like an arrow:

```
arrow._rotation = 90;
var targetRotation:Number = 270;
```

And then ease it:

```
arrow._rotation += (targetRotation - arrow._rotation) * easing;
```

Colors

If you are up for a real challenge, try easing on 24-bit colors. You'll need to start with red, green, and blue initial values and target values, perform the easing on each separate component color, and then combine them into a 24-bit color. For instance, you could ease from red to blue. Start with the initial and target colors:

```
red = 255;
green = 0;
blue = 0;
redTarget = 0;
greenTarget = 0;
blueTarget = 255;
```

Then in your `enterFrame` handler, perform easing on each one. Here is just the red value:

```
red += (redTarget - red) * easing;
```

Then combine the three into a single value (as described in Chapter 4):

```
col = red << 16 | green << 8 | blue;
```

And use that for `setRGB`, or for a line, a fill color, or another element.

Advanced easing

Now that you've seen how simple easing works, you might consider using more complex easing formulas for additional effects. For instance, you might want something to start slowly, build up speed, and then slow down as it approaches its target. Or you might want to ease something into position over a certain time period or number of frames.

Robert Penner has become famous for collecting a lot of formulas, cataloging them, and implementing them in ActionScript. You can find his easing formulas at `www.robertpenner.com`.

OK, let's move on to perhaps my most favorite subject in Flash: springing.

Springing

Maybe it's just me, but I've always found springing to be one of the most powerful and useful physics concepts in ActionScripted animation. It seems like you can do almost anything with a spring. Of course, it's just another technique that has its specific uses. I've just gotten so much mileage out of this one that I get a bit enthusiastic about it. So, let's look at what a spring is and how you can program it in Flash.

As I mentioned at the beginning of the chapter, a spring's acceleration is proportional to its distance from a target. Think about a real, physical spring, or better yet, a ball on the end of a rubber band. You attach the other end to something solid. As the ball is hanging there with no force applied, that's its target point. That's where it wants to be. Now pull it away a tiny bit and let it go. At that point, the ball's velocity is zero, but the rubber band applies force to it, pulling it back to the target. Now pull it away as far as you can and let it go. The rubber band applies a lot more force. The ball zooms right past its target and starts going the other way. Its velocity is very high. But when it gets a little bit past the target, the rubber band starts pulling it back a bit—changes its velocity. The ball keeps going, but the farther it goes, the more the band pulls back on it. Eventually, the velocity reaches zero, the direction reverses, and the whole thing starts over again. Finally, after bouncing back and forth a few times, it slows down and comes to a stop at—you guessed where—its target.

Now, let's start translating this into ActionScript so you can use it. To keep things simple, let's start off with one dimension.

Springing in one dimension

Let's drag our good friend, the red ball movie clip, back into active service. You'll stick it over on the left hand side of the screen and have it spring to the middle. As with easing, you'll need a variable to hold the proportionate value of the spring. You can think of this as the proportion of the distance that will be added to the velocity. A high spring value will make a very stiff spring. Something lower will look more like a loose rubber band. You'll start off with 0.1. Here's what you have so far:

```
spring = 0.1;
ball._x = 0;
targetX = Stage.width / 2;
```

Again, don't worry about where to put this just yet. Just make sure you know what these variables and statements are about.

Then find the distance to the target.

```
dist = targetX - ball._x;
```

Now, compute some acceleration. The acceleration will be proportional to that distance. In fact, it will be the distance multiplied by the spring value.

```
ax = dist * spring;
```

Once you have a value for acceleration, you should be back on familiar ground. Add the acceleration to the velocity and add the velocity to the position, right?

```
vx += ax;
ball._x += vx;
```

Before you write any code, let's simulate it with some sample numbers. Let's say the x position is 0, vx is 0, the target x is 100, and the spring variable is 0.1. Here is how it might progress:

1. Multiply distance (100) by spring, and you get 10. Add that to vx, which then becomes 10. Add velocity to position, making the x position 10.
2. Next round, distance is 90. Acceleration is 90 times 0.1, or 9 this time. This gets added to vx, which becomes 19. The x position becomes 29.

3. Next round, distance is 71, acceleration is 7.1, added to vx makes it 26.1. The x position becomes 55.1.

4. Next round, distance is 44.9, acceleration is 4.49, and vx becomes 30.59. The x position is then 85.69.

The thing to note is that the acceleration on each frame becomes less and less as the object approaches its target, but the velocity continues to build. It's not building as rapidly as it was on previous frames, but it's still moving faster and faster.

After a couple more rounds, the object goes right past the target to an x position of around 117. The distance is now –17. A fraction of this gets added to the velocity, slowing the object down a bit.

Now that you understand how springing works, let's make a real file. As usual, place a ball movie clip on the stage, and then add the following code on frame 1 (ch08_05.fla):

```
var spring:Number = 0.1;
ball._x = 0;
ball._y = Stage.height / 2;
var targetX:Number = Stage.width / 2;
var vx:Number = 0;
onEnterFrame = function () {
      var ax:Number = (targetX - ball._x) * spring;
      vx += ax;
      ball._x += vx;
};
```

Test this, and you'll see you definitely have something spring-like going on there. The only problem is that it kind of goes on forever. Earlier, when I described a spring, I said that "it slows down and comes to a stop." As is though, the ball builds up the same velocity on each leg of its swing, so it keeps bouncing back and forth at the same speed. You need something to reduce its velocity and slow it down. Hmmm . . . sound familiar? That's right, you need to apply some friction. Easy enough—just make a friction variable, with a value like 0.95 for starters. Then multiply vx by friction somewhere in the enterFrame handler. Here's the corrected code (ch08_06.fla):

```
var spring:Number = 0.1;
var friction:Number = 0.95;
ball._x = 0;
ball._y = Stage.height / 2;
var targetX:Number = Stage.width / 2;
var vx:Number = 0;
onEnterFrame = function () {
      var ax:Number = (targetX - ball._x) * spring;
      vx += ax;
      vx *= friction;
      ball._x += vx;
};
```

At this point, you have a full-fledged, albeit one-dimensional, spring. Definitely play with this one a lot. See what different values for spring and friction do and how they interact. Check out how a different starting position or target position affects the action of the system, the speed of the ball, and the rate at which it slows down and comes to a stop. Knowing this one file well will take you a long way. When you've got it down cold, you're ready to move on to a two-dimensional spring.

Springing in two dimensions

If you are thinking that a two-dimensional spring is as simple as adding a second target, velocity, and acceleration, I have news for you: You're right. So, without further ado, here is a two-dimensional spring (ch08_07.fla):

```
var spring:Number = 0.1;
var friction:Number = 0.9;
ball._x = 0;
ball._y = 0;
var targetX:Number = Stage.width / 2;
var targetY:Number = Stage.height / 2;
var vx:Number = 0;
var vy:Number = 0;
onEnterFrame = function () {
      var ax:Number = (targetX - ball._x) * spring;
      var ay:Number = (targetY - ball._y) * spring;
      vx += ax;
      vy += ay;
      vx *= friction;
      vy *= friction;
      ball._x += vx;
      ball._y += vy;
};
```

As you can see, the only difference is adding in all the y-axis stuff. The problem is, it still seems rather one-dimensional. Yes, the ball is now moving on the x and y axes, but it's just going in a straight line. That's because its velocity starts out as zero, and the only force acting on it is the pull towards the target, so it goes in a straight line towards its target.

To make things a little more interesting, initialize vx to something other than 0. Try something nice and big like 50. Now, you have something that looks a little more loose and fluid. But you're only getting started. It gets a lot cooler.

Springing to a moving target

You probably won't be surprised to hear that springing doesn't require the target to be the same on each frame. When I covered easing, I gave you a quick and easy example of the ball following the mouse. It's pretty easy to adapt that example to make the ball spring to the mouse. Instead of the targetX and targetY you've been using, use the mouse coordinates. In springing, as with easing, the distance to the target is always calculated newly on each frame. Acceleration is based on that, and that acceleration is added to the velocity.

The effect is so cool, I feel like I should be writing on and on about it. But the fact is, there's really not much more to say on the subject, and the code isn't all that different. In the preceding example, simply change these lines:

```
var ax:Number = (targetX - ball._x) * spring;
var ay:Number = (targetY - ball._y) * spring;
```

to read like this:

```
var ax:Number = (_xmouse - ball._x) * spring;
var ay:Number = (_ymouse - ball._y) * spring;
```

You can also remove the lines that declare the targetX and targetY variables, though they are not going to hurt anything if you leave them in. The updated file is available as ch08_08.fla.

This is another good point to stop and play. Get a really good feeling for how all these variables work, and try out many variations. Break it. Find out what breaks it. Have fun with it!

So where's the spring?

At this point, you have a very realistic looking ball on the end of a rubber band. But it seems to be an invisible rubber band. Well, you can remedy that pretty easily with a few lines of drawing API code!

Since you have a fairly simple file without much else going on, you can safely apply your drawing code directly to the stage. In a more complex application, you might want to create an empty movie clip and use that as a kind of drawing layer.

The strategy is simple. In each frame, after the ball is in position, you call clear() to erase any previous lines. Then you reset the lineStyle and draw a line from the ball to the mouse. You just need the following code in the enterFrame handler, immediately after you set the ball's position (you'll see it in the full code shortly):

```
clear();
lineStyle(1, 0, 100);
moveTo(ball._x, ball._y);
lineTo(_xmouse, _ymouse);
```

Well, this is fun! What else can you do? How about adding some gravity so the ball looks like it's actually hanging off the end of the mouse? That's easy. Just add a gravity variable and add that to the vy for each frame. You know the drill by now. The following code incorporates the line drawing and gravity additions (ch08_09.fla):

```
var spring:Number = 0.1;
var friction:Number = 0.9;
var gravity:Number = 5;
ball._x = 0;
ball._y = 0;
var vx:Number = 0;
var vy:Number = 0;
onEnterFrame = function () {
```

```
        var ax:Number = (_xmouse - ball._x) * spring;
        var ay:Number = (_ymouse - ball._y) * spring;
        vx += ax;
        vy += ay;
        vy += gravity;
        vx *= friction;
        vy *= friction;
        ball._x += vx;
        ball._y += vy;
        clear();
        lineStyle(1, 0, 100);
        moveTo(ball._x, ball._y);
        lineTo(_xmouse, _ymouse);
};
```

When you test this version, you should see something like Figure 8-2.

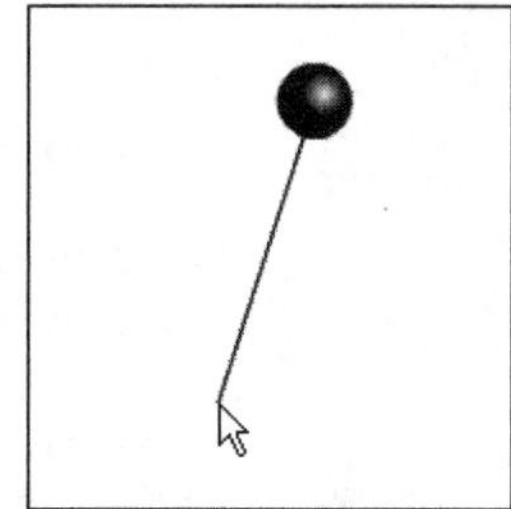

Figure 8-2. Springing from the mouse, with a visible spring

Notice how you needed to increase the gravity variable to 5 in order to get the ball to actually hang down. Much less than that, and the force of the spring overcomes the force of gravity and you don't see the effect.

Now, here's another point where I've just butchered real-world physics. Of course, you can't go around "increasing gravity" on objects! Gravity is a constant, based on the size and mass of the planet you happen to be on. What you can do is increase the mass of the object, so that gravity has more of an effect on it. So, technically I should keep gravity at something like 0.5, and then create a mass property and make it something like 10. Then I could multiply mass by gravity and come up with 5 again. Or I could change the name of the gravity variable to something like forceThatGravityIsExertingOnThisObjectBasedOnItsMass. But as long as you know that's what I mean, I'll save the space and shorten it to gravity.

Again, experiment with this one. Try decreasing the gravity and spring values. Try changing the friction value. You'll see you can have a nearly endless number of combinations, allowing you to create all kinds of systems.

Chaining springs

Moving right along, let's chain a few springs together. In the easing section, I discussed mouse trailers briefly, where one object eases to the mouse, another object eases to that object, and so on. I didn't give you an example because it's an old, and somewhat cheesy, effect. But, when you apply the same concept using springing instead, well, that's just different.

Here's the plan: Start off with three balls on stage, named ball0, ball1, and ball2. The first one, ball0, will behave pretty much like the single ball did in the previous example. Then ball1 will spring to ball0, and ball2 will spring to ball1. All will have gravity, so they should kind of hang down in a chain. The code isn't really anything you haven't seen before, just a little more complex. Here it is, assuming that the three balls are already on stage (ch08_10.fla):

```
var spring:Number = 0.1;
var friction:Number = 0.8;
var gravity:Number = 5;
ball0.vx = 0;
ball0.vy = 0;
ball1.vx = 0;
ball1.vy = 0;
ball2.vx = 0;
ball2.vy = 0;
onEnterFrame = function () {
	ball0.vx += (_xmouse - ball0._x) * spring;
	ball0.vy += (_ymouse - ball0._y) * spring;

	ball1.vx += (ball0._x - ball1._x) * spring;
	ball1.vy += (ball0._y - ball1._y) * spring;

	ball2.vx += (ball1._x - ball2._x) * spring;
	ball2.vy += (ball1._y - ball2._y) * spring;

	clear();
	lineStyle(1, 0, 100);
	moveTo(_xmouse, _ymouse);

	for(var i:Number=0;i<3;i++)
	{
		var ball:MovieClip = this["ball" + i];
		ball.vy += gravity;
		ball.vx *= friction;
		ball.vy *= friction;
		ball._x += ball.vx;
		ball._y += ball.vy;
		lineTo(ball._x, ball._y);
	}
};
```

Notice that you now assign each ball its own vx and vy and initialize them to 0. Then in the onEnterFrame function, you perform all the springing. Then you set up a line style and move the drawing cursor to the mouse position. Then you loop through the three balls, getting a reference to each one using array notation (this["ball" + i]), and apply basic motion code to them. At the end of the function, you draw a line to each successive ball, creating the rubber band holding them all together.

Actually, this code could be a lot more concise. I left a lot of stuff out of for loops that could have gone into them, such as the spring code itself. I did this just to make it very clear what the code is doing. But if you want to extend this to add a chain of a dozen balls or more—something like

Figure 8-3—you'll probably want to put that in a loop as well, rather than having several dozen extra lines of code. Here's an example of one way of doing that (ch08_11.fla):

```
var spring:Number = 0.1;
var friction:Number = 0.8;
var gravity:Number = 5;
var ballCount:Number = 5;
for(var i=0;i<ballCount;i++)
{
      var ball:MovieClip = attachMovie("ball", "ball" + i, i);
      ball.vx = 0;
      ball.vy = 0;
}
onEnterFrame = function () {
      clear();
      lineStyle(1, 0, 100);
      moveTo(_xmouse, _ymouse);

      ball0.vx += (_xmouse - ball0._x) * spring;
      ball0.vy += (_ymouse - ball0._y) * spring;

      for(var i=0;i<ballCount;i++)
      {
            var ballA:MovieClip = this["ball" + i];
            if(i > 0)
            {
                  var ballB:MovieClip = this["ball" + (i-1)];
                  ballA.vx += (ballB._x - ballA._x) * spring;
                  ballA.vy += (ballB._y - ballA._y) * spring;
            }
               ballA.vy += gravity;
               ballA.vx *= friction;
               ballA.vy *= friction;
               ballA._x += ballA.vx;
               ballA._y += ballA.vy;
               lineTo(ballA._x, ballA._y);
      }
};
```

This code will allow you to enter any number of objects just by changing the ballCount variable. But make sure the ball movie clip symbol is now set to export with the linkage name ball, as you are attaching the instances (this is the setup in the ch08_11.fla file).

Here, you still need to handle ball0's spring by itself, as that springs to the mouse. By checking if(i>0) in the for loop, you can ignore ball0 for the spring action there. You just find ballB, which is the previous ball in the chain, and ballA, which is the current one, and spring ballA to ballB. I also made gravity and friction less so the chain kind of sticks together a little better.

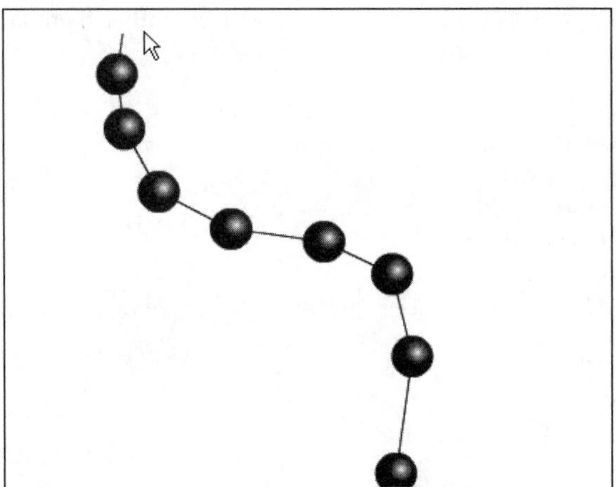

Figure 8-3. Chained springs

Springing to multiple targets

Back when I introduced the subjects of velocity and acceleration in Chapter 5, I talked about how you could have multiple forces acting on an object. Each force is an acceleration, and you just add them on to the velocity, one by one. Well, since a spring is nothing more than something exerting acceleration on an object, it's pretty simple to create multiple springs acting on a single object.

Here's the setup for demonstrating springing to multiple targets: You'll create three "handles," which will just be movie clips with simple drag-and-drop functionality, but they will also be targets for the ball to spring to. The ball will try to spring to all three of them at once and find its equilibrium somewhere between them. Or, to put it another way, each target will exert a certain amount of acceleration on the ball, and its motion will be the sum total of all of those forces.

For this example, place these handles on stage and name them handle0, handle1, and handle2. Then add the code (ch08_12.fla):

```
var spring:Number = 0.1;
var friction:Number = 0.9;
var vx:Number = 0;
var vy:Number = 0;

handle0.onPress = doDrag;
handle0.onRelease = handle0.onReleaseOutside = doDrop;
handle1.onPress = doDrag;
handle1.onRelease = handle1.onReleaseOutside = doDrop;
handle2.onPress = doDrag;
handle2.onRelease = handle2.onReleaseOutside = doDrop;

onEnterFrame = function () {
      vx += (handle0._x - ball._x) * spring;
      vy += (handle0._y - ball._y) * spring;
```

```
        vx += (handle1._x - ball._x) * spring;
        vy += (handle1._y - ball._y) * spring;

        vx += (handle2._x - ball._x) * spring;
        vy += (handle2._y - ball._y) * spring;

        vx *= friction;
        vy *= friction;
        ball._x += vx;
        ball._y += vy;

        clear();
        lineStyle(1, 0, 100);
        moveTo(ball._x, ball._y);
        lineTo(handle0._x, handle0._y);
        moveTo(ball._x, ball._y);
        lineTo(handle1._x, handle1._y);
        moveTo(ball._x, ball._y);
        lineTo(handle2._x, handle2._y);
};

function doDrag()
{
        this.startDrag();
}
function doDrop()
{
        this.stopDrag();
}
```

Figure 8-4 shows an example of the results of this code.

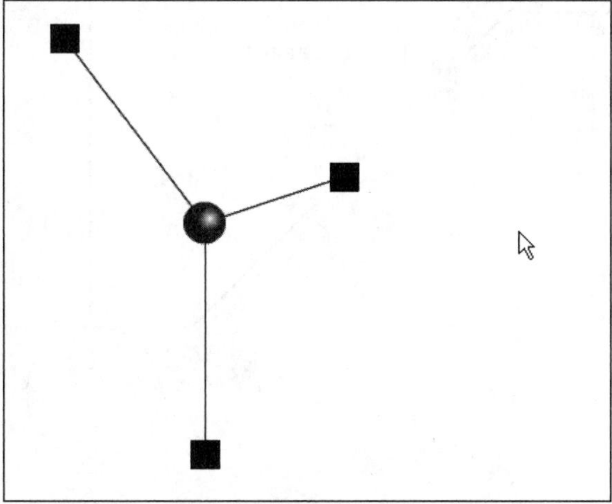

Figure 8-4. Multiple springs

Again, you could use a for loop several places in this code. I kept it unlooped just so it is easier to see exactly what you're doing. You should have enough knowledge under your belt now to be able to alter the code to use a for loop. If you do that, you can add as many handles as you want. Or try making the handles throwable—that should create some interesting effects.

By now, I'm sure you've already started taking many detours and creating a few things that I haven't even mentioned (or perhaps, thought of). If so, that's excellent! That's exactly my goal in writing this book.

Offsetting the target

If you took a real spring—an actual coil of bouncy metal—and attached one end of it to something solid and the other end to a ball or some other object, what would be the target? Would the target be the point where the spring is attached? No, not really. The ball would never be able to reach that point, because the spring itself would be in the way. Furthermore, once the spring had contracted to its normal length, it wouldn't be applying any more force on the ball. So, the target would actually be the position of the loose end of the spring in its unstretched state. But that point could vary as the spring pivots around the fixed point.

To find the actual target, you need to first find the angle between the object and the fixed point, and then move out from the fixed point at that angle—the length of the spring. In other words, if the length of the spring were 50, and the angle between the ball and fixed point were 45, you would move out 50 pixels from the fixed point, at an angle of 45 degrees, and that would be the ball's target to spring to. Figure 8-5 illustrates how this works.

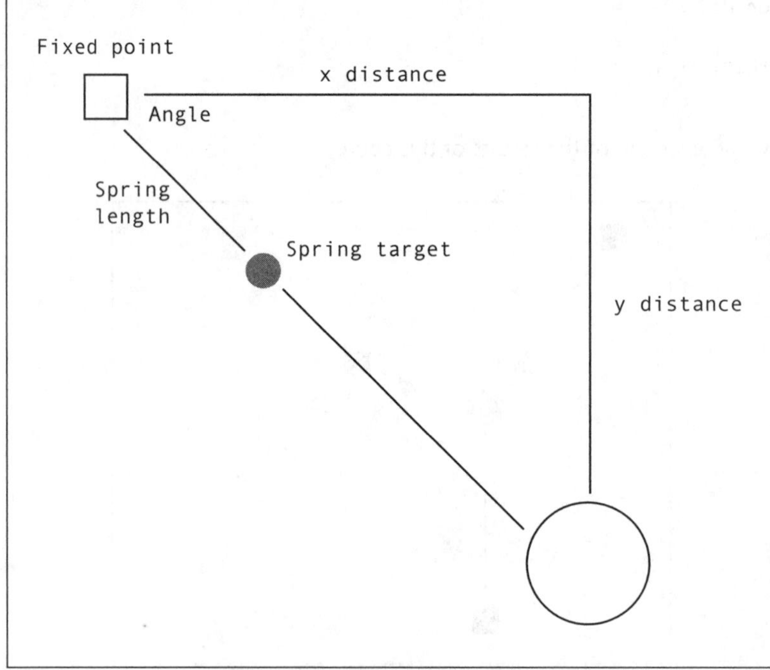

Figure 8-5. Offsetting a spring

The code to find the target in this case is roughly as follows:

```
var dx:Number = ball._x - fixedX;
var dy:Number = ball._y - fixedY;
var angle:Number = Math.atan2(dy, dx);
var targetX:Number = fixedX + Math.cos(angle) * springLength;
var targetY:Number = fixedY + Math.sin(angle) * springLength;
```

So, the result is that the object will spring *towards* the fixed point, but will come to rest some distance away from it. Also, note that although I'm calling it a "fixed point," this just means the point to which the spring is fixed. It doesn't mean that point cannot move. Perhaps it's better just to see it in action. You'll go back to using the mouse position, but this time, it will be the spring's fixed point. The spring's length will be 75. Here's the code (`ch08_13.fla`):

```
var spring:Number = 0.1;
var friction:Number = 0.9;
var springLength:Number = 75;
var vx:Number = 0;
var vy:Number = 0;

onEnterFrame = function () {
      var dx:Number = ball._x - _xmouse;
      var dy:Number = ball._y - _ymouse;
      var angle:Number = Math.atan2(dy, dx);
      var targetX:Number = _xmouse + Math.cos(angle) * springLength;
      var targetY:Number = _ymouse + Math.sin(angle) * springLength;
      vx += (targetX - ball._x) * spring;
      vy += (targetY - ball._y) * spring;

      vx *= friction;
      vy *= friction;
      ball._x += vx;
      ball._y += vy;

      clear();
      lineStyle(1, 0, 100);
      moveTo(ball._x, ball._y);
      lineTo(_xmouse, _ymouse);
};
```

Even though you can see what is happening here, it might not be too obvious exactly where you would find this technique particularly useful. Well, the next section will give you a specific example.

Attaching multiple objects with springs

I remember the exact moment I realized I could do this. It was something like, "OK, I know how to spring an object to a point. And I know that point does not have to be fixed. I can even have one object spring to another object. Well, how about if the other object sprang back to the first object? So these two objects were linked to each other by a spring. Move either one and the other one springs to it."

My initial impression was that it would probably cause some weird feedback loop that would crash Flash, or at least bring up some kind of warning message. But I bravely went ahead and tried it anyway. And to my complete amazement, it worked perfectly!

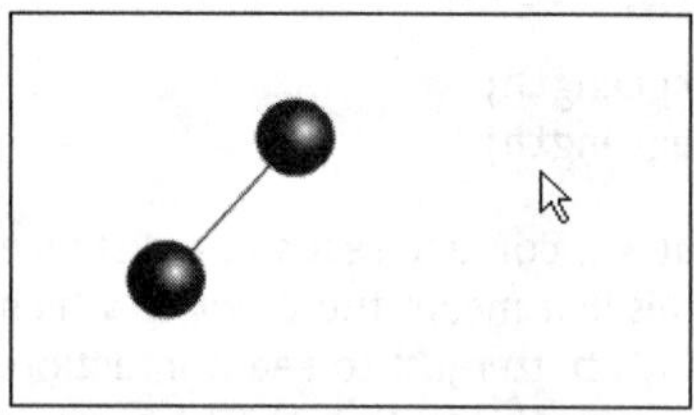

Figure 8-6. Two objects connected by a spring

I've already pretty much described the strategy, but to recap: Object A has object B as its target. It springs towards it. Object B in turn has object A as its target. Actually, this is the point where the offset has a great role. If each object had the other as a direct target, they would collapse in on each other and occupy the same point. By applying an offset, you keep them apart a bit, as shown in Figure 8-6.

For this next example, you'll need two ball movie clips on stage. I'll call them ball0 and ball1. ball0 springs to ball1 with an offset. And ball1 springs to ball0 with an offset. Rather than writing out all the offset, spring, and motion code twice, I put it all into a function called springTo. So, you can spring ball0 to ball1 by saying springTo(ball0, ball1), and then spring ball1 to ball0 by saying springTo(ball1, ball0). Here's the code (ch08_14.fla):

```
var spring:Number = 0.1;
var friction:Number = 0.9;
var springLength:Number = 75;
ball0.vx = 0;
ball0.vy = 0;
ball0.onPress = doDrag;
ball0.onRelease = ball0.onReleaseOutside = doDrop;
ball1.vx = 0;
ball1.vy = 0;
ball1.onPress = doDrag;
ball1.onRelease = ball1.onReleaseOutside = doDrop;

onEnterFrame = function () {
      springTo(ball0, ball1);
      springTo(ball1, ball0);
      clear();
      lineStyle(1, 0, 100);
      moveTo(ball0._x, ball0._y);
      lineTo(ball1._x, ball1._y);
}

function springTo(ballA, ballB)
{
      if(!ballA.dragging)
      {
            var dx:Number = ballA._x - ballB._x;
            var dy:Number = ballA._y - ballB._y;
            var angle:Number = Math.atan2(dy, dx);
            var targetX:Number = ballB._x +
```

```
                                    Math.cos(angle) * springLength;
            var targetY:Number = ballB._y +
                                    Math.sin(angle) * springLength;
            ballA.vx += (targetX - ballA._x) * spring;
            ballA.vy += (targetY - ballA._y) * spring;
            ballA.vx *= friction;
            ballA.vy *= friction;
            ballA._x += ballA.vx;
            ballA._y += ballA.vy;
        }
};

function doDrag()
{
        this.dragging = true;
        this.startDrag();
}
function doDrop()
{
        this.dragging = false;
        this.stopDrag();
}
```

For this file, the balls are placed on stage and are set up for drag-and-drop. The enterFrame handler function simply calls the springTo function twice:

```
springTo(ball0, ball1);
springTo(ball1, ball0);
```

The springTo function is where all the action happens and is identical in both versions. Everything in this function should be familiar to you. First, it makes sure the ball in question is not being dragged. It finds the distance and angle to the other ball, and calculates a target point based on that. It then performs basic spring mechanics on that target point. When the function is called again, with the parameters reversed, the balls swap roles, and the original target ball springs towards the other one. This may not be the most efficient code, but it demonstrates what is happening as clearly as possible.

You'll see that neither ball is attached to any fixed point or the mouse; they are both free-floating. Their only constraint is that they maintain a certain distance from each other. The great thing about this setup is that it is now very easy to incorporate additional objects. For example, if you create a third ball (ball2) and set it up like the others, you can add that into the mix like so:

```
springTo(ball0, ball1);
springTo(ball1, ball0);
springTo(ball1, ball2);
springTo(ball2, ball1);
springTo(ball2, ball0);
springTo(ball0, ball2);
```

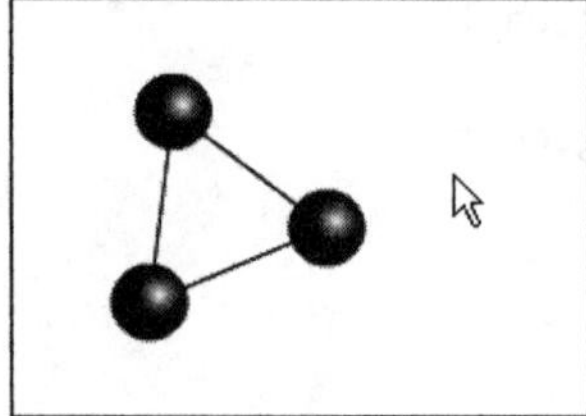

Figure 8-7. Three objects connected by a spring

This will create a triangle formation, as shown in Figure 8-7, which to me is pretty cool. I'm sure once you get the hang of this, you'll quickly move onto a square, and from there, all kinds of complex springy structures.

Important formulas in this chapter

Once again, it's time to review the important formulas presented in this chapter.

Simple easing, long form:

```
var dx:Number = targetX - movieclip._x;
var dy:Number = targetY - movieclip._y;
vx = dx * easing;
vy = dy * easing;
movieclip._x += vx;
movieclip._y += vy;
```

Simple easing, abbreviated form:

```
vx = (targetX - movieclip._x) * easing;
vy = (targetY - movieclip._y) * easing;
movieclip._x += vx;
movieclip._y += vy;
```

Simple easing, short form:

```
movieclip._x += (targetX - movieclip._x) * easing;
movieclip._y += (targetY - movieclip._y) * easing;
```

Simple spring, long form:

```
var ax:Number = (targetX - movieclip._x) * spring;
var ay:Number = (targetY - movieclip._y) * spring;
vx += ax;
vy += ay;
vx *= friction;
vy *= friction;
movieclip._x += vx;
movieclip._y += vy;
```

Simple spring, abbreviated form:

```
vx += (targetX - movieclip._x) * spring;
vy += (targetY - movieclip._y) * spring;
vx *= friction;
vy *= friction;
movieclip._x += vx;
movieclip._y += vy;
```

Simple spring, short form:

```
vx += (targetX - movieclip._x) * spring;
vy += (targetY - movieclip._y) * spring;
movieclip._x += (vx *= friction);
movieclip._y += (vy *= friction);
```

Offset spring:

```
var dx:Number = movieclip._x - fixedX;
var dy:Number = movieclip._y - fixedY;
var angle:Number = Math.atan2(dy, dx);
var targetX:Number = fixedX + Math.cos(angle) * springLength;
var targetY:Number = fixedX + Math.sin(angle) * springLength;
// spring to targetX, targetY as above
```

Summary

This chapter covered the two basic techniques of proportional motion: easing and springing. You've learned that easing is proportional motion and springing is proportional velocity, and you should have a very good understanding of how to apply both of these techniques.

I hope that you now understand why I get so excited about springs, and that you have begun to play with them and create some really fun and interesting effects yourself.

Now that you've learned all sorts of ways of moving things around, let's move on to the next chapter, where you'll find out what to do when they start hitting each other!

this._height += (this.targetHeight - this._height)/speed;
};Shape.targetHeight = shape._height;
var speed = 5;
this._width += (this.targetWidth - this._width)/speed;
this._height += (this.targetHeight - this._height)/speed;
};

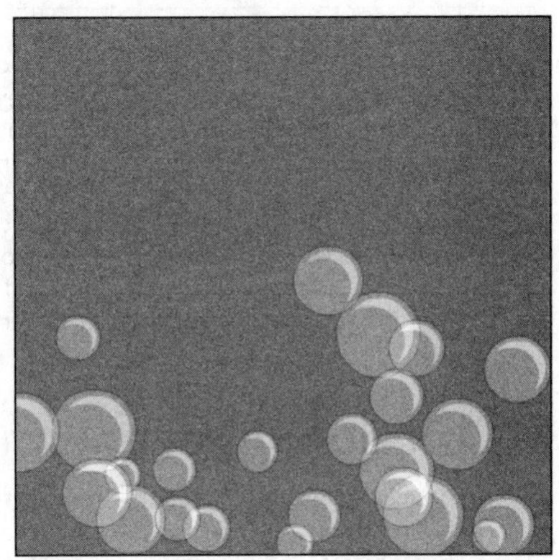

Chapter 9

COLLISION DETECTION

What we'll cover in this chapter:

- Collision detection methods
- Built-in hitTest
- Distance-based collision detection
- Multiple-object collision detection strategies
- Important formulas in this chapter

As you've progressed through the book to this point, you've seen how to make objects move and make them interact with the space they occupy. Now, you're going to delve into making these objects interact with each other. For the most part, this will involve determining when two objects have touched each other. This is a subject known as *collision detection* or *hit testing*.

In this chapter, I'll attempt to cover just about everything you need to know about detecting collisions. This includes hit testing between two movie clips, hit testing between a movie clip and a point, distance-based collision detection, and multiple-object collision testing strategies. First, let's see what options are available for collision detection.

Collision detection methods

Basically, collision detection, or hit testing, is a very simple concept. You want to know if two objects are occupying any part of the same space at the same time. Of course, you may have a lot more than two objects, and you may want to know if any of them are hitting any others. But when you break it down, you need to test each object one at a time against each other object. So, it always comes down to testing one object against another.

As the title of this section indicates, you have a couple of ways of doing collision detection:

- You can base the test on the actual pixels of each object (movie clip); that is, does the shape of this movie clip overlap the shape of that movie clip? And for that test, are you considering the actual visible pixels that make up the graphics of that movie clip, or are you going to base it on the rectangular bounds of that movie clip? So, this method has several options for how it is applied. This form of collision detection is built into Flash.
- You can base the test on distance. You get the distance between the two objects and you ask, "Is that close enough for them to be colliding?" This is more of a "roll your own" method of collision detection. You need to calculate the distance and decide when the objects are close enough.

Each method has its uses. I'll cover both in detail in this chapter, and you'll get a good chance to see how they are used.

One thing I won't go into in too much detail in this chapter is what to do when you *do* get a collision. How are two objects supposed to react when they bump into each other? I'll cover that subject in exhaustive detail in Chapter 11, when I talk about conservation of momentum.

Built-in hitTest

For quite a while now, Flash movie clips have had a built-in method called `hitTest`. You can use this method a couple of different ways: to test if one movie clip is hitting another or to test if a specific point is hitting a movie clip. Which technique it uses depends on what you pass it as parameters. If you pass `hitTest` a reference to another movie clip, it will perform a hit test against that movie clip. If you feed it two numbers, it will take those as x, y coordinates and test against the point they define. Let's start out with how to detect if two movie clips are colliding.

Hit testing two movie clips

Using hitTest to see if two movie clips are hitting each other is probably the simplest method of collision detection. It is also the easiest to program and the quickest to execute. You call the function as a method of one movie clip and pass it in a reference to another movie clip. It looks like this:

```
mc1.hitTest(mc2)
```

This would normally go within an if statement, like so:

```
if(mc1.hitTest(mc2))
{
   // react to collision
}
```

The method will return true if there is a collision, and the statements within the if block will execute.

However, as with all things, there is a trade-off. As collision detection methods get easier, they get less accurate. As they get more accurate, they become more complex and time-consuming. So, while this is the easiest method, it is also the least accurate.

Now, what do we mean by accuracy in hit testing? Either something is hitting or it's not, right? I wish it were that easy. It goes back to this question: Based on the positions of two movie clips, how do you determine if they are hitting?

Here's the simplest method of determining if a collision has occurred: You take the first object and draw a rectangle around it. The top edge of the rectangle goes on the topmost visible pixel of the object's graphics, the bottom edge goes on the lowest visible pixel, and the left and right edges are on their furthest visible pixels. Then you do the same for the object you're testing against. Then you check if these two rectangles are intersecting in any way. If so, you have a collision.

This rectangle around the object is known as a *bounding box*. Every movie clip has one. If you click on a movie clip on the stage, you'll see it as a blue outline, as shown in Figure 9-1.

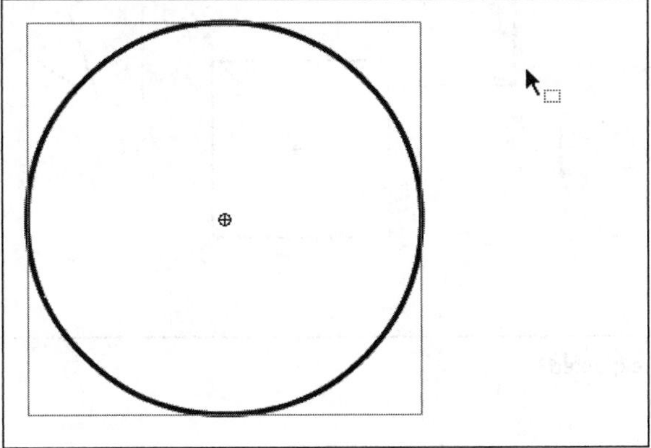

Figure 9-1. A bounding box

Of course, in the Flash player, nothing is actually drawing rectangles and checking them. It's all done mathematically, based on the movie clips' positions and sizes.

Now, why would this be inaccurate? One would think that if the bounding boxes intersected, the objects must be touching. Well, take a look at the pictures in Figure 9-2. Which pairs would you say are touching each other?

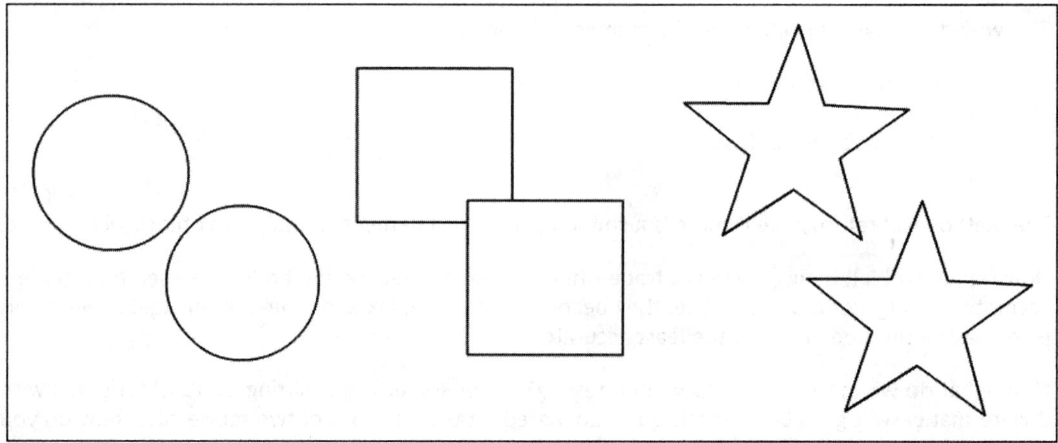

Figure 9-2. Which ones are touching?

Obviously, only the squares are actually hitting, right? Well, let's draw in the bounding boxes and see what Flash sees. Figure 9-3 shows the results.

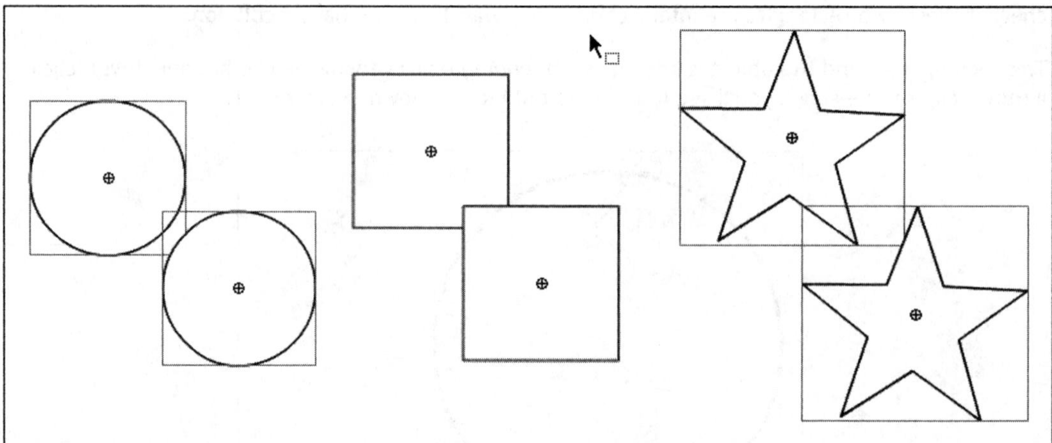

Figure 9-3. Not what you expected?

What do you know? All of these pairs are colliding as far as Flash is concerned. If you don't believe me, do this simple test. Create any two shapes and convert them to movie clips. Leave them on stage and give them the instance names mc1 and mc2. Add the following code to frame 1 (available in the file ch09_01.fla):

```
mc1.startDrag(true);
onEnterFrame = function()
{
	if(mc1.hitTest(mc2))
	{
		trace("hit");
	}
}
```

Test it with a variety of shapes. You'll find that anything but a roughly rectangular shape is going to give you a false positive on the corners. The more irregular the shape, the more inaccuracies you'll find. So, you should be very careful about using this method for anything other than rectangular shapes. For rectangles though, it works just wonderfully.

Let's try an example that demonstrates a simple hitTest with rectangles. The idea is that when you click on the stage with your mouse, a box is attached. So, you'll need a movie clip in the library with the linkage name of box. This should contain a square graphic, with the registration point centered. When the box is placed, it falls down until it hits the bottom of the stage or collides with another box. If it hits another box, it positions itself so it is sitting right on top of it. Here's the code (ch09_02.fla):

```
var count:Number = 0;
var gravity:Number = 0.3;
onMouseDown = function()
{
	// create a box
	var box:MovieClip = attachMovie("Box", "box" + count, count);
	count++;
	// position it on the mouse position
	box._x = _xmouse;
	box._y = _ymouse;
	// randomly scale it
	box._xscale = box._yscale = Math.random() * 100 + 10;
	// set it up to fall
	box.vy = 0;
	box.onEnterFrame = drop;
}
function drop(Void):Void
{
	// general motion code
	this.vy += gravity;
	this._y += this.vy;
```

```
        // if it reached the bottom, stop it
        if(this._y > Stage.height - this._height / 2)
        {
            this._y = Stage.height - this.height / 2;
            delete this.onEnterFrame;
        }
        // loop through all the other boxes
        for(var i=0;i<count;i++)
        {
            var testBox:MovieClip = _root["box" + i];
            // make sure you are not testing it against itself
            if(this != testBox && this.hitTest(testBox))
            {
                // it hit; position it on top of the box it hit
                this._y = testBox._y -
                          testBox._height / 2 -
                          this._height / 2;
                delete this.onEnterFrame;
            }
        }
    }
```

The heart of this is the hitTest line, where you determine if the box has hit any other box, reposition it to be on top of the one it hit, and turn off the falling action. If you really want to see the inaccuracy of this method in action, change the box graphic to a circle or some other irregular shape, and see the objects hovering in mid air as they "hit" other objects.

You might notice that this example presents the possibility of potentially testing many objects against each other. I showed you a simple brute-force method for clarity in this case. In the "Multiple-object collision detection strategies" section later in this chapter, I'll show you a much more efficient method of doing the same thing.

Hit testing a movie clip and a point

The second version of hitTest works quite a bit differently, and even has a couple of options of its own. The truth be told, this method by itself is not usually very useful for testing for the collision between two movie clips. This method takes two numbers as arguments and uses them to define a point. It then returns true or false, based on whether or not that point is hitting the movie clip in question. In its most basic form, it might be used like this (where 100, 100 refers to the x and y locations of a point):

```
mc.hitTest(100, 100)
```

Again, you would use this within an if statement to designate some conditional code to run only if the hit test is true.

But once again, we come back to the question: What constitutes a hit? And, once again, we see our old friend the bounding box coming into play. Flash merely checks if the point provided is within the movie clip's bounding box.

Let's do a quick test to see that in action. Place a movie clip on stage with either a circle or some irregular-shaped graphic inside. Name the instance mc and put this code on frame 1 (ch09_03.fla):

```
function onEnterFrame():Void
{
	if(mc.hitTest(_xmouse, _ymouse))
	{
		trace("hit");
	}
}
```

This uses the x, y coordinates of the mouse position as the point the movie clip will test against. As you move the mouse close to the movie clip, you will see that it probably starts registering a hit before you actually hit the graphics of the clip.

So again, this method seems to be useful only for rectangle-shaped objects. But there is another option here, called shapeFlag.

Hit testing with shapeFlag

shapeFlag is the third and optional parameter to the hitTest method. It is a Boolean value, so it's true or false. Setting shapeFlag to true means that now your hit test will check against the visible graphics of movie clip, rather than just the bounding box. Note that shapeFlag is applicable only for testing a movie clip against a point. If you are testing two movie clips, you cannot use shapeFlag as an option.

Let's play with this one for a bit. It's as simple as adding in that one value. Just take the preceding example and add to it. Change your code so that the hitTest line reads like this:

```
if(mc.hitTest(_xmouse, _ymouse, true))
```

(If you want to explicitly say that you don't want to use shapeFlag, you could set the parameter to false, but this would be the same as if you left it off entirely.) Test this version with an irregular shape. You'll see that now you must actually touch the shape itself with the mouse in order to trigger a hit.

So, here you have a perfectly accurate hit test. Accurate, but perhaps not entirely useful for collision detection. The problem is that it tests only a single point, which makes it rather difficult to see if any part of a movie clip is touching any part of another. Your first impulse might be to do something like this:

```
mc1.hitTestPoint(mc2._x, mc2._y, true)
```

But in that case, all you're checking is whether or not the registration point of mc2 is within mc1. That's pretty limited. Any other part of the clip could be touching mc1. In fact, half of mc2 could be overlapping mc1. But as long as that registration point were outside, Flash would consider it as not colliding. In practice, hit testing against a point is best used for mouse interaction or for very small movie clips, where there might be only a pixel or two between the registration point and outer edges.

One way people have attempted to use this method for collision detection is to test several points along the perimeter of the object. For example, say you had a star-shaped movie clip. You could calculate where the five points of the star were, and do a hit test from another movie clip to each of those five points. But then if you had two stars, you would need to test each one against the other's five points. For a star, this would probably work pretty well. A more complex shape would obviously need a few more points. You can see this gets very complex and CPU-intensive pretty quickly. Just two stars, and you're up to ten times the number of hit tests you would use for the more simple method. Accuracy costs you.

> *I even saw an example once where someone had set up a motion path around the edge of a complex shape, and created a motion tween of an empty movie clip going around that path. On each frame, he stepped the tween through all of its frames, using* `gotoAndStop`. *Then he used the position of the tweened empty movie clip as a point for the hit test. While this wound up being pretty accurate, it seemed much more like a trick than something I'd consider doing in a real project.*

Summary of hitTest

So, how do you do collision detection between two irregularly shaped movie clips, so that if any part of one touches the other, you get a hit? Sadly, the answer is that this is not supported in movie clips with the `hitTest` methods.

To summarize, your basic options are as follows:

- For roughly rectangular clips, use `hitTest(mc)`.
- For very small movie clips, you can get away with `hitTest(x, y, true)` (note that `shapeFlag` is set to `true`).
- For very irregularly shaped movie clips, you either live with the inaccuracy or custom program some sort of solution, probably using `hitTest(x, y, true)`.

Of course, the chapter is far from done yet, and there are solutions beyond `MovieClip`'s `hitTest`. If you have circular or roughly circular objects, distance-based collision detection will probably be your best bet. Actually, you'd be surprised at how many shapes fall into the "roughly rectangular" or "roughly circular" categories.

Distance-based collision detection

In this section, you'll abandon the built-in `hitTest` family of methods and take collision detection into your own hands. This involves using the distance between two objects to determine if they have collided.

Taking it to the real world, if the center of your car is 100 feet from the center of my car, you know that the two cars are far enough apart that they couldn't possibly be touching. However, if both of our cars are 6 feet wide and 12 feet long, and the center of my car is 5 feet from the center of your car, you can be pretty certain there is some twisted metal involved, and some insurance papers to fill out. In other words, there is no way for the centers to be that close together without some parts of the car touching. That's the whole concept behind distance-based testing. You determine the minimum distance required to separate the two objects, calculate the current distance, and compare the two. If the current distance is less than the minimum, you know they are hitting.

Naturally, there is a catch. Where the simplest hitTest method worked perfectly with rectangles, but degraded with any departure from that shape, this method favors perfect circles. In fact, it works perfectly for perfect circles. So, if that's what you're dealing with, this is the way to go.

As you depart from a circular shape, you are going to see less accuracy. But rather than the problem of reporting things that aren't hitting as collisions, as you saw earlier with hitTest and the bounding box, you may have the opposite problem: Things that appear to be touching don't register a collision because their centers are still not close enough.

Simple distance-based collision detection

Let's start out with the ideal situation: a couple of perfectly round circles as movie clips. Also, the registration point should be in the exact center of the circle. And as before, you'll set up one of them to drag. You'll also perform your collision detection in an enterFrame handler. So, up to this point, it is pretty much identical to the first example in this chapter. But instead of using if(mc1.hitTest(mc2)) to check for a collision, you'll be using distance in the if statement. You should already know how to compute the distance between two objects. Remember the good old Pythagorean Theorem from back in Chapter 3. So, you start off with something like this:

```
var dx:Number = mc2._x - mc1._x;
var dy:Number = mc2._y - mc1._y;
var dist:Number = Math.sqrt(dx * dx + dy * dy);
```

OK, now you have the distance, but how do you know if that distance is small enough to consider that a collision has occurred? Well, take a look at the picture in Figure 9-4.

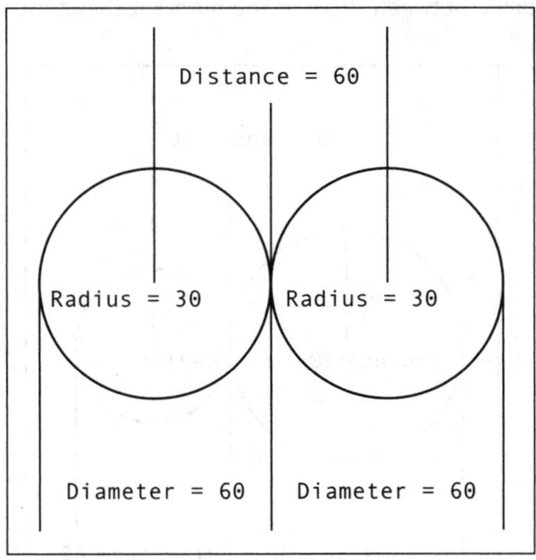

Figure 9-4. The distance of a collision

Here, you see the two circular movie clips in a position where they are just touching. Consider that each movie clip is 60 pixels across (only because the ones I made are that size). This would give it a radius of 30. Thus, at the exact moment they touch, they are exactly 60 pixels apart. Aha! There's the answer. For two circular movie clips of the same size, if the distance is less than their diameter, they are colliding. Here's the code to test that in the example (ch09_04.fla):

```
mc1.startDrag(true);
onEnterFrame = function()
{
        var dx:Number = mc2._x - mc1._x;
        var dy:Number = mc2._y - mc1._y;
        var dist:Number = Math.sqrt(dx * dx + dy * dy);
        if(dist < 60)
        {
                trace("hit");
        }
}
```

When you run this, you'll notice that it doesn't matter from which angle you approach the target movie clip. It doesn't register a hit until that exact point when the graphics actually overlap.

Now, I've already covered the fact that hard-coding numbers into code like that is generally a bad idea. You would need to change the code every time you had different-sized objects. Furthermore, what about the case where the two movie clips are not the same size? You need to abstract this concept into some kind of formula that will fit any situation.

Consider the picture shown in Figure 9-5. It shows two movie clips of different sizes, again, just touching. The one on the left is 60 pixels across, and the one on the right is 40 pixels. You can get this programmatically by inspecting their _width properties. Thus, the radius of one is 30, and the radius of the other is 20. So, the distance between them at the moment they touch is exactly 50.

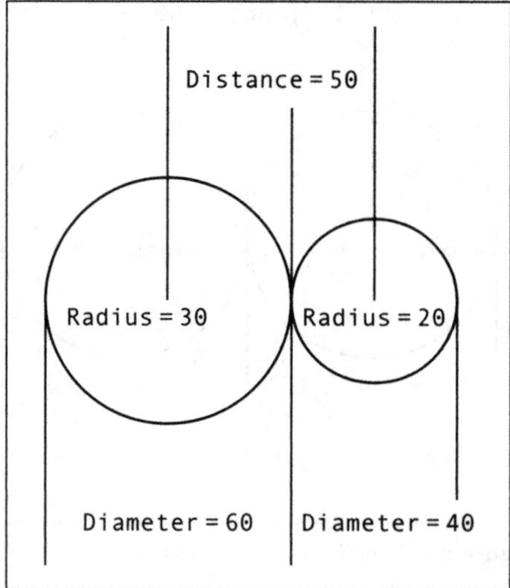

Figure 9-5. The distance of a collision of two different sized objects

A pattern begins to emerge. The magic distance is half the _width of one movie clip, plus half the _width of the other. Actually, it doesn't matter whether you use _width or _height. Since the objects are circular, these values should be the same anyway. You can now remove all hard-coded numbers from the code and get something like this (ch09_05.fla):

```
mc1.startDrag(true);
onEnterFrame = function()
{
	var dx:Number = mc2._x - mc1._x;
	var dy:Number = mc2._y - mc1._y;
	var dist:Number = Math.sqrt(dx * dx + dy * dy);
	if(dist < mc1._width / 2 + mc2._width / 2)
	{
		trace("hit");
	}
}
```

Go ahead and change the size of one of the movie clips and see that this code works, even if one circle is huge and one circle is tiny.

Collision-based springing

The problem with giving you a good working example of distance-based hit testing is that a complete program would involve a lot of issues related to things I haven't covered yet, such as the reaction of two objects when they hit and how to efficiently handle interactions between many objects. But I did manage to create something that demonstrates hit testing without too much stuff that you haven't already seen.

Here is the idea: Place one large circular movie clip, called centerBall, in the center of the stage. Then add in a bunch of smaller circular movie clips, giving them random sizes and velocities. These will move with basic motion code and bounce off the walls. On each frame, do a distance-based collision check between each moving ball and the center ball. If you get a collision, calculate an offset spring target based on the angle between the two balls and the minimum distance to avoid collision. OK, that might not be crystal clear. All it really means is that if a moving ball collides with the center ball, you make it spring back out again. You do this by setting a target just outside the center ball. The moving ball springs to that target. Then, once it reaches the target, it is no longer colliding, so the spring action ends, and it just moves with its regular motion code.

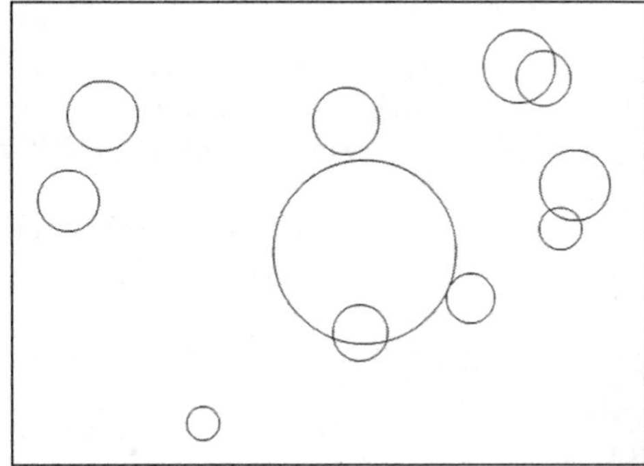

Figure 9-6. Collision-based springing

The result is kind of like bubbles bouncing off a large bubble, as shown in Figure 9-4. The little bubbles enter into the big one a bit, depending on how fast they are going, but then spring back out. (Ah, you see my obsession with springs has resurfaced.)

Here is the code (ch09_06.fla):

```
var left:Number = 0;
var right:Number = Stage.width;
var top:Number = 0;
var bottom:Number = Stage.height;
var centerBall:MovieClip;
var numBalls:Number = 10;
init();

function init()
{
      for (var i = 0; i<numBalls; i++)
      {
            var ball:MovieClip = attachMovie("Ball", "ball" + i, i);
            ball._x = Math.random() * Stage.width;
            ball._y = Math.random() * Stage.height;
            ball._width = ball._height = Math.random() * 40 + 20;
            ball.vx = Math.random() * 4 - 2;
            ball.vy = Math.random() * 4 - 2;
      }
      centerBall = attachMovie("Ball", "centerball", i);
      centerBall._width = centerBall._height = 150;
      centerBall._x = Stage.width / 2;
      centerBall._y = Stage.height / 2;
}
function onEnterFrame(Void):Void
{
      for (var i = 0; i<numBalls; i++)
{
            var ball:MovieClip = this["ball" + i];
            move(ball);
      }
}
function move(ball:MovieClip)
{
      ball._x += ball.vx;
      ball._y += ball.vy;
      if (ball._x + ball._width / 2 > right)
      {
            ball._x = right-ball._width / 2;
            ball.vx *= -1;
      }
      else if (ball._x - ball._width / 2 < left)
      {
            ball._x = left+ball._width / 2;
```

```
            ball.vx *= -1;
        }
        if (ball._y + ball._width / 2 > bottom)
        {
            ball._y = bottom-ball._width / 2;
            ball.vy *= -1;
        }
        else if (ball._y - ball._width / 2 < top)
        {
            ball._y = top+ball._width / 2;
            ball.vy *= -1;
        }
        var dx:Number = ball._x - centerBall._x;
        var dy:Number = ball._y - centerBall._y;
        var dist:Number = Math.sqrt(dx * dx + dy * dy);
        var minDist = ball._width/2+centerBall._width/2;
        if (dist < minDist)
        {
            var angle:Number = Math.atan2(dy, dx);
            var targetX:Number = centerBall._x +
                                 Math.cos(angle) * minDist;
            var targetY:Number = centerBall._y +
                                 Math.sin(angle) * minDist;
            ball.vx += (targetX-ball._x) * .1;
            ball.vy += (targetY-ball._y) * .1;
        }
    }
```

Yes, this is a whole lot of code, but you've already seen most of these techniques in earlier chapters. Let's walk through it quickly.

Starting with the `init` function, you loop through and create the smaller, moving balls. They are given a random size, position, and velocity. Then you create the `centerBall`.

The `enterFrame` handler just loops through and gets a reference to each ball. To separate functionality, I've moved the motion code to a function called `move`. This takes a reference to one of the balls and applies all the motion code to it. The first half of this function should be old hat to you. It's basic velocity code with bouncing. Then you find the distance from this ball to the `centerBall`, and compute the minimum distance to determine a collision. If there is a collision, you find the angle between the two, and use that plus the minimum distance to calculate a target x and y. This target will be right on the outer edge of the `centerBall`.

From there, you just apply basic spring code to spring to that point (as described in Chapter 8). Of course, once it reaches that point, it's no longer colliding and will fly off in whatever direction it's heading.

See how you can build up and layer simple techniques to wind up with some very complex motion?

Multiple-object collision detection strategies

When you have just a couple of objects moving around the screen, it's pretty simple to test them against each other. But when you get several objects, or even dozens, you need some kind of strategy for how to test them so that you don't miss any possible collisions. Furthermore, as you have more and more objects being tested, it becomes very important to perform your tests with some kind of efficiency in mind.

Basic multiple-object collision detection

With just two objects, only one collision is possible—A versus B. With three objects, you have three possibilities: A-B, B-C, and C-A. Four objects give you six collisions, and five objects give you ten collisions. When you get up to twenty objects, you need to take into account 190 separate collisions! That means that in every `enterFrame` handler, you need to run an `if` statement with a `hitTest` call or a distance calculation.

That's enough as it is. You certainly don't need to be adding any unnecessary hit testing to the game plan. But many people who dive into this type of calculation for the first time wind up doing not just a few extra hit tests, but exactly *twice* as many as necessary! For 20 objects, they do 380 `if` statements (20 clips each testing 19 others, or 20 × 19 = 380). So, you can see why you should have a solid understanding of this subject.

To see the problem, let's take a look at what needs to be done, and how it is often approached. Say you have six movie clips, named `mc0`, `mc1`, `mc2`, `mc3`, `mc4`, and `mc5`. You have them moving around nicely, bouncing or whatever, and you want to know when any one of the clips hits any other one. The normal thing to do, when you've thought it through a bit, is to make two nested `for` loops. The outer one loops through each of the six clips, gets a reference to each one in turn, and then loops through again, comparing it to each of the others. Here it is in a sort of pseudocode:

```
numClips = 6;
for(i=0; i<numClips; i++)
{
        clipA = this["mc" + i];
        for(j=0; j<numClips; j++)
        {
                clipB = this["mc" + j];
                if(clipA.hitTest(clipB))
                {
                        // do whatever
                }
        }
}
```

That's 36 hit tests for six clips. Seems reasonable, right? Well, this code has two huge problems.

First, take a look what happens the first time through it. The variables `i` and `j` will both equal 0. So `clipA` will hold a reference to `mc0`, as will `clipB`. Hey, you're testing a clip against itself! That's kind of dumb. Well, you could make sure that clipA != clipB before performing the hitTest, or you could even go simpler and just make sure i != j. Then you get something like this:

```
numClips = 6;
for(i=0; i<numClips; i++)
{
      clipA = this["mc" + i];
      for(j=0; j<numClips; j++)
      {
            clipB = this["mc" + j];
            if(i != j && clipA.hitTest(clipB))
            {
                  // do whatever
            }
      }
}
```

OK, so you've eliminated six hit tests with that. Now you're down to 30. But this is still way too many. Let's chart out the exact tests you're doing. You are comparing the following:

```
mc0   with   mc1, mc2, mc3, mc4, mc5
mc1   with   mc0, mc2, mc3, mc4, mc5
mc2   with   mc0, mc1, mc3, mc4, mc5
mc3   with   mc0, mc1, mc2, mc4, mc5
mc4   with   mc0, mc1, mc2, mc3, mc5
mc5   with   mc0, mc1, mc2, mc3, mc4
```

Look at the very first test: mc0 with mc1. Now look at the first test on the second row: mc1 with mc0. Well, that's the same thing, isn't it? If mc0 is not hitting mc1, then mc1 is surely not hitting mc0. Or if one is hitting the other, then you can be sure the other is hitting the first. It turns out that you have a whole lot of these double checks in there. If you remove all the duplicate checks, you get a table like this:

```
mc0   with   mc1, mc2, mc3, mc4, mc5
mc1   with   mc2, mc3, mc4, mc5
mc2   with   mc3, mc4, mc5
mc3   with   mc4, mc5
mc4   with   mc5
mc5   with   nothing!
```

You see that in the first round of tests, you're testing mc0 with every other movie clip. So no other movie clip needs to test against that one again. You drop mc0 off the list. Then mc1 tests against the remaining clips, and you drop it off the list. By the time you get to the last clip, mc5, every other clip has already tested itself for a collision with it. There's no need to test it against anything. The result is that you're down to 15 tests. So, you see why I said the initial solution usually ends up being double what is needed.

Now, how do you code this thing? Well, you still have two nested for loops. But now it looks like this:

```
numClips
for(i=0; i<numClips-1; i++)
{
	clipA = this["mc" + i];
	for(j=i+1; j<numClips; j++)
	{
		clipB = this["mc" + j];
		if(clipA.hitTest(clipB))
		{
			// do whatever
		}
	}
}
```

Notice that the first, outer for loop now goes to one less than the total number of clips. As you just saw in the final comparison chart, you don't need to test the last clip against anything, as it's already been thoroughly tested.

In the inner loop, you always start with one higher than the index of the outer loop. This is because you've already tested everything lower, and you don't want to test the same index, which, as you saw, would be testing a clip against itself. So, this even lets you get rid of that check. The result is just a few characters different from the original code, but gives you a 100% performance increase!

Also, even beyond its performance impact, in many cases, doing double hit testing might have unwanted results. If you're changing the velocity or some other value when you detect a collision, you may wind up changing it twice, resulting in who knows what kind of effect. Of course, the specifics would vary according to the actions you're taking, but in general, you want one collision to result in one action.

Multiple-object springing

Let's make another quick application to see this in action. Again, you'll go with the bubble-type reaction, but this time, all bubbles can bounce off of each other. This will require a ball-shaped movie clip in the library with the linkage ball. I even made mine look more like a bubble this time. Figure 9-7 illustrates the effect.

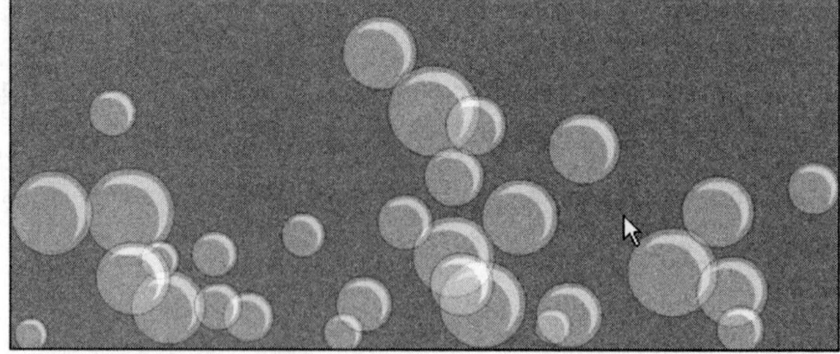

Figure 9-7. Multiple-object collision

Here's the code to put right on frame 1 (`ch09_07.fla`):

```
var left:Number = 0;
var right:Number = Stage.width;
var top:Number = 0;
var bottom:Number = Stage.height;
var numBalls:Number = 30;
var spring:Number = 0.05;
var gravity:Number = 0.3;
init();

function init()
{
      for (var i = 0; i<numBalls; i++)
      {
            var ball:MovieClip = attachMovie("ball", "ball" + i, i);
            ball._x = Math.random() * Stage.width;
            ball._y = Math.random() * Stage.height;
            ball._width = ball._height = Math.random() * 40 + 20;
            ball.vx = 0;
            ball.vy = 0;
      }
}
function onEnterFrame(Void):Void
{
      for(var i=0;i<numBalls-1;i++)
      {
            var ballA:MovieClip = this["ball" + i];
            for(var j=i+1;j<numBalls;j++)
            {
                  var ballB:MovieClip = this["ball" + j];
                  var dx:Number = ballB._x - ballA._x;
                  var dy:Number = ballB._y - ballA._y;
                  var dist:Number = Math.sqrt(dx*dx + dy*dy);
                  var minDist:Number = ballA._width / 2 +
                                       ballB._width / 2;
                  if(dist < minDist)
                  {
                        var angle:Number = Math.atan2(dy, dx);
                        var targetX:Number = ballA._x +
                                             Math.cos(angle) * minDist;
                        var targetY:Number = ballA._y +
                                             Math.sin(angle) * minDist;
                        var ax:Number = (targetX - ballB._x) *
                                        spring;
                        var ay:Number = (targetY - ballB._y) *
                                        spring;
```

```
                        ballA.vx -= ax;
                        ballA.vy -= ay;
                        ballB.vx += ax;
                        ballB.vy += ay;
                    }
                }
            }
            for (var i = 0; i<numBalls; i++)
            {
                var ball:MovieClip = this["ball" + i];
                move(ball);
            }
        }
        function move(ball:MovieClip)
        {
            ball.vy += gravity;
            ball._x += ball.vx;
            ball._y += ball.vy;
            if (ball._x + ball._width / 2 > right)
            {
                ball._x = right-ball._width / 2;
                ball.vx *= -.9;
            }
            else if (ball._x - ball._width / 2 < left)
            {
                ball._x = left+ball._width / 2;
                ball.vx *= -.9;
            }
            if (ball._y + ball._width / 2 > bottom)
            {
                ball._y = bottom-ball._width / 2;
                ball.vy *= -.9;
            }
            else if (ball._y - ball._width / 2 < top)
            {
                ball._y = top+ball._width / 2;
                ball.vy *= -.9;
            }
        }
```

Here, you are simply using the double-nested `for` loop to perform collision detection. In this case, the reaction might need some additional explanation. Here's the collision reaction code:

```
if(dist < minDist)
{
      var angle:Number = Math.atan2(dy, dx);
          var targetX:Number = ballA._x + Math.cos(angle) * minDist;
          var targetY:Number = ballA._y + Math.sin(angle) * minDist;
          var ax:Number = (targetX - ballB._x) * spring;
          var ay:Number = (targetY - ballB._y) * spring;
          ballA.vx -= ax;
          ballA.vy -= ay;
          ballB.vx += ax;
          ballB.vy += ay;
}
```

Remember that this occurs once a collision is found between ballA and ballB. Essentially, it starts out the same as the earlier example with the unmoving center ball. For now, let ballA take the place of that center ball. You find the angle between the two, and get a target x and y. This is the point that you would need to place ballB so that the two balls would not be touching. Based on that, you get the x and y acceleration that would cause ballB to spring to that point. These are ax and ay.

But then you do something a little tricky. In this case, not only does ballB need to spring away from ballA, but ballA must spring away from ballB. The acceleration would be the same force and exactly the opposite direction. So rather than calculate it twice, you just add ax and ay to ballB's velocity, and subtract them from ballA's velocity! You get the same result, and you just saved a bunch of calculation right there. You might be thinking that this doubles the final acceleration, as it's being applied twice. That's true. To compensate, you make the spring variable quite a bit lower than usual.

While we're on the subject of optimization tricks, I'd like to mention another one here. The preceding code calculates the angle using Math.atan2, and then uses Math.cos and Math.sin to find the target point:

```
var angle:Number = Math.atan2(dy, dx);
var targetX:Number = ballA._x + Math.cos(angle) * minDist;
var targetY:Number = ballA._y + Math.sin(angle) * minDist;
```

But remember that sine is opposite over hypotenuse, and cosine is adjacent over hypotenuse. And realize that the opposite side of the angle is dy, the adjacent side is dx, and the hypotenuse is dist. Thus, you could actually shorten these three lines to just these two:

```
var targetX:Number = ballA._x + dx / dist * minDist;
var targetY:Number = ballA._y + dy / dist * minDist;
```

Voila! You've just wiped out three calls to trig functions and replaced them with two simple divisions.

Before you move on, take some time to play with the springing bubbles example. You can adjust many variables. Try changing the spring, gravity, number, and size of the balls. You might want to try adding some friction or some mouse interaction.

Important formulas in this chapter

It's time to review the two important formulas presented in this chapter.

Distance-based collision detection:

```
// starting with mcA and mcB
var dx:Number = mcB._x - mcA._x;
var dy:Number = mcB._y - mcA._y;
var dist:Number = Math.sqrt(dx*dx+dy*dy);
if(dist < mcA._width / 2 + mcB._width / 2)
{
        // handle collision
}
```

Multiple-object collision detection:

```
var numObjects:Number = 10; // for example
for(var i:Number = 0; i<numObjects-1; i++)
{
        // evaluate reference using variable i. For example:
        var objectA = this["object" + i];
        for(var j:Number = i+1; j<numObjects;j++)
        {
                // evaluate reference using j. For example:
                var objectB = this["object" + j];

                // perform collision detection
                // between objectA and objectB
        }
}
```

Summary

This chapter covered just about everything you need to know about collision detection, including the built-in hitTest function in all its variations, distance-based collision checking, and how to efficiently track collisions among many objects. You should know the pluses and minuses of each method, and situations where each works well or does not perform satisfactorily. You'll be using all of this material as you move forward in the book, and no doubt, you'll be using it extensively in your own projects.

In the next chapter, you'll find out what to do to create a realistic reaction to the collisions you have now detected.

this._height += (this.targetHeight - this._height)/speed;
};shape.targetHeight = shape._height;
shape.onEnterFrame = function() {
var speed = 5;
this._width += (this.targetWidth - this._width)/speed;
this._height += (this.targetHeight - this._height)/speed;

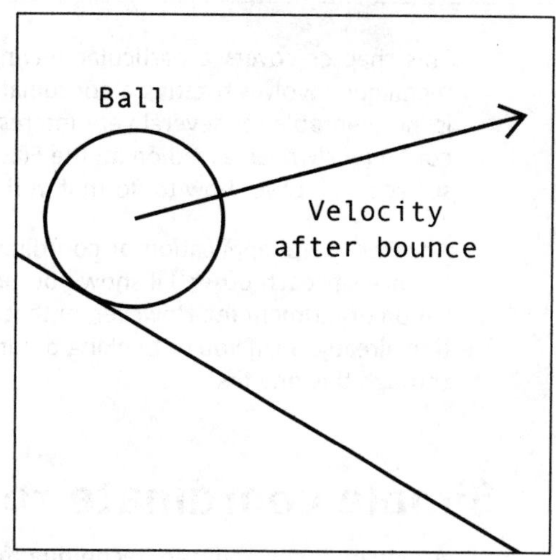

Chapter 10

COORDINATE ROTATION AND BOUNCING OFF ANGLES

What we'll cover in this chapter:

- Simple coordinate rotation
- Advanced coordinate rotation
- Bouncing off an angle
- Important formulas in this chapter

This chapter covers a particular technique known as *coordinate rotation*. As its name implies, this technique involves rotating a coordinate around a point. While useful all by itself, coordinate rotation is indispensable for several very interesting effects. One of those is the answer to a question that has continuously been asked on all the Flash boards for years: "How do I bounce something off an angled surface?" I'll cover how to do that in this chapter.

Another useful application of coordinate rotation is for calculating the reactions of two objects that bounce off each other. I'll show you how to do that in the next chapter, where I discuss the conservation of momentum. However, in that chapter, I'm going to assume you know about coordinate rotation already. So, if you're thinking of jumping ahead to that chapter, I recommend you sit tight and get through this one first.

Simple coordinate rotation

Although I covered the technique for simple coordinate rotation in Chapter 3's discussion of trigonometry, let's do a quick recap. You have a center point, an object, a radius, and an angle. You just keep increasing or decreasing the angle, and use basic trigonometry to place the object around the center point. You can set a variable such as vr (velocity of rotation) to control how much the angle is increased or decreased. And don't forget that the angle is in radians.

The structure of the code would be something like this pseudocode:

```
vr = 0.1;
angle = 0;
radius = 100;
centerX = 250;
centerY = 200;

// and in an enterFrame handler:
   mc._x = centerX + cos(angle) * radius;
   mc._y = centerY + sin(angle) * radius;
   angle += vr;
```

You're just using basic trig to set the _x and _y properties of the object based on the angle and the radius, and changing the angle on each frame. Let's make a couple of sample Flash movies to demonstrate this in action.

This first example just has a movie clip on stage named ball and the following code on the main timeline (`ch10_01.fla`):

```
var angle:Number = 0;
var radius:Number = 150;
var vr:Number = .05;
function onEnterFrame():Void
{
      ball._x = Stage.width / 2 + Math.cos(angle) * radius;
      ball._y = Stage.height / 2 + Math.sin(angle) * radius;
      angle += vr;
}
```

As you can see, this has nothing brand new to you in terms of code. Go ahead and try it out. This approach works great when you know or specify the angle and radius from a center point.

But what if all you have is the position of the object and the center point. Well, naturally it isn't too hard to calculate the current angle and radius based on the x and y positions. Once you have them, you can carry on as before. It looks something like this (`ch10_02.fla`):

```
var dx:Number = ball._x - Stage.width / 2;
var dy:Number = ball._y - Stage.height / 2;
var angle:Number = Math.atan2(dy, dx);
var radius:Number = Math.sqrt(dx * dx + dy * dy);
var vr:Number = .05;
function onEnterFrame():Void
{
        ball._x = Stage.width / 2 + Math.cos(angle) * radius;
        ball._y = Stage.height / 2 + Math.sin(angle) * radius;
        angle += vr;
}
```

Try moving the ball to different spots on the stage before testing. You'll see that its starting position and distance from the center are both based on where you first place the ball.

This method of rotation based on coordinates might be fine for a single object, especially in a situation where you are just determining the angle and radius the one time. But in a more dynamic example, you could have many objects to rotate, and their relative positions to the center rotation point could be changing. So, for each object, you would need to compute its distance, angle, and radius, then add the `vr` to the angle, and calculate the new x, y position, on each frame. That's not too elegant, and probably not too efficient. Fortunately, there is a better way.

Advanced coordinate rotation

If you are going to be rotating objects around a point, and you are starting with just their positions, I've got a formula for you. The formula just needs the x, y position of the object in relation to the center point and the angle to rotate by. It returns the new x, y position of the object, relative to the center. Here's the basic formula:

```
x1 = cos(angle) * x - sin(angle) * y;
y1 = cos(angle) * y + sin(angle) * x;
```

If that just seems like a bunch of letters and symbols that happen to have a somewhat pleasing symmetry in the way they are arranged, don't feel bad. That's the way I felt about it when I first started. Actually, even though I use this formula quite often, I still feel pretty much that way about it. I have sat down a couple of times and figured out with diagrams exactly how the sines and cosines, x's and y's, pluses and minuses, and so forth work in terms of triangles and coordinates. And when I did that, it made complete sense to me. And 30 minutes later, it looked like a bunch of symbols with nice symmetry.

So, although I usually strive to give you a complete conceptual understanding of the techniques I'm presenting, I'd be a hypocrite if I did that here. Because, personally, I've just memorized the formula so that I can type it in my sleep. The good news is that if you know more trigonometry than I do, you'll probably be able to get a deeper understanding of this technique, but even if you aren't a rocket scientist, you can memorize the formula and still get great results.

So, let's just look at what this formula is saying, which I've illustrated in Figure 10-1. The x and the y are, of course, the coordinates of the thing you are rotating. More specifically, they are the coordinates of that object in relation to the center point it is rotating around. Thus, if your center point is at 200, 100, and your object is at 300, 150, x will be 300 – 200, or 100, and y will be 150 – 100, or 50.

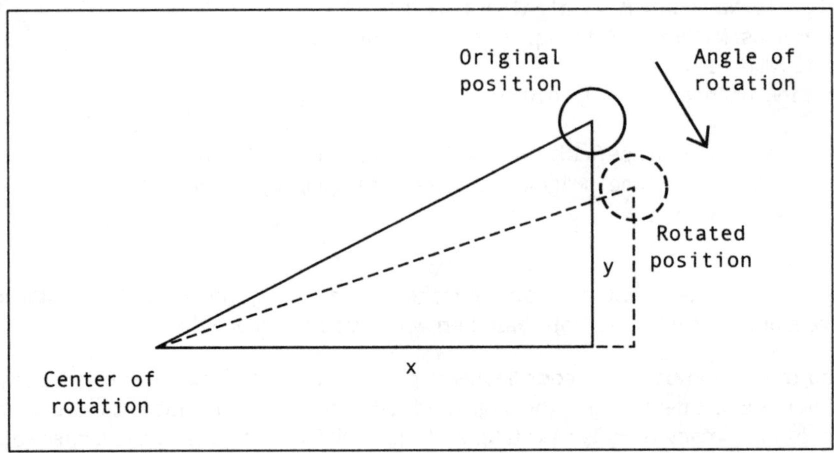

Figure 10-1. Rotating coordinates

The angle is how much you are rotating the object this particular time. It's not the current angle, or the resulting angle, but the difference between the two. In other words, talking in degrees for just a moment, if the object is at a 45-degree angle from the center point, and the angle here is 5 degrees, you will be rotating it another 5 degrees to put it at 50. Remember though, in this technique, you probably don't know, and don't really care about, the initial and final angles. You're just interested in how much rotation is occurring. Also, I'm sure I don't have to mention it, but as usual, this angle will be in radians, not degrees.

OK, so let's see it in action.

Rotating a single object

To begin, just change the code on the first frame of the previous example to read like this (`ch10_03.fla`):

```
var vr:Number = .05;
var cosine:Number = Math.cos(vr);
var sine:Number = Math.sin(vr);
function onEnterFrame():Void {
      var x:Number = ball._x - Stage.width / 2;
      var y:Number = ball._y - Stage.height / 2;
      var x1:Number = cosine * x - sine * y;
```

```
        var y1:Number = cosine * y + sine * x;
        ball._x = Stage.width / 2 + x1;
        ball._y = Stage.height / 2 + y1;
}
```

Here, you are setting the vr to the same value of .05 you used before. Then you're calculating the sine and cosine of that angle. Since it isn't going to change in this simple example, you can do it once outside the enterFrame handler, rather than inside, where it would need to be recalculated every frame. The x and y positions are calculated in relation to the point they will rotate around—the center of the stage. Then you apply the coordinate rotation formula as just described. This gives you x1 and y1, the new position of the ball. Again, this is in relation to the center point, so you need to add x1 and y1 to the center point to get the final position of the ball.

Try it out, and you'll see it should work exactly the same as the earlier version. Now, I'm sure you're thinking, if it works exactly the same, why bother going through this new formula, which actually looks more complex? Well, in a very simple situation like this, you'd probably be right. But let's look at some situations where this setup actually simplifies things. First, consider rotating multiple objects.

Rotating multiple objects

Suppose there are many objects to rotate. The for loop would look something like this:

```
for(var i:Number = 0;i<mcCount;i++)
{
        var mc:MovieClip = this["mc" + i];
        var dx:Number = mc._x - centerX;
        var dy:Number = mc._y - centerY;
        var angle:Number = Math.atan2(dy, dx);
        var dist:Number = Math.sqrt(dx * dx + dy * dy);
        angle += vr;
        mc._x = centerX + Math.cos(angle) * dist;
        mc._y = centerY + Math.sin(angle) * dist;
}
```

Whereas, the advanced coordinate rotation method would look like this:

```
var cosine:Number = Math.cos(vr);
var sine:Number = Math.sin(vr);
for(var i:Number = 0;i<mcCount;i++)
{
        var mc:MovieClip = this["mc" + i];
        var x:Number = mc._x - centerX;
        var y:Number = mc._y - centerY;
        var x1:Number = cosine * x - sine * y;
        var y1:Number = cosine * y + sine * x;
        mc._x = centerX + x1;
        mc._y = centerY + y1;
}
```

Notice that the first version includes four calls to Math functions within the loop, meaning that all four are executed once for each object being rotated. The second version has just two calls to Math functions, both outside the loop, meaning they are executed only once, regardless how many objects there are. So, for example, if you have 30 movie clips, you're looking at 120 Math calls on each frame with the first version, as compared to two with the second version. You decide which is going to be more efficient.

In the previous example, you were able to remove the sine and cosine calculations right outside the enterFrame handler. This is because you were sticking with a fixed angle, so you could set it and forget it. In many cases, however, these angles of rotation may be changing, and you'll need to recalculate the sine and cosine each time it changes.

To demonstrate these latest couple of concepts, let's build a quick example where the mouse position is controlling the speed of rotation of multiple objects. If the mouse is in the center of the screen, no rotation happens. As it moves to the left, the objects move faster and faster in a counterclockwise direction. As it moves to the right, they rotate in a clockwise direction. This example will start out quite similar to the previous one, except you'll need four movie clip instances on stage, named ball0 through ball3. Here's the code for frame 1 (ch10_04.fla):

```
function onEnterFrame():Void {
        var angle:Number = (_xmouse - 270) * .001;
        var cosine:Number = Math.cos(angle);
        var sine:Number = Math.sin(angle);
        for(var i:Number = 0;i<4;i++)
        {
                var ball:MovieClip = this["ball" + i];
                var x:Number = ball._x - Stage.width / 2;
                var y:Number = ball._y - Stage.height / 2;
                var x1:Number = cosine * x - sine * y;
                var y1:Number = cosine * y + sine * x;
                ball._x = Stage.width / 2 + x1;
                ball._y = Stage.height / 2 + y1;
        }
}
```

You can see that the code here isn't all that complex. If you're up to it, try recoding it using the angle and radius method, and see if it looks better or worse and how it performs.

You'll revisit this formula when you get to the discussion of 3D in Chapter 15. In fact, you'll be using it twice within the same method, to rotate things around two axes and three dimensions. But don't let me scare you off yet. You have a lot to do before you get there.

Bouncing off an angle

I remember when I was first becoming addicted to Flash, math, and physics. I had figured out how to bounce things off a wall, floor, and ceiling. If a barrier was dead horizontal or vertical, I knew just what to do. But it didn't take too long for me to get bored. In real situations, things are not always horizontal or vertical. Sometimes, things are angled. And I couldn't figure out how to simulate this in Flash with the ease I could do bouncing off a flat surface. I went to the various online Flash forums and asked around. I wasn't the only one. I remember one board had three separate threads going with the exact title as this section: "Bouncing off an angle."

A few wise math gurus attempted answers. Something about the angle of reflection being equal to the angle of incidence. I remember it being a pretty straightforward formula that told you the angle at which a moving object would travel after hitting an angled surface. In and of itself, that was fine. But it solved only part of the problem. If you recall back to the discussion on bouncing off barriers, a few steps are involved:

1. Determine when you have passed a boundary.
2. Reset the object so it is resting directly on the boundary.
3. Reverse its velocity on the axis of the collision.

Knowing the final angle solved about half of step 3. But it didn't give me a way to discover when the collision with an angled surface had occurred, or where to position the object so it looked like it had stopped on the surface before bouncing. Nobody seemed to be able to answer all of those points. I tried everything I could think of. I drew enough diagrams to fill a warehouse and wrote enough test code to fill a hard drive. I was getting frustrated. It was so easy if the surfaces were flat. But when they were rotated, it was so complex. Perhaps you're starting to see where I'm going with this, and why I'm talking about this subject in this chapter.

At the time, Stuart Schoneveld of `www.illogicz.com` had an incredible physics engine online that handled such collisions smoothly and cleanly. I begged him for information on how he did it. Although he didn't show me any code, he gave me a general idea of what he did, in a sentence or two. It was one of those moments of revelation when the light comes shining through, and you feel like an idiot for not having seen it before.

What he told me was something like, "Bouncing off an angled surface? Just rotate the system so the surface is flat, do your bounce, and rotate it all back."

Wow! That was all I needed. You need to rotate the whole system to make your angle surface like a flat floor. This means rotating the surface, rotating the coordinates of the object in question, and rotating the object's velocity vector.

Now, rotating a velocity seems a bit complex, but think about it. You've been storing velocity in vx and vy variables. The vx and vy simply define a vector, which is angle and a magnitude, or length. If you know the angle, you can rotate it directly. But if you just know the vx and vy, you can apply the advanced coordinate rotation formula to it and get the same result, just as you did for the position of the ball.

Some diagrams should help you visualize it a little better than words ever could. In Figure 10-2, you see the angled surface, the ball, which has obviously just hit the surface, and the vector arrow representing the ball's direction and speed.

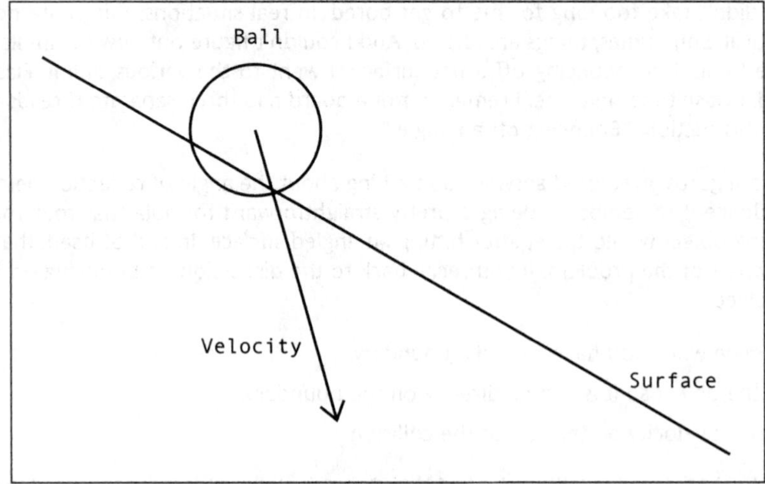

Figure 10-2. A ball hitting an angled surface

In Figure 10-3, you see that the whole thing has been rotated and the surface is now horizontal, just like the bottom barrier on the original bouncing example. Note that the velocity vector has been rotated right along with everything else.

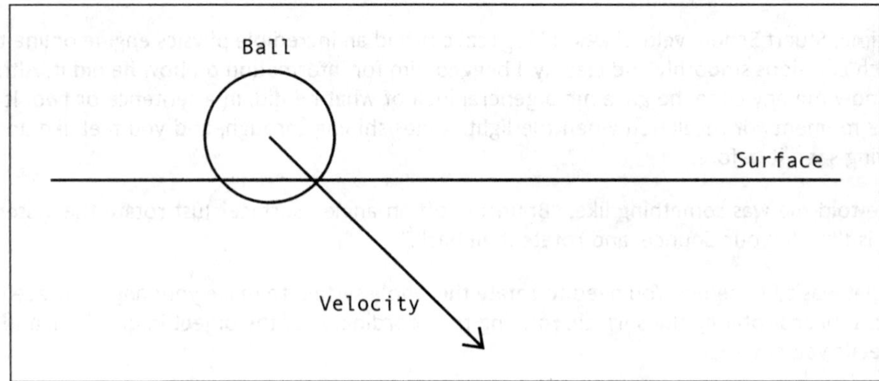

Figure 10-3. The same scene, rotated

The way the picture now looks, it's pretty simple to perform a bounce, right? Adjust the position, and change the y velocity, as in Figure 10-4.

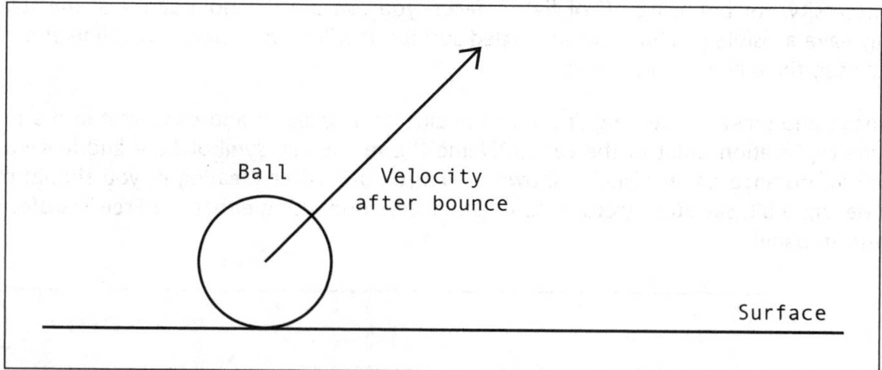

Figure 10-4. After the bounce

You now have a new position and velocity for the ball. Next, rotate everything back to the original angle, as shown in Figure 10-5.

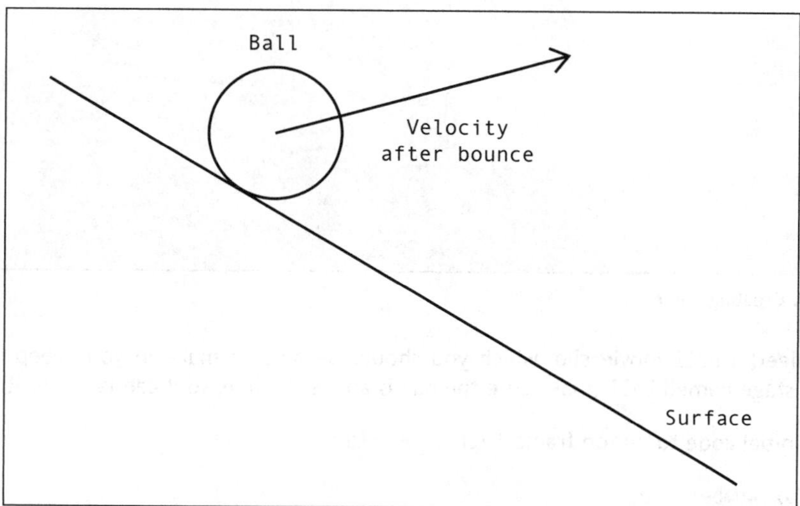

Figure 10-5. After rotating back

Voila! You've detected the collision, adjusted the position, and changed the velocity, all on an angled surface. Assuming that the pictures make sense to you, let's move on to some code and real graphics.

Performing the rotation

First, you need something to act as an angled surface. This is more for your eyes than for any mathematical necessity. For bouncing off of flat surfaces, you can use the boundaries of the stage, which inherently have a visible position. For an angled surface, it will help to have a real line at a real angle, so you can see the ball bouncing on it.

So, go ahead and make a nice long line with the Line tool. Select it and convert it into a movie clip, making the registration point in the center. Name the movie clip symbol `line` and leave a copy on stage with an instance name `line`, as shown in Figure 10-6. After creating it, you should rotate the `line` movie clip a bit, say 30 degrees or so in either direction, using either the Free Transform tool or the Transform panel.

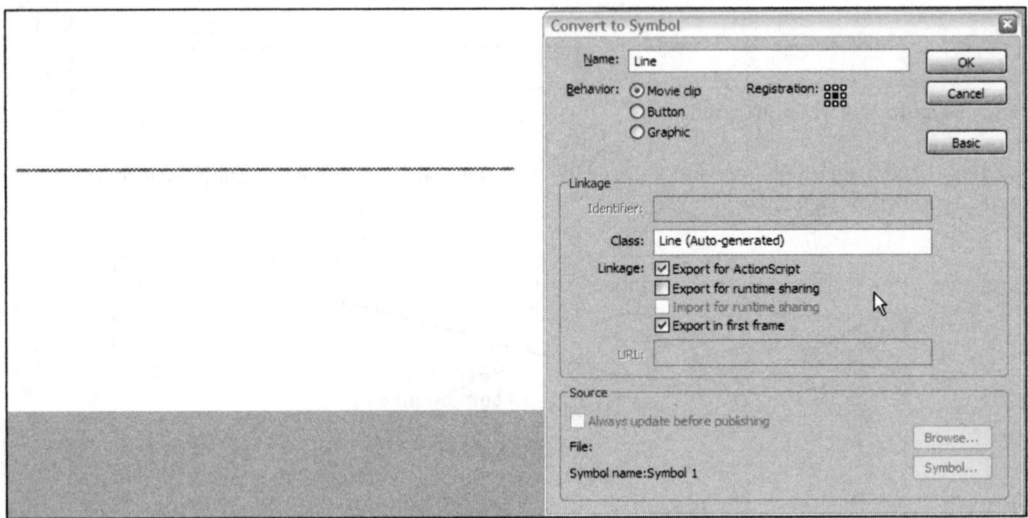

Figure 10-6. Creating a line

You'll also need a `ball` movie clip, which you should be able to make in your sleep now, with an instance on stage named `ball` (make sure the ball is above the line, so it can fall onto it).

Here is the initial code to put on frame 1 (`ch10_05.fla`):

```
var vx:Number = 0;
var vy:Number = 0;
var gravity:Number = .5;
var bounce:Number = -0.7;

function onEnterFrame():Void
{
	vy += gravity;
	ball._x += vx;
	ball._y += vy;
```

```
        // get angle, sine and cosine
        var angle:Number = line._rotation * Math.PI / 180;
        var cosine:Number = Math.cos(angle);
        var sine:Number = Math.sin(angle);

        // get position of ball, relative to line
        var x:Number = ball._x - line._x;
        var y:Number = ball._y - line._y;

        // rotate line
        var x1:Number = cosine * x + sine * y;
        var y1:Number = cosine * y - sine * x;

        // rotate velocity
        var vx1:Number = cosine * vx + sine * vy;
        var vy1:Number = cosine * vy - sine * vx;

        // perform bounce with rotated values
        if(y1 > -ball._height / 2)
        {
            y1 = -ball._height / 2;
            vy1 *= bounce;
        }

        // rotate everything back
        x = cosine * x1 - sine * y1;
        y = cosine * y1 + sine * x1;
        vx = cosine * vx1 - sine * vy1;
        vy = cosine * vy1 + sine * vx1;

        // reset actual ball position
        ball._x = line._x + x;
        ball._y = line._y + y;
}
```

You start out by declaring variables for vx, vy, gravity, and bounce, as usual. The enterFrame handler begins with basic motion code.

You then get the angle of the line and convert it to radians. Once you have the angle, you get the sine and cosine of that angle.

Then you get the initial x, y position of the ball in relation to the line, by subtracting the line position from the ball position.

Finally, you're ready to rotate something! Now, when you look at the next couple of lines of code, you may notice something wrong.

```
var x1:Number = cosine * x + sine * y;
var y1:Number = cosine * y - sine * x;
```

The plus and minus are reversed from the original formula I gave you for coordinate rotation, which is as follows:

```
x1 = cos(angle) * x - sin(angle) * y;
y1 = cos(angle) * y + sin(angle) * x;
```

That's not a mistake. Think about what you're doing. Say the line is rotated 17 degrees. Using the original formula, you would wind up rotating it 17 degrees more, making it 34 degrees! Oops. You actually want to rotate it –17 degrees to put it at 0. Now, you could have calculated the sine and cosine to be `Math.sin(-angle)` and `Math.cos(-angle)`, respectively. But eventually, you'll need the sine and cosine of the original angle, in order to rotate everything back.

So, rather than making two `cosine` and `sine` variables (at double the cost of calculation), you can use an alternate form of coordinate rotation to rotate everything in the opposite direction. It's as simple as reversing the plus and minus, as you just saw. If the line is at 17 degrees rotation, this will rotate everything –17 degrees, putting it at zero degrees, or flat. Then do the same to the velocity.

Note that you don't need to actually rotate the `line` movie clip. Again, it's mostly there for your eyes—to let you see where the ball is supposed to bounce. It's also a handy place to store the angle and position of the surface, since you can move and rotate it by hand.

Then you can perform the bounce. You do this using the `x1`, `y1` position values and the `vx1`, `vy1` velocity values. Realize that because `y1` is in relation to the `line` movie clip, the "bottom" boundary is the line itself, which will be 0. Taking into account the size of the ball, you check to see if `y1` is greater than `0 - ball._height / 2`. This check is shortcut to the following:

```
if(y1 > -ball._height / 2)
```

The rest of the bounce should be obvious.

Then you rotate everything back, using the original formula. This gives you updated values for `x`, `y`, `vx`, and `vy`. All you need to do at that point is reset the actual position of the `ball` movie clip by adding `x` and `y` to `line._x` and `line._y`.

Take some time to test this example. Try different rotations of the line, and different positions of both the line and ball. Make sure it all works fine.

Optimizing the code

You've already seen some examples of changing code a bit to make it more optimized. This usually involves doing things once instead of multiple times, or not doing them at all, unless you're really sure they need to be done.

I wrote the code in the previous example for clarity only. So, there is a lot happening on every frame that doesn't need to be. Most of that code needs to execute only when the ball has actually hit the line. Most of the time, you just need the basic motion code, and the bare minimum of calculation to check if the ball has hit the line. In other words, all you need is the data that goes into the `if` statement:

```
if(y1 > -ball._height / 2)
```

So, you do need the y1 variable. And in order to get that, you need x and y, and sine and cosine. But if the ball hasn't hit the line, you don't need x1, or vx1 and vy1. So, those can go *inside* the if statement.

Also, if there's no hit, there's no need to rotate anything back or reset the ball position. So, all the stuff *after* the if statement can go inside the if statement as well. You wind up with this optimized version (ch10_06.fla):

```
var vx:Number = 0;
var vy:Number = 0;
var gravity:Number = .5;
var bounce:Number = -0.7;

onEnterFrame = function()
{
      vy += gravity;
      ball._x += vx;
      ball._y += vy;

      // get angle, sine and cosine
      var angle:Number = line._rotation * Math.PI / 180;
      var cosine:Number = Math.cos(angle);
      var sine:Number = Math.sin(angle);

      // get position of ball, relative to line
      var x:Number = ball._x - line._x;
      var y:Number = ball._y - line._y;

      // rotate line
      var y1:Number = cosine * y - sine * x;


      if(y1 > -ball._height / 2)
      {
            // rotate line
            var x1:Number = cosine * x + sine * y;

            // rotate velocity
            var vx1:Number = cosine * vx + sine * vy;
            var vy1:Number = cosine * vy - sine * vx;

            // perform bounce with rotated values
            y1 = -ball._height / 2;
            vy1 *= bounce;

            // rotate everything back
            x = cosine * x1 - sine * y1;
            y = cosine * y1 + sine * x1;
            vx = cosine * vx1 - sine * vy1;
            vy = cosine * vy1 + sine * vx1;
```

```
            // reset actual ball position
            ball._x = line._x + x;
            ball._y = line._y + y;
        }
    }
```

All the stuff in bold has been moved from outside the if statement to inside the statement, so it will happen only if a hit actually occurs, rather than every single frame. Can you imagine how many CPU cycles you just saved? It's pretty important to think about things like this, especially as your movies get more and more complex.

Making it dynamic

You can now start to make the action a little more dynamic. Let's adjust the angle of the line in real time, just to see how robust this thing is. You can do this with a single line of code, as the very first line inside the onEnterFrame function:

```
line._rotation = (Stage.width / 2 - _xmouse) * .1;
```

Now you can move your mouse back and forth, and the line will tilt one way or the other. The ball should constantly adjust itself accordingly.

Fixing the "falling off the edge" problem

What you're probably noticing now is that the ball will continue to roll along the angle of the line, even if it has gone past the edge of it. This may look a bit strange. But remember that the ball is not actually interacting with the line movie clip at all. It's all done mathematically. But the results are so exact, it's easy to forget that nothing is actually "hitting" anything. And since the ball doesn't "know" anything about the line movie clip, it doesn't know where it starts or ends. But you can tell it where the line is—using either a simple hit test or a more precise bounds check. Let's look at both methods, so you can decide which to use.

Hit testing

The easiest way to find the line's location is to wrap everything but the basic motion code inside an if statement with a hit test, as follows:

```
function onEnterFrame ():Void
{
    vy += gravity;
    ball._x += vx;
    ball._y += vy;

    if(ball.hitTest(line))
    {
        // all the rest of the stuff that was in this function
    }
}
```

While that is pretty simple, and might suffice for many implementations, there's another way to do it that's a little more exact, and which I prefer. Naturally, that means it's a little more complex and processor-intensive.

Bounds checking

I personally think that the getBounds method is one of the most underappreciated functions in ActionScript. I thought about mentioning it in Chapter 9, as it fits in nicely with collision detection, but I had enough to cover there, and one of the best uses I've found for it is exactly what I'm going to describe next. So I saved it for this chapter.

If you recall the discussion on hitTest, then you may also remember what a bounding box is. In case your memory is like mine, I'll recap. The bounding box is the rectangle described by the visible graphic elements of a movie clip instance on stage. If you took any movie clip on stage and drew a rectangle around it so that the top edge touched the very top part of the movie clip, the bottom edge touched the bottom part of the clip, and the same with the left and right edges, you'd have the bounding box. Or you could simply select a movie clip that is on stage and see this rectangle outlined in blue.

This bounding box is used in two out of three of the possible ways of calling the hitTest function. In that case, the location of the bounding box is handled behind the scenes, and you get a true or a false in response to the function.

The getBounds function gives you direct access to the numerical values of the position and size of that box. Here's the basic signature of the function:

```
bounds = mc.getBounds(targetCoordinateSpace)
```

As you can see, it's called as a method of any movie clip, and it returns an object that contains data about the bounding box. I'll get to that in a moment. First, let's look at that single parameter, targetCoordinateSpace. What's that all about?

You use the targetCoordinateSpace parameter to specify from which viewpoint this bounding box will be described. In most cases, this will be the timeline or movie clip where that mc is located. For example, if you're writing your code directly on the main timeline, you could say mc.getBounds(this), meaning, "Give me the bounding box for this movie clip, in terms of the stage's coordinates." On the other hand, if you were creating or attaching a movie clip inside another movie clip, you might want the bounding box in terms of the exterior movie clip's registration point, as that might be different from the 0, 0 point of the stage. In that case, you could do something like this:

```
holder.mc.getBounds(holder)
```

This means you want the bounding box for the movie clip named mc, which is inside the movie clip holder, and you want it described in terms of holder's coordinate space.

Naturally, the targetCoordinateSpace needs to be a movie clip, or an instance of some class that extends the MovieClip class. And the stage, _root, and _level0 and above are movie clips in essence, so they all count.

Now, on to what the getBounds function returns. I said earlier that it returns an object that contains data about the bounding box. It returns a generic object (of type Object), which I'll call bounds. This bounds object contains four properties: xMin, xMax, yMin, and yMax.

Let's try it out. Put any movie clip on stage and name it mc, and then put the following code on the timeline:

```
var bounds:Object = mc.getBounds(this);
trace("xMax: " + bounds.xMax);
trace("xMin: " + bounds.xMin);
trace("yMax: " + bounds.yMax);
trace("yMin: " + bounds.yMin);
```

For an interesting experiment, change the first line to read as follows:

```
var bounds:Object = mc.getBounds(mc);
```

Now, you're getting the movie clip's bounds from its own viewpoint; in other words, in relationship to its own registration point. If its registration point is in its center, the xMin and yMin values should be negative and exactly equal to –xMax and –yMax. If the registration point is in the upper-left corner, xMin and yMin should be 0, and xMax and yMax should be equal to the height and width of the clip. It's also worth mentioning that if you call getBounds without a parameter, you'll get the same result, as the object you are checking the bounds of will be used as the target coordinate space.

Just about now, you're probably starting to forget why I'm talking about bounds in the first place, so let's get back on track. We were trying to figure out when the ball has fallen off of the edge of the line, remember? So, you can call getBounds on the line, and find its xMin and xMax. If the ball's x position is less than the bounds' xMin, or if it is greater than the bounds' xMax, it has gone over the edge. It's far more complex to describe than it is to just show, so here's the code:

```
function onEnterFrame ():Void
{
	vy += gravity;
	ball._x += vx;
	ball._y += vy;

	var bounds:Object = line.getBounds(this);
	if(ball._x > bounds.xMin && ball._x < bounds.xMax)
	{
		// all the rest of the stuff that was in this function
	}
}
```

You can see these changes implemented in the file ch10_07.fla.

Fixing the "under the line" problem

In either method—hitTest or bounds checking—you're first finding out if the ball is in the vicinity of the line, and then doing coordinate rotation to get the adjusted positions and velocities. At that point, you check if the y1 rotated y position of the ball is past the line, and if so, perform a bounce. But what if the ball passes *under* the line? Say the line is up in the middle of the stage, and the ball is bouncing around on the "floor." If either the hitTest or the bounds check comes back true, Flash will think the ball has just bounced on the line, and will transport the ball from below the line to above it.

The way I've come up with to solve this is to compare vy1 with y1, and bounce only if vy1 is greater. How did I come up with that? Take a look at the diagram in Figure 10-7.

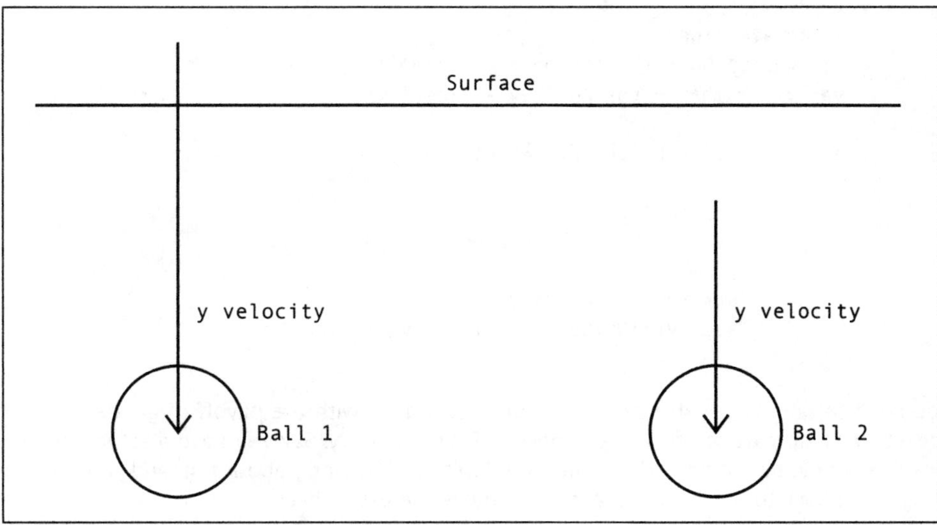

Figure 10-7. Did it go through, or just pass under?

With the ball on the left, the y velocity is greater than the y position in relation to the line. This means that just before it moved, it had to be above the line. With the ball on the right, the velocity is less than the relative y position. In other words, it's below the line on this frame, and it was below the line on the last frame. So it's just moving underneath the frame. The only time you want to do a bounce is when the ball goes from above the line to below it. Now, let's look at how to fix the code to do that. Here's a section of the code out of the enterFrame handler:

```
...
// rotate line
    var y1:Number = cosine * y - sine * x;

if(y1 > -ball._height / 2)
    {
          // rotate line
          var x1:Number = cosine * x + sine * y;

          // rotate velocity
          var vx1:Number = cosine * vx + sine * vy;
          var vy1:Number = cosine * vy - sine * vx;
...
```

You just need to add that y1 < vy1 into your if statement:

```
if(y1 > -ball._height / 2 && y1 < vy1)
```

But in order to do that, you need to calculate vy1 beforehand. So that comes out of the `if` statement, and the snippet becomes corrected to this:

```
. . .
// rotate line
    var y1:Number = cosine * y - sine * x;
var vy1:Number = cosine * vy - sine * vx;

if(y1 > -ball._height / 2 && y1 < vy1)
    {
          // rotate line
          var x1:Number = cosine * x + sine * y;

          // rotate velocity
          var vx1:Number = cosine * vx + sine * vy;
. . .
```

So, you need to do a little extra calculation on each frame, with the payoff of greater accuracy and realism—that familiar trade-off. You can decide if it's necessary. Say you have a setup where it's just not possible for the ball to go under a line. You don't need to worry about this, and you can move the vy1 calculation back to the `if` statement and remove the extra check.

OK, we're bouncing, we're dynamic, we've got edges! Let's move on to the final, large-scale example of the chapter.

Bouncing off multiple angles

So far, you've just been dealing with a single line, or angled surface. Dealing with multiple surfaces is not really all that complicated. You just make a bunch of surfaces and loop through them. You can abstract the angle bouncing code into its own function and just call that from within the loop.

Also, in all the examples in this chapter up to now, I've tried to keep things as simple as possible, giving you only the minimum amount of code necessary to demonstrate the principle at hand. However, the next example is a complete program, using all the techniques you've seen in prior chapters (with some comments to jar your memory).

The library setup for this example is similar to the last few examples, with the same `line` and `ball` movie clips, except I made the lines a bit smaller so there would be room for more of them. I've placed five lines and one ball on stage. The ball instance is named `ball`, and the lines are named `line0` through `line4`. I then positioned everything in a nice layout, as shown in Figure 10-8.

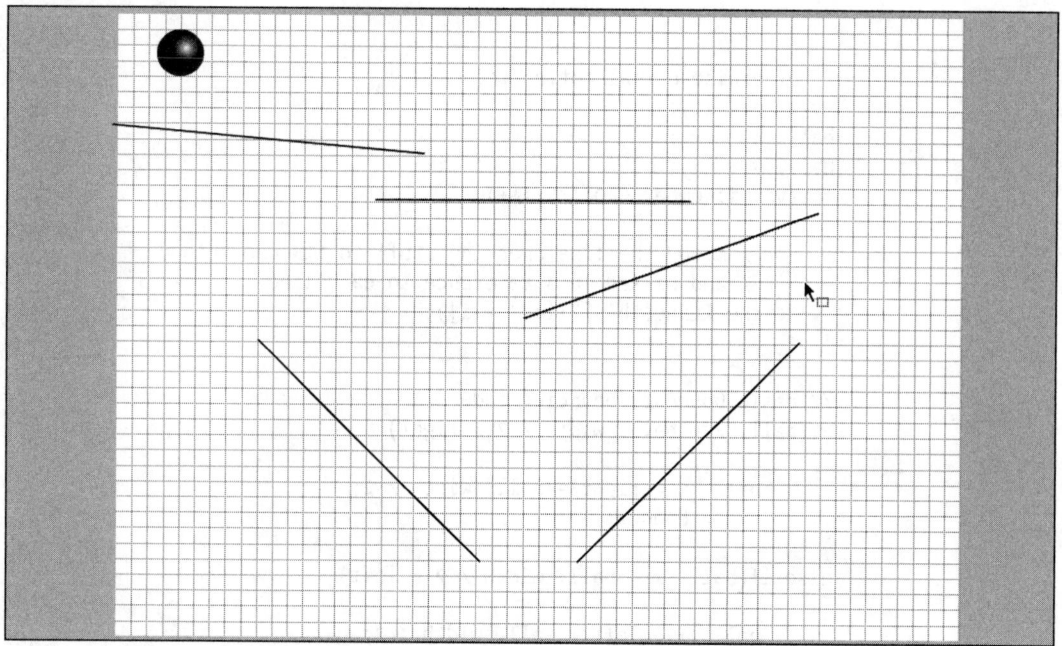

Figure 10-8. Maybe a pinball machine?

Here's the code (ch10_08.fla):

```
var vx:Number = 0;
var vy:Number = 0;
var gravity:Number = .5;
var bounce:Number = -0.7;
var left:Number = 0;
var right:Number = Stage.width;
var top:Number = 0;
var bottom:Number = Stage.height;
var dragging:Boolean = false;
var oldX:Number;
var oldY:Number;

function onEnterFrame ():Void
{
	if(dragging)
	{
		// keep track of velocity while dragging
		vx = ball._x - oldX;
		vy = ball._y - oldY;
		oldX = ball._x;
		oldY = ball._y;
	}
```

```
        else
        {
            // otherwise normal motion code
            vy += gravity;
            ball._x += vx;
            ball._y += vy;
            for(var i:Number = 0;i<5;i++)
            {
                // moved the line checking stuff to its own method
                // and passed in a reference to each line
                checkLine(this["line" + i]);
            }

            // basic boundary bouncing code
            if(ball._x + ball._width / 2 > right)
            {
                ball._x = right - ball._width / 2;
                vx *= bounce;
            }
            else if(ball._x - ball._width / 2 < left)
            {
                ball._x = left + ball._width / 2;
                vx *= bounce;
            }
            if(ball._y + ball._height / 2 > bottom)
            {
                ball._y = bottom - ball._height / 2;
                vy *= bounce;
            }
            else if(ball._y - ball._height / 2< top)
            {
                ball._y = top + ball._height / 2;
                vy *= bounce;
            }
        }
    }

    function checkLine(line:MovieClip)
    {
        // nothing new here!
        var bounds:Object = line.getBounds(this);
        if(ball._x > bounds.xMin && ball._x < bounds.xMax)
        {
            // get angle, sine and cosine
            var angle:Number = line._rotation * Math.PI / 180;
            var cosine:Number = Math.cos(angle);
            var sine:Number = Math.sin(angle);
```

```
            // get position of ball, relative to line
            var x:Number = ball._x - line._x;
            var y:Number = ball._y - line._y;

            // rotate line
            var y1:Number = cosine * y - sine * x;
            var vy1:Number = cosine * vy - sine * vx;


            if(y1 > -ball._height / 2 && y1 < vy1)
            {
                  // rotate line
                  var x1:Number = cosine * x + sine * y;

                  // rotate velocity
                  var vx1:Number = cosine * vx + sine * vy;

                  // perform bounce with rotated values
                  y1 = -ball._height / 2;
                  vy1 *= bounce;

                  // rotate everything back
                  x = cosine * x1 - sine * y1;
                  y = cosine * y1 + sine * x1;
                  vx = cosine * vx1 - sine * vy1;
                  vy = cosine * vy1 + sine * vx1;

                  // reset actual ball position
                  ball._x = line._x + x;
                  ball._y = line._y + y;
            }
      }
}

// basic drag and drop functionality
ball.onPress = function()
{
      oldX = this._x;
      oldY = this._y;
      dragging = true;
      this.startDrag();
}
ball.onRelease = ball.onReleaseOutside = function()
{
      dragging = false;
      this.stopDrag();
}
```

Yes, it's a lot of code, but as I've become fond of saying, it's all stuff you should recognize by now. Complex programs are not necessarily composed of complex pieces, but they are frequently built from a lot of familiar pieces, put together just right.

There is a bit of optimization you can try here if you are interested. Say you have many surfaces to check, and you are looping through them and checking each one. In many systems, once you have found a surface that the ball is hitting, and handled that reaction, you don't need to continue checking all the other surfaces. So you could just break out of the for loop at that point. To do such a thing, you might want to have the checkLine function return true or false based on whether or not it has hit a line. Then your for loop in the onEnterFrame function could look like this:

```
for(var i:Number = 0;i<5;i++)
{
	// moved the line checking stuff to its own method
	// and passed in a reference to each line
	if(checkLine(this["line" + i]))
	{
		break;
	}
}
```

In some cases though, particularly in a dense area of lines, you might want to check all of the lines on every frame. So, I'll leave it to you to decide if such an optimization is appropriate.

Important formulas in this chapter

Here's a reminder of the two main formulas introduced in this chapter.

Coordinate rotation:

```
x1 = Math.cos(angle) * x - Math.sin(angle) * y;
y1 = Math.cos(angle) * y + Math.sin(angle) * x;
```

Reverse coordinate rotation:

```
x1 = Math.cos(angle) * x + Math.sin(angle) * y;
y1 = Math.cos(angle) * y - Math.sin(angle) * x;
```

Summary

As you've seen in this chapter, coordinate rotation can give you some very complex behavior, but it all boils down to a couple of formulas that never change. Once you're comfortable with the formulas, you can use them anywhere. I hope you're starting to see how you can create very complicated and richly realistic motion just by adding in more and more simple techniques.

You'll be using the coordinate rotation formula quite a bit in the next chapter, where you'll learn how to handle the results of collisions of objects with different velocities and masses.

};shape.targetHeight = shape._height;
shape.onEnterFrame = function() {
var speed = 5;
this._width += (this.targetWidth - this._width)/speed;
this._height += (this.targetHeight - this._height)/speed;
};

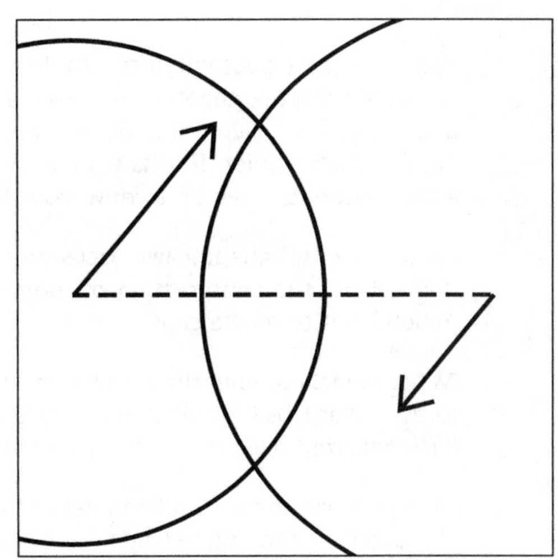

Chapter 11

BILLIARD BALL PHYSICS

What we'll cover in this chapter:

- Mass
- Momentum
- Conservation of momentum
- Important formulas in this chapter

As you might expect in a technical book like this, things start off simple and gradually become more complex. With this chapter, you reach a pinnacle of complexity. Not that the rest of the chapters after this are all downhill, but I think this one in particular requires that you have not skimped on the material that came earlier. That said, I'll walk you through the concepts step by step, and if you've followed along reasonably well up to now, you should be fine.

Specifically, this chapter will focus on momentum: What happens to the momentum of two objects that collide, the conservation of momentum, and how to apply this conservation of momentum in ActionScript to movie clips.

As the objects used in these examples are all round, for simplicity's sake, this subject is often referred to as "billiard ball physics." And you'll soon see that these examples really do look like a bunch of different-sized billiard balls hitting each other.

As in previous chapters, when I get to the code, I'll start you out on one dimension to keep things simpler and easier to understand. Then I'll move into two dimensions, at which point you'll need to jump into some coordinate rotation (the subject of the previous chapter). Essentially, you'll be rotating the two-dimensional scene so it lies flat. You can then ignore one axis and treat it as a one-dimensional scene. But all that is just to whet your appetite for what's coming up. Let's start with the simple concepts of mass and momentum.

Mass

The earlier chapters of the book have gone into several aspects of motion: velocity, acceleration, vectors, friction, bouncing, easing, springing, and gravity. One thing that I have pretty successfully gotten away with ignoring is the concept of the mass of the object being moved around. Now, I'm going to reissue my standard disclaimer here, and say that there are probably several points in the book so far where, scientifically speaking, mass should have been in the equation. But I've generally concentrated on doing things *mostly* correctly, and kept the emphasis on making sure it *looks* right. Most important, the final result must be efficient enough that it won't totally kill Flash in the process.

Unfortunately, or maybe fortunately, I have reached a point where I just can't ignore mass any longer. Mass is just so tied up in the subject of momentum that I'm just going to have to confront it head on.

So just what is mass? Here on earth, we usually think of mass as how much something weighs. And that's pretty close, as weight is proportional to mass. The more mass something has, the more it weighs. In fact, we use the same terms to measure mass and velocity: kilograms, pounds, and so on. Technically speaking though, mass is the measurement of how much an object resists change in velocity. Thus, the more mass an object has, the harder it is to move that object or to change how that object is moving (slow it down, speed it up, or change its direction).

This also relates to acceleration and force. The more mass something has, the more force you need to apply to it to produce a given acceleration. The engine in my Chevy Cavalier is designed to produce enough force to provide reasonable acceleration on the mass of a Chevy Cavalier (barely). It's not going to produce enough force to accelerate a large truck. The engine would need a lot more force, because the truck has a lot more mass.

Momentum

Now we move on to momentum. This is basically the product of an object's mass and velocity. In other words, mass *times* velocity. Momentum is usually indicated by the letter p, and mass by m. Thus, the following should be pretty self-explanatory:

```
p = m * v
```

This means that something with a small mass and high velocity could have a similar momentum to something with a large mass and low velocity. The aforementioned large truck moving at a mere 20 miles an hour could easily kill you. A bullet, on the other hand, has a relatively tiny mass but a much higher velocity, and it's just as deadly.

Because velocity is a vector (direction and magnitude), that means momentum must also be a vector. The direction of the momentum vector is the same as the direction of the velocity vector. Thus, to fully describe momentum, you say something like this (where m/s is meters per second):

```
5 kg * 20 m/s at 23 degrees
```

Pretty complex, eh? Now you know why I've waited until now to bring it up.

Conservation of momentum

Finally, we get to the meat of the chapter: conservation of momentum. What does that mean? Momentum is conserved? When? Where? How? OK, let's slow down. Momentum conservation has everything to do with collisions, which is something you're very familiar with by now. You've gone through a whole chapter on collision detection and even faked some collision reactions between two objects. Conservation of momentum is the exact principle you need to respond very realistically to a collision.

Conservation of momentum allows you to say, "This object was moving at velocity A and that object was moving at velocity B before the collision. Now, *after* the collision, this object will move at velocity C and that object will move at velocity D." To break it down further, knowing that velocity is speed and direction, you can say that if you know the speed and direction of two objects just before they collide, you can figure out the speed and direction they will move in after the collision. A very useful thing, as I'm sure you'll agree.

There's one catch though: You'll need to know each object's mass. Again, you see why I've put off this discussion until now. So, in reality, you're saying if you know the mass, speed, and direction of each object before the collision, you can figure out where and how fast the objects will go after they collide.

OK, so that's what conservation of momentum can do for you. But what is it? Basically, the Law of Conservation of Momentum says that the total momentum for a system before a collision will be equal to the total momentum after a collision. But what is this *system* the law refers to? This is just a collection of objects with momentum. Most discussions also specify that this would be a *closed system*, which is a system with no other forces or influences acting on it. In other words, you can just ignore anything but the actual collision itself. For our purposes, we will always be considering just the reaction between two objects, so our system will always be something like object A and object B.

The total momentum of the system is simply the combined momentum of all the objects in the system. For us, this will mean the combined momentum of object A and object B. So, if you combine the momentums before the collision, and combine the momentums afterwards, the result should be the same. Well, that's great, you say, but it doesn't really tell me how to find out the new momentums. Patience, we're getting there. I told you we'll be walking through this step by step. A few paragraphs from now, you'll probably be wanting me to slow down, because here come the formulas!

Before I jump into the math, here's a suggestion. Don't worry too much at first about trying to figure out how to convert this to real code. You'll get to that soon enough. Just try to look at the next few formulas from a conceptual viewpoint. "This plus that equals that plus this. Sure, that makes sense." It will all translate very neatly into code by the end of this chapter.

OK, if combined momentum before and after the collision is the same, and momentum is velocity times mass, then for two objects—object 0 and object 1—you can come up with something like this:

```
momentum0 + momentum1 = momentum0Final + momentum1Final
```

or

```
(m0 * v0) + (m1 * v1) = (m0 * v0Final) + (m1 * v1Final)
```

Now, what you want to know is the final velocities for object 0 and object 1. Those would be `v0Final` and `v1Final`. The way to solve an equation with two unknowns is to find *another* equation that has the same two unknowns in it. It just so happens there is such an equation floating around the halls of the physics departments of the world. It has to do with kinetic energy. The funny thing is, you don't even have to know or even care what kinetic energy is all about. You just borrow the formula to help you solve your own problem, dust it off, and give it back when you're done. Here's the formula for kinetic energy:

$$KE = 0.5 * m * v^2$$

Technically, kinetic energy is not a vector, so although you use the v for velocity in there, it deals with only the magnitude of the velocity. It doesn't care about the direction. But that won't hurt your calculations.

Now, it happens that the kinetic energy before and after a collision remains the same. So, you can do something like this:

```
KE0 + KE1 = KE0Final + KE1Final
```

or

$$(0.5 * m0 * v0^2) + (0.5 * m1 * v1^2) =$$
$$(0.5 * m0 * v0Final^2) + (.5 * m1 * v1Final^2)$$

You can then factor out the `0.5` values to get this:

$$(m0 * v0^2) + (m1 * v1^2) = (m0 * v0Final^2) + (m1 * v1Final^2)$$

What do you know? You have a different equation with the same two unknown variables: `v0Final` and `v1Final`. You can now factor these out and come up with a single equation for each unknown. I'll save us both a headache in the intervening algebra and just give you the formulas that you wind up with when all is said and done. If you're one of those people who actually like doing algebra equations, or you need some extra credit for school, I invite you to sit down with some paper and a few sharp pencils, and figure it out on your own. You will wind up with the equations that follow (if not, either you made a mistake or I'm in big trouble with my publisher).

```
           (m0 - m1) * v0 + 2 * m1 * v1
v0Final = ----------------------------
                    m0 + m1

           (m1 - m0) * v1 + 2 * m0 * v0
v1Final = ----------------------------
                    m0 + m1
```

And now you see why I said at the beginning of this chapter that you have reached a pinnacle of complexity. Actually, you haven't quite reached it yet. You're about to apply this to one axis, and after that, you're going to dive in and add coordinate rotation to it when you move to two axes. Hold on!

Conservation of momentum on one axis

Now that you've got some formulas, you can start making things move with them. For this first example, start with the same basic ball movie clip FLA file you've been using all along, but place two balls on stage. Name them `ball0` and `ball1`, and scale `ball0` down a bit (or scale `ball1` up, if you prefer). Place `ball0` way over on the left side and `ball1` on the right. You'll be ignoring the y axis this time around, so make sure both movie clips are in the same position vertically. Otherwise, it will be strange to see them bounce if they haven't visually touched each other. You can see the basic setup in Figure 11-1 (in `ch11_01.fla`).

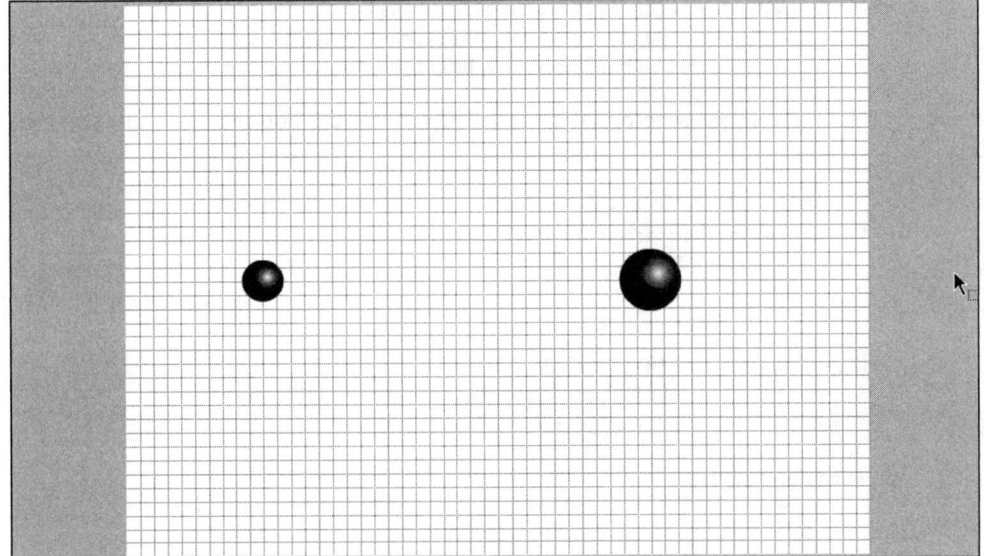

Figure 11-1. Setting up the stage for conservation of momentum on one axis

Start off by giving each clip a mass and a velocity on the x axis:

```
ball0.vx = 1;
ball0.mass = 1;
ball1.vx = -1;
ball1.mass = 2;
```

Then do some basic motion code for one-axis velocity and simple distance-based collision detection:

```
function onEnterFrame ():Void
{
      ball0._x += ball0.vx;
      ball1._x += ball1.vx;
      var dist:Number = ball1._x - ball0._x;
      if(Math.abs(dist) < ball0._width / 2 + ball1._width / 2)
      {
            // reaction will go here
      }
}
```

Now, the only question is how to code in the reaction. Well, let's take ball0 first. Considering that ball0 is object 0 and ball1 is object 1, you need to apply the following formula:

```
              (m0 - m1) * v0 + 2 * m1 * v1
v0Final = ----------------------------
                        m0 + m1
```

In ActionScript, this becomes the following code:

```
var vx0Final:Number = ((ball0.mass - ball1.mass) *
                       ball0.vx + 2 * ball1.mass * ball1.vx)
                       / (ball0.mass + ball1.mass);
```

It shouldn't be too hard to see where that came from. You can then do the same thing with ball1, so this:

```
              (m1 - m0) * v1 + 2 * m0 * v0
v1Final = ----------------------------
                    m0 + m1
```

becomes this:

```
var vx1Final:Number = ((ball1.mass - ball0.mass) *
                       ball1.vx + 2 * ball0.mass * ball0.vx)
                       / (ball0.mass + ball1.mass);
```

The final code winds up like this:

```
ball0.vx = 1;
ball0.mass = 1;
ball1.vx = -1;
ball1.mass = 2;
```

```
function onEnterFrame ():Void
{
	ball0._x += ball0.vx;
	ball1._x += ball1.vx;
	var dist:Number = ball1._x - ball0._x;
	if(Math.abs(dist) < ball0._width / 2 + ball1._width / 2)
	{
		var vx0Final:Number = ((ball0.mass - ball1.mass) *
		                       ball0.vx + 2 * ball1.mass *
		                       ball1.vx)
		                       / (ball0.mass + ball1.mass);
		var vx1Final:Number = ((ball1.mass - ball0.mass) *
		                       ball1.vx + 2 * ball0.mass *
		                       ball0.vx)
		                       / (ball0.mass + ball1.mass);

		ball0.vx = vx0Final;
		ball1.vx = vx1Final;

		ball0._x += ball0.vx;
		ball1._x += ball1.vx;
	}
}
```

Note that the calculation for vx0Final uses ball1.vx and vice versa. Thus, I had to store both of them in temporary variables, rather than assigning them directly to the ball0.vx and ball1.vx properties.

Placing the objects

The last two lines of the preceding ActionScript deserve some explanation. After you figure out the new velocities for each ball, you add them back to the ball's position. That's something new. Why do that? Well, remember that in all previous bouncing examples, you needed to reposition the movie clip so that it wasn't embedded in the wall. You just moved it out so it was touching the edge of the wall. You need to do the same thing here, but now you have two moving objects. You don't want them embedded in each other. That would not only look wrong, but it would usually result in the two objects becoming stuck together permanently.

You could place one of the balls just on the edge of the other one. But which one should you move? Whichever one you moved would kind of jump into its new position unnaturally, which would be especially noticeable at low speeds.

There are probably a number of ways to determine the correct placement of the balls, ranging from simple to complex and accurate to totally faked. The simple solution I used for this first example is just to add the new velocity back to the objects, moving them apart again. I've found that this is pretty realistic and quite simple—accomplished in two lines of code. Later, in the "Solving a potential problem" section, I'll show you a problem that can crop up with this method and give you a solution that's a little more robust.

Go ahead and run the ch11_01.fla file. Then change the masses and velocities of each ball until you see what's going on. Change the sizes of each, too. Note that the size doesn't really have anything to do with the reaction. In most cases, the larger object would have a higher mass, and you could probably figure out the relative volume of the two balls and come up with realistic masses for their sizes. However, usually, I just mess around with numbers for mass until things look and feel right. I say something very scientific like, "Well, this ball is roughly twice as big, so I'll give it twice the mass."

Optimizing the code

The worst part of this solution is that huge equation right in the middle. Actually, the very worst part is the fact that the code has almost exactly the same equation in there twice. If you could somehow get rid of one of them, I'm sure you'd feel a lot better. The good news is that you can.

It's going to take a bit more math and algebra, which I'm not going to explain in mind-numbing detail. Basically, you need to find the total velocity of the two objects before the condition. Then, after you get the final velocity of one object, you can find the difference between it and the total velocity to get the final velocity for the other object.

You actually find the total velocity by *subtracting* the velocities of the two objects. That may seem strange, but think of it from the viewpoint of the system. Say the system is two cars on a highway. One is going at 50 mph and the other at 60 mph. Depending on which car you're in, you could see the other car going at 10 mph or –10 mph. In other words, it's either slowly moving ahead of you or falling behind you.

So, before you do anything in terms of collisions, you find out the total velocity (from ball1's viewpoint) by subtracting ball1.vx from ball0.vx.

```
var vxTotal:Number = ball0.vx - ball1.vx;
```

Finally, after calculating vx0Final, add that to vxTotal, and you'll have vx1Final. Again, this may seem counterintuitive, but try it out, and you'll see it works.

```
vx1Final = vxTotal + vx0Final;
```

Fantastic! That's better than that horrible double formula. Also, now that the formula for ball1.vx doesn't reference ball0.vx anymore, you can even get rid of the temporary variables. Here's the full code (ch11_02.fla):

```
ball0.vx = 2;
ball0.mass = 1;
ball1.vx = -1;
ball1.mass = 3;

onEnterFrame = function()
{
	ball0._x += ball0.vx;
	ball1._x += ball1.vx;
	var dist:Number = ball1._x - ball0._x;
	if(Math.abs(dist) < ball0._width / 2 + ball1._width / 2)
	{
		var vxTotal:Number = ball0.vx - ball1.vx;
```

```
                ball0.vx = ((ball0.mass - ball1.mass) *
                            ball0.vx + 2 * ball1.mass * ball1.vx)
                            / (ball0.mass + ball1.mass);
                ball1.vx = vxTotal + ball0.vx;

                ball0._x += ball0.vx;
                ball1._x += ball1.vx;
          }
    }
```

You've gotten rid of quite a few math operations and still have the same result—not bad.

Now, this isn't one of those formulas that you're necessarily going to understand inside out, unless perhaps you have a physics background. You may not even memorize it, unless you're using it on a very regular basis. Personally, I have this stuff written down somewhere, and I need to pull it out and read it whenever I want to use it. I'll be happy when this book gets published, so I'll know right where to find this formula and not have to dig through piles of paper looking for my notes!

Conservation of momentum on two axes

OK, take a deep breath. You're going to the next level. So far, you've applied a long-winded formula, but it's pretty much plug-and-play. You take the mass and the velocity of the two objects, plug them into the formula, and get your result.

Now I'm going to throw one more layer of complexity onto it—namely, another dimension. I've already given away the strategy at the beginning of the chapter, so you know that you'll be using coordinate rotation. Let's take a look at why.

Understanding the theory and strategy

Figure 11-1 illustrates the example you just saw: collision on one dimension.

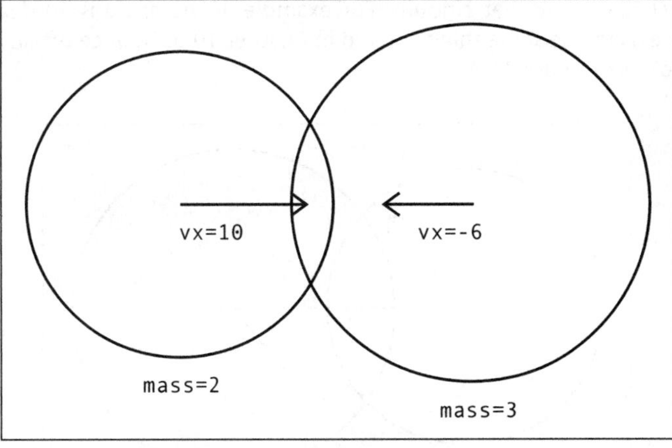

Figure 11-2. A one-dimensional collision

As you can see, the objects have different sizes, different masses, and different velocities. The velocities are represented by the arrows coming out from the center of each ball. These are vectors. To refresh your memory, a velocity vector points in the direction of the motion, and its length indicates the speed.

The one-dimensional example was pretty simple, because both velocity vectors were along the x axis. So, you could just add and subtract their magnitudes directly. Now, take a look at Figure 11-3, which shows two balls colliding in two dimensions.

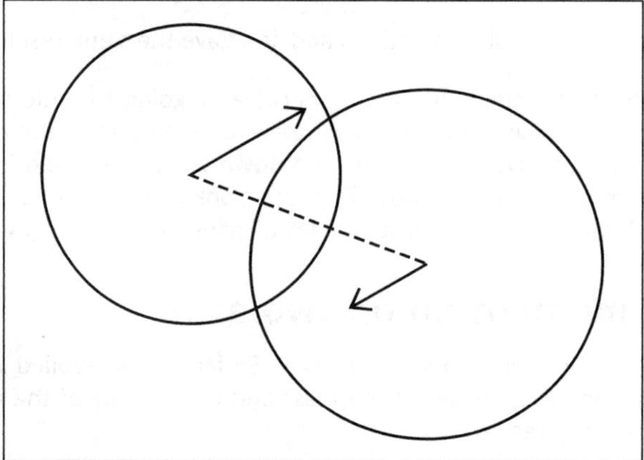

Figure 11-3. A two-dimensional collision

Now the velocities are in completely different directions. You can't just plug the velocities into the momentum-conservation formula. That would give you completely incorrect results. So, how do you solve this?

Well, you start by making the second diagram look a bit more like the first, by rotating it. First, figure out the angle formed by the positions of the two balls and rotate the whole scene—positions and velocities—counterclockwise by that amount. For example, if the angle is 30 degrees, rotate everything by –30. This is exactly the same thing you did in Chapter 10 to bounce off an angled surface. The resulting picture looks like Figure 11-4.

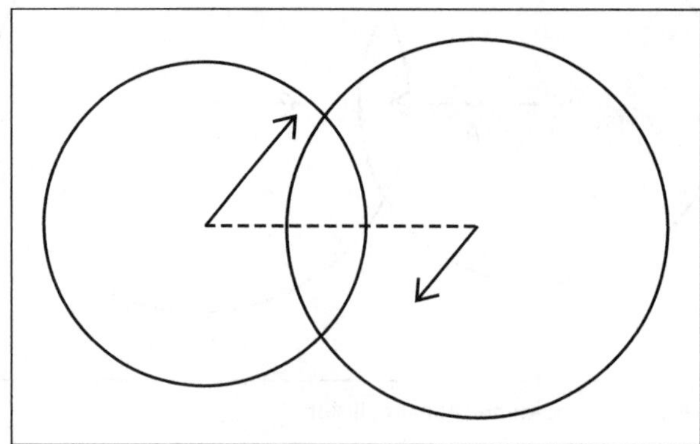

Figure 11-4. A two dimensional collision, rotated

That angle between the two balls is pretty important, and not just to make things look pretty, either. That angle can be called the *angle of collision*. It's important because it's the only part of the ball's velocities that you care about—the portion of the velocity that lies on that angle.

Now, take a look at the diagram in Figure 11-5. Here, I've added in vector lines for the vx and vy for both velocities. Note that the vx for both balls lies exactly along the angle of collision.

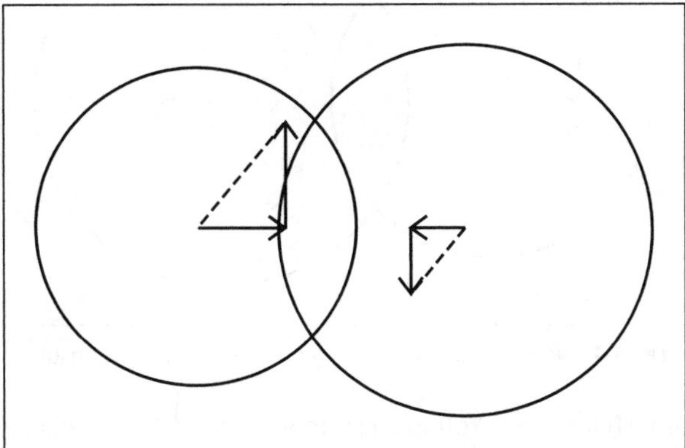

Figure 11-5. Draw in the x and y velocities.

As I just said, the only portion of the velocity you care about is the part that lies on the angle of collision. That is now your vx. In fact, you can just forget all about vy for now. I'll take it right out of the picture, as you can see in Figure 11-6.

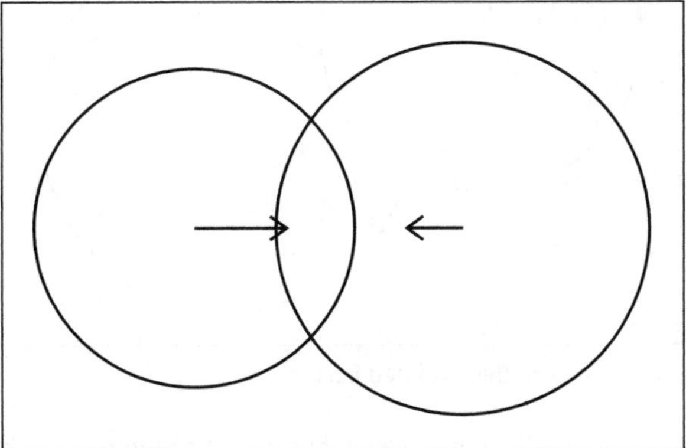

Figure 11-6. All you care about is the x velocity.

Does this look familiar? It's the first diagram again! You can easily solve this with the plug-and-play momentum formula. (Notice how I'm brainwashing you! You've already started agreeing with me that the formula for conservation of momentum is easy, haven't you?)

When you apply the formula, you wind up with two new vx values. Remember that the vy values never change. But the alteration of the vx alone changed the overall velocity to look something Figure 11-7.

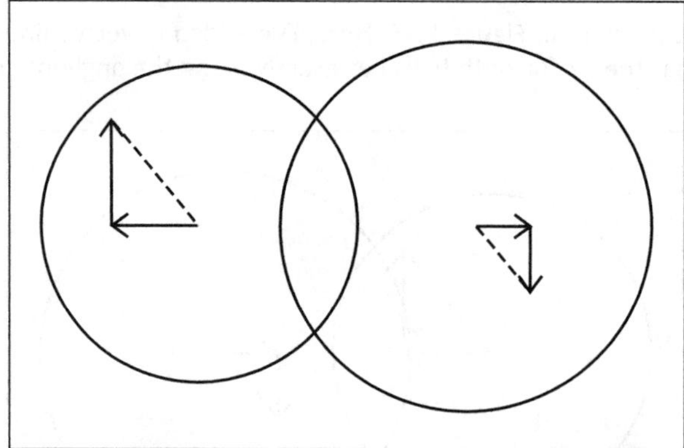

Figure 11-7. New x velocities, same y velocities, with the result of a new overall velocity

Have you already guessed what's next? You just rotate everything back again, as shown in Figure 11-8, and you have the final real vx and vy for each ball.

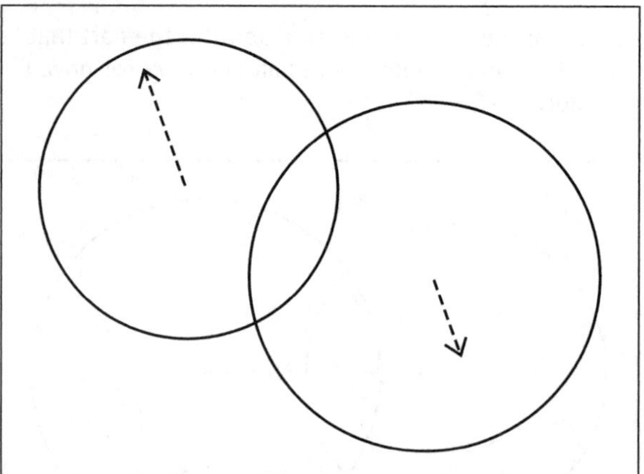

Figure 11-8. Everything rotated back

Well, that all looks very nice in a little line drawing, but now it's time to somehow convert all this into code. The hardest part for me is trying to continue to convince you that it's easy.

Writing the code

To begin, you need to make a base file that will allow two balls to move at any angles and eventually hit each other. Starting off with pretty much the same FLA file as before, you have two ball movie clips: ball0 and ball1. I made them a little larger now, as you can see in Figure 11-9, so there's a good chance of them bumping into each other often.

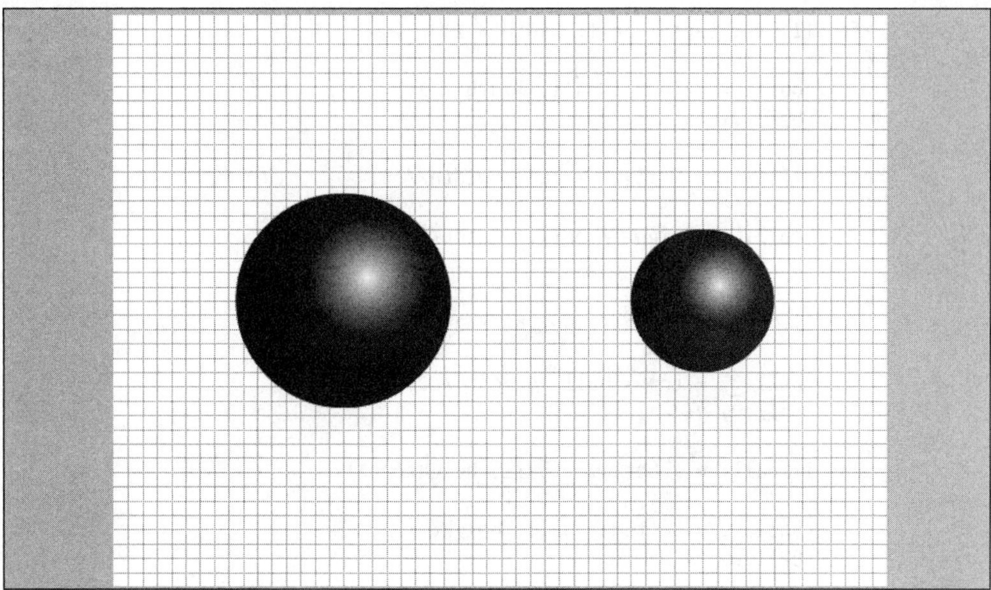

Figure 11-9. Setting up the stage for conservation of momentum on two axes

Then you need to set up some basic motion code and allow the balls to bounce off the walls.

```
var left:Number = 0;
var right:Number = Stage.width;
var top:Number = 0;
var bottom:Number = Stage.height;

ball0.vx = Math.random() * 4-2;
ball0.vy = Math.random() * 4-2;
ball0.mass = 2;

ball1.vx = Math.random() * 4-2;
ball1.vy = Math.random() * 4-2;
ball1.mass = 1;

function onEnterFrame():Void
{
      ball0._x += ball0.vx;
      ball0._y += ball0.vy;
      ball1._x += ball1.vx;
```

```
        ball1._y += ball1.vy;
        checkWalls(ball0);
        checkWalls(ball1);
}

function checkWalls(ball:MovieClip):Void
{
        if(ball._x < left + ball._width / 2)
        {
                ball._x = left + ball._width / 2;
                ball.vx *= -1;
        }
        else if(ball._x > right - ball._width / 2)
        {
                ball._x = right - ball._width / 2;
                ball.vx *= -1;
        }
        if(ball._y < top + ball._height / 2)
        {
                ball._y = top + ball._height / 2;
                ball.vy *= -1;
        }
        else if(ball._y > bottom - ball._height / 2)
        {
                ball._y = bottom - ball._height / 2;
                ball.vy *= -1;
        }
}
```

Now, that's all stuff you should be able to do in your sleep by now. You set boundaries, set some random velocities, throw in some mass, move each ball according to its velocity, and check the boundaries. Notice that I pulled the boundary-checking stuff out into its own function, checkWalls, so I could use it twice without typing it in again.

I do the same thing with the collision-checking routine, putting it into a function called checkCollision. So, onEnterFrame becomes this:

```
function onEnterFrame():Void
{
        ball0._x += ball0.vx;
        ball0._y += ball0.vy;
        ball1._x += ball1.vx;
        ball1._y += ball1.vy;
        checkCollision(ball0, ball1);
        checkWalls(ball0);
        checkWalls(ball1);
}
```

From this point on, I'll show you only the checkCollision function and any other functions I happen to come up with. The rest of the code doesn't change. If you want to see the finished product in all its glory, it's in ch011_03.fla.

The beginning of that function is pretty simple. It's just a distance-based collision detection setup.

```
function checkCollision(ball0:MovieClip, ball1:MovieClip):Void
{
	var dx:Number = ball1._x - ball0._x;
	var dy:Number = ball1._y - ball0._y;
	var dist:Number = Math.sqrt(dx*dx + dy*dy);
	if(dist < ball0._width / 2 + ball1._width / 2)
	{
		// collision handling code here
	}
}
```

See? You have about two-thirds of the code written already, and so far it has been a piece of cake!

The first thing that the collision-handling code needs to do is figure out the angle between the two balls. You can do that with Math.atan2(dy, dx). (If that didn't spring to your mind even as you were reading it, you might want to review the trigonometry in Chapter 3.) Then you store the cosine and sine calculations, as you'll be using them over and over.

```
		// calculate angle, sine and cosine
		var angle:Number = Math.atan2(dy, dx);
		var sine:Number = Math.sin(angle);
		var cosine:Number = Math.cos(angle);
```

Next, you need to do coordinate rotation for the velocity and position of both balls. Let's call the rotated positions x0, y0, x1, and y1 and the rotated velocities vx0, vy0, vx1, and vy1.

Since you are using ball0 as the "pivot point," its coordinates will be 0, 0. That won't change even after rotation, so you can just say this:

```
		// rotate ball0's position
		var x0:Number = 0;
		var y0:Number = 0;
```

Next, ball1's position is in relation to ball0's position. This corresponds to the distance values you've already figured out, dx and dy. So, you can just rotate those to get ball1's rotated position:

```
		// rotate ball1's position
		var x1:Number = dx * cosine + dy * sine;
		var y1:Number = dy * cosine - dx * sine;
```

Finally, rotate all the velocities. You should see a pattern forming:

```
// rotate ball0's velocity
var vx0:Number = ball0.vx * cosine + ball0.vy * sine;
var vy0:Number = ball0.vy * cosine - ball0.vx * sine;

// rotate ball1's velocity
var vx1:Number = ball1.vx * cosine + ball1.vy * sine;
var vy1:Number = ball1.vy * cosine - ball1.vx * sine;
```

Here's all the rotation code in place:

```
function checkCollision(ball0:MovieClip, ball1:MovieClip):Void
{
	var dx:Number = ball1._x - ball0._x;
	var dy:Number = ball1._y - ball0._y;
	var dist:Number = Math.sqrt(dx*dx + dy*dy);
	if(dist < ball0._width / 2 + ball1._width / 2)
	{
		// calculate angle, sine and cosine
		var angle:Number = Math.atan2(dy, dx);
		var sine:Number = Math.sin(angle);
		var cosine:Number = Math.cos(angle);

		// rotate ball0's position
		var x0:Number = 0;
		var y0:Number = 0;

		// rotate ball1's position
		var x1:Number = dx * cosine + dy * sine;
		var y1:Number = dy * cosine - dx * sine;

		// rotate ball0's velocity
		var vx0:Number = ball0.vx * cosine + ball0.vy * sine;
		var vy0:Number = ball0.vy * cosine - ball0.vx * sine;

		// rotate ball1's velocity
		var vx1:Number = ball1.vx * cosine + ball1.vy * sine;
		var vy1:Number = ball1.vy * cosine - ball1.vx * sine;
	}
}
```

That's not so horrible yet, right? Well, hang in there. You're already one-third of the way through the painful stuff.

You can now do a simple one-dimensional collision reaction with vx0 and ball0.mass, and vx1 and ball1.mass. For the earlier one-dimensional example, you had the following code:

```
var vxTotal:Number = ball0.vx - ball1.vx;
ball0.vx = ((ball0.mass - ball1.mass) *
            ball0.vx + 2 * ball1.mass * ball1.vx)
            / (ball0.mass + ball1.mass);
ball1.vx = vxTotal + ball0.vx;
```

You can now rewrite that as follows:

```
var vxTotal:Number = vx0 - vx1;
vx0 = ((ball0.mass - ball1.mass) *
       vx0 + 2 * ball1.mass * vx1)
      / (ball0.mass + ball1.mass);
vx1 = vxTotal + vx0;
```

All you did was replace the ball0.vx and ball1.vx with the rotated version, vx0 and vx1. Let's plug that into the function:

```
function checkCollision(ball0:MovieClip, ball1:MovieClip):Void
{
      var dx:Number = ball1._x - ball0._x;
      var dy:Number = ball1._y - ball0._y;
      var dist:Number = Math.sqrt(dx*dx + dy*dy);
      if(dist < ball0._width / 2 + ball1._width / 2)
      {
            // calculate angle, sine and cosine
            var angle:Number = Math.atan2(dy, dx);
            var sine:Number = Math.sin(angle);
            var cosine:Number = Math.cos(angle);

            // rotate ball0's position
            var x0:Number = 0;
            var y0:Number = 0;

            // rotate ball1's position
            var x1:Number = dx * cosine + dy * sine;
            var y1:Number = dy * cosine - dx * sine;

            // rotate ball0's velocity
            var vx0:Number = ball0.vx * cosine + ball0.vy * sine;
            var vy0:Number = ball0.vy * cosine - ball0.vx * sine;

            // rotate ball1's velocity
            var vx1:Number = ball1.vx * cosine + ball1.vy * sine;
            var vy1:Number = ball1.vy * cosine - ball1.vx * sine;
```

```
                // collision reaction
                var vxTotal:Number = vx0 - vx1;
                vx0 = ((ball0.mass - ball1.mass) *
                       vx0 + 2 * ball1.mass * vx1)
                       / (ball0.mass + ball1.mass);
                vx1 = vxTotal + vx0;

                // update position
                x0 += vx0;
                x1 += vx1;
            }
        }
```

This code also adds the new x velocities to the x positions, to move them apart, as in the one-dimensional example.

Now that you have updated, postcollision positions and velocities, rotate everything back. Start by getting the unrotated, final positions.

```
// rotate positions back
var x0Final:Number = x0 * cosine - y0 * sine;
var y0Final:Number = y0 * cosine + x0 * sine;
var x1Final:Number = x1 * cosine - y1 * sine;
var y1Final:Number = y1 * cosine + x1 * sine;
```

Remember to reverse the + and - in the rotation equations, as you are going in the other direction now. These "final" positions are actually not quite final. They are in relation to the pivot point of the system, which is ball0's original position. So, you need to add all of these to ball0's position to get the actual screen positions. Let's do ball1 first, so that it's using ball0's original position, not the updated one:

```
// adjust positions to actual screen positions
ball1._x = ball0._x + x1Final;
ball1._y = ball0._y + y1Final;
ball0._x = ball0._x + x0Final;
ball0._y = ball0._y + y0Final;
```

Last, but not least, rotate back the velocities. These can be applied directly to the balls' vx and vy properties:

```
// rotate velocities back
ball0.vx = vx0 * cosine - vy0 * sine;
ball0.vy = vy0 * cosine + vx0 * sine;
ball1.vx = vx1 * cosine - vy1 * sine;
ball1.vy = vy1 * cosine + vx1 * sine;
```

Let's take a look at the entire, completed function:

```
function checkCollision(ball0:MovieClip, ball1:MovieClip):Void
{
      var dx:Number = ball1._x - ball0._x;
      var dy:Number = ball1._y - ball0._y;
      var dist:Number = Math.sqrt(dx*dx + dy*dy);
      if(dist < ball0._width / 2 + ball1._width / 2)
      {
            // calculate angle, sine and cosine
            var angle:Number = Math.atan2(dy, dx);
            var sine:Number = Math.sin(angle);
            var cosine:Number = Math.cos(angle);

            // rotate ball0's position
            var x0:Number = 0;
            var y0:Number = 0;

            // rotate ball1's position
            var x1:Number = dx * cosine + dy * sine;
            var y1:Number = dy * cosine - dx * sine;

            // rotate ball0's velocity
            var vx0:Number = ball0.vx * cosine + ball0.vy * sine;
            var vy0:Number = ball0.vy * cosine - ball0.vx * sine;

            // rotate ball1's velocity
            var vx1:Number = ball1.vx * cosine + ball1.vy * sine;
            var vy1:Number = ball1.vy * cosine - ball1.vx * sine;

            // collision reaction
            var vxTotal:Number = vx0 - vx1;
            vx0 = ((ball0.mass - ball1.mass) *
                   vx0 + 2 * ball1.mass * vx1)
                   / (ball0.mass + ball1.mass);
            vx1 = vxTotal + vx0;

            // update position
            x0 += vx0;
            x1 += vx1;

            // rotate positions back
            var x0Final:Number = x0 * cosine - y0 * sine;
            var y0Final:Number = y0 * cosine + x0 * sine;
            var x1Final:Number = x1 * cosine - y1 * sine;
            var y1Final:Number = y1 * cosine + x1 * sine;
```

```
                // adjust positions to actual screen positions
                ball1._x = ball0._x + x1Final;
                ball1._y = ball0._y + y1Final;
                ball0._x = ball0._x + x0Final;
                ball0._y = ball0._y + y0Final;

                // rotate velocities back
                ball0.vx = vx0 * cosine - vy0 * sine;
                ball0.vy = vy0 * cosine + vx0 * sine;
                ball1.vx = vx1 * cosine - vy1 * sine;
                ball1.vy = vy1 * cosine + vx1 * sine;
        }
}
```

Play around with this example. Change the size of the ball movie clip instances, the initial velocities, masses, and so on. Become convinced that it works pretty well.

As for that checkCollision function, it's a doozy, yes. But if you read the comments, you see it's broken up into (relatively) simple chunks. You could probably optimize this, or you could refactor it a bit to remove some of the duplication. In fact, in the name of good practice, I've gone ahead and done this in `ch11_04.fla`, which you can see here:

```
function checkCollision(ball0:MovieClip, ball1:MovieClip):Void
{
        var dx:Number = ball1._x - ball0._x;
        var dy:Number = ball1._y - ball0._y;
        var dist:Number = Math.sqrt(dx*dx + dy*dy);
        if(dist < ball0._width / 2 + ball1._width / 2)
        {
                // calculate angle, sine and cosine
                var angle:Number = Math.atan2(dy, dx);
                var sine:Number = Math.sin(angle);
                var cosine:Number = Math.cos(angle);

                // rotate ball0's position
                var pos0:Object = {x:0, y:0};

                // rotate ball1's position
                var pos1:Object = rotate(dx, dy, sine, cosine, true);

                // rotate ball0's velocity
                var vel0:Object = rotate(ball0.vx,
                                         ball0.vy,
                                         sine,
                                         cosine,
                                         true);
```

```
// rotate ball1's velocity
var vel1:Object = rotate(ball1.vx,
                         ball1.vy,
                         sine,
                         cosine,
                         true);

// collision reaction
var vxTotal:Number = vel0.x - vel1.x;
vel0.x = ((ball0.mass - ball1.mass) *
          vel0.x + 2 * ball1.mass * vel1.x)
          / (ball0.mass + ball1.mass);
vel1.x = vxTotal + vel0.x;

// update position
pos0.x += vel0.x;
pos1.x += vel1.x;

// rotate positions back
var pos0F:Object = rotate(pos0.x,
                          pos0.y,
                          sine,
                          cosine,
                          false);
var pos1F:Object = rotate(pos1.x,
                          pos1.y,
                          sine,
                          cosine,
                          false);

// adjust positions to actual screen positions
ball1._x = ball0._x + pos1F.x;
ball1._y = ball0._y + pos1F.y;
ball0._x = ball0._x + pos0F.x;
ball0._y = ball0._y + pos0F.y;

// rotate velocities back
var vel0F:Object = rotate(vel0.x,
                          vel0.y,
                          sine,
                          cosine,
                          false);
var vel1F:Object = rotate(vel1.x,
                          vel1.y,
                          sine,
                          cosine,
                          false);
```

```
                ball0.vx = vel0F.x;
                ball0.vy = vel0F.y;
                ball1.vx = vel1F.x;
                ball1.vy = vel1F.y;
        }
}

function rotate(x:Number,
                y:Number,
                sine:Number,
                cosine:Number,
                reverse:Boolean):Object
{
        var result:Object = new Object();
        if(reverse)
        {
                result.x = x * cosine + y * sine;
                result.y = y * cosine - x * sine;
        }
        else
        {
                result.x = x * cosine - y * sine;
                result.y = y * cosine + x * sine;
        }
        return result;
}
```

Here, I've made a `rotate` function that takes in the values it needs and returns an object with updated _x and _y properties. This version isn't quite as easy to read when you're learning the principles involved, but it results in a lot less duplicated code.

Adding more objects

Now, having two movie clips colliding and reacting was no easy task, but you made it. Congratulations. Now let's go for a few more colliding objects—say eight. That sounds like it's going to be four times more complex, but it's really not. The functions you have now just check two balls at a time, but that's all you really want to do anyway. You put more objects on stage, move them around, and check each one against all the others. And you've already done just that in the collision detection examples (Chapter 9). All you need to do is to plug in the `checkCollision` function where you would normally do the collision detection.

For this example (`ch11_05.fla`), start with eight balls on the stage, named `ball0` through `ball7`, as shown in Figure 11-10.

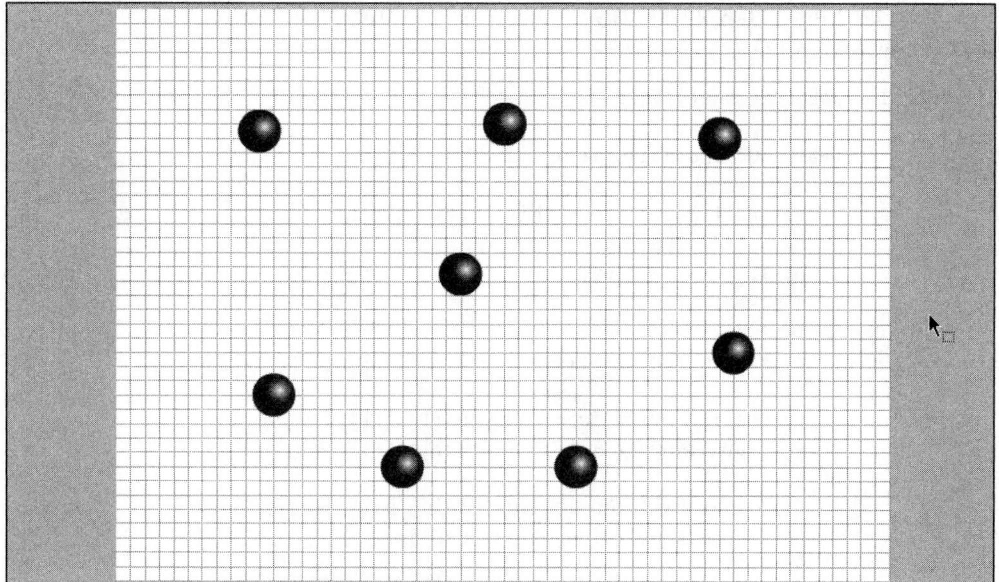

Figure 11-10. Setting up the stage with multiple objects

After the usual setting of boundaries, you loop through the on-stage balls and assign various properties to them:

```
var numBalls:Number = 8;
for(var i:Number = 0;i<numBalls;i++)
{
	var ball:MovieClip = this["ball" + i];
	ball.vx = Math.random() * 10 - 5;
	ball.vy = Math.random() * 10 - 5;
	ball._xscale = ball._yscale =
	               ball.mass =
	               Math.random() * 250 + 20;
}
```

Now, you might be asking, why didn't I just attach them at runtime, rather than go through the trouble of putting them on stage, laying them out, and naming each one? The reason is that you need to make sure that when each ball first appears, it does not collide with any of the existing balls. Otherwise, it will become stuck to it, probably for eternity. While there are certainly ways of avoiding that via code, I decided to keep the code simple and clean, and place the movie clips by hand.

The onEnterFrame function is surprisingly simple. It has just two loops: one for basic movement and one for collision detection.

```
function onEnterFrame():Void
{
	for(var i=0;i<numBalls;i++)
	{
		var ball:MovieClip = this["ball" + i];
		ball._x += ball.vx;
		ball._y += ball.vy;
		checkWalls(ball);
	}
	for(var i=0;i<numBalls-1;i++)
	{
		var ballA:MovieClip = this["ball" + i];
		for(var j:Number = i+1;j<numBalls;j++)
		{
			var ballB:MovieClip = this["ball" + j];
			checkCollision(ballA, ballB);
		}
	}
}
```

The first for loop just runs through each ball on stage, moving it and bouncing it off the walls. Then you have a nested loop that compares each ball with every other one, as I covered in the discussion of collision detection (in Chapter 9). In this, you get a reference to two of the balls at a time, name them ballA and ballB, and pass these to the checkCollision function. And, amazingly enough, that's all there is to it! The checkCollision and rotate functions are exactly the same.

To add more balls, just put them on stage, name them ball8, ball9, and so on, and update the numBalls variable to the new total.

Solving a potential problem

One word of warning regarding the setup I've described in this chapter: It's still possible for a pair of movie clips to get kind of stuck together. This mostly happens in a crowded environment with many movie clips bouncing off each other, and it seems worse when they are moving at high speeds. You can also occasionally see this behavior if two or three balls collide in a corner of the stage.

Say you have three balls on stage—ball0, ball1, and ball2—and they all happen to be really close together. Here's basically what happens:

- The code moves all three according to their velocities.
- The code checks ball0 vs. ball1, and ball0 vs. ball2. It finds no collision.
- The code checks ball1 vs. ball2. These two happen to be hitting, so it does all the calculations for their new velocities and updates their positions so that they are no longer touching. This inadvertently puts ball1 in contact with ball0. However, this particular combination has already been checked for a collision, so it now goes unnoticed.

- On the next loop, the code again moves each according to its velocity. This potentially drives ball1 and ball0 even further together.
- Now the code does notice that ball0 and ball1 are hitting. It calculates their new velocities and adds the new velocities to the positions, to move them apart. But, since they were already touching, this might not be enough to actually separate them. They become stuck.

Again, this mostly occurs when you have a lot of objects in a small space, moving at higher speeds. You probably won't see it happen in the file you just created, which is why I'm bringing it up as an afterthought. (If it isn't broken, don't fix it.) But, if you add a bunch more balls into the equation, you'll probably see it crop up now and then. So, it's good to know where the problem lies. The exact point is in the checkCollision function, specifically the following lines:

```
// update position
pos0.x += vel0.x;
pos1.x += vel1.x;
```

This just assumes that the collision occurred due to only the two ball's own velocities, and that adding back on the new velocities will separate them. Most of the time, this is true. But the situation I just described is an exception. If you are running into this situation, you need something more stringent in ensuring that the movie clips are definitely separated before moving on. I came up with the following method:

```
// update position
var absV:Number = Math.abs(vel0.x) + Math.abs(vel1.x);
var overlap:Number = (ball0._width / 2 + ball1._width / 2)
                     - Math.abs(pos0.x - pos1.x);
pos0.x += vel0.x / absV * overlap;
pos1.x += vel1.x / absV * overlap;
```

This is totally my own creation, so I'm not sure how accurate it is, but it seems to work pretty well. It first determines the absolute velocity (a term I made up!). This is the sum of the absolute values of both velocities. For instance, if one velocity is –5 and the other is 10, the absolute values are 5 and 10, and the total is 5 + 10, or 15.

Next, it determines how much the balls are actually overlapping. It does this by getting their total radii, and subtracting their distance.

Then it moves each ball a portion of the overlap, according to their percent of the absolute velocity. The result is that the balls should be exactly touching each other, with no overlap. It's a bit more complex than the earlier version, but it pretty much clears up the bugs.

In fact, in the next version, I just attached 20 instances and randomly placed them on stage. The ones that overlap still freak out for a few frames, but eventually, due to this new code, they all settle down.

Here's the setup code from ch11_06.fla, which starts with an empty stage and the ball movie clip exported from the library.

```
var numBalls:Number = 20;
for(var i:Number = 0;i<numBalls;i++)
{
	var ball:MovieClip = attachMovie("ball", "ball" + i, i);
	ball._x = Math.random() * Stage.width;
	ball._y = Math.random() * Stage.height;
	ball.vx = Math.random() * 10 - 5;
	ball.vy = Math.random() * 10 - 5;
	ball._xscale = ball._yscale =
	               ball.mass =
	               Math.random() * 200 + 50;
}
```

The rest is all the same, except that it includes the fix I just mentioned.

Of course, you're free to investigate your own solutions to the problem, and if you come up with something that is simpler, more efficient, and more accurate, please share!

Important formulas in this chapter

The important formula in this chapter is the one for conservation of momentum.

Conservation of momentum, in straight mathematical terms:

```
          (m0 - m1) * v0 + 2 * m1 * v1
v0Final = ----------------------------
                    m0 + m1

          (m1 - m0) * v1 + 2 * m0 * v0
v1Final = ----------------------------
                    m0 + m1
```

Conservation of momentum in ActionScript, with a shortcut:

```
var vxTotal:Number = vx0 - vx1;
vx0 = ((ball0.mass - ball1.mass) * vx0
      + 2 * ball1.mass * vx1) / (ball0.mass + ball1.mass);
vx1 = vxTotal + vx0;
```

Summary

Congratulations! You've made it through what will probably be the heaviest math in the book. You now have in your repertoire the methods for handling accurate collision reactions. This is one of the most common things that people write to me asking about. With what you have under your belt right now, you could whip up a pretty decent game of billiards, which would be a fitting thing to do with billiard ball physics! One thing I've totally ignored in these examples, just to keep them simple, is the concept of friction. You might want to try adding that into the system. You certainly know enough at this point to do so. You might also want to check out Chapter 19, where I give you a little trick to use in the case that both objects have the same mass.

In the next chapter, I'll tone things down a bit and look into particle attraction, though adding in some billiard ball physics to the examples there would be quite fitting.

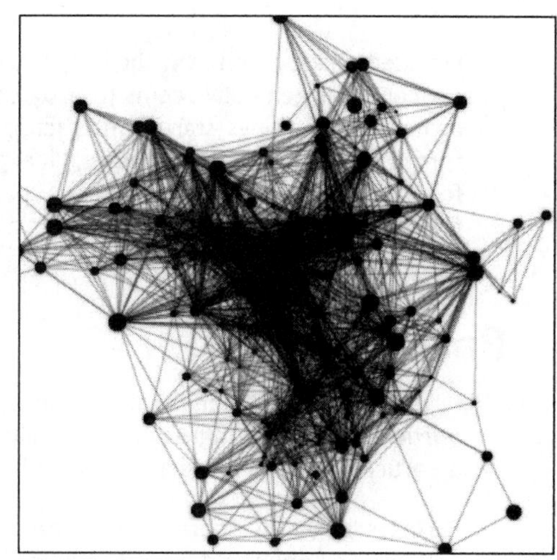

Chapter 12

PARTICLE ATTRACTION AND GRAVITY

What we'll cover in this chapter:

- Particles
- Gravity
- Springs
- Important formulas in this chapter

I'm pretty happy with how the progression of these chapters has turned out. Each chapter adds a new concept that generally seems to progress in terms of interaction. At first, you just had things moving around. Then things started interacting with the environment, then the user, and then each other through collisions. In this chapter, I'll expand on the ways objects interact with each other, particularly from a distance. Specifically, I'll cover particles, gravity (a little different this time), springs (again!), and the world-famous Node Garden. Let's dive right in!

Particles

I guess I should define what I mean by a particle. For me, and for the purposes of this chapter, a *particle* is simply a single unit, generally in the company of several (or many) other similar units. Thus, a particle could be a speck of dust, a beach ball, or a planet.

Particles generally share a common type of behavior, but also can have their own individuality. Followers of object-oriented programming will see an analogy here to *objects*. All objects of a particular class usually share the same behavior, defined by the methods of the class, and individual instances are customized by assigning values to various properties. You've already seen how this works with the ball movie clips you've been using in the examples. Each had its own properties: velocity, mass, size, and so on, but all of the balls moved with the same rules.

> *Actually, creating a class for a particle is a great way to proceed. In* New Masters of Flash Volume 3 *(another friends of ED book, published in 2004), I walked through the creation of just such a class. For this book, however, I'll keep things on the timeline.*

Why don't you go ahead and create some kind of graphic to use as a particle. For these examples, I'll stick with the red ball I've been using all along (I'm *really* proud of that thing!), but make it a lot smaller—just 10 pixels across. Whatever you come up with, convert it to a movie clip, keep the registration point centered as usual, and call it `particle`. Make sure that it is also set to export for ActionScript, with the linkage name `particle`.

The general setup will be the same in each case. Most of the variations will be in the interaction and attraction between the particles, and they will come in the `onEnterFrame` function. The setup basically consists of attaching a bunch of particles and sprinkling them randomly around the screen. Here's that code:

```
var numParticles:Number = 30;
init();
function init():Void
{
      for(var i:Number=0;i<numParticles;i++)
      {
            var particle:MovieClip = attachMovie("particle",
                                                 "p" + i, i);
            particle._x = Math.random() * Stage.width;
            particle._y = Math.random() * Stage.height;
```

```
                particle.vx = 0;
                particle.vy = 0;
                particle.mass = 1;
            }
        }
```

Here, you initialize each particle's vx and vy to 0, and leave them at their default size. You're also continuing to use mass, setting the particle mass to 1. You'll probably want to try changing that around to get different effects later. You might also want to start off the particles with a random velocity or randomly size them.

All the rest of the examples in this chapter assume this basic setup, and will occasionally add something to it. But mainly I'll be describing the onEnterFrame and any other functions that need to be written. First, I'll describe some background theory, but hold on to the file you just created, because you'll be getting back to it very soon.

Gravity

The first kind of particle attraction I'm going to talk about is gravity. Now, I can hear you saying, "Didn't you cover that way back in Part Two of the book?" True, I did, but that was gravity as seen from very close up.

Standing on earth, gravity has a pretty simple description: It pulls things down. In fact, it pulls things down at a very specific rate. The acceleration it applies is equal to about 32 feet per second per second. One way of expressing acceleration is by how much velocity it adds over a specific time period. Gravity makes things go 32 feet per second faster, every second it pulls on them. You can go to the tallest mountain or the lowest valley, and that number 32 isn't going to change enough for you to notice (that is, without some sensitive instruments).

Gravitational force

When you start stepping back, you see that actually, the farther away you are from a planet or large body, the less the gravity becomes. This is a very good thing. Otherwise, we would all be sucked into the sun, which would be sucked into every other sun and planet, which would all wind up smashed together pretty quickly. So, when you get out to the point where you can refer to planets as particles, the distance between them very much affects the gravitational pull.

How much the distance affects the force is very easy to describe. It's inversely proportional to the square of the distance. Well, maybe that needs some explanation. First, gravity is also very tied in with mass. The more mass something has, the more force it will pull on other things, and the more it will be pulled by them. There is also something called the *gravitational constant* (abbreviated G) that fits in there. Here's the full equation for the force of gravity:

$$force = G * m1 * m2 / distance^2$$

In plain English, the force of gravity on an object by another object is equal to this gravitational constant, times both masses, divided by the square of the distance between them. Hmmm. . . that looks pretty simple. You just need to know what this gravitational constant is, and you'll be all set. Well, here's the official definition of it:

$$G = (6.6742 \pm 0.0010) * 10^{-11} * m^3 * kg^{-1} * s^{-2}$$

Now, if you want to figure out coding that in ActionScript, go for it. For me, when I see something like that, I immediately know I'm going to be doing some faking soon. You want to know how I usually fake it? I write my gravity formula like this:

$$force = m1 * m2 / distance^2$$

Yup, that's right, I ignore G. And now I'll plug in my usual disclaimer. If you are doing a Flash-based space shuttle guidance system for NASA, you should probably leave G in there. But if you're coding up the next great online space wars game, you're probably going to be able to live without it.

Now that you have a formula, let's put it into code. Set up the `onEnterFrame` function first, and have it call a `gravitate` function so you can separate the code that handles gravity:

```
function onEnterFrame():Void
{
	for(var i:Number = 0;i<numParticles;i++)
	{
		var particle:MovieClip = this["p" + i];
		particle._x += particle.vx;
		particle._y += particle.vy;
	}
	for(i=0;i<numParticles-1;i++)
	{
		var partA:MovieClip = this["p" + i];
		for(var j:Number = i+1;j<numParticles;j++)
		{
			var partB:MovieClip = this["p" + j];
			gravitate(partA, partB);
		}
	}
}
```

Here, you're just moving all the particles with basic motion code in a single `for` loop, and then doing a double `for` loop to get their interactions. Once you have `partA` and `partB`, you pass these two particles to the gravitate function. Here's that function:

```
function gravitate(partA:MovieClip, partB:MovieClip):Void
{
	var dx:Number = partB._x - partA._x;
	var dy:Number = partB._y - partA._y;
	var distSQ:Number = dx*dx + dy*dy;
	var dist:Number = Math.sqrt(distSQ);
	var force:Number = partA.mass * partB.mass / distSQ;
	var ax:Number = force * dx / dist;
	var ay:Number = force * dy / dist;
	partA.vx += ax / partA.mass;
```

```
        partA.vy += ay / partA.mass;
        partB.vx -= ax / partB.mass;
        partB.vy -= ay / partB.mass;
    }
```

First, you find the dx and dy between the two particles, and the total distance. Remember that the formula for gravity—force = G × m1 × m2 / distance2—contains the distance squared. Normally, I would calculate distance all at once using `dist = Math.sqrt(dx*dx + dy*dy)`. But then to get distance squared, I would be squaring something that was a square root! That's double work. If I just use the variable `distSQ` to grab a reference to `dx*dx + dy*dy` before I take the square root, I save myself that calculation.

Then I find the total force by multiplying the masses and dividing by the distance squared. Then I figure out the total acceleration on the x and y axes. Again, I'm using the shortcut I discussed at the very end of Chapter 9, using `dx / dist` instead of `Math.cos(angle)` and `dy / dist` instead of `Math.sin(angle)`. This saves me from needing to use `Math.atan2(dy, dx)` to find the angle in the first place.

Now, notice that I keep talking about the *total* force and the *total* acceleration. This is the combined force acting between the two objects. You need to divvy it up between the two, based on their masses. If you think of the earth and the sun, there is a particular force between them. It is the product of their masses, divided by the square of their distance. So, they are pulling towards each other with that total force. The earth is being pulled towards the sun, and the sun is being pulled towards the earth. Obviously, the earth gets a lot more of that acceleration because it has much less mass than the sun. So, to get the individual acceleration for either object in the system, you divide the total acceleration by that object's mass. Thus, you have the last four lines of the formula. Notice that `partA` gets the acceleration added, and `partB` gets it subtracted. This is merely due to the order of subtraction I used to get dx and dy.

The final code for this example can be found in `ch12_01.fla`. Go ahead and test it. You should see that the particles start out motionless, but are slowly attracted to each other, something like Figure 12-1. Occasionally, a couple of them will start sort of orbiting around each other. But mostly what happens is that they hit and fly off in opposite directions.

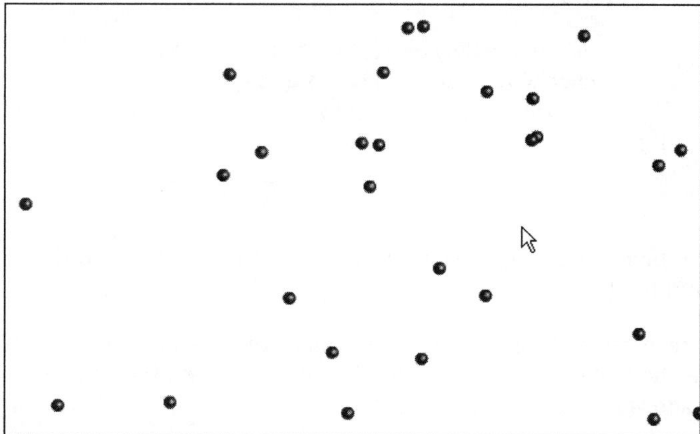

Figure 12-1. We have particles!

Is this speeding off a bug? Well, yes and no. It's not a bug in the code. It's actually expected behavior, and is something called the *slingshot effect*. It's what NASA uses to send probes into deep space. As an object gets closer and closer to a planet, it feels more and more acceleration, and it starts traveling with a very high velocity. If you aim it just right, so it comes very close to the planet, but just misses it, that object will whip off into space too fast for the planet's gravity to capture it. All that speed with zero fuel—now that's efficiency.

But back to Flash. What is happening here is that the objects are getting to within a very small distance of each other—almost zero distance. Thus, the force between them becomes huge, almost infinite. So, mathematically, it's correct, but from a simulation viewpoint, it's unrealistic. What should happen is that if the objects get close enough together, they collide. If you aimed that space probe directly at the planet, it would not zoom past it at infinite speed. It would make a crater.

Collision detection and reaction

So, for your particles, you need to have some kind of collision detection and reaction. What you do is up to you. You could have them explode and disappear. You could have one particle disappear and add its mass to the other one, as if they had joined.

For this example, I realized that I had some very nice collision and reaction code left over from the previous chapter, in a function called checkCollision. Let's just plug that right in here, like so (ch12_02.fla):

```
function onEnterFrame():Void
{
        for(var i:Number = 0;i<numParticles;i++)
        {
                var particle:MovieClip = this["p" + i];
                particle._x += particle.vx;
                particle._y += particle.vy;
        }
        for(i=0;i<numParticles-1;i++)
        {
                var partA:MovieClip = this["p" + i];
                for(var j:Number = i+1;j<numParticles;j++)
                {
                        var partB:MovieClip = this["p" + j];
                        checkCollision(partA, partB);
                        gravitate(partA, partB);
                }
        }
}
```

Only that one line in bold has changed. Plus, of course, I copied and pasted the checkCollision and rotate functions into the file.

Now the particles are attracted to each other, but bounce off when they hit. Try changing the mass of the particles and see how they attract differently. You can even do bizarre things like giving the particles negative mass and watching them repel each other!

In the file ch12_03.fla, I kept everything the same, but added a couple of lines to the init function:

```
function init():Void
{
	for(var i:Number=0;i<numParticles;i++)
	{
		var particle:MovieClip = attachMovie("particle",
		                                     "p" + i, i);
		particle._x = Math.random() * Stage.width;
		particle._y = Math.random() * Stage.height;
		particle.vx = 0;
		particle.vy = 0;
		particle._xscale = particle._yscale = 100 +
		                   Math.random() * 500;
		particle.mass = particle._xscale / 100;
	}
}
```

This just gives each particle a random size and a mass based on that size, as you can see in Figure 12-2. Things start to get interesting.

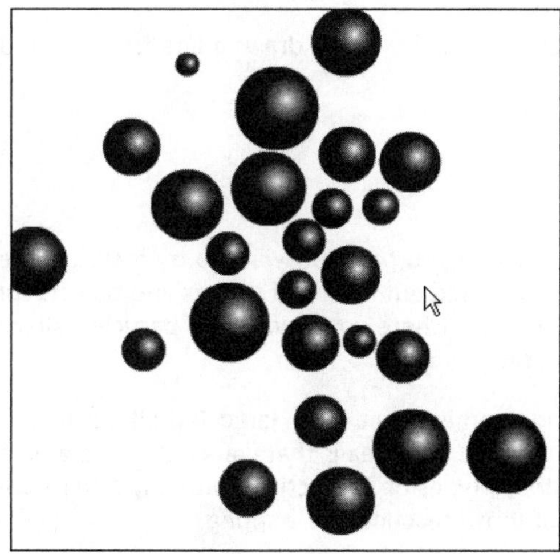

Figure 12-2. Colliding planets?

Orbiting

Finally, just to show you how realistic this gets, let's set up a simple planetary system, with a sun and planet. Make a large sun with a mass of 10,000, and a planet with a mass of 1. Then move the planet a distance away from the sun and give it some velocity perpendicular to the line between it and the sun. The setup looks something like Figure 12-3.

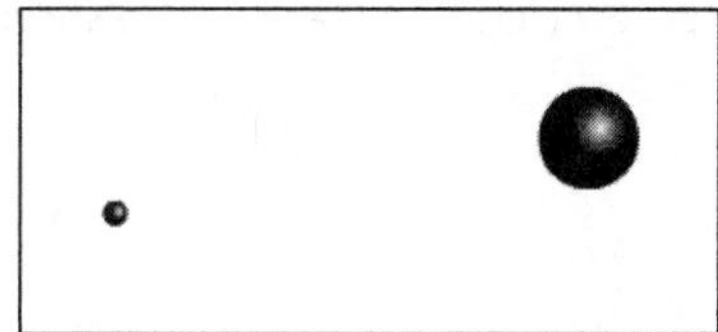

Figure 12-3. Setting up the stage

If you get the masses, distance, and velocity just right, you should be able to get the planet into orbit. It took some trial and error, but I came up with what's in ch12_04.fla. All I'm going to show you here is the init code. The only other change to the file was to set the numParticles variable to 2.

```
function init():Void
{
	var sun:MovieClip = attachMovie("particle", "p" + 0, 0);
	sun._x = Stage.width / 2;
	sun._y = Stage.height / 2;
	sun._xscale = sun._yscale = 400;
	sun.vx = 0;
	sun.vy = 0;
	sun.mass = 10000;

	var planet:MovieClip = attachMovie("particle", "p" + 1, 1);
	planet._x = Stage.width / 2+ 200;
	planet._y = Stage.height / 2;
	planet.vx = 0;
	planet.vy = 7;
	planet.mass = 1;
}
```

As a little extra, check out ch12_04a,fla, which draws a line tracing the orbit. You can wind up with some interesting patterns.

Springs

The other kind of particle attraction you probably want to try is springs. Yes, springs, my favorite subject! Recall that in Chapter 8, you tried out chains of springs and objects springing to each other. Here, you'll look at a broader application, where you have many particles, all springing to each other, as in the gravity examples you just saw.

The inspiration for this example came from a piece Jared Tarbell did at www.levitated.net, called The Node Garden, shown in Figure 12-4. The idea is that you could have a field of these nodes (particles), and they could each have various types of interactions with any other nodes that were nearby. I think it was my idea to have one of those reactions be a spring.

Gravity vs. springs

If you look at gravity and springs, you see they are very similar, yet almost exactly opposite. Both apply acceleration to two objects to pull them together. But in gravity, the farther apart the objects are, the less acceleration there is. In a spring, the acceleration gets *larger* as the distance increases.

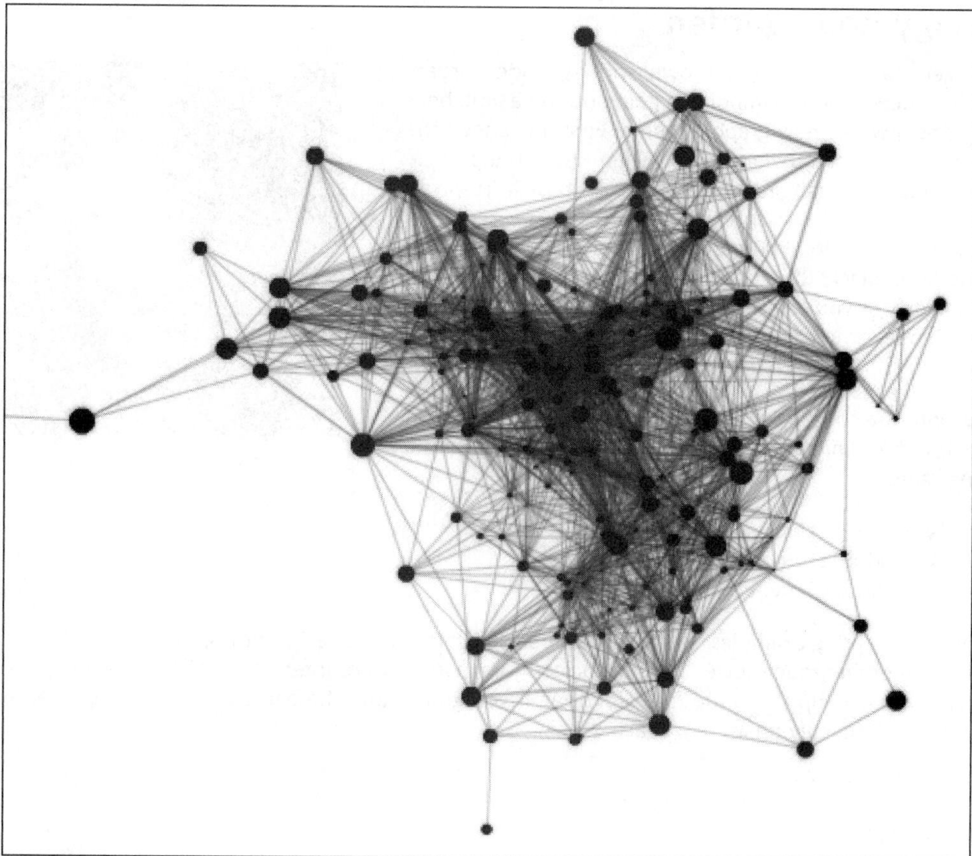

Figure 12-4. Jared Tarbell's Node Garden

So, while you could just swap out the gravity code and plug the spring code into the previous examples, the effect might not be too interesting, because the particles would eventually just lump into a mass. Springs can't tolerate distance. If gravity's motto is "out of sight, out of mind," a spring's credo is "absence makes the spring grow fonder."

So you have a dilemma. You want to have particles attract with a spring force, but you want them to tolerate some distance and not be pulling themselves together. My solution for this was to come up with a minimum distance variable. Mathematically speaking, it might be more like a maximum distance, because it is the largest distance at which a reaction will still take place. But minimum distance always seemed right to my brain, because it means that particles must be *at least* this close together to react. If they are farther apart, they ignore each other.

A springy node garden

Let's get started making our own springy node garden. First, you need a node symbol. I'm going out on a limb here and using a whole new graphic theme! First, I changed the background of the movie to black. Then I took the particle movie clip and changed the graphic in it to a 10-pixel-diameter circle with a centered gradient fill. The center of the fill is pure white, 100 percent opaque. The outer edge of the fill is black, 0% alpha. The result is a kind of small, glowing orb, as you can see in Figure 12-5. That's how I picture a "node." You can make your own, or use what I came up with in ch12_05.fla.

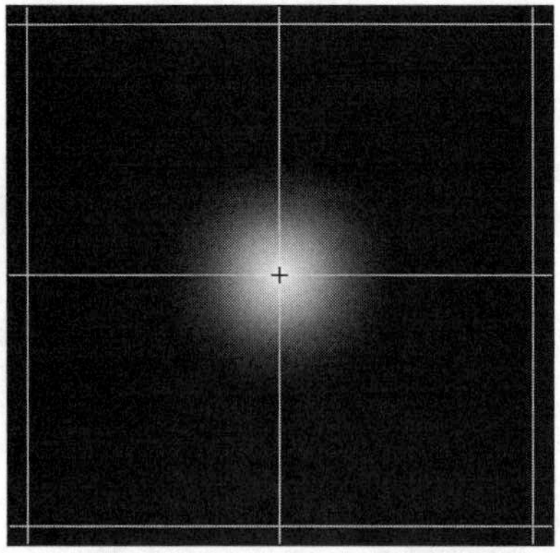

Figure 12-5. My version of a node

Now, onto the code. First, set some variables for number of particles, the minimum distance I just talked about, and a spring value.

```
var numParticles:Number = 30;
var minDist:Number = 100;
var springAmount:Number = .001;
```

In the earlier spring examples in Chapter 8, you used something like 0.2 for a spring amount. You need to use something much lower here, as a lot more particles are interacting. If you go too high, the velocity will build up much too fast. However, if you go too low, the particles will just meander about the screen, seemingly unaware of each other.

Then initialize things:

```
init();
function init():Void
{
	for(var i:Number=0;i<numParticles;i++)
	{
		var particle:MovieClip = attachMovie("particle",
		                                     "p" + i, i);
		particle._x = Math.random() * Stage.width;
		particle._y = Math.random() * Stage.height;
		particle.vx = Math.random() * 6 - 3;
		particle.vy = Math.random() * 6 - 3;
	}
}
```

This just creates a bunch of particles, throws them around the screen, and gives them random velocities. Note that I got rid of mass for this example. Later, in the "Node with mass" section, I'll show you an experiment with adding mass back in.

Next comes the onEnterFrame action function:

```
function onEnterFrame():Void
{
	for(var i:Number = 0;i<numParticles;i++)
	{
		var particle:MovieClip = this["p" + i];
		particle._x += particle.vx;
		particle._y += particle.vy;
		if(particle._x > Stage.width)
		{
			particle._x = 0;
		}
		else if(particle._x < 0)
		{
			particle._x = Stage.width;
		}
		if(particle._y > Stage.height)
		{
			particle._y = 0;
		}
		else if(particle._y < 0)
		{
			particle._y = Stage.height;
		}
	}

	for(i=0;i<numParticles-1;i++)
	{
		var partA:MovieClip = this["p" + i];
		for(var j:Number = i+1;j<numParticles;j++)
		{
			var partB:MovieClip = this["p" + j];
			spring(partA, partB);
		}
	}
}
```

This should look pretty familiar. It's basically the same as the gravity setup. I just added in screen wrapping and called a spring function instead of gravitate.

Now to the meat of it, the spring function itself:

```
function spring(partA:MovieClip, partB:MovieClip):Void
{
	var dx:Number = partB._x - partA._x;
	var dy:Number = partB._y - partA._y;
	var dist:Number = Math.sqrt(dx*dx + dy*dy);
	if(dist < minDist)
	{
```

```
                var ax:Number = dx * springAmount;
                var ay:Number = dy * springAmount;
                partA.vx += ax;
                partA.vy += ay;
                partB.vx -= ax;
                partB.vy -= ay;
            }
        }
```

First, you find the distance between the two particles. If it's not less than minDist, you move on. If it is less, however, you figure out the acceleration on each axis, based on the distance and springValue. You add that acceleration to partA's velocity and subtract it from partB's velocity. This pulls the particles together.

Go ahead and try it out. You'll see something like Figure 12-6. Notice how the particles kind of clump together like flies buzzing around a . . . whatever flies like to buzz around. But even those clumps move around, break up, join other clumps, and so on. It's interesting emergent behavior. Try changing the minDist and springValue values to see what happens.

Figure 12-6. Nodes in action

Nodes with connections

While it is pretty obvious that something is going on between the nodes here, I wanted to really point out the specific interaction between each pair of nodes. What better way than to draw a line between any two nodes that are interacting? That's simple enough to do. I just altered the spring function a little bit:

```
function spring(partA:MovieClip, partB:MovieClip):Void
{
      var dx:Number = partB._x - partA._x;
      var dy:Number = partB._y - partA._y;
      var dist:Number = Math.sqrt(dx*dx + dy*dy);
      if(dist < minDist)
      {
            lineStyle(1, 0xffffff, 50);
            moveTo(partA._x, partA._y);
            lineTo(partB._x, partB._y);
            var ax:Number = dx * springAmount;
            var ay:Number = dy * springAmount;
            partA.vx += ax;
            partA.vy += ay;
            partB.vx -= ax;
            partB.vy -= ay;
      }
}
```

If two nodes are interacting, Flash sets a line style and draws a line between them. You should also add the following as the first line in the onEnterFrame function, so you are starting fresh each frame:

```
clear();
```

So, the nodes are now connected, as shown in Figure 12-7. This is OK, but I don't like the way the lines kind of snap on and off as nodes came in and out of range of each other.

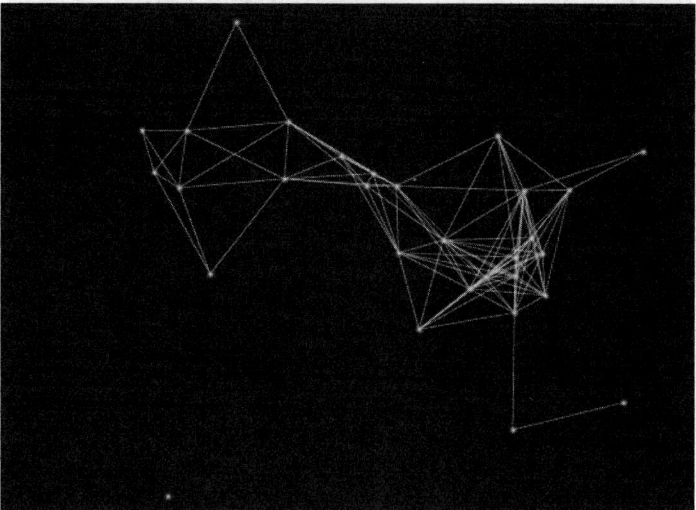

Figure 12-7. Connect the dots

I want a more gradient approach. I figure that if two nodes are just under minDist apart, the line should be almost completely transparent. As they got closer and closer, the line should become brighter and brighter. So, if I say dist / minDist, this gives me a fraction from 0 to 1. Multiply by 100, and I get 0 to 100 for alpha. But this is backwards, because if dist equals minDist, then alpha will be 100, and as dist approaches 0, alpha will approach 0. OK, so take that number and *subtract* it from 100, which effectively reverses the effect. Here's the final line-drawing code:

```
lineStyle(1, 0xffffff, 100 - dist / minDist * 100);
moveTo(partA._x, partA._y);
lineTo(partB._x, partB._y);
```

This, to me, is a very beautiful effect, as shown in Figure 12-8. The result is in ch12_06.fla.

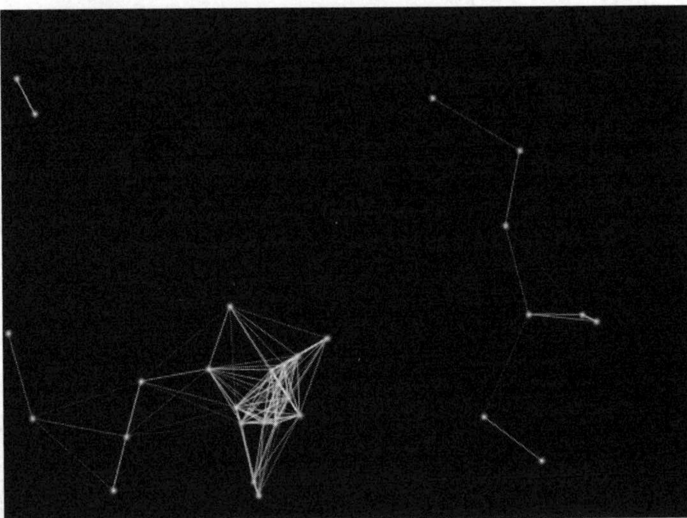

Figure 12-8. Subtle change, but a world of difference

Nodes with mass

While writing the chapter, I intrigued myself with the idea of nodes having mass, something I never thought of before. So, I tried it out and came up with ch12_07.fla. In it, I assign each node a random scale and mass based on that scale.

```
function init():Void
{
	for(var i:Number=0;i<numParticles;i++)
	{
		var particle:MovieClip = attachMovie("particle",
		                                     "p" + i, i);
		particle._x = Math.random() * Stage.width;
		particle._y = Math.random() * Stage.height;
		particle.vx = Math.random() * 6 - 3;
		particle.vy = Math.random() * 6 - 3;
```

```
            particle._xscale = particle._yscale = 50 +
                                Math.random() * 600;
            particle.mass = particle._xscale / 100;
        }
    }
```

This is used only when I'm adding in the velocities in the spring function. I divide the velocity by the mass of each particle. This gives the larger ones more inertia.

```
    function spring(partA:MovieClip, partB:MovieClip):Void
    {
        var dx:Number = partB._x - partA._x;
        var dy:Number = partB._y - partA._y;
        var dist:Number = Math.sqrt(dx*dx + dy*dy);
        if(dist < minDist)
        {
            lineStyle(1, 0xffffff, 100 - dist / minDist * 100);
            moveTo(partA._x, partA._y);
            lineTo(partB._x, partB._y);
            var ax:Number = dx * springAmount;
            var ay:Number = dy * springAmount;
            partA.vx += ax / partA.mass;
            partA.vy += ay / partA.mass;
            partB.vx -= ax / partB.mass;
            partB.vy -= ay / partB.mass;
        }
    }
```

Since I was cutting down the overall effect of the spring, I increased the springValue to .0025. I like the overall effect, which you can see in Figure 12-9.

Figure 12-9. One more for the road

So what can you use nodes for? Personally, I think they are pretty cool to look at, and I even made a nice screensaver with them once. But I can imagine all kinds of game scenarios you could build with them for starters. Throw an Asteroids-type spaceship in there, and try to make it avoid the nodes. I bet that would be a nice challenge!

Important formulas in this chapter

Obviously, the big formula here is gravity.

Basic gravity:

```
force = G * m1 * m2 / distance²
```

ActionScript-friendly gravity implementation:

```
function gravitate(partA:MovieClip, partB:MovieClip):Void
{
      var dx:Number = partB._x - partA._x;
      var dy:Number = partB._y - partA._y;
      var distSQ:Number = dx*dx + dy*dy;
      var dist:Number = Math.sqrt(distSQ);
      var force:Number = partA.mass * partB.mass / distSQ;
      var ax:Number = force * dx / dist;
      var ay:Number = force * dy / dist;
      partA.vx += ax / partA.mass;
      partA.vy += ay / partA.mass;
      partB.vx -= ax / partB.mass;
      partB.vy -= ay / partB.mass;
}
```

Summary

This chapter covered interaction between particles at a distance, and how you can use gravity and springing for interesting effects. As a result, you have two new ways to make some *very* dynamic motion graphics involving many objects.

In the next couple of chapters, I'm going to talk about some very new subjects: *forward kinematics* and *inverse kinematics*. These techniques allow you to make cool things like robot arms and walking figures.

this._height += (this.targetHeight - this._height)/speed;
};shape.targetHeight = shape._height;
shape.onEnterFrame = function() {
var speed = 5;
this._width += (this.targetWidth - this._width)/speed;
this._height += (this.targetHeight - this._height)/speed;

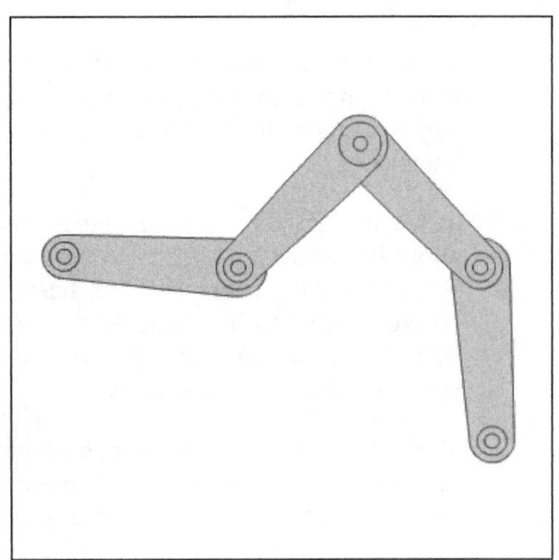

Chapter 13

FORWARD KINEMATICS: MAKING THINGS WALK

What we'll cover in this chapter:

- Introducing forward and inverse kinematics
- Getting started programming forward kinematics
- Automating the process
- Making it really walk

Up to now, you've been going down a particular path, and it has all flowed very nicely. In fact, the previous chapters covered just about all the basics of interactive ActionScripted animation, even all the very advanced "basics." Now, I'm going to branch off to some other interesting techniques that use kinematics.

So, what exactly is this thing called *kinematics*? It always seemed kind of scary when I tried to find out about it. I know it's built into some advanced 3D animation programs, and if you look it up online, you'll find some pages that will barrage you with strange symbols in equations that make anything you've done so far in this book look like first-grade arithmetic. So, first, I want to say that it's really not that tough. The previous chapters covered just about all the concepts you need. You just have to put them together in the right way.

Kinematics is basically the branch of mathematics that deals with the motion of objects without regard for force or mass. So, it's speed, direction, and velocity. Sounds pretty basic, eh? Well, that's a pretty simple definition, and I'm sure it gets into some complex stuff, but for our purposes, yeah, that's pretty much it.

When people in computer science, graphics, games, and so on start talking about kinematics, they are talking about two specific branches of kinematics: forward kinematics and inverse kinematics. Let's start there.

Introducing forward and inverse kinematics

Forward and inverse kinematics generally have to do with a system of connected parts, such as a chain or a jointed arm. They have to do with how that system moves, and how each part moves in relation to the other parts and to the whole.

Often, a kinematics system has two ends: the base and the free end. A jointed arm is usually attached to something fixed at one end, and the other end moves around to reach and grab things. A chain might be attached to something on one or both ends, or not at all.

Forward kinematics (FK) deals with motion that originates at the base of the system and moves out to the free end. *Inverse kinematics* (IK) deals with the opposite: motion originating at, or determined by, the free end and going back to the base, if there is one.

Some examples are in order. In most cases, the limbs of a body in a walk cycle will be done with forward kinematics. The thigh moves, which moves the calf. The calf moves, which moves the foot. The foot moves. In this case, the foot isn't determining anything. It winds up wherever it winds up, based on the positions of all the limbs before it.

An example of inverse kinematics would be pulling someone by the hand. Here, the force applied on the free end—the hand—controls the position and movements of the hand, forearm, upper arm, and eventually the whole body.

Another, more subtle example of inverse kinematics is an arm reaching for something. Again, the hand is what is driving the system. Of course, you can say that, in this example, the upper arm and forearm are moving and they control the position of the hand. That's true, but there is a direct intention to put that hand in a specific place. That is the driving force. In this case, it's not a physical force, but an intention. The forearm and upper arm are simply arranging themselves in whatever configuration necessary to position that hand.

The differences will become clearer as you go through the examples in this and the next chapter. But for now, remember that dragging and reaching are generally inverse kinematics, while a repeated cycle of motion, such as walking, is usually forward kinematics, which is the subject of this chapter.

Getting started programming forward kinematics

Programming both types of kinematics involves a few basic elements:

- The parts of the system. I'll call them *segments*.
- The position of each segment.
- The rotation of each segment.

Each segment in these examples will be an oblong shape like a forearm or upper arm, or any part of a leg. Of course, the last segment could be some other shape, such as a hand, a foot, a gripper, a stinger, or a device that shoots green laser beams at intruders.

Each segment will have a pivot point at one end, around which it can rotate. If that segment has any subsegments, they will pivot on the opposite end of that segment. Just like your upper arm pivots on your shoulder, your forearm pivots on your elbow, and your hand pivots on your wrist.

Of course, in many real systems, that pivoting can be in many directions. Think of how many ways you can move your wrist. By the end of this book, you might want to try to do something like that in Flash on your own, but right now, the system is going to be strictly two-dimensional.

Moving one segment

Let's start with a single segment and get it moving somehow. First, you need something to use as a segment. If you're guessing that might be a movie clip, you're right. A movie clip can have graphics, it can have a position, and it can be rotated. We'll take it. Figure 13-1 shows what I came up with.

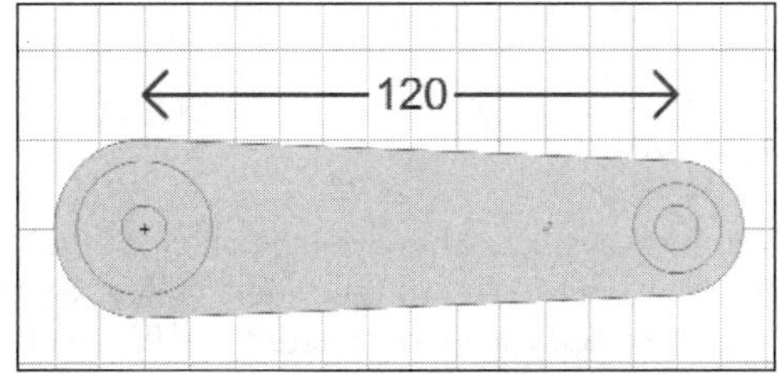

Figure 13-1. A single segment

Notice two things in the segment illustrated in Figure 13-1, which apply regardless of what graphic you create for your segment:

- The little crosshair inside the circles on the left, which is the position of the registration point, or pivot point
- The distance from that point to the pivot point of this segment's subsegment, marked as 120 in the figure

The position of the registration point (the little crosshair) is the pivot point of the movie clip. When you position the movie clip with its _x and _y properties, this is the point that will be placed at those coordinates. When you rotate the clip, it will rotate around this point.

Most likely, the only way you're going to get your movie clip's registration point in the right place is by manually positioning the graphics after you create it. As you know, when you create a movie clip, you can set its registration point to any one of nine positions: the corners, center of any edge, or center of the movie clip. None of those are particularly useful for what you are doing here. So, after you create your movie clip symbol, go inside and edit it. Select all the graphics and move them so that the point you want to pivot on is right on that registration point. You can do this numerically. For example, I knew that the center of that inner circle was 20 pixels from the left edge. So I centered my graphics vertically and moved them to be 20 pixels left of the registration point.

The next thing to take note of is the distance from that pivot point to the pivot point of this segment's subsegment. In other words, how long from the shoulder to the elbow? Obviously, you're dealing with just a single segment for the moment, but I might as well cover this now, as you'll need to know it. On the right side of the segment in Figure 13-1, I have another circle. This is where I want to position the next segment eventually. And I've measured and found that the distance between the two pivot points is 120 pixels. It's important to find this out manually, because there's no way to do it automatically. Flash has no way of knowing where you want that next limb to be placed. Of course, there could be other solutions to this, such as placing another movie clip inside the segment to represent where the next pivot point would be, and calculating that distance. But the point is that somehow you need to tell Flash where that point is.

Now that you have your first segment, get an instance on stage and name it seg0. In the file `ch13_01.fla`, I've included a slider component, which you're free to use for whatever you want. It's pretty useful for adjusting numeric values on the fly. You can use that or any other similar component for this example. If you look at the component parameters (in the Property inspector or Component panel), you'll see that I set `maximum` to –90, `minimum` to 90, and value to 0. Yes, I know that `maximum` and `minimum` look backwards, but the slider supports this kind of use, and you'll see that it makes sense in a moment. I've named the slider instance `slider0`. Now, you just need a small code snippet to tie it all together:

```
slider0.changeHandler = update;
function update():Void
{
	seg0._rotation = slider0.value;
}
```

This just says that whenever the value of the slider changes, it will call the `update` function, which sets the rotation of seg0 to the slider's value. Try that out, and you should see something like Figure 13-2. If it all works, you've completed the first phase of forward kinematics.

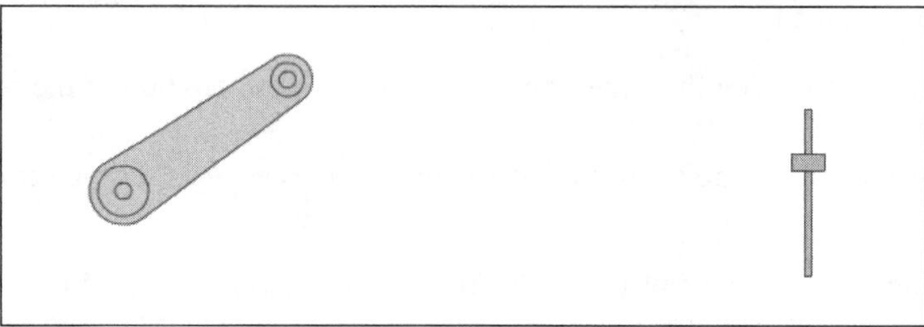

Figure 13-2. It moves!

Moving two segments

Working with one segment was very simple and rather boring, but necessary. It's time to move on. Throw another copy of the segment movie clip on stage and name the instance seg1. You might want to arrange it so it's behind seg0, but that's a purely cosmetic issue. Don't worry about seg1's position on stage for now. You'll be handling that with code. You can also throw another slider instance down there and call it `slider1`.

Now for the code:

```
update();
slider0.changeHandler = update;
slider1.changeHandler = update;
function update():Void
{
	seg0._rotation = slider0.value;
	seg1._rotation = slider1.value;

	var radians:Number = seg0._rotation * Math.PI / 180;
	seg1._x = seg0._x + Math.cos(radians) * 120;
	seg1._y = seg0._y + Math.sin(radians) * 120;
}
```

Take a quick look down at the bottom of the `update` function, and you'll see that it now contains code to position seg1. Since you didn't do that manually, you better call `update` as your first action, so that segment isn't just floating out in space when the viewer first sees it.

You set up `slider1` to call the `update` function in the same way as `slider0`. And, obviously, you have seg1's rotation now based on `slider1`.

The rest of the code should be pretty simple if you've followed the trigonometry stuff (introduced in Chapter 3). It simply converts seg0's rotation to radians and uses that angle with the cosine and sine to find the next pivot point, which will be seg1's new position. Remember that 120 is the distance measured between the two pivot points. If you made your own graphic for the segment, you'll want to use whatever distance you came up with.

You can find this example in the `ch13_02.fla` file. If you test this file, you'll see that as you rotate seg0 around, seg1 remains attached to the end of it, as shown in Figure 13-3. Realize that there is no actual physical attachment between the two movie clips. It's all being done with math. You can also rotate seg1 independently with its slider.

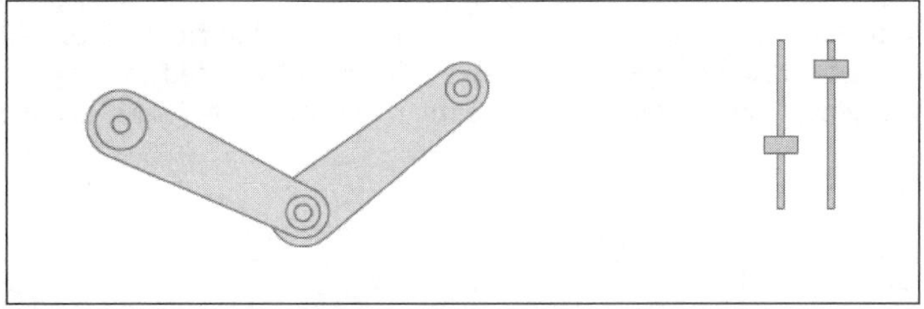

Figure 13-3. Forward kinematics with two segments

One thing that looks a bit strange is that while seg1 *moves* with seg0; it doesn't *rotate* with it. It's like there's some gyro-stabilizer inside of it, holding its orientation steady. I don't know about you, but my forearm doesn't have a gyro-stabilizer in it (though that might be kind of cool), so to me, this looks unnatural. What really should be happening is that seg1's rotation should be seg0's rotation plus the value of slider1. The ch13_03.fla file handles this with the following code:

```
update();
slider0.changeHandler = update;
slider1.changeHandler = update;
function update():Void
{
      seg0._rotation = slider0.value;
      seg1._rotation = seg0._rotation + slider1.value;

      var radians:Number = seg0._rotation * Math.PI / 180;
      seg1._x = seg0._x + Math.cos(radians) * 120;
      seg1._y = seg0._y + Math.sin(radians) * 120;
}
```

Now, that looks more like a real arm. Of course, if you're talking about a human arm, you might not like the way the elbow can bend in both directions. Just change the range of slider1 so minimum is 0 and maximum is something like -160, and that should look more normal.

This might be a good time to reflect on the term *forward kinematics* again. The base of this system is the pivot point of seg0. The free end is the other end of seg1. If you want, you can imagine a hand there. The rotation and position of the base determine the position of seg1. And seg1's rotation and position determine the position of the free end. The free end has no say at all in where it is, should be, or would like to be. It just goes along for the ride. Thus, control is moving forward from the base to the free end.

Automating the process

All these sliders for rotation give you a lot of control, but what you've created is something like a piece of construction machinery with hydraulic levers to move around the parts. If you want to make something really walk, you're going to have to step back and give it some self-control.

You just need a way for each segment to smoothly swing back and forth, and then somehow synchronize them all. That sounds like a job for a sine wave.

In ch13_04.fla, I've replaced the sliders with a trig function. It takes the sine of the cycle variable (which is initialized to 0), and multiplies it by 90, resulting in a value from 90 to –90. The cycle variable is constantly increased, so you get an oscillation. For now, I've used the resulting angle variable to control both segments. I made update the handler for the enterFrame event so the motion is constant.

```
var cycle:Number = 0;
update();
onEnterFrame = update;
function update():Void
{
	var angle:Number = Math.sin(cycle) * 90;
	cycle += .05;

	seg0._rotation = angle;
	seg1._rotation = seg0._rotation + angle;

	var radians:Number = seg0._rotation * Math.PI / 180;
	seg1._x = seg0._x + Math.cos(radians) * 120;
	seg1._y = seg0._y + Math.sin(radians) * 120;
}
```

Building a natural walk cycle

OK, now you have something moving around looking vaguely arm-like. Let's turn it into a leg. Start with the following changes:

- Make the system point down, by adding 90 to seg0's rotation and reducing its range of motion from 90 degrees in both directions to 45 degrees.
- Use a separate angle for each segment, so you'll have angle0 and angle1.
- Reduce angle1's range to 45, and then add 45 to it. This makes its final range 0 to 90, so that it bends in only one direction, like a real knee. If that isn't totally clear, try it with and without the added 45 to see what it's doing, and try some other numbers in there, until you get a feel for how it all fits together.

You end up with the following (`ch13_05.fla`):

```
var cycle:Number = 0;
update();
onEnterFrame = update;
function update():Void
{
	var angle0:Number = Math.sin(cycle) * 45 + 90;
	var angle1:Number = Math.sin(cycle) * 45 + 45;
	cycle += .05;

	seg0._rotation = angle0;
	seg1._rotation = seg0._rotation + angle1;

	var radians:Number = seg0._rotation * Math.PI / 180;
	seg1._x = seg0._x + Math.cos(radians) * 120;
	seg1._y = seg0._y + Math.sin(radians) * 120;
}
```

Well, you're getting there, as shown in Figure 13-4. This is starting to look like a leg, or at least starting to move like one.

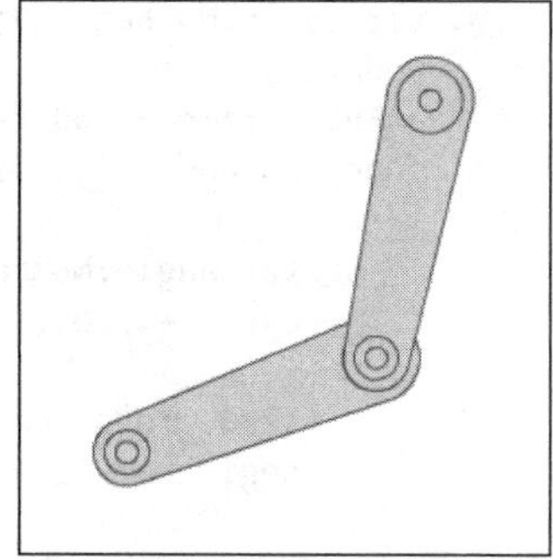

Figure 13-4. The beginnings of a walk cycle

The problem is it doesn't really look like it's walking. Maybe it's kicking a half-hearted field goal, or perhaps practicing some ballet moves, but it's not walking. What's happening now is that both segments are moving in the same direction at the same time. They are totally in sync, which, if you were to analyze an actual walk cycle, is not how it works.

The segments are in sync because they are both using the `cycle` variable to calculate their angle. To throw them out of sync, you could resort to using `cycle0` and `cycle1` variables, but you don't need to go that far with it. Instead, you can just offset `cycle` a bit when using it to find `angle1`, like so:

```
var angle1:Number = Math.sin(cycle + offset) * 45 + 45;
```

Of course, you'll need to define `offset` earlier in the code. But how much should `offset` be? I don't know that there's any set amount. Experiment until you find something that looks good. I'll give you a hint: It should be something between `Math.PI` and `-Math.PI` (or 3.14 and –3.14). Anything more or less than that is just going to kind of double back on itself. For instance, I used `-Math.PI / 2`, which puts it a quarter of a cycle behind `angle0`. Of course, `-Math.PI / 2` is about –1.57, so you might want to try other numbers around that value, like –1.7 or -1.3, and see if that looks better or worse. A little later, I'll throw in a slider to do it all dynamically. The file with this offset in it is `ch13_06.fla`.

Now, this whole "one leg walking" thing sounds a bit too Zen for me, so let's add another leg. You'll start by throwing in two more segments, named `seg2` and `seg3`. The `seg2` movie clip should be in the exact same position as `seg0`, as it will also be the top level, or base, of the whole leg, but `seg3` can be anywhere, as it will be positioned by code. Figure 13-5 shows the setup.

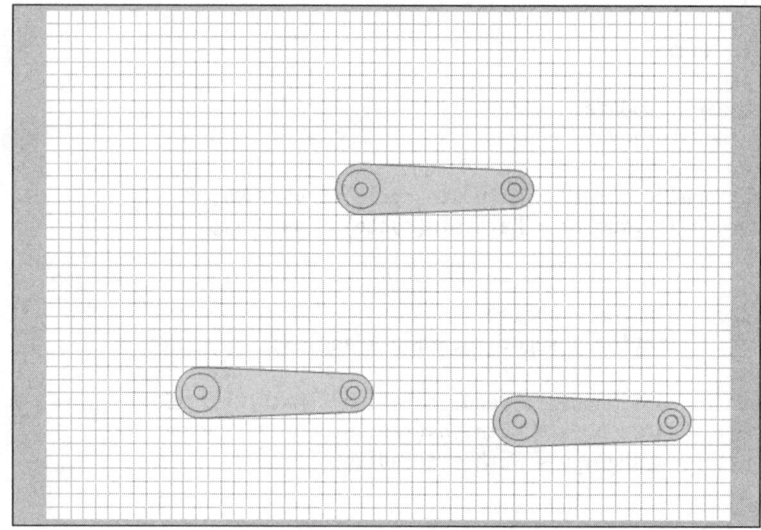

Figure 13-5. Clips seg0 and seg2 appear as one, and seg1 and seg3 are below.

Now, rather than duplicate all the code that makes seg0 and seg1 walk, I abstracted it into its own function, called walk:

```
function walk(segA:MovieClip, segB:MovieClip, cyc:Number)
{
	var angleA:Number = Math.sin(cyc) * 45 + 90;
	var angleB:Number = Math.sin(cyc + offset) * 45 + 45;

	segA._rotation = angleA;
	segB._rotation = segA._rotation + angleB;

	var radians:Number = segA._rotation * Math.PI / 180;
	segB._x = segA._x + Math.cos(radians) * 120;
	segB._y = segA._y + Math.sin(radians) * 120;
}
```

Notice that the function takes three parameters: two movie clips, segA and segB, which are the two segments, and cyc, which stands for cycle. The rest of the code is pretty much what you've been using. Now, to make seg0 and seg1 walk, just call it like this:

```
walk(seg0, seg1, cycle);
```

By now, you see where I'm going with this, and you're ready to make seg2 and seg3 walk as well. If you jump right into it, you'll end up with this as your update function:

```
function update():Void
{
	walk(seg0, seg1, cycle);
	walk(seg2, seg3, cycle);
	cycle += .05;
}
```

But if you try that, you're going to be wondering where the second leg is. The problem is that both legs are moving exactly in sync, so they appear as one. Once again, you need to desynchronize. Last time, you offset the bottom segment's position on the cycle from the top segment's position. This time, you'll offset the second leg from the first. Again, this comes down to changing the value it's using for cycle. And once again, rather than keeping track of two different variables, just add something to or subtract something from cycle before you send it into the walk function. So the update function becomes this:

```
function update():Void
{
	walk(seg0, seg1, cycle);
	walk(seg2, seg3, cycle + Math.PI);
	cycle += .05;
}
```

Why `Math.PI`? The long answer is that value puts the second leg 180 degrees out of sync with the first, so the first leg will move forward while the second is moving back, and vice versa. The short answer is because it works! You can try it out with some different values, say `Math.PI / 2`, and see that it looks a lot more like a gallop than a walk or run. But keep that in mind—you may need to make something gallop someday!

The file as it stands is available as `ch13_07.fla` and looks like Figure 13-6. In the next version, you're going to make a lot of things dynamic with sliders, but I highly recommend that you play around with some of these variables now manually, by changing the values in the code and seeing how the values affect things.

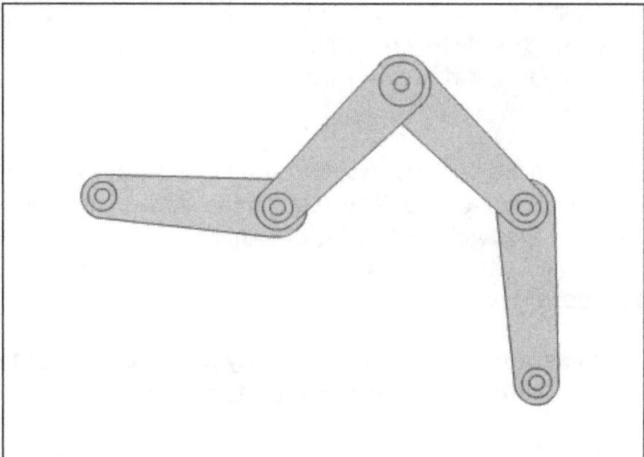

Figure 13-6. Behold! It walks!

Making it dynamic

Next, let's really play around with this walk cycle and see just how much you can change it by altering the various values that go into it. The `ch13_08.fla` file has a slider component in it that you can use for this project (or anything else you might need a slider for). You simply put it on stage and set the minimum, maximum, and initial values of the slider. Don't forget to name the instance. After that, you can read the current setting of the slider with its value property.

For the next example, I set up five of these sliders across the top of the stage, as shown in Figure 13-7.

Table 13-1 shows the slider instance names (from left to right), what they do, and the settings to use for them. These are just ranges and values I found to work well. By all means, feel free to experiment with other values.

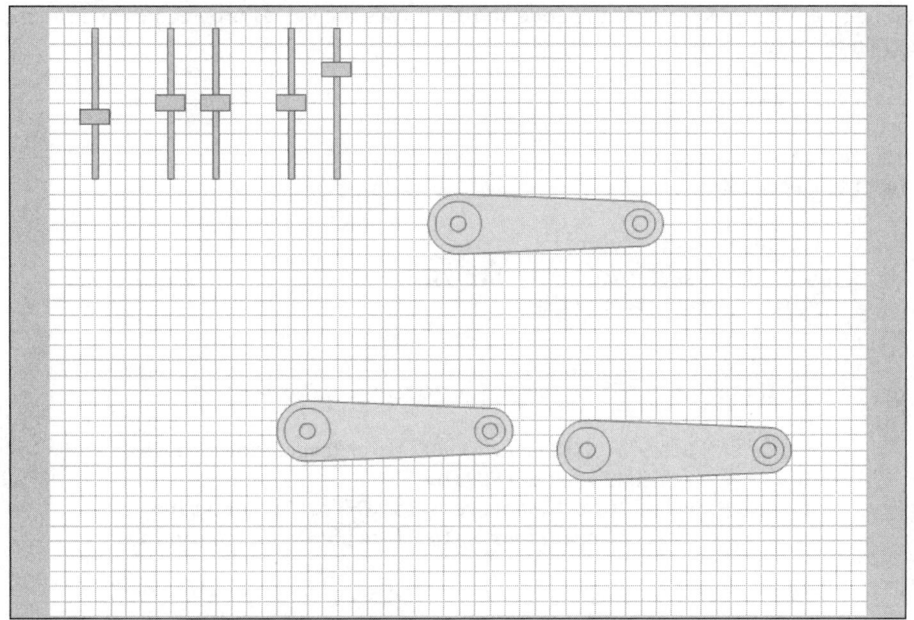

Figure 13-7. Adding the sliders

Table 13-1. The Sliders for Controlling the Walk Cycle

Instance	Description	Settings
`speedSlider`	Controls the speed at which the system moves.	`maximum`: 0.3, `minimum`: 0, `value`: 0.12
`thighRangeSlider`	Controls how far back and forth the top-level segments (thighs) can move.	`maximum`: 90, `minimum`: 0, `value`: 45
`thighBaseSlider`	Controls the base angle of the top-level segments. So far, this has been 90, meaning that the legs will point straight down, and move back and forth from there. But you can get some interesting effects by changing this value.	`maximum`: 0, `minimum`: 180, `value`: 90
`calfRangeSlider`	Controls how much range of motion the lower segments (calves) have.	`maximum`: 90, `minimum`: 0, `value`: 45
`calfOffsetSlider`	Controls the offset value (you've been using `-Math.PI / 2`).	`maximum`: –3.14, `minimum`: 3.14, `value`: –1.57

Now, you need to go in and change the code so that it uses the values provided by the sliders, rather than hard-coded values.

```
var cycle:Number = 0;
update();
onEnterFrame = update;
function update():Void
{
      walk(seg0, seg1, cycle);
      walk(seg2, seg3, cycle + Math.PI);
      cycle += speedSlider.value;
}

function walk(segA:MovieClip, segB:MovieClip, cyc:Number)
{
      var angleA:Number = Math.sin(cyc) * thighRangeSlider.value
                  + thighBaseSlider.value;
      var angleB:Number = Math.sin(cyc + calfOffsetSlider.value)
                  * calfRangeSlider.value + calfRangeSlider.value;

      segA._rotation = angleA;
      segB._rotation = segA._rotation + angleB;

      var radians:Number = segA._rotation * Math.PI / 180;
      segB._x = segA._x + Math.cos(radians) * 120;
      segB._y = segA._y + Math.sin(radians) * 120;
}
```

This code is exactly as it was before, but now it's using the slider values rather than values hard-coded into the file. I'm sure you can have a lot of fun with this file, exploring different variations of the walk cycle.

Making it really walk

So far, you have a couple of legs moving around in a manner that looks pretty realistic. But they are just kind of floating in space there. Earlier in the book, you got something moving with velocity and acceleration, and then had it interact with the environment. It's time to do the same thing here.

This portion of the chapter gets pretty complex, so I'll go through the code one concept at a time. The final file, with all of these concepts incorporated, is `ch13_09.fla`.

Giving it some space

Since this thing is actually going to be walking around and so forth, let's make all the parts a bit smaller so that there is room for it to move around. I took the original four segments and scaled them all to 50%. Remember that earlier, you were using 120 as the distance between the two pivot points.

This distance becomes 60. Since this is now changing, you'll do what you should have done earlier, and make this a variable defined at the top of the code:

```
var legLength:Number = 60;
```

Then substitute that variable the two places where it is used in the walk function:

```
segB._x = segA._x + Math.cos(radians) * legLength;
segB._y = segA._y + Math.sin(radians) * legLength;
```

Next, because it will be moving around and reacting with boundaries, you'll define a vx, a vy, and boundary values. So, the top part of the file looks like this:

```
var cycle:Number = 0;
var legLength:Number = 60;
var vx:Number = 0;
var vy:Number = 0;
var top:Number = 0;
var bottom:Number = Stage.height;
var left:Number = 0;
var right:Number = Stage.width;

update();
onEnterFrame = update;
```

Following that is the update function, which hasn't changed at all yet, and the walk function, which has the one change just mentioned. At this point, you should have a miniature, working version of the previous file.

Adding gravity

Next, you need to create some gravity. Otherwise, even if you program in the boundary reaction, the legs are just going to float in space anyway. You'll even make the gravity variable at runtime, with another slider! So, create a new slider instance and name it gravitySlider. Set maximum to 1, minimum to 0, and value to 0.2. I put this slider next to the first one, and moved seg0 and seg2 down a bit and to the left, so the setup looks like Figure 13-8.

Now, you need to do the velocity calculations, along with the gravity acceleration. Rather than jamming all this into the update function, just make a call to another function called doVelocity:

```
function update():Void
{
      doVelocity();
      walk(seg0, seg1, cycle);
      walk(seg2, seg3, cycle + Math.PI);
      cycle += speedSlider.value;
}
```

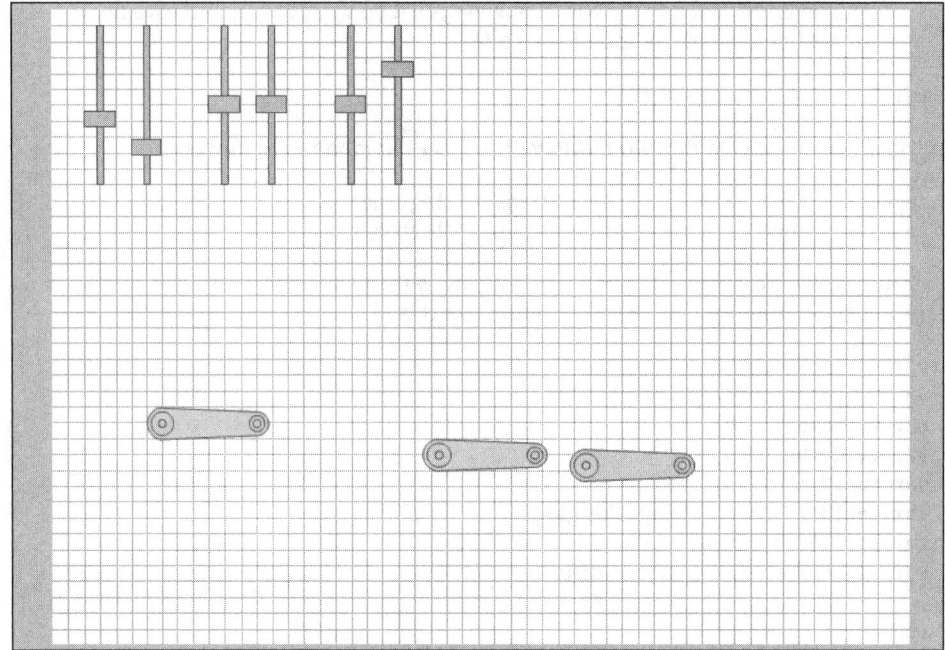

Figure 13-8. Setup for real walking

And in that function, just add gravity to vy, and then add vx and vy to the position of seg0 and seg2. Remember that you don't need to worry about seg1 and seg3, as their positions are calculated in relationship to the higher-level segments.

```
function doVelocity():Void
{
    vy += gravitySlider.value;
    seg0._x += vx;
    seg0._y += vy;
    seg2._x += vx;
    seg2._y += vy;
}
```

You can test this version if you want, but it won't be very exciting. There's no x velocity happening yet, and gravity just pulls the legs right through the floor. So, you need to check the floor to see if the legs have hit it. That means it's time for collision detection.

Handling the collision

To start, make update call another function, checkFloor. This will happen after the calls to walk, so it's operating on the latest positions. Generally speaking, you'll need to check only seg1 and seg3—the lower-level segments—to see if they hit the floor. So, call checkFloor with both of them.

```
function update():Void
{
	doVelocity();
	walk(seg0, seg1, cycle);
	walk(seg2, seg3, cycle + Math.PI);
	cycle += speedSlider.value;
	checkFloor(seg1);
	checkFloor(seg3);
}
```

Now comes the first interesting part: the collision detection. Note that I said "interesting" and not "impossibly difficult." It's really pretty simple. You want to know if any part of the segment in question has gone below the bottom boundary (as specified by the bottom variable). In Figure 13-9, I've drawn bounding boxes around a couple of segments. In one, you can plainly see the segment has gone beyond the bottom boundary; in the other, the segment hasn't passed the bottom boundary.

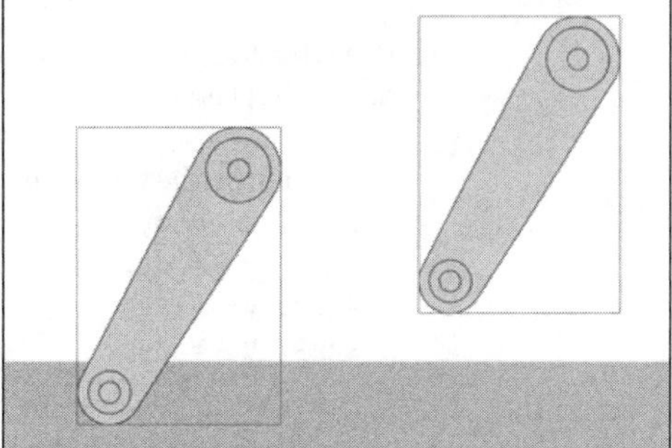

Figure 13-9. Has it hit bottom or not?

So, what you need to do is use getBounds on the segment, and see if its yMax is greater than bottom. That's how you'll start the checkFloor function:

```
function checkFloor(seg:MovieClip)
{
	var yMax:Number = seg.getBounds(_root).yMax;
	if(yMax > bottom)
	{

	}
}
```

I took a little shortcut there in the first line of the function, which may look a bit odd to you.

```
var yMax:Number = seg.getBounds(_root).yMax;
```

Normally, you might expect to do that in two steps, like so:

```
var bounds:Object = seg.getBounds(_root);
var yMax:Number = bounds.yMax;
```

But what not everyone realizes is that since seg.getBounds(_root) is a statement that returns an object, you can directly access the properties of the object from that statement like so: seg.getBounds(_root).yMax. Flash first evaluates the call to setBounds as an object, and then it sees the dot and property, and looks for that property of that object. If that syntax is confusing to you, go ahead and use the two-line method. If you were going to do anything else with the bounds object, such as read additional properties, you would want to store it first. But in this case, you're interested in only yMax, so you grab it right off the bat and don't have an extra variable sitting around.

OK, now say you've determined that yMax is indeed greater than bottom, or in real-world terms, the leg has hit the floor. What do you do? Well, just as in other boundary collisions, you first want to move the object so it's resting right on the boundary. Taking another look at Figure 13-9, you see that if yMax is the lowest edge of the segment, and bottom is the floor, you need to move the segment back up exactly the distance between them. In other words, say bottom is 600, and yMax is 620, you'll need to change the segment's y position by –20. But you don't just want to move the segment. You want to move *all* the segments by that amount, since they are all part of the same body and must move as one. So, you get something like this:

```
function checkFloor(seg:MovieClip)
{
        var yMax:Number = seg.getBounds(_root).yMax;
        if(yMax > bottom)
        {
                var dy:Number = yMax - bottom;
                seg0._y -= dy;
                seg1._y -= dy;
                seg2._y -= dy;
                seg3._y -= dy;
        }
}
```

This iteration is worth playing with some more. Adjust the slider values to see the different walk cycles in action. You'll get more of a feel for them with the legs actually interacting with the environment. Of course, it's still not really walking yet. That's up next.

Handling the reaction

Now, you have the legs successfully colliding with the floor, but other than repositioning themselves, there's no real reaction. The whole reason you walk is to get some horizontal motion going—x velocity, in this case. Furthermore, your walk cycle should give you a bit of y velocity as well—at least enough to counteract gravity briefly. You see this more in a fast run, where you might get slightly airborne for a brief period of the cycle.

One way of looking at this is that your foot is moving down. When it hits the floor, it can't move down any more, so that vertical momentum goes back up to your body, moving it up. The stronger your foot is moving down, the more lift you get. Likewise, if your foot is moving backwards when it hits, that horizontal momentum goes back to your body, moving it forwards. The faster your foot is moving back, the more horizontal thrust you get.

OK, we have a theory here. If you can keep track of the "foot's" x and y velocity, then when you get a collision, you can subtract that x and y velocity from the vx and vy values.

The first problem you run into is that you don't have any feet yet. Actually, although you are free to add some physical feet yourself, figuring out their locations the same way you did the positions for the second segments, I'm not going to use real feet in this example. Instead, I'm just going to calculate the position of the virtual feet, which, you may have guessed, is the position of the second pivot point in the lower segments.

If you can track where that pivot point is on each frame, and compare that to where it was on the last frame, you can subtract the two and get the "foot's" velocity on both x and y.

So, the main project becomes finding the foot's position. By now, you should have a pretty good idea of how to calculate that, using the sine and cosine. Just take the segment's position and the sine or cosine of the rotation (in radians) times the legLength variable. That will give you the location of that pivot point.

You'll do this calculation in the walk function. In fact, you'll do it twice. First you'll use it to get the old x and y, then you'll do the usual calculations to position and rotate the segments, and then you'll use it again to get the new x and y. You can then subtract the two to get the foot's vx and vy, which you'll just make properties of the segment itself. Here's the new walk function:

```
function walk(segA:MovieClip, segB:MovieClip, cyc:Number)
{
      var oldx:Number = segB._x +
                        Math.cos(segB._rotation * Math.PI / 180) *
                        legLength;
      var oldy:Number = segB._y +
                        Math.sin(segB._rotation * Math.PI / 180) *
                        legLength;

      var angleA:Number = Math.sin(cyc) * thighRangeSlider.value
                        + thighBaseSlider.value;
      var angleB:Number = Math.sin(cyc + calfOffsetSlider.value)
                      * calfRangeSlider.value + calfRangeSlider.value;

      segA._rotation = angleA;
      segB._rotation = segA._rotation + angleB;

      var radians:Number = segA._rotation * Math.PI / 180;
      segB._x = segA._x + Math.cos(radians) * legLength;
      segB._y = segA._y + Math.sin(radians) * legLength;

      var newx:Number = segB._x +
                        Math.cos(segB._rotation * Math.PI / 180) *
                        legLength;
      var newy:Number = segB._y +
                        Math.sin(segB._rotation * Math.PI / 180) *
                        legLength;
      segB.vx = newx - oldx;
      segB.vy = newy - oldy;
}
```

It's entirely possible that this function could be optimized, but let's leave it as is for the sake of clarity. Now, each bottom segment has a vx and vy property, which represents not the velocity of the segment itself, but the velocity of that bottom pivot point, or virtual foot.

So, what do you do with this velocity? Well, you wait until you have a collision with the floor, and then you subtract it from the overall velocity. In other words, if the foot is moving down at 3 pixels per frame (a vy of 3) when it hits, you'll subtract 3 from the overall vy. You'll do the same with the vx. In code, it's really simple:

```
function checkFloor(seg:MovieClip)
{
	var yMax:Number = seg.getBounds(_root).yMax;
	if(yMax > bottom)
	{
		var dy:Number = yMax - bottom;
		seg0._y -= dy;
		seg1._y -= dy;
		seg2._y -= dy;
		seg3._y -= dy;
		vx -= seg.vx;
		vy -= seg.vy;
	}
}
```

At this point, I'll throw in my usual disclaimer about how this is an extremely simplified and probably totally inaccurate representation of how the forces involved in walking actually work. But then I'll smile and say "test the movie." See if you like the effect. It looks pretty darned cool to me. I've got a pair of legs walking across my screen!

Screen wrapping, revisited

You've probably noticed that the legs walk off screen, never to return. A little screen wrapping will fix that. When the legs go off to the right, you move them back to the left. It's a little more complex than before, because now you're moving four pieces around in unison, instead of a single object. But then again, remember that you need to check only either one of the two top segments, as they are always in the same position, and the lower segments' positions are totally determined by the upper ones. Add a call to a function named checkWalls at the end of update:

```
function update():Void
{
	doScale();
	doVelocity();
	walk(seg0, seg1, cycle);
	walk(seg2, seg3, cycle + Math.PI);
	cycle += speedSlider.value;
	checkFloor(seg1);
	checkFloor(seg3);
	checkWalls();
}
```

Let's leave a general margin of 100 pixels, so that either leg can go 100 pixels off the right of the stage before wrapping. If it goes past that, you reposition everything way over to the left. How far to the left? The width of the stage (which is stored in the variable, `right`), plus 200, for the 100-pixel margin on each side. So, start your `if` statement in the `checkWalls` function like so:

```
if(seg0._x > right + 100)
{
	seg0._x -= (right + 200);
	seg1._x -= (right + 200);
	seg2._x -= (right + 200);
	seg3._x -= (right + 200);
}
```

Then do the exact same thing for the left edge, as some walk cycles can actually make the legs go backwards. Here's the final `checkWalls` function:

```
function checkWalls()
{
	if(seg0._x > right + 100)
	{
		seg0._x -= (right + 200);
		seg1._x -= (right + 200);
		seg2._x -= (right + 200);
		seg3._x -= (right + 200);
	}
	else if(seg0._x < - 100)
	{
		seg0._x += (right + 200);
		seg1._x += (right + 200);
		seg2._x += (right + 200);
		seg3._x += (right + 200);
	}
}
```

And there you have it. In case it got confusing, the code for the whole thing follows (and can be found in `ch13_09.fla`).

```
var cycle:Number = 0;
var legLength:Number = 60;
var vx:Number = 0;
var vy:Number = 0;
var top:Number = 0;
var bottom:Number = Stage.height;
var left:Number = 0;
var right:Number = Stage.width;
```

```
update();
onEnterFrame = update;

function update():Void
{
      doVelocity();
      walk(seg0, seg1, cycle);
      walk(seg2, seg3, cycle + Math.PI);
      cycle += speedSlider.value;
      checkFloor(seg1);
      checkFloor(seg3);
      checkWalls();
}

function walk(segA:MovieClip, segB:MovieClip, cyc:Number)
{
      var oldx:Number = segB._x +
                        Math.cos(segB._rotation * Math.PI / 180) *
                        legLength;
      var oldy:Number = segB._y +
                        Math.sin(segB._rotation * Math.PI / 180) *
                        legLength;

      var angleA:Number = Math.sin(cyc) * thighRangeSlider.value
                        + thighBaseSlider.value;
      var angleB:Number = Math.sin(cyc + calfOffsetSlider.value)
                      * calfRangeSlider.value + calfRangeSlider.value;

      segA._rotation = angleA;
      segB._rotation = segA._rotation + angleB;

      var radians:Number = segA._rotation * Math.PI / 180;
      segB._x = segA._x + Math.cos(radians) * legLength;
      segB._y = segA._y + Math.sin(radians) * legLength;

      var newx:Number = segB._x +
                        Math.cos(segB._rotation * Math.PI / 180) *
                        legLength;
      var newy:Number = segB._y +
                        Math.sin(segB._rotation * Math.PI / 180) *
                        legLength;
      segB.vx = newx - oldx;
      segB.vy = newy - oldy;
}

function doVelocity():Void
{
```

```
        vy += gravitySlider.value;
        seg0._x += vx;
        seg0._y += vy;
        seg2._x += vx;
        seg2._y += vy;

        if(seg0._x > right + 100 || seg2._x > right + 100)
        {
                seg0._x -= (right + 200);
                seg2._x -= (right + 200);
        }
        if(seg0._x < - 100 || seg2._x < - 100)
        {
                seg0._x += (right + 200);
                seg2._x += (right + 200);
        }
}

function checkFloor(seg:MovieClip)
{
        var yMax:Number = seg.getBounds(_root).yMax;
        if(yMax > bottom)
        {
                var dy:Number = yMax - bottom;
                seg0._y -= dy;
                seg1._y -= dy;
                seg2._y -= dy;
                seg3._y -= dy;
                vx -= seg.vx;
                vy -= seg.vy;
        }
}
function checkWalls()
{
        if(seg0._x > right + 100)
        {
                seg0._x -= (right + 200);
                seg1._x -= (right + 200);
                seg2._x -= (right + 200);
                seg3._x -= (right + 200);
        }
        else if(seg0._x < - 100)
        {
                seg0._x += (right + 200);
                seg1._x += (right + 200);
                seg2._x += (right + 200);
                seg3._x += (right + 200);
        }
}
```

Summary

You've done some pretty powerful stuff in this chapter, conquering the basics of forward kinematics. Note that the methods I gave you here are probably not the only solutions to the subject. They're obviously tailored toward a particular application of the technology: making something walk. Feel free to leave things out, change things, or add whatever you want to this system. Experiment and see what you can come up with.

As a bonus, I've provided another file, `ch13_10.fla`, in which you'll see a much fuller application of forward kinematics, building on what you've done here. Check out that code for a few extra tips and tricks.

Next up, you'll look at the other side of the coin: inverse kinematics.

};shape.targetHeight = shape._height;
shape.onEnterFrame = function() {
var speed = 5;
this._width += (this.targetWidth - this._width)/speed;
this._height += (this.targetHeight - this._height)/speed;
};

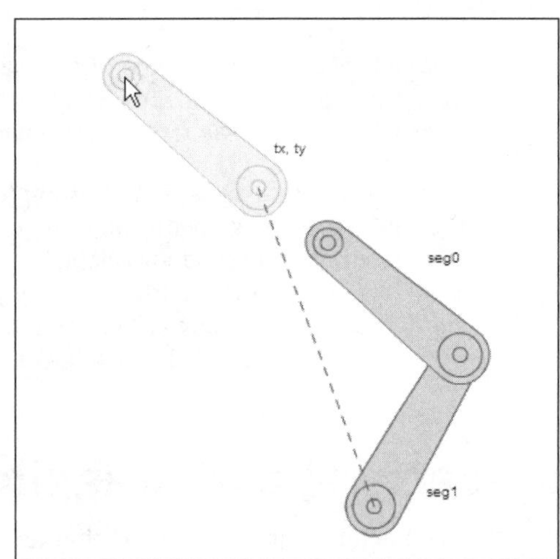

Chapter 14

INVERSE KINEMATICS: DRAGGING AND REACHING

What we'll cover in this chapter:

- Reaching and dragging single segments
- Dragging multiple segments
- Reaching with multiple segments
- Using the standard inverse kinematics method
- Important formulas in this chapter

In Chapter 13, I covered some of the basics of kinematics and the difference between inverse and forward kinematics. That chapter went into forward kinematics. Now, you're ready for its close relative, inverse kinematics. The movements involved are dragging and reaching.

As with the forward kinematics examples, the examples in this chapter build systems from individual segments. You'll begin with single segments, and then move on to multiple segments. First, I'll show you the simplest method for calculating the various angles and positions. This just approximates measurements using the basic trigonometry you've already seen in action. Finally, I'll briefly cover another method using something called the law of cosines, which can be more accurate at the cost of being more complex—that familiar trade-off.

Reaching and dragging single segments

As I mentioned in the previous chapter, inverse kinematics systems can be broken down into a couple of different types: reaching and dragging.

When the free end of the system is reaching for a target, the other end of the system, the base, may be unmovable, so the free end may never be able to get all the way to the target if it is out of range. An example of this is when you're trying to grab hold of something. Your fingers move toward the object, your wrist pivots to put your fingers as close as possible, and your elbow, shoulder, and the rest of your body move in whatever way they can to try to give you as much reach as possible. Sometimes, the combination of all these positions will put your fingers in contact with the object; sometimes, you won't be able to reach it. If the object were to move from side to side, all your limbs would constantly reposition themselves to keep your fingers reaching as close as they could to the object. Inverse kinematics will show you how to position all those pieces to give the best reach.

The other type of inverse kinematics is when something is being dragged. In this case, the free end is being moved by some external force. Wherever it is, the rest of the parts of the system follow along behind it, positioning themselves in whatever way is physically possible. For this, imagine an unconscious or dead body (sorry, that's all I could come up with). You grab it by the hand and drag it around. The force you apply to the hand causes the wrist, elbow, shoulder, and rest of the body to pivot and move in whatever way they can as they are dragged along. In this case, inverse kinematics will show you how those pieces will fall into the correct positions as they are dragged.

To give you a quick idea of the difference between these two methods, let's run through an example of each one with a single segment. To start with, place whatever movie clip you're using as a segment on stage and name it seg0. I'll continue to use the same segment movie clip symbol I used in Chapter 13. You can use that one or anything similar. If you prefer to make your own movie clip, just review the section in the previous chapter that describes what this segment needs to contain. Then you'll add the code to frame 1.

Reaching with a single segment

For reaching, all the segment will be able to do is turn toward the target. The target, if you haven't read my mind already, will be the mouse. To turn the segment toward the target, you need the distance between the two, on the x and y axes. You then can use `Math.atan2` to get the angle between them in radians. Converting that to degrees, you know how to rotate the segment. Here's the code (`ch14_01.fla`):

```
function onEnterFrame():Void
{
    var dx:Number = _xmouse - seg0._x;
    var dy:Number = _ymouse - seg0._y;
    var angle:Number = Math.atan2(dy, dx);
    seg0._rotation = angle * 180 / Math.PI;
}
```

Figure 14-1 shows the result, Test this and watch how the segment follows the mouse around. Even if the segment is too far away, you can see how it seems to be reaching for the mouse.

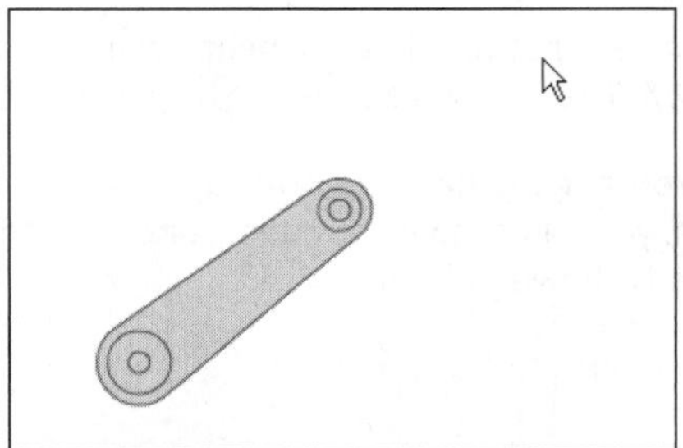

Figure 14-1. A single segment reaching toward the mouse

Dragging with a single segment

Now, let's try dragging. Here, you're not actually dragging using the `startDrag` and `stopDrag` movie clip methods (though you could conceivably do it that way). Instead, you'll just assume that the segment is attached to the mouse right at that second pivot point.

The first part of the dragging method is exactly the same as the reaching method: You rotate the clip toward the mouse. But then you go a step further and move the segment to a position that will place the second pivot point exactly where the mouse is. To do that, you need to know the distance between the two pivot points (see Chapter 13), and the angle, which you just calculated. From there, it's a simple matter of using sine and cosine to place the segment where it needs to go. Here's the code (`ch14_02.fla`):

```
var segLength:Number = 120;

function onEnterFrame():Void
{
    var dx:Number = _xmouse - seg0._x;
    var dy:Number = _ymouse - seg0._y;
    var angle:Number = Math.atan2(dy, dx);
    seg0._rotation = angle * 180 / Math.PI;
    seg0._x = _xmouse - Math.cos(angle) * segLength;
    seg0._y = _ymouse - Math.sin(angle) * segLength;
}
```

You can see how the segment is permanently attached to the mouse and rotates to drag along behind it. You can even push the segment around in the opposite direction.

Dragging multiple segments

Dragging a system with inverse kinematics is actually a bit simpler than reaching, so I'll cover that first. Let's begin with a couple of segments.

Dragging two segments

Starting with the previous example, I put another segment down on stage and named it seg1. I then scaled both of them down to 50%. Then I changed the seglength variable to 60 to reflect that change.

The strategy is pretty simple. You already have seg0 dragging on the mouse position. You just have seg1 drag on seg0. To start with, you can simply copy and paste the code, and change some of the references. The new block of code is shown in bold.

```
var segLength:Number = 60;

function onEnterFrame():Void
{
	var dx:Number = _xmouse - seg0._x;
	var dy:Number = _ymouse - seg0._y;
	var angle:Number = Math.atan2(dy, dx);
	seg0._rotation = angle * 180 / Math.PI;
	seg0._x = _xmouse - Math.cos(angle) * segLength;
	seg0._y = _ymouse - Math.sin(angle) * segLength;

	var dx:Number = seg0._x - seg1._x;
	var dy:Number = seg0._y - seg1._y;
	var angle:Number = Math.atan2(dy, dx);
	seg1._rotation = angle * 180 / Math.PI;
	seg1._x = seg0._x - Math.cos(angle) * segLength;
	seg1._y = seg0._y - Math.sin(angle) * segLength;
}
```

You see how in the new block of code, you figure the distance from seg1 to seg0, and use that for the angle and rotation and position of seg1. You can test this example and see how it's a pretty realistic two-segment system.

Now, you have a lot of duplicated code there, which is not good. If you wanted to add more segments, this file would get longer and longer, all with the same code. The solution is to move the duplicated code out into its own function, called drag. This function needs to know what segment to drag and what x, y point to drag to. Then you can drag seg0 to _xmouse, _ymouse, and seg1 to seg0._x, seg0._y. Here's the code (ch14_03.fla):

```
var segLength:Number = 60;

function onEnterFrame():Void
{
	drag(seg0, _xmouse, _ymouse);
	drag(seg1, seg0._x, seg0._y);
}

function drag(seg:MovieClip, x:Number, y:Number)
{
	var dx:Number = x - seg._x;
	var dy:Number = y - seg._y;
	var angle:Number = Math.atan2(dy, dx);
	seg._rotation = angle * 180 / Math.PI;
	seg._x = x - Math.cos(angle) * segLength;
	seg._y = y - Math.sin(angle) * segLength;
}
```

Dragging more segments

Now you can add as many segments as you want. Say you throw down a total of six segments, named seg0 through seg5. You can even use a for loop to call the drag function for each segment. You can find this example in ch14_04.fla. Here's the enterFrame code for this file, as it's the only part that changes:

```
function onEnterFrame():Void
{
	drag(seg0, _xmouse, _ymouse);
	for(var i=0;i<5;i++)
	{
		var segA:MovieClip = this["seg" + i];
		var segB:MovieClip = this["seg" + (i+1)];
		drag(segB, segA._x, segA._y);
	}
}
```

Here, segA is the segment being dragged to, and segB is the next segment in line—the one that is being dragged. You just pass these to the drag function. Figure 14-2 shows the result.

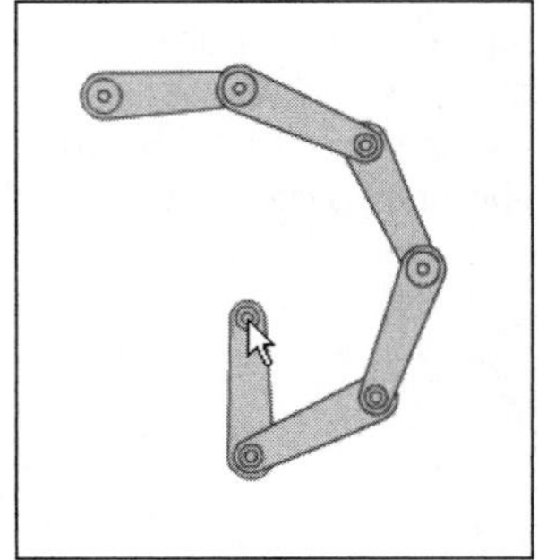

Figure 14-2. Multiple-segment dragging

Well, there you have the basics of inverse kinematics. That's not too complex, huh? In ch14_05.fla, I've dynamically attached 50 segments and scaled them down a bit more. Using the same code, they form a nice long chain, as you can see in Figure 14-3, showing just how robust this system is.

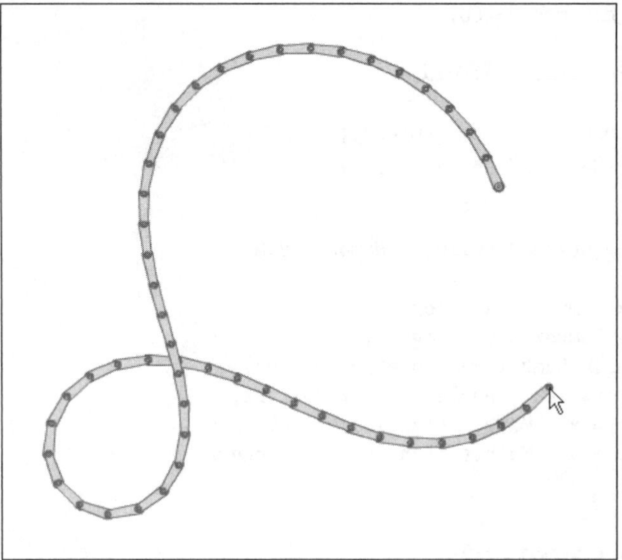

Figure 14-3. Dragging 50 segments

Reaching with multiple segments

To start with inverse kinematics reaching, you'll take this chapter's initial example, `ch14_01.fla`, and add to that. That file simply had the segment rotating to a target, which was the mouse position.

Reaching for the mouse

First, you need to determine where the segment should be to exactly touch that target. This is the same calculation you use to position the segment when you're dragging. However, in this case, you don't actually move the segment. You just find that position. So, what do you do with that position? You use that as the target of the next segment up the line, and have that segment rotate to that position. When you reach the base of the system, you then work back down, positioning each piece on the end of its parent. Figure 14-4 illustrates how this works.

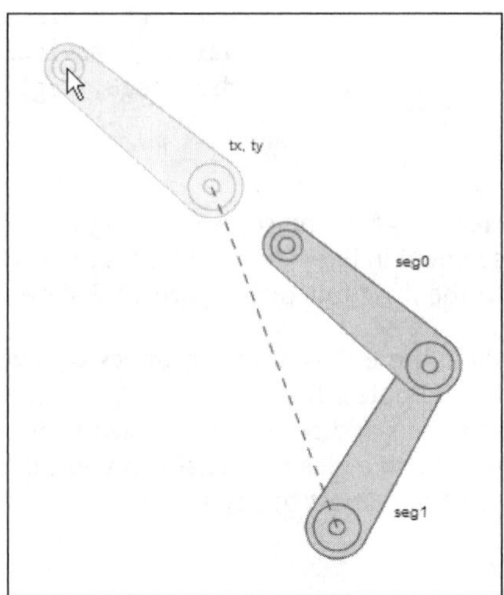

Figure 14-4. seg0 rotates to the mouse. tx, ty is where it would like to be. seg1 will rotate to tx, ty.

The first file from this chapter, ch14_01.fla, had a single segment, seg0, reaching for the mouse:

```
function onEnterFrame():Void
{
	var dx:Number = _xmouse - seg0._x;
	var dy:Number = _ymouse - seg0._y;
	var angle:Number = Math.atan2(dy, dx);
	seg0._rotation = angle * 180 / Math.PI;
}
```

Shrink that segment down to 50% and make another one the same size, named seg1. The next step is to find the target point where seg0 would be hitting the target. And to do that, you need to know the length of the segment. So, you get this:

```
var segLength:Number = 60;

function onEnterFrame():Void
{
	var dx:Number = _xmouse - seg0._x;
	var dy:Number = _ymouse - seg0._y;
	var angle:Number = Math.atan2(dy, dx);
	seg0._rotation = angle * 180 / Math.PI;

	var tx:Number = _xmouse - Math.cos(angle) * segLength;
	var ty:Number = _ymouse - Math.sin(angle) * segLength;
}
```

I called that point tx, ty, because it will be the target for seg1 to rotate to.

Next, you can copy and paste and adjust the rotation code to have seg1 rotate to its target:

```
var segLength:Number = 60;

function onEnterFrame():Void
{
	var dx:Number = _xmouse - seg0._x;
	var dy:Number = _ymouse - seg0._y;
	var angle:Number = Math.atan2(dy, dx);
	seg0._rotation = angle * 180 / Math.PI;

	var tx:Number = _xmouse - Math.cos(angle) * segLength;
	var ty:Number = _ymouse - Math.sin(angle) * segLength;

	var dx:Number = tx - seg1._x;
	var dy:Number = ty - seg1._y;
	var angle:Number = Math.atan2(dy, dx);
	seg1._rotation = angle * 180 / Math.PI;
}
```

This code is the same as the first four lines of the function, but using a different segment and different target.

Finally, reposition seg0 so it's sitting on the end of seg1, since seg1 has now rotated to a different position.

```
var segLength:Number = 60;

function onEnterFrame():Void
{
	var dx:Number = _xmouse - seg0._x;
	var dy:Number = _ymouse - seg0._y;
	var angle:Number = Math.atan2(dy, dx);
	seg0._rotation = angle * 180 / Math.PI;

	var tx:Number = _xmouse - Math.cos(angle) * segLength;
	var ty:Number = _ymouse - Math.sin(angle) * segLength;

	var dx:Number = tx - seg1._x;
	var dy:Number = ty - seg1._y;
	var angle:Number = Math.atan2(dy, dx);
	seg1._rotation = angle * 180 / Math.PI;

	seg0._x = seg1._x + Math.cos(seg1._rotation * Math.PI / 180)
	                    * segLength;
	seg0._y = seg1._y + Math.sin(seg1._rotation * Math.PI / 180)
	                    * segLength;
}
```

When you test this example, you'll see that the segments do work as a unit to reach for the mouse. The file as it stands is `ch14_06.fla`.

Now, let's clean up the code so you can add more segments to it easily. First, let's move all of the rotation stuff into its own function, called reach.

```
function reach(seg:MovieClip, x:Number, y:Number):Object
{
	var dx:Number = x - seg._x;
	var dy:Number = y - seg._y;
	var angle:Number = Math.atan2(dy, dx);
	seg._rotation = angle * 180 / Math.PI;

	var tx:Number = x - Math.cos(angle) * segLength;
	var ty:Number = y - Math.sin(angle) * segLength;

	return {tx:tx, ty:ty};
}
```

Note that the return type of the function is `Object`, and the last line returns a generic object with two properties. The `tx` property is assigned the value of the local `tx` variable you just created, and the same for `ty`. This last line is the same as if you had said this:

```
var result:Object = new Object();
result.tx = tx;
result.ty = ty;
return result;
```

This allows you to call the `reach` function to rotate the segment, and it will return the target, which you can pass to the next call. So, the `onEnterFrame` function becomes this:

```
var numSegments:Number = 2;

function onEnterFrame():Void
{
	var target = reach(seg0, _xmouse, _ymouse);
	for(var i:Number = 1;i<numSegments;i++)
	{
		target = reach(this["seg" + i], target.tx, target.ty);
	}
	seg0._x = seg1._x + Math.cos(seg1._rotation * Math.PI / 180)
	                  * segLength;
	seg0._y = seg1._y + Math.sin(seg1._rotation * Math.PI / 180)
	                  * segLength;
}
```

Here, `seg0` always reaches toward the mouse, and you can add any number of additional segments that will reach toward the last target.

Now, let's clean up the last bit. This has to start at the base and work toward the free end, so you'll need to loop backwards. The final code for everything looks like this (`ch14_07.fla`):

```
var segLength:Number = 60;
var numSegments:Number = 2;

function onEnterFrame():Void
{
	var target = reach(seg0, _xmouse, _ymouse);
	for(var i:Number = 1;i<numSegments;i++)
	{
		target = reach(this["seg" + i], target.tx, target.ty);
	}
	for(i = numSegments-1;i>=1;i--)
	{
		position(this["seg" + i], this["seg" + (i-1)]);
	}
}
```

```
function position(segA:MovieClip, segB:MovieClip):Void
{
      var angle:Number = segA._rotation * Math.PI / 180;
      segB._x = segA._x + Math.cos(angle) * segLength;
      segB._y = segA._y + Math.sin(angle) * segLength;
}

function reach(seg:MovieClip, x:Number, y:Number):Object
{
      var dx:Number = x - seg._x;
      var dy:Number = y - seg._y;
      var angle:Number = Math.atan2(dy, dx);
      seg._rotation = angle * 180 / Math.PI;

      var tx:Number = x - Math.cos(angle) * segLength;
      var ty:Number = y - Math.sin(angle) * segLength;

      return {tx:tx, ty:ty};
}
```

The second for loop gets references to the next two segments and passes them to the position function, which positions them. This file functions the same as the previous one, but it is much more scalable. Just add more segments with sequentially numbered names (seg2, seg3, and so on) and update the numSegments variable. You should be able to create an arm of any length. Figure 14-5 shows an example.

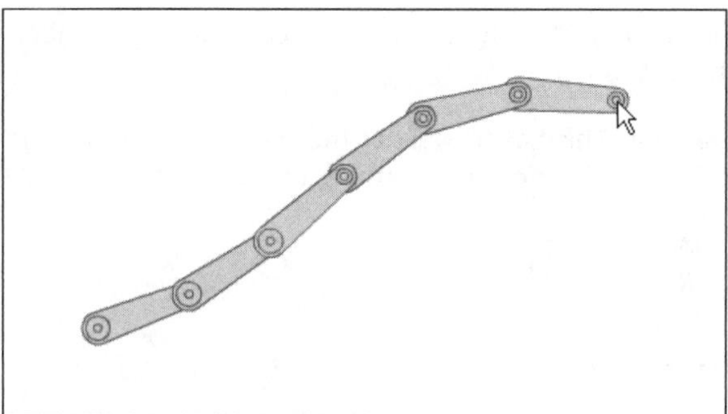

Figure 14-5. Multiple-segment reaching

Now, this is a lot better than what you started out with. But why does the segment chain have to chase the mouse all day? It seems to have some will of its own. Let's see what happens if you give it a toy!

Reaching for an object

For the next example, I resurrected that little red ball from the earlier chapters. I put it on stage and gave it the instance name ball (at least I'm consistent).

Then create some new variables for the ball to use as it moves around. Note that this code builds on the last example, so you can just add or change the following.

```
var vx:Number = 5;
var vy:Number = 0;
var grav:Number = 0.5;
var bounce:Number = -0.9;
var top:Number = 0;
var bottom:Number = Stage.height;
var left:Number = 0;
var right:Number = Stage.width;
```

Then, in onEnterFrame, you call a function named moveBall. This just separates all the ball-moving code so it doesn't clutter things up:

```
function onEnterFrame():Void
{
      moveBall();
      var target = reach(seg0, _xmouse, _ymouse);
      for(var i:Number = 1;i<numSegments;i++)
      {
            target = reach(this["seg" + i], target.tx, target.ty);
      }
      for(i = numSegments-1;i>=1;i--)
      {
            position(this["seg" + i], this["seg" + (i-1)]);
      }
}
```

And here is that function:

```
function moveBall():Void
{
      vy += grav;
      ball._x += vx;
      ball._y += vy;
      if(ball._x > right - ball._width / 2)
      {
            ball._x = right - ball._width / 2;
            vx *= bounce;
      }
      else if(ball._x < left + ball._width / 2)
      {
            ball._x = left + ball._width / 2;
            vx *= bounce;
      }
      if(ball._y > bottom - ball._height / 2)
      {
            ball._y = bottom - ball._height / 2;
            vy *= bounce;
```

```
        }
        else if(ball._y < top + ball._height / 2)
        {
            ball._y = top + ball._height / 2;
            vy *= bounce;
        }
}
```

Then change the second line of the onEnterFrame function to have it reach for the ball instead of the mouse:

```
var target = reach(seg0, ball._x, ball._y);
```

And that's all there is to it. You should see something like Figure 14-6. The ball now bounces around, and the arm follows it. Pretty amazing, right?

But, you can do better. Right now, the arm does well at touching the ball, but the ball pretty much ignores the arm. Let's have them interact.

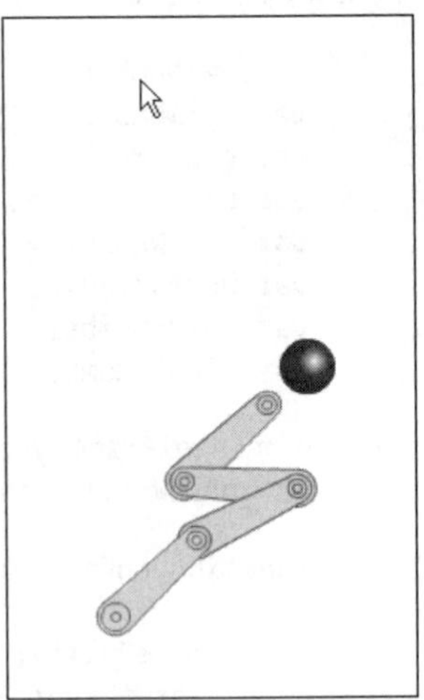

Figure 14-6. It likes to play ball.

Adding some interaction

How the ball and the arm interact depends on what you want them to do. But, no matter what you do, the first thing you need is some collision detection. Then you can have the reaction if there is a collision. Again, you'll pull all that stuff into its own function and call it from onEnterFrame.

```
function onEnterFrame():Void
{
    moveBall();
    var target = reach(seg0, ball._x, ball._y);
    for(var i:Number = 1;i<numSegments;i++)
    {
        target = reach(this["seg" + i], target.tx, target.ty);
    }
    for(i = numSegments-1;i>=1;i--)
    {
        position(this["seg" + i], this["seg" + (i-1)]);
    }
    checkHit();
}
```

I've named this function checkHit, and placed it last in the function, so everything is in its final position. Here's the start of the checkHit function:

```
function checkHit():Void
{
    var angle:Number = seg0._rotation * Math.PI / 180;
    var tx:Number = seg0._x + Math.cos(angle) * segLength;
    var ty:Number = seg0._y + Math.sin(angle) * segLength;
```

```
        var dx:Number = tx - ball._x;
        var dy:Number = ty - ball._y;
        var dist:Number = Math.sqrt(dx * dx + dy * dy);
        if(dist < ball._width / 2)
        {
            // reaction goes here
        }
    }
```

The first thing you do is find the end point, tx and ty. Now you can get the distance of that point and use distance-based collision detection to see if it's hitting the ball.

Now we get back to the question of what to do when you do get a hit. Here's my plan: The arm will throw the ball up in the air (negative y velocity) and move it randomly on the x axis (random x velocity), like so:

```
    function checkHit():Void
    {
        var angle:Number = seg0._rotation * Math.PI / 180;
        var tx:Number = seg0._x + Math.cos(angle) * segLength;
        var ty:Number = seg0._y + Math.sin(angle) * segLength;

        var dx:Number = tx - ball._x;
        var dy:Number = ty - ball._y;
        var dist:Number = Math.sqrt(dx * dx + dy * dy);
        if(dist < ball._width / 2)
        {
            vx += Math.random() * 2 - 1;
            vy -= 1;
        }
    }
```

This works out pretty well, and the final code can be found in ch14_08.fla. I actually left it running overnight, and the next morning, the arm was still happily playing with its toy! But don't take it as anything "standard" that you are supposed to do. You might want to have it catch the ball and throw it towards a target. A game of basketball maybe? Or have two arms play catch? Play around with different reactions. You surely have enough tools under your belt now to do something interesting in there.

Using the standard inverse kinematics method

I'll be perfectly honest with you. The method of calculating inverse kinematics I've described so far is something I came up with completely on my own. I think the first time I did it, I didn't even know that what I was doing was called inverse kinematics. I simply wanted something to reach for something else, and I worked out what each piece had to do in order to accomplish that, fooled around with it, got it working, and got it down to a system that I could easily duplicate and describe to others. It works pretty well, looks pretty good, and doesn't kill the CPU, so I'm happy with it. I hope you are too.

But, shocking as this may seem to you, I was not the first one to consider this problem. Many others, with much larger IQs and much more formal training in math, have tackled this problem and come up with alternate solutions that are probably much more in line with how physical objects actually move. So let's take a look at the "standard" way of doing inverse kinematics. Then you'll have a couple different methods at your disposal and can choose whichever one you like.

Introducing the law of cosines

The usual way for doing inverse kinematics uses, as the section title implies, something called the *law of cosines*. Uh-oh, more trigonometry? Yup. Recall that in Chapter 3, all the examples use right triangles—triangles with one right angle (90 degrees). The rules for such triangles are fairly simple: sine equals opposite over hypotenuse, cosine equals adjacent over hypotenuse, and so on. I've used these rules quite extensively throughout the book.

But what if you have a triangle that doesn't have a 90-degree angle? Are you just left out in the cold? No, the ancient Greeks thought of that one, too, and gave us the law of cosines to help us figure out the various angles and lengths of even this kind of shape. Of course, it is a little more complex, but if you have enough information about the triangle, you can use this law to figure out the rest.

The question you should be asking now is "What the heck does this have to do with inverse kinematics?" Well, take a look at the diagram in Figure 14-7.

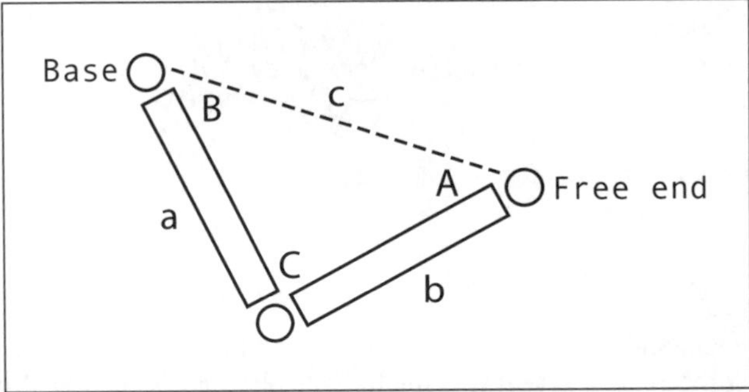

Figure 14-7. Two segments form a triangle with sides a, b, c, and angles A, B, C.

Here, you have two segments. The one on the left is the base. It's fixed, so you know that location. You want to put the free end at the location shown. You've formed an arbitrary triangle.

What do you know about this triangle? You can easily find out the distance between the two ends—side c. And you know the length of each segment—sides a and b. So, you know all three lengths.

What do you need to know about this triangle? You just need to know the two angles of the two segments—angles B and C. This is what the law of cosines helps you discover. Let me introduce you to it:

$$c^2 = a^2 + b^2 - 2 * a * b * \cos C$$

Now, you need to know angle C, so you can isolate that on one side. I won't go through every step, as it's pretty basic algebra. You should wind up with this:

```
C = acos ((a2 + b2 - c2) /  (2 * a * b))
```

The acos there is arccosine, or inverse cosine. The cosine of an angle gives you a ratio, or decimal. The arccosine of that ratio gives you back the angle. The Flash function for this is `Math.acos()`. Since you know sides a, b, and c, you can now find angle C. Similarly, you need to know angle B. The law of cosines says this:

$$b^2 = a^2 + c^2 - 2 * a * c * \cos B$$

And that boils down to this:

$$B = \operatorname{acos}((a^2 + c^2 - b^2) / (2 * a * c))$$

Converting to ActionScript gives you something like this:

```
B = Math.acos((a * a + c * c - b * b) / (2 * a * c));
C = Math.acos((a * a + b * b - c * c) / (2 * a * b));
```

Now you have *almost* everything you need to start positioning things. Almost, because the angles B and C aren't really the angles of rotation you'll be using for the segment movie clips. Look at the next diagram in Figure 14-8.

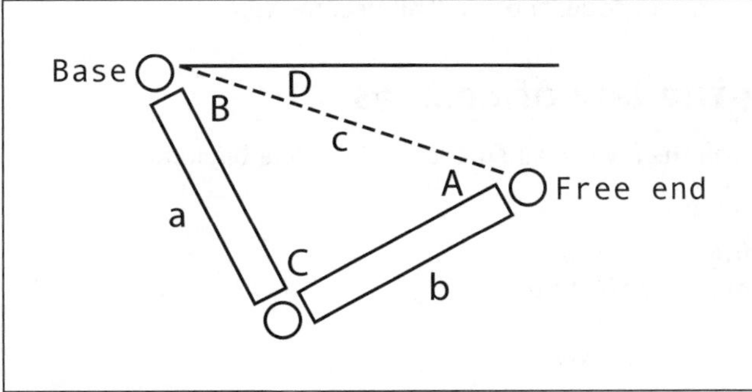

Figure 14-8. Figuring the rotation of seg1

While you know angle B, what you need to determine is how much to actually rotate seg1. This is how far from zero, or horizontal, it's going to be, and is represented by angles D plus B. Luckily, you can get angle D by figuring out the angle between the base and free end, as illustrated in Figure 14-9.

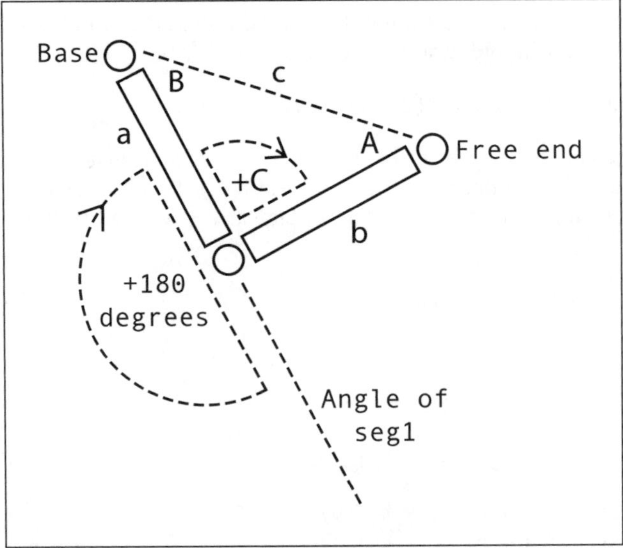

Figure 14-9. Figuring the rotation of seg0

Then you know angle C, but that is only in relation to seg1. What you need for rotation is seg1's rotation, plus 180, plus C. I'll call that angle E.

OK, enough talk. Let's see it in code, and it will all become clear.

ActionScripting the law of cosines

I'm just going to give you the inverse kinematics code in one big lump, and then explain it. Here's the code (`ch14_09.fla`):

```
var segLength:Number = 60;
function onEnterFrame():Void
{
	var dx:Number = _xmouse - seg1._x;
	var dy:Number = _ymouse - seg1._y;
	var dist:Number = Math.sqrt(dx * dx + dy * dy);

	var a:Number = segLength;
	var b:Number = segLength;
	var c:Number = Math.min(dist, a + b);

	var B:Number = Math.acos((b * b - a * a - c * c) /
	                         (-2 * a * c));
	var C:Number = Math.acos((c * c - a * a - b * b) /
```

```
                                        (-2 * a * b));
        var D:Number = Math.atan2(dy, dx);
        var E:Number = D + B + Math.PI + C;

        seg1._rotation = (D + B) * 180 / Math.PI;

        seg0._x = seg1._x + Math.cos(D + B) * segLength;
        seg0._y = seg1._y + Math.sin(D + B) * segLength;

        seg0._rotation = E * 180 / Math.PI;
}
```

Here's the procedure:

1. Get the distance from seg1 to the mouse.
2. Get the three sides' lengths. Sides a and b are easy. They are equal to segLength. Side c is equal to dist or a + b, whichever is smaller. This is because one side of a triangle can't be longer than the other two sides added together. If you don't believe me, try to draw such a shape. This also gets back into the reaching paradigm. If the distance from the base to the mouse is 200, but the length of the two segments adds up to only 120, it just isn't going to make it.
3. Figure out angles B and C using the law of cosines formula, and angle D using Math.atan2. E, as mentioned, is D + B + 180 + C. Of course, in code, you substitute Math.PI radians for 180 degrees.
4. Just as the diagram in Figure 14-9 shows, convert angle D + B to degrees, and that's seg1's rotation. Use the same angle to find the end point of seg1 and position seg0 on it.
5. Finally, seg0's rotation is E, converted to degrees.

There you have it: inverse kinematics using the law of cosines. You might notice that the joint always bends the same way. This might be good if you're building something like an elbow or a knee that can bend only one way.

When you're figuring out the angles analytically like this, there are two solutions to the problem: It could bend this way, or it could bend that way. You've hard-coded it to bend one way by *adding* D and B, and then *adding* C. If you subtracted them all, you'd get the same effect, but the limb would bend in the other direction.

```
var segLength:Number = 60;
function onEnterFrame():Void
{
        var dx:Number = _xmouse - seg1._x;
        var dy:Number = _ymouse - seg1._y;
        var dist:Number = Math.sqrt(dx * dx + dy * dy);

        var a:Number = segLength;
        var b:Number = segLength;
        var c:Number = Math.min(dist, a + b);

        var B:Number = Math.acos((b * b - a * a - c * c) /
                                        (-2 * a * c));
        var C:Number = Math.acos((c * c - a * a - b * b) /
```

```
                        (-2 * a * b));
        var D:Number = Math.atan2(dy, dx);
        var E:Number = D - B + Math.PI - C;

        seg1._rotation = (D - B) * 180 / Math.PI;

        seg0._x = seg1._x + Math.cos(D - B) * segLength;
        seg0._y = seg1._y + Math.sin(D - B) * segLength;

        seg0._rotation = E * 180 / Math.PI;
}
```

If you want it to bend either way, you'll need to figure out some kind of conditional logic to say, "If it's in this position, bend this way; otherwise, bend that way." Unfortunately, I have only enough space to give you this brief introduction to the law of cosines method. But if this is the kind of thing you're interested in doing, I'm sure you'll be able to find plenty of additional data on the subject. A quick web search for "inverse kinematics" just gave me more than 90,000 results. So yeah, you'll be able to dig up something!

Important formulas in this chapter

For the standard form of inverse kinematics, you use the law of cosines formula.

Law of cosines:

```
a2 = b2 + c2 - 2 * b * c * cos A
b2 = a2 + c2 - 2 * a * c * cos B
c2 = a2 + b2 - 2 * a * b * cos C
```

Law of cosines in ActionScript:

```
A = Math.acos((b * b + c * c - a * a) / (2 * b * c));
B = Math.acos((a * a + c * c - b * b) / (2 * a * c));
C = Math.acos((a * a + b * b - c * c) / (2 * a * b));
```

Summary

Inverse kinematics is a vast subject—far more than could ever be covered in a single chapter. Even so, I think this chapter described some pretty cool and useful things. You saw how to set up an inverse kinematics system and two ways of looking at it: dragging and reaching. If nothing else, I hope I've at least sparked some excitement in you for the subject. The main ideas I've tried to convey are that you can do some really fun stuff with it, and it doesn't have to be all that complex. There's much more that can be done in Flash with inverse kinematics, and I'm sure that you're now ready to go discover it and put it to use.

In the next chapter, you're going to enter a whole new dimension, which will allow you to add some depth to your movies. Yes, we're going 3D.

Part Four

3D ANIMATION

};shape.targetHeight = shape._height;
shape.onEnterFrame = function() {
var speed = 5;
this._width += (this.targetWidth - this._width)/speed;
this._height += (this.targetHeight - this._height)/speed;
};

Chapter 15

3D BASICS

What we'll cover in this chapter:

- The third dimension and perspective
- Velocity and acceleration
- Bouncing
- Gravity
- Wrapping
- Easing and springing
- Coordinate rotation
- Collision detection
- Important formulas in this chapter

Everything you've done so far in the book has been in just two (and sometimes only one) dimension, and you've done some pretty cool stuff. Now, let's take it to the next level.

Creating graphics in 3D is always exciting. That extra dimension seems to make things really come to life. How to do 3D in Flash has been covered in innumerable books and tutorials. So, while I don't plan on skimping on anything, I'm going to move through the basics pretty quickly. After that, I'll explain how the motion effects discussed in the previous chapters can be done with a third dimension. Specifically, this chapter covers velocity, acceleration, friction, gravity, bouncing, wrapping, easing, springing, coordinate rotation, and collision detection.

For now, you'll primarily be concerned with taking a movie clip and moving it around in 3D space, using perspective to calculate its size and position on the screen. The movie clip itself will be flat, of course. It won't have a back, side, top, or bottom that you can see. In the next couple of chapters, you'll do some modeling of points, lines, shapes, and solids in 3D.

The third dimension and perspective

It goes without saying that the main concept behind 3D is the existence of another dimension beyond x and y. This is the dimension of depth, and it is usually labeled z.

Flash does not have a built-in z dimension, but it isn't too difficult to create one with ActionScript. It's actually far less complex than a lot of the stuff you've just done in the previous chapters!

The z axis

To begin with, you need to decide which direction the z axis is going to go: in or out. Let me explain. If you recall back to Chapter 2's discussion of Flash's coordinate system, you'll remember that it is in some ways opposite to most other common coordinate systems. The y axis goes down instead of up, and angles are measured clockwise instead of counterclockwise.

So, should you make the z axis so that as an object's z position increases, it is going away from you or towards you? Neither way is necessarily more *correct* than the other. In fact, this subject has been addressed enough times that there are even names to describe the two methods: left-hand system and right-hand system.

Take your right hand and form an *L* with your thumb and forefinger, and then bend your middle finger 90 degrees from your index finger, each one will be pointing in another dimension. Now point your index finger in the direction the positive x axis goes, and your middle finger in the direction of the positive y axis. In a right-hand system, your thumb will now be pointing in the direction of the positive z axis. For Flash, this means the z axis will increase as it goes away from the viewer, and decrease as it goes toward the viewer, as shown in Figure 15-1.

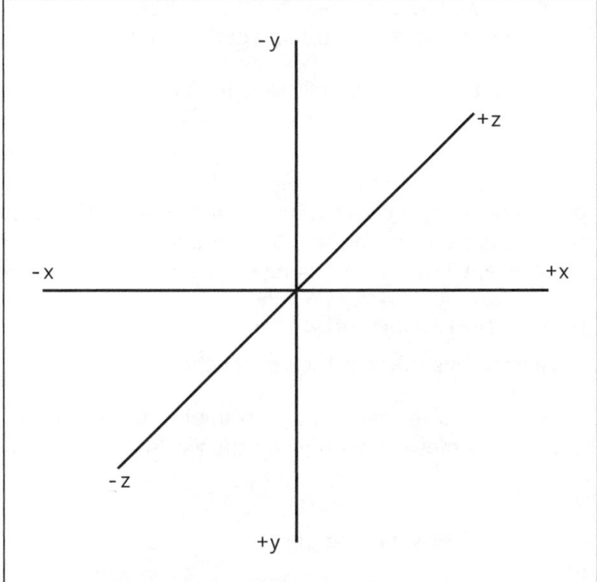

Figure 15-1. Right-hand coordinate system

If you try it with your left hand, you'll get the opposite result. Figure 15-2 shows the left-hand coordinate system.

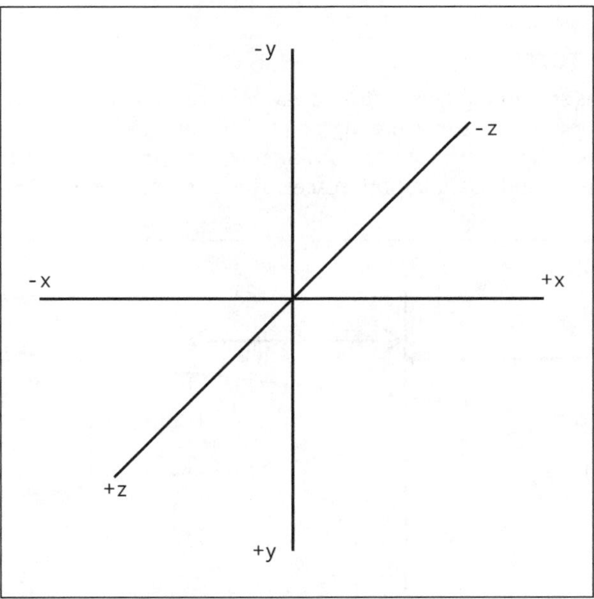

Figure 15-2. Left-hand coordinate system

I use the right-hand coordinate system (Figure 15-1) for the examples here. There's no reason that you couldn't make a left-hand system, but it seems to fall together a little better to make the z axis go in.

The next step in creating a third (z) dimension in Flash is to figure out how to simulate perspective.

Perspective

Perspective is how we tell if something is closer to us or farther away. Or, to put it another way, how we make something look like it is closer or farther. While the field of fine arts has a number of techniques for presenting perspective, I'll be concentrating on two here:

- Things get smaller as they get farther away.
- Things converge on a vanishing point as they get farther away.

I won't labor the point—I'm sure you've seen enough examples of train tracks coming to a point on the horizon. So basically, when you move something on the z axis, you need to do two things:

- Scale it up or down.
- Move it closer or further to the vanishing point.

In working with only two dimensions, you can generally get away with using the screen x and y coordinates for your object's x and y position. You just do a one-to-one mapping. This isn't going to work in 3D, because two objects can have the same x and y position, and yet, due to their depth, have a different position on the screen. So, each object you move in 3D will need to have its own x, y, and z coordinates that have nothing to do with the screen position. These now describe a location in virtual space. The perspective calculation will tell you where to put the object on the screen.

The perspective formula

The basic idea is that as something gets further away (z increases), its scale approaches 0 and its x, y position converges on the 0, 0 of the vanishing point. The good news is that the ratio of distance to scale is the same as the ratio of distance to convergence. So, you just need to figure out what that ratio is for a given distance and use it in both places. The diagram in Figure 15-3 helps to explain.

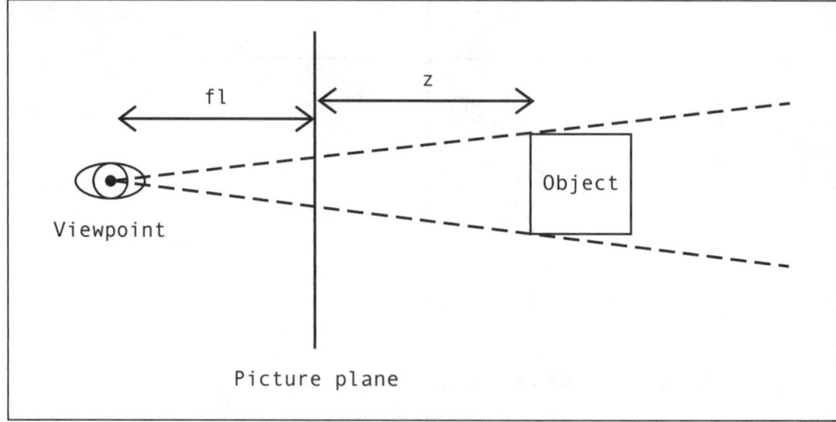

Figure 15-3. Perspective seen from the side

You have an object off in the distance. You have a viewpoint: your eyes. And you have a picture plane, which you can consider the computer screen. You have the distance of the object to the picture plane, which is the z value, and, finally, you have the distance from the viewpoint to the picture point. This last one is the key. It's not exactly the same as the focal length of a camera lens, but it is analogous, so I usually use the variable `fl` to represent it.

Here's the formula:

```
scale = fl / (fl + z)
```

This will usually yield a number between 0.0 and 1.0, which is your ratio for scaling and converging on the vanishing point. However, as z goes negative, `fl + z` approaches 0 and `scale` approaches infinity. This is the ActionScript equivalent to being poked in the eye.

So, what do you do with this `scale` value? Well, assuming you are dealing with a movie clip (which you will be throughout this chapter), you multiply `scale` by 100 and assign that to the clip's `_xscale` and `_yscale`. You then multiply the object's x and y position by this factor to find its screen x and y position.

Let's look at an example. Usual values of `fl` are around 200 to 300. Let's use 250. If z is zero—in other words, the object is exactly on the picture plane—then scale will be 250 / (250 + 0). This comes out to exactly 1.0. Multiplied by 100, you get 100 for `_xscale` and `_yscale`. And multiplied by the object's x and y positions, this gives the same numbers as result, so the object's screen position is exactly equal to its x and y.

Now move it out so that z is 250. That makes `scale` 250 / (250 + 250), or 0.5, which makes `_xscale` and `_yscale` 50. It also moves the object's screen position. If the object were at 200, 300 on x, y, its screen position would now be 100, 150. So, it has moved halfway to the vanishing point. (Actually, the screen position would be in relation to the vanishing point, which you'll see shortly.)

Now, move z way out to 9750. This makes `scale` 250 / 10000, or 0.025, and `_xscale` and `_yscale` are just 2.5. The object will become just a speck, very close to the vanishing point.

OK, enough theory. Time for some code.

Perspective in ActionScript

Start with a new FLA file. Create some new movie clip and put an instance of it on stage. I'll continue to use the red ball that I've grown so attached to, and name it `ball`. For interaction, let's get fancy and use the mouse *and* keyboard. You'll use the mouse to control the ball's x and y position, and the up and down keys to move it forward and back on the z axis.

Here's the code to put on frame 1 of the main timeline (`ch15_01.fla`):

```
var x:Number = 0;
var y:Number = 0;
var z:Number = 0;
var fl:Number = 250;
var vpX:Number = Stage.width / 2;
var vpY:Number = Stage.height / 2;
```

```
function onEnterFrame():Void
{
        x = _xmouse - vpX;
        y = _ymouse - vpY;
        if(Key.isDown(Key.UP))
        {
                z+=5;
        }
        else if(Key.isDown(Key.DOWN))
        {
                z-=5;
        }
        var scale:Number = fl / (fl + z);
        ball._xscale = ball._yscale = scale * 100;
        ball._x = vpX + x * scale;
        ball._y = vpY + y * scale;
}
```

First, you create variables for x, y, and z, as well as fl. Then you create a vanishing point, vpX, vpY. Remember that as things go off in the distance, they converge on 0, 0. If you don't offset this somehow, everything will converge at the top-left corner of the screen, which is not what you want. You'll use vpX, vpY to make the center of the stage the vanishing point.

Next, set x and y to equal the mouse position, as offset by the vanishing point. In other words, if the mouse is 200 pixels right of center, x will be 200. If it's 200 pixels left of center, x will be –200.

Then check the state of the up and down cursor keys, and change z accordingly. If the up key is being pressed, z increases, and down decreases it. This will make the ball move farther or closer to the viewer.

Finally, calculate scale using the formula I just covered, and size and position the ball accordingly. Note that the screen x and y positions (_x and _y) are calculated from the vanishing point, adding on the x and y times the scale. Thus, as scale becomes very small, the ball will converge on the vanishing point.

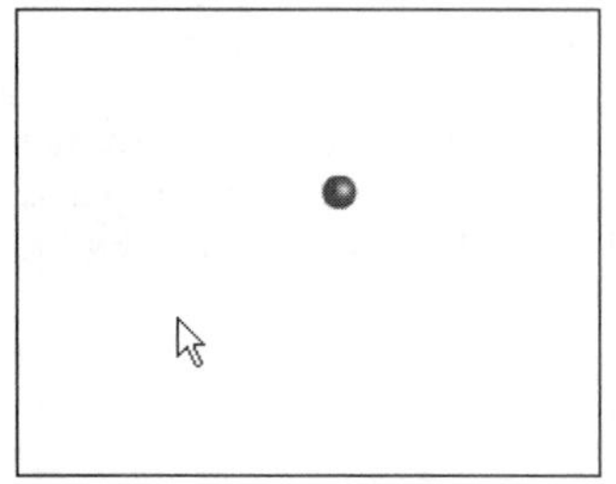

Figure 15-4. Perspective in action.

When you test it, at first it looks like you're simply dragging the ball with the mouse. This is because z is zero, making scale 1.0. So, no noticeable perspective is being applied. As you press the up cursor key, the ball appears to slide into the distance, as shown in Figure 15-4. Now as you move the mouse around, the ball moves with it, but much less, giving you a parallax effect.

One thing you might notice is that if you hold down the cursor key too long, the ball starts getting very large. This is fine. If you held a pebble up close to your eye, it would look like a boulder. If you keep holding the key down, though, you'll see that it grows to an infinite size and then shrinks down again, but now it's upside down and reversed. What has happened is that the ball has gone behind the viewpoint. So, I guess this must be what you would see if your eyes could look behind you.

Mathematically, what happens is that when z is equal to -fl, the formula scale = fl / (fl + z) becomes scale = fl / 0. In many languages, dividing by zero gives you an error. In Flash, it gives you Infinity. As you decrease z even more, you're now dividing fl by a negative number. Scale becomes negative, which is why your ball goes upside down and backwards.

How can you handle this? A simple way is to just make the ball invisible if it goes past a certain point. If z is less than or equal to -fl, you'll have a problem, so you can test for that condition and handle it like so (ch15_02.fla):

```
var x:Number = 0;
var y:Number = 0;
var z:Number = 0;
var fl:Number = 250;
var vpX:Number = Stage.width / 2;
var vpY:Number = Stage.height / 2;

function onEnterFrame():Void
{
	x = _xmouse - vpX;
	y = _ymouse - vpY;
	if(Key.isDown(Key.UP))
	{
		z+=5;
	}
	else if(Key.isDown(Key.DOWN))
	{
		z-=5;
	}
	if(z <= -fl)
	{
		ball._visible = false;
	}
	else
	{
		ball._visible = true;
		var scale:Number = fl / (fl + z);
		ball._xscale = ball._yscale = scale * 100;
		ball._x = vpX + x * scale;
		ball._y = vpY + y * scale;
	}
}
```

Note that if the ball is not visible, you don't need to worry about scaling and positioning it. Also note that if the ball is in visible range, you need to make sure it is visible. It adds a little extra overhead, but it's necessary overall.

Well, there you have it, the barebones basics of 3D. Not so painful is it? Make sure you play around with this example a bit to get a good feel for it. In particular, try changing the value for fl and see the different effects you get. This is equivalent to changing the lens of a camera. High values for fl are like a telephoto lens, giving you a small field of view, with less visible perspective. A low fl will create a wide-angle lens, with exaggerated perspective.

The rest of the chapter is devoted to ActionScripting the various motion effects covered in previous chapters, but now in 3D.

Velocity and acceleration

Accomplishing velocity and acceleration in 3D is surprisingly easy. For 2D, you had vx and vy variables to represent velocity on two axes. You just need to add a vz for the third dimension. Similarly, if you have something like ax and ay for acceleration, you just add an az variable.

You can alter the last example to make it work sort of like the Asteroids spaceship, but in 3D. Let's make it all keyboard-controlled now. Cursor keys can provide thrust on the x and y axes, and we'll grab a couple other keys, say *Shift* and *Ctrl*, for z thrust.

Here's the code (ch15_03.fla):

```
var x:Number = 0;
var y:Number = 0;
var z:Number = 0;
var vx:Number = 0;
var vy:Number = 0;
var vz:Number = 0;
var friction:Number = .98;
var fl:Number = 250;
var vpX:Number = Stage.width / 2;
var vpY:Number = Stage.height / 2;

function onEnterFrame():Void
{
	if(Key.isDown(Key.UP))
	{
		vy -= 1;
	}
	else if(Key.isDown(Key.DOWN))
	{
		vy += 1;
	}
	if(Key.isDown(Key.LEFT))
	{
		vx -= 1;
	}
	else if(Key.isDown(Key.RIGHT))
	{
		vx += 1;
	}
	if(Key.isDown(Key.SHIFT))
```

```
        {
            vz += 1;
        }
        else if(Key.isDown(Key.CONTROL))
        {
            vz -= 1;
        }

        x += vx;
        y += vy;
        z += vz;

        vx *= friction;
        vy *= friction;
        vz *= friction;

        if(z <= -fl)
        {
            ball._visible = false;
        }
        else
        {
            ball._visible = true;
            var scale:Number = fl / (fl + z);
            ball._xscale = ball._yscale = scale * 100;
            ball._x = vpX + x * scale;
            ball._y = vpY + y * scale;
        }
    }
```

All you've done here is add variables for velocity on each axis and some friction. When one of the six keys is pressed, it adds or subtracts from the appropriate velocity (remember that acceleration changes velocity). Then it adds the velocity to the position on each axis and computes friction.

Now you have a 3D object moving with acceleration, velocity, and friction. Wow, three birds with one stone. I told you it was easy.

Bouncing

For the purposes of this section, I'll be talking about bouncing off a flat surface. In other words, one that aligns perfectly with the x, y, or z axis. This is analogous to the bouncing off the sides of the screen you did in 2D.

Single object bouncing

With bouncing in 3D, again you detect when the object has gone past a boundary, adjust it to sit on that boundary, and then reverse its velocity on the appropriate axis. One of the differences with 3D is in how you decide where the boundaries are. In 2D, you generally use the stage coordinates or some other visible rectangular area. In 3D, things aren't quite so simple. There is no real concept of a visible edge, unless you draw one in 3D. You'll get to drawing in 3D in the next chapter, so for now, you'll be bouncing off arbitrarily placed invisible walls.

So, you set up your boundaries the same as before, but now you are setting them up in a 3D space, which means that they can be negative as well as positive. You also have the option of setting up a boundary on the z axis. The boundaries now look something like this:

```
var top:Number = -250;
var bottom:Number = 250;
var left:Number = -250;
var right:Number = 250;
var front:Number = 250;
var back:Number = -250;
```

Then, after determining the object's new position, you need to check it against all six boundaries. Remember that you take half of the object's width into account in checking for the collision. Rather than recalculate that six times per frame, I stored it in a variable called `radius`. Here's the full code for 3D bouncing (`ch15_04.fla`):

```
var x:Number = 0;
var y:Number = 0;
var z:Number = 0;
var vx:Number = Math.random() * 10 - 5;
var vy:Number = Math.random() * 10 - 5;
var vz:Number = Math.random() * 10 - 5;
var top:Number = -100;
var bottom:Number = 100;
var left:Number = -100;
var right:Number = 100;
var front:Number = 100;
var back:Number = -100;
var radius:Number = 15;
var fl:Number = 250;
var vpX:Number = Stage.width / 2;
var vpY:Number = Stage.height / 2;

function onEnterFrame():Void
{
      x += vx;
      y += vy;
      z += vz;

      if(x + radius > right)
      {
```

```
            x = right - radius;
            vx *= -1;
        }
        else if(x - radius < left)
        {
            x = left + radius;
            vx *= -1;
        }
        if(y + radius > bottom)
        {
            y = bottom - radius;
            vy *= -1;
        }
        else if(y - radius < top)
        {
            y = top + radius;
            vy *= -1;
        }
        if(z + radius > front)
        {
            z = front - radius;
            vz *= -1;
        }
        else if(z - radius < back)
        {
            z = back + radius;
            vz *= -1;
        }

        if(z <= -fl)
        {
            ball._visible = false;
        }
        else
        {
            ball._visible = true;
            var scale:Number = fl / (fl + z);
            ball._xscale = ball._yscale = scale * 100;
            ball._x = vpX + x * scale;
            ball._y = vpY + y * scale;
        }
    }
```

Note that I removed all of the key-handing stuff and just gave the ball a random velocity on each axis. Now you can see it is definitely bouncing around, but you can't really tell what it is bouncing against—as I said, these are arbitrarily placed invisible boundaries.

Multiple object bouncing

One thing you could do to help visualize the walls a little better would be to fill up the space with more objects. In ch15_05.fla, I've removed the ball from the stage and attached 50 of them dynamically instead. Each one now gets its own x, y, z and vx, vy, vz. The onEnterFrame function now loops through, doing the same thing to each ball instead of just one. Here's the code:

```
var numBalls:Number = 50;
var top:Number = -100;
var bottom:Number = 100;
var left:Number = -100;
var right:Number = 100;
var front:Number = 100;
var back:Number = -100;
var radius:Number = 15;
var fl:Number = 250;
var vpX:Number = Stage.width / 2;
var vpY:Number = Stage.height / 2;

init();
function init() {
      for (var i:Number = 0; i<numBalls; i++) {
            var ball:MovieClip = attachMovie("ball", "ball" + i, i);
            ball.x = Math.random() * 200 - 100;
            ball.y = Math.random() * 200 - 100;
            ball.z = Math.random() * 200 - 100;

            ball.vx = Math.random() * 10 - 5;
            ball.vy = Math.random() * 10 - 5;
            ball.vz = Math.random() * 10 - 5;
      }
}

function onEnterFrame():Void {
      for (var i:Number=0;i<numBalls;i++) {
            var ball:MovieClip = this["ball" + i];

            ball.x += ball.vx;
            ball.y += ball.vy;
            ball.z += ball.vz;

            if (ball.x + radius > right) {
                  ball.x = right - radius;
                  ball.vx *= -1;
            } else if (ball.x - radius < left) {
                  ball.x = left + radius;
                  ball.vx *= -1;
```

```
                }
                if (ball.y + radius > bottom) {
                    ball.y = bottom - radius;
                    ball.vy *= -1;
                } else if (ball.y - radius < top) {
                    ball.y = top + radius;
                    ball.vy *= -1;
                }
                if (ball.z + radius > front) {
                    ball.z = front - radius;
                    ball.vz *= -1;
                } else if (ball.z - radius < back) {
                    ball.z = back + radius;
                    ball.vz *= -1;
                }
                if (ball.z <= -fl) {
                    ball._visible = false;
                } else {
                    ball._visible = true;
                    var scale:Number = fl / (fl + ball.z);
                    ball._xscale = ball._yscale=scale*100;
                    ball._x = vpX + ball.x * scale;
                    ball._y = vpY + ball.y * scale;
                }
            }
        }
```

When you run this file, the balls largely fill up the space between the six boundaries, as shown in Figure 15-5, and you can get an idea of the shape of this space.

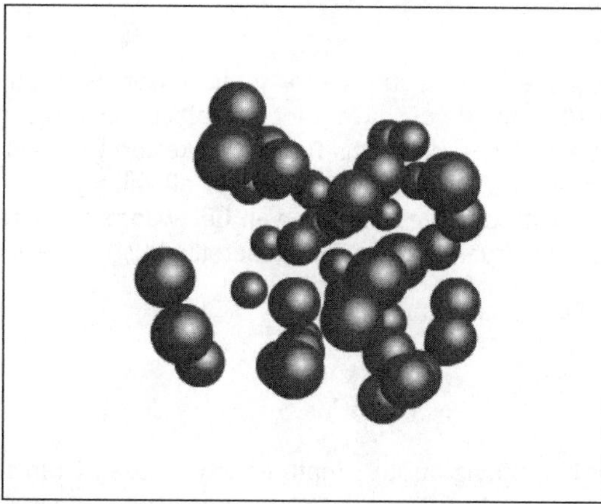

Figure 15-5. Bouncing 3D balls

Z-sorting

Now, this addition of multiple objects reveals something lacking in the code you have so far—something called *z-sorting*. Z-sorting is pretty much what it sounds like: how things are sorted on the z axis, or which one goes in front of another one. In Flash, z-sorting is done by the depth of the object, which is determined when you place the object on stage or when you attach it. Movie clips with a higher depth appear in front of ones with a lower depth.

Flash doesn't know that you are simulating 3D. It just knows that you're moving and scaling movie clips. And it certainly doesn't know if you're using a left-hand or right-hand coordinate system. So, it has no idea that because this ball is farther away, it should appear behind this other one that is closer. It just sorts them according to the depth they were originally given. If you want to change that, you need to tell Flash the order you want to use for them. You can do that by using the `MovieClip` method `swapDepths` to send the clip to the appropriate depth.

The problem is that the z-sorting you're using is opposite to Flash's ordering. With the right-hand system, objects with a higher z value are farther away. But there's a simple fix. Just use `-z` to determine the depth, like so: `ball.swapDepths(-ball.z)`. It's no problem to swap a movie clip to a negative depth. As you may recall from Chapter 2, movie clips placed on stage already have a negative depth. The only caveat is that if you want to remove these clips at some point with `removeMovieClip`, you'll need to swap them back to a higher depth.

Here's the updated block of code from the `onEnterFrame` function:

```
} else {
      ball._visible = true;
      var scale:Number = fl / (fl + ball.z);
      ball._xscale = ball._yscale=scale*100;
      ball._x = vpX + ball.x * scale;
      ball._y = vpY + ball.y * scale;
      ball.swapDepths(-ball.z);
}
```

If you thought the example looked a little strange for some reason, you can add this single line to the file. Note that this is not a 100% fix. If you have a lot of objects on stage, there may be several very close to each other on the z axis. The `swapDepths` function takes only integers, so if you use it on three movie clips at z positions of –100.3, –100.0, and –99.7, they all will try to change their depths to 100. The last one will wind up at 100, but the first two will be swapped out to some other coordinate, possibly giving you some minor visual glitches. But generally, this is a very quick, easy, and effective technique for z-sorting.

Gravity

I should mention that here I'm talking about simple gravity as seen from the earth's surface, and as described in Chapter 5. In this case, gravity works pretty much the same in 3D as it does in 2D. All you need to do is choose a number for the force gravity is exerting on the object, and add that number to the object's y velocity on each frame or iteration.

Since gravity in 3D is so simple, I could be tempted to gloss it over and say, "Yup, same as 2D. OK, next subject . . ." But I decided to throw in a nice example that demonstrates how something so simple can create a really great effect, like 3D fireworks.

To start with, you need a movie clip to represent a single "firework," you know, one of those dots of glowing light that can be combined with others to make a big explosion. I made a 10-pixel white circle and converted it to a movie clip symbol named dot, exported for ActionScript, also with the name dot. I also made the background of the movie black.

Since I'm sure you can handle it by now, I'm going to dump the entire code listing on you (ch15_06.fla), and then explain it.

```
var numDots:Number = 100;
var gravity:Number = .5;
var fl:Number = 250;
var vpX:Number = Stage.width / 2;
var vpY:Number = Stage.height / 2;

init();
function init() {
      for (var i:Number = 0; i<numDots; i++) {
            var dot:MovieClip = attachMovie("dot", "dot" + i, i);
            reset();
      }
}

onMouseDown = reset;
function reset():Void
{
      var x:Number = Math.random() * 400 - 200;
      var y:Number = Math.random() * 50 - 200;
      var z:Number = Math.random() * 100 + 200;
      var color:Number = Math.random() * 0xffffff;

      for (var i:Number = 0; i<numDots; i++) {
            var dot = this["dot" + i];
            var dotColor:Color = new Color(dot);
            dotColor.setRGB(color);

            dot.x = x;
            dot.y = -200;
            dot.z = 250;

            dot.vx = Math.random() * 10 - 5;
            dot.vy = Math.random() * 10 - 10;
            dot.vz = Math.random() * 10 - 5;
      }
}
```

```
function onEnterFrame():Void {
	for (var i:Number=0;i<numDots;i++) {
		var dot:MovieClip = this["dot" + i];
		dot.vy += gravity;
		dot.x += dot.vx;
		dot.y += dot.vy;
		dot.z += dot.vz;

		if (dot.z <= -fl) {
			dot._visible = false;
		} else {
			dot._visible = true;
			var scale:Number = fl / (fl + dot.z);
			dot._xscale = dot._yscale=scale*100;
			dot._x = vpX + dot.x * scale;
			dot._y = vpY + dot.y * scale;
			dot.swapDepths(-dot.z);
		}
	}
}
```

First, you set up your variables: numDots, gravity, fl, vpX, and vpY. If you find that 100 dots are slowing down your computer too much, you can reduce the number to 50 or so.

Then call the init function to attach all the dots. The init function then calls the reset function to set up the properties of each dot. I separated this out because I wanted to be able to reset all the dots (hence the function name) to create another explosion later. You can see that this is done by assigning this function to onMouseDown. So each time you click, reset is called again, and you get a new fireworks display.

The reset function determines a random x, y, z point and color for the explosion. It then loops through each dot, coloring and positioning the dot at that point. It also gives the dot a random velocity on all three axes. The following line causes the dots to tend to have an upward initial velocity, creating a nicer explosion:

```
dot.vy = Math.random() * 10 - 10;
```

The code for random upward velocity is just something I found through experimentation, which I hope you've now learned to do as well. Again, I want to stress that you shouldn't just be copying and pasting this code. Play with it. Change it until you break it, and then put it back together again some new way. And if it works, share the result!

It's funny that the most complex code is all the setup stuff you just went through. The actual 3D and gravity code is pretty simple. You loop through each dot, add gravity to its y velocity, add velocity to its position, and apply perspective to it. The result looks something like Figure 15-6.

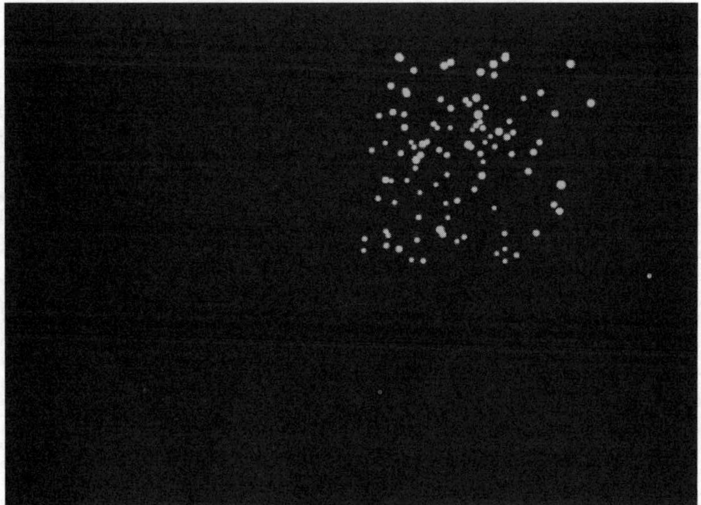

Figure 15-6. Fireworks! (Trust me, it looks much better in motion.)

For homework, create a "ground" and have the dots bounce off it when they hit.

Wrapping

If you can remember back to Chapter 5, I talked about three possible reactions when an object hit a boundary. I just covered bouncing. There was also wrapping and regeneration. For 3D, I have found wrapping to be pretty useful, but really only on the z axis.

In 2D wrapping, you check if the object went off the screen on the x or y axes. This works pretty well, because when the object goes beyond one of those boundaries, you can't see it anymore, so you can easily reposition it without jarring the viewer's attention. You don't have that luxury in 3D.

With 3D, there are really only two points where it's safe to remove and reposition an object. One is when the object has gone behind the viewpoint. The previous examples test for this and turn the object invisible in such a case. The other is when the object is so far in the distance and shrunk to such a small size that it's invisible or nearly so. This means that you can safely wrap on the z axis. When something goes behind you, you toss it way out in front of you, and let it come at you again. Or, if something has gone so far out that you can barely see it, remove it and replace it behind you. If you want, you can try wrapping on the x or y axis as well, but in most cases, you're going to wind up with an unnatural popping in and out of existence effect.

The good news is that z-axis wrapping can be pretty useful. I've used it to create a realistic 3D racing-type game, which I'll partially re-create here.

The idea is to place various 3D objects out in front of the viewpoint. Then you move those objects toward the viewpoint. In other words, you give them some negative z velocity. Depending on how you set it up, this can either look like a lot of objects coming towards you or it can trick the eye to look like you're moving towards them. Once an object has gone behind the viewpoint, you'll replace it way out in the distance. That way, there is a never-ending supply of objects to drive past.

The objects I used in ch15_07.fla are simple stylized trees, as you can see in Figure 15-7.

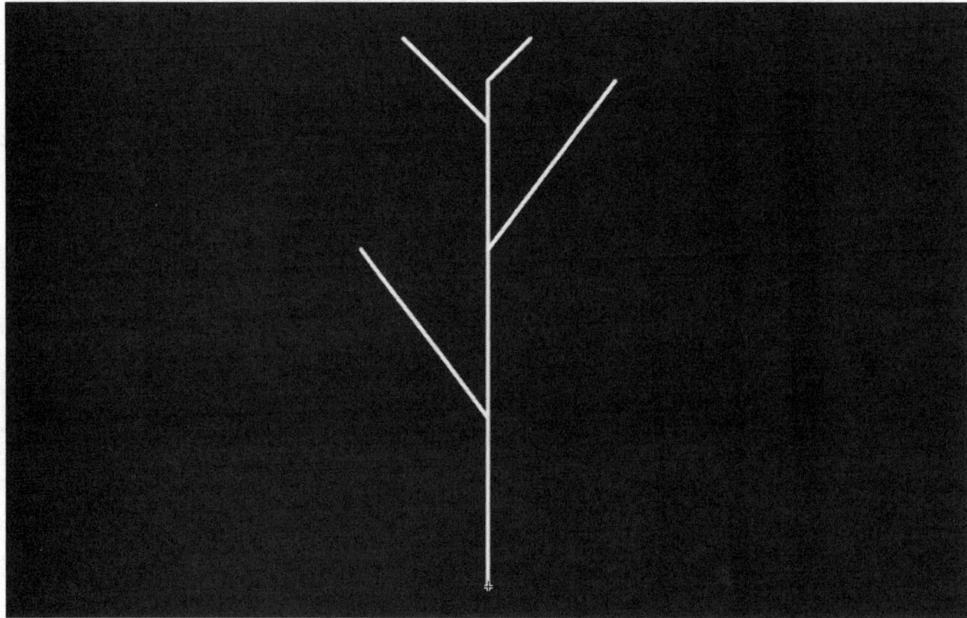

Figure 15-7. My tree. (By now you know why I became a programmer instead of a designer.)

The tree symbol is named tree and exported with the same name. Again, I went with white on a black background. But you can make any kind of objects you want, and make them as complex as you want. The code merely attaches a whole bunch (100 to be exact) of these trees. They are spread out randomly on the x axis, 1,000 pixels in either direction. They are also spread out on the z axis, from 0 to 10,000. They all have the same y position though, forming the impression of a ground plane.

Here's the code (ch15_07.fla):

```
var numTrees:Number = 100;
var fl:Number = 250;
var vz:Number = 0;
var friction:Number = .98;
var vpX:Number = Stage.width / 2;
var vpY:Number = Stage.height / 2;

init();
function init() {
      for (var i:Number = 0; i<numTrees; i++) {
            var tree:MovieClip = attachMovie("tree", "tree" + i, i);
            tree.x = Math.random() * 2000 - 1000;
            tree.y = 50;
            tree.z = Math.random() * 10000;
      }
}
```

```
function onEnterFrame():Void {
      if(Key.isDown(Key.UP))
      {
            vz -= 1;
      }
      else if(Key.isDown(Key.DOWN))
      {
            vz += 1;
      }
      vz *= friction;
      for (var i:Number=0;i<numTrees;i++) {
            var tree:MovieClip = this["tree" + i];
            tree.z += vz;

            if (tree.z <= -fl) {
                  tree.z += 10000;
            }
            else if(tree.z > 10000 - fl)
            {
                  tree.z -= 10000;
            }
            var scale:Number = fl / (fl + tree.z);
            tree._xscale = tree._yscale=scale*100;
            tree._x = vpX + tree.x * scale;
            tree._y = vpY + tree.y * scale;
            tree._alpha = scale * 60 + 40;
            tree.swapDepths(-tree.z);
      }
}
```

Notice that now there is only a single variable for z velocity, as the trees won't be moving on the x or y axis, and all will be moving in unison on the z axis. In the `onEnterFrame` function, you check for the up or down cursor key being pressed and increment or decrement vz accordingly. A little friction keeps the speed from increasing infinitely, and slows you down if no key is being pressed.

The code then loops through each tree, updating its z position with the current z velocity. Then it checks if a tree has gone behind you. If so, rather than turning it invisible, it moves it 10,000 pixels into the z axis. Likewise, if it has gone past 10,000 – `fl`, it moves it back 10,000.

You then do the standard perspective actions. Here, I also added another little tidbit to further enhance the illusion of depth:

```
tree._alpha = scale * 60 + 40;
```

This sets the transparency of the clip in relation to its depth on the z axis. The farther away it goes, the more it fades out. This is atmospheric perspective, simulating the effect of the atmosphere between the viewer and the object. This is particularly effective when you have objects moving way out in the distance, as in this example. I could have simply written:

```
tree._alpha = scale * 100;
```

But I found that made the trees *too* faded. Doing it as scale * 60 + 40 makes them anywhere from 40% transparent to 100% transparent, which looked about right to me. You can see how this comes out in Figure 15-8.

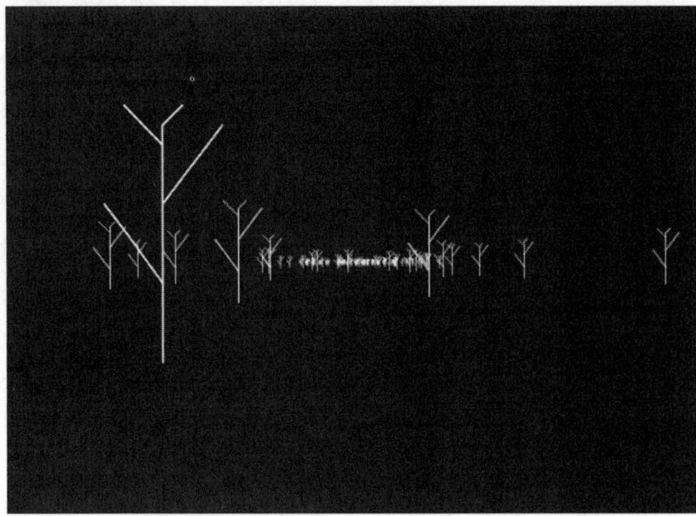

Figure 15-8. Watch out for the trees!

Again, I'm just showing you what you can do. Please try all kinds of combinations. You can even try something like this:

```
tree._alpha = scale * 40;
```

This gives the effect of a dark, spooky night. There are no right or wrong values for most of this stuff—just different values that create different effects.

I liked this example so much that I added a few enhancements beyond the scope of the subject of wrapping, just to give you an idea of where this could go. Here is the result (ch15_08.fla):

```
var numTrees:Number = 100;
var fl:Number = 250;
var gravity:Number = .5;
var vx:Number = 0;
var vy:Number = 0;
var vz:Number = 0;
var friction:Number = .98;
var vpX:Number = Stage.width / 2;
var vpY:Number = Stage.height / 2;

init();
function init() {
```

```
        for (var i:Number = 0; i<numTrees; i++) {
            var tree:MovieClip = attachMovie("tree", "tree" + i, i);
            tree.x = Math.random() * 2000 - 1000;
            tree.y = 50;
            tree.z = Math.random() * 10000;
        }
    }

    function onEnterFrame():Void {
        if(Key.isDown(Key.UP))
        {
            vz -= 1;
        }
        else if(Key.isDown(Key.DOWN))
        {
            vz += 1;
        }
        if(Key.isDown(Key.LEFT))
        {
            vx += 1;
        }
        else if(Key.isDown(Key.RIGHT))
        {
            vx -= 1;
        }
        if(Key.isDown(Key.SPACE))
        {
            vy += 1;
        }
        vy -= gravity;
        vx *= friction;
        vy *= friction;
        vz *= friction;
        for (var i:Number=0;i<numTrees;i++) {
            var tree:MovieClip = this["tree" + i];

            tree.x += vx;
            tree.y += vy;
            tree.z += vz;
            if(tree.y < 50)
            {
                tree.y = 50;
                vy = 0;
            }
            if (tree.z <= -fl) {
                tree.z += 10000;
```

```
                }
                else if(tree.z > 10000 - fl)
                {
                      tree.z -= 10000;
                }
                var scale:Number = fl / (fl + tree.z);
                tree._xscale = tree._yscale=scale*100;
                tree._x = vpX + tree.x * scale;
                tree._y = vpY + tree.y * scale;
                tree._alpha = scale * 60 + 40;
                tree.swapDepths(-tree.z);
          }
    }
```

Here, I've added velocity for the x and y axes, as well as some gravity. The left and right cursor keys were obvious choices for the x velocity, and I used the spacebar for y. One interesting point is that I am actually *subtracting* gravity from vy. This is because I want it to seem like the *viewer* is the one who is falling down to where the trees are, as shown in Figure 15-9. Really, the trees are "falling up" to where the viewpoint is, but it winds up looking the same. Notice also that I limit the trees' y position to 50, which makes it look like you've landed on the ground.

Figure 15-9. Look, I'm flying!

I didn't do anything to limit movement on the x axis, which means you can go way off to the side of the forest if you want. It wouldn't be too hard for you to set up some limitation, but I think I've done enough here to get you started.

Easing and springing

Easing and springing are also not much more complex in 3D than they are in 2D (the subject of Chapter 8). You mainly need to add in another variable or two for the z axis, and you're all set.

Easing

There's not a whole lot to cover on easing. In 2D, you have tx and ty as a target point. You just add tz for the z axis. On each frame, you measure the distance from the object to the target on each axis, and move it a fraction of the way there.

Let's look at a simple example that eases an object to a random target, and when it gets there, it picks another target and moves the object there. Note that I went back to my red ball again for the next couple of examples. Here's the code (ch15_09.fla):

```
var x:Number = 0;
var y:Number = 0;
var z:Number = 0;

var tx:Number = Math.random() * 500 - 250;
var ty:Number = Math.random() * 500 - 250;
var tz:Number = Math.random() * 500;

var easing:Number = .1;
var fl:Number = 250;
var vpX:Number = Stage.width / 2;
var vpY:Number = Stage.height / 2;

function onEnterFrame():Void
{
      var dx:Number = tx - x;
      var dy:Number = ty - y;
      var dz:Number = tz - z;
      x += dx * easing;
      y += dy * easing;
      z += dz * easing;

      var dist:Number = Math.sqrt(dx*dx + dy*dy + dz*dz);

      if(dist < 1)
      {
            tx = Math.random() * 500 - 250;
            ty = Math.random() * 500 - 250;
            tz = Math.random() * 500
      }
```

```
        if(z <= -fl)
        {
            ball._visible = false;
        }
        else
        {
            ball._visible = true;
            var scale:Number = fl / (fl + z);
            ball._xscale = ball._yscale = scale * 100;
            ball._x = vpX + x * scale;
            ball._y = vpY + y * scale;
        }
    }
```

The most interesting point of this code is the following line:

```
var dist:Number = Math.sqrt(dx*dx + dy*dy + dz*dz);
```

If you remember, in 2D, you measure the distance between two points by the following equation:

```
var dist:Number = Math.sqrt(dx*dx + dy*dy);
```

To move into 3D distances, just add the square of the distance on the third axis. This always strikes me as too simple. It seems like I should be using a cube root instead of a square root, now that I've added on an extra term. But it doesn't work that way.

Springing

Springing, being a close cousin to easing, requires a similar adjustment for 3D. You just use the distance to the target to change the velocity, rather than the position. I'll give you another quick example. In this one (file ch15_10.fla), clicking the mouse will create a new random target for the ball to spring to.

```
var x:Number = 0;
var y:Number = 0;
var z:Number = 0;

var vx:Number = 0;
var vy:Number = 0;
var vz:Number = 0;

var tx:Number = Math.random() * 500 - 250;
var ty:Number = Math.random() * 500 - 250;
var tz:Number = Math.random() * 500;
```

```
var friction:Number = .98;
var spring:Number = .1;
var fl:Number = 250;
var vpX:Number = Stage.width / 2;
var vpY:Number = Stage.height / 2;

function onMouseDown():Void
{
      tx = Math.random() * 500 - 250;
      ty = Math.random() * 500 - 250;
      tz = Math.random() * 500;

}

function onEnterFrame():Void
{
      var dx:Number = tx - x;
      var dy:Number = ty - y;
      var dz:Number = tz - z;

      vx += dx * spring;
      vy += dy * spring;
      vz += dz * spring;
      x += vx;
      y += vy;
      z += vz;
      vx *= friction;
      vy *= friction;
      vz *= friction;

      if(z <= -fl)
      {
            ball._visible = false;
      }
      else
      {
            ball._visible = true;
            var scale:Number = fl / (fl + z);
            ball._xscale = ball._yscale = scale * 100;
            ball._x = vpX + x * scale;
            ball._y = vpY + y * scale;
      }
}
```

As you can see, this uses the basic spring formula (from Chapter 8) with a third axis.

Coordinate rotation

Next up is coordinate rotation in 3D. This does get a bit more complex than 2D, which you saw in Chapters 10 and 11. Not only can you choose between three different axes to rotate on, you can even rotate on more than one of them at once.

In 2D coordinate rotation, the points are rotated around the z axis, as shown in Figure 15-10. Think of a "Wheel of Fortune" type spinning wheel with an axle through the center. The axle is the z axis. Only the x and y coordinates change.

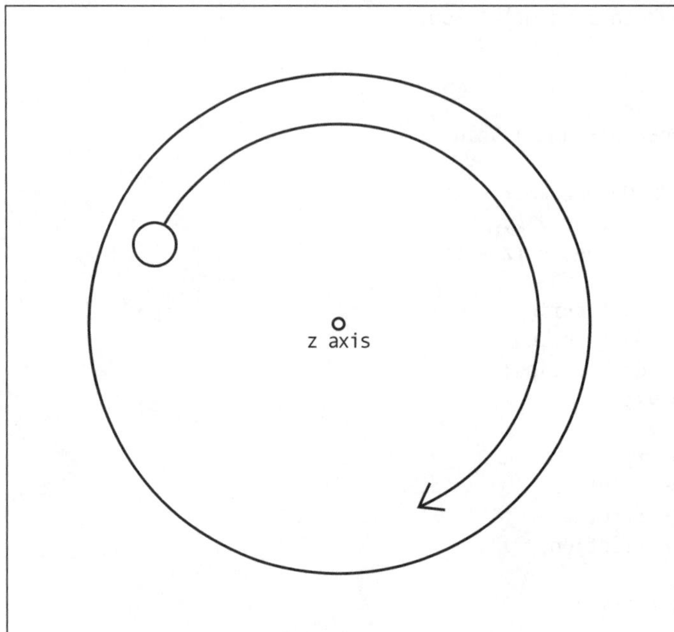

Figure 15-10. Rotation on the z axis

In 3D, you can also rotate on the x or y axis. An x-axis rotation would look like a car tire rolling towards you, as shown in Figure 15-11. The axle is on the x axis. Points rotate around that and change their y and z positions.

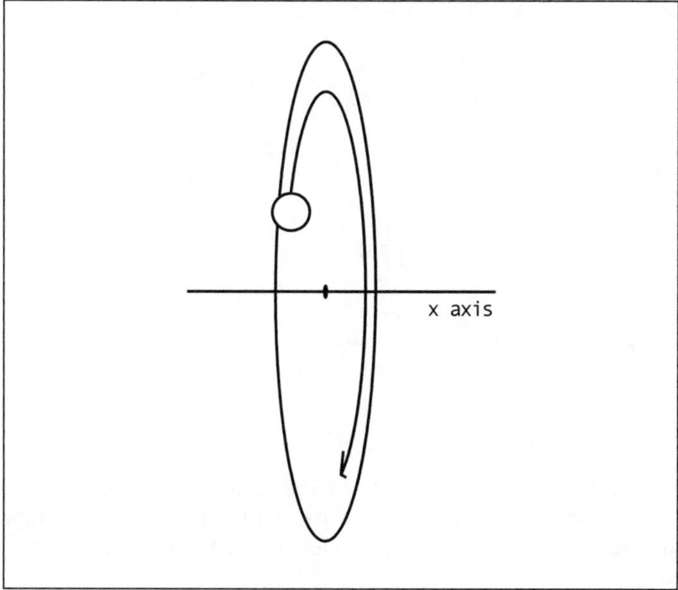

Figure 15-11. Rotation on the x axis

For y-axis rotation, imagine an old record player, something like Figure 15-12. The spindle is the y axis. Points change on the x and z axes.

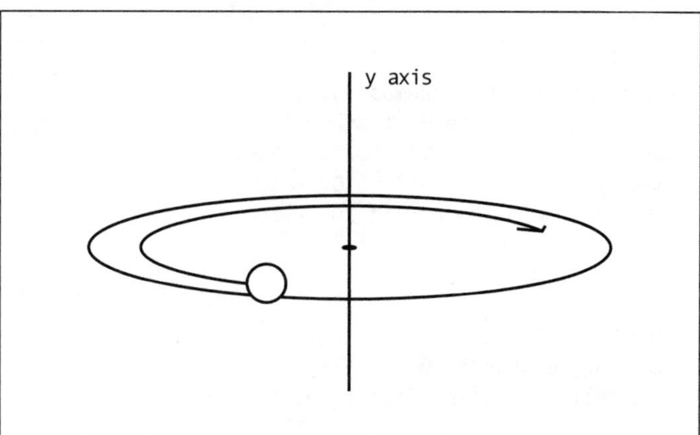

Figure 15-12. Rotation on the y axis

Thus, for 3D, when you rotate an object on one axis, its position will change on the other two axes.

If you check back to Chapter 10, you'll find the following formula for 2D rotation:

```
x1 = cos(angle) * x - sin(angle) * y;
y1 = cos(angle) * y + sin(angle) * x;
```

In 3D, you do basically the same thing, but you need to specify *which* angle you're talking about: x, y, or z. Thus, you get the following three formulas:

```
x1 = cos(angleZ) * x - sin(angleZ) * y;
y1 = cos(angleZ) * y + sin(angleZ) * x;

x1 = cos(angleY) * x - sin(angleY) * z;
z1 = cos(angleY) * z + sin(angleY) * x;

y1 = cos(angleX) * y - sin(angleX) * z;
z1 = cos(angleX) * z + sin(angleX) * y;
```

Let's try a y-axis rotation. The following code can be found in `ch15_11.fla`. It attaches 50 movie clips and randomly positions them. Then it gets a y angle based on the mouse's x position. The further right the mouse goes, the higher the number for the angle. This makes the movie clips seem to follow the mouse in their rotation.

```
var numBalls:Number = 50;
var fl:Number = 250;
var vpX:Number = Stage.width / 2;
var vpY:Number = Stage.height / 2;

init();
function init() {
	for (var i:Number = 0; i<numBalls; i++) {
		var ball:MovieClip = attachMovie("ball", "ball" + i, i);
		ball.x = Math.random() * 200 - 100;
		ball.y = Math.random() * 200 - 100;
		ball.z = Math.random() * 200 - 100;
	}
}

function onEnterFrame():Void {
	for (var i:Number=0;i<numBalls;i++) {
		var ball:MovieClip = this["ball" + i];

		var angleY:Number = (_xmouse - vpX) * .001;
		var cosY:Number = Math.cos(angleY);
		var sinY:Number = Math.sin(angleY);

		var x1:Number = ball.x * cosY - ball.z * sinY;
		var z1:Number = ball.z * cosY + ball.x * sinY;

		ball.x = x1;
		ball.z = z1;
```

```
            if (ball.z <= -fl) {
                ball._visible = false;
            } else {
                ball._visible = true;
                var scale:Number = fl / (fl + ball.z);
                ball._xscale = ball._yscale = scale*100;
                ball._x = vpX + ball.x * scale;
                ball._y = vpY + ball.y * scale;
                ball.swapDepths(-ball.z);
            }
        }
    }
```

The important parts are in bold. You get an angle, get the sine and cosine of that angle, do the rotation, and assign x1 and z1 back to ball.x and ball.z. Figure 15-13 shows the result.

Figure 15-13. 3D coordinate rotation on the y axis

Once you've tried that, you can try switching it over to x-axis rotation. Just change the bold lines in the preceding code to the following:

```
var angleX:Number = (_ymouse - vpY) * .001;
var cosX:Number = Math.cos(angleX);
var sinX:Number = Math.sin(angleX);

var y1:Number = ball.y * cosX - ball.z * sinX;
var z1:Number = ball.z * cosX + ball.y * sinX;

ball.y = y1;
ball.z = z1;
```

Now, angleX is based on the mouse's y position. You take the cosine and sine of that, and use them to get y1 and z1, which are passed to the ball's y and z properties.

Next, let's combine the two rotations. Here's the code (ch15_12.fla):

```
var numBalls:Number = 50;
var fl:Number = 250;
var vpX:Number = Stage.width / 2;
var vpY:Number = Stage.height / 2;

init();
function init() {
    for (var i:Number = 0; i<numBalls; i++) {
        var ball:MovieClip = attachMovie("ball", "ball" + i, i);
        ball.x = Math.random() * 200 - 100;
        ball.y = Math.random() * 200 - 100;
        ball.z = Math.random() * 200 - 100;
    }
}
```

```
function onEnterFrame():Void {
      for (var i:Number=0;i<numBalls;i++) {
            var ball:MovieClip = this["ball" + i];

            var angleY:Number = (_xmouse - vpX) * .001;
            var cosY:Number = Math.cos(angleY);
            var sinY:Number = Math.sin(angleY);

            var angleX:Number = (_ymouse - vpY) * .001;
            var cosX:Number = Math.cos(angleX);
            var sinX:Number = Math.sin(angleX);

            var x1:Number = ball.x * cosY - ball.z * sinY;
            var z1:Number = ball.z * cosY + ball.x * sinY;

            var y1:Number = ball.y * cosX - z1 * sinX;
            var z2:Number = z1 * cosX + ball.y * sinX;

            ball.x = x1;
            ball.y = y1;
            ball.z = z2;

            if (ball.z <= -fl) {
                  ball._visible = false;
            } else {
                  ball._visible = true;
                  var scale:Number = fl / (fl + ball.z);
                  ball._xscale = ball._yscale = scale*100;
                  ball._x = vpX + ball.x * scale;
                  ball._y = vpY + ball.y * scale;
                  ball.swapDepths(-ball.z);
            }
      }
}
```

The changes from the previous example are in bold. Now, you find both angleY and angleX, and the sine and cosine of each. Then you calculate x1 and z1, based on the y rotation as before. Next, you need to take those rotated values and rotate them *again* on the x axis. Because the z position is being rotated twice, you need a new variable, z2, for the second rotation. When both rotations are done, you have new values for x, y, and z. The rest is just perspective.

Play around with this one. By combining 3D coordinate rotation with some of the concepts from the racing game examples in the "Wrapping" section earlier in this chapter, you can create some rich, interactive 3D environments.

Collision detection

The last thing I want to cover in this introduction to 3D is collision detection. The only feasible way of doing collision detection in 3D in Flash is distance-based. This is not too much different from collision detection in 2D. You find the distance between two objects (using the 3D distance formula), and if that is less than the sum of their radii, you have a hit.

For a 3D collision detection example, I altered one of the earlier 3D bouncing examples, giving it fewer movie clips and more space. I also altered the ball movie clip, giving it two frames. The first has a red ball on it, the second has an identical ball in blue. It has a stop(); action on the first frame to prevent it from looping back and forth between the two.

In the code, I first do the normal 3D motion and perspective, and then do a double for loop to compare all the balls' locations. If any are less distance apart than twice their radius, I turn them both blue, by sending them to frame 2. It's pretty simple. Here's the code (ch15_13.fla):

```
var numBalls:Number = 20;
var top:Number = -200;
var bottom:Number = 200;
var left:Number = -200;
var right:Number = 200;
var front:Number = 200;
var back:Number = -200;
var radius:Number = 15;
var fl:Number = 250;
var vpX:Number = Stage.width / 2;
var vpY:Number = Stage.height / 2;

init();
function init() {
      for (var i:Number = 0; i<numBalls; i++) {
            var ball:MovieClip = attachMovie("ball", "ball" + i, i);
            ball.x = Math.random() * 500 - 250;
            ball.y = Math.random() * 500 - 250;
            ball.z = Math.random() * 500 - 250;

            ball.vx = Math.random() * 10 - 5;
            ball.vy = Math.random() * 10 - 5;
            ball.vz = Math.random() * 10 - 5;
      }
}

function onEnterFrame():Void {
      for (var i:Number=0;i<numBalls;i++) {
            var ball:MovieClip = this["ball" + i];

            ball.x += ball.vx;
            ball.y += ball.vy;
            ball.z += ball.vz;
```

```
                if (ball.x + radius > right) {
                    ball.x = right - radius;
                    ball.vx *= -1;
                } else if (ball.x - radius < left) {
                    ball.x = left + radius;
                    ball.vx *= -1;
                }
                if (ball.y + radius > bottom) {
                    ball.y = bottom - radius;
                    ball.vy *= -1;
                } else if (ball.y - radius < top) {
                    ball.y = top + radius;
                    ball.vy *= -1;
                }
                if (ball.z + radius > front) {
                    ball.z = front - radius;
                    ball.vz *= -1;
                } else if (ball.z - radius < back) {
                    ball.z = back + radius;
                    ball.vz *= -1;
                }
                if (ball.z <= -fl) {
                    ball._visible = false;
                } else {
                    ball._visible = true;
                    var scale:Number = fl / (fl + ball.z);
                    ball._xscale = ball._yscale=scale*100;
                    ball._x = vpX + ball.x * scale;
                    ball._y = vpY + ball.y * scale;
                    ball.swapDepths(-ball.z);
                }
            }
            for(var i:Number = 0;i<numBalls-1;i++)
            {
                var ballA:MovieClip = this["ball" + i];
                for(var j:Number = i+1;j<numBalls;j++)
                {
                    var ballB:MovieClip = this["ball" + j];
                    var dx:Number = ballA.x - ballB.x;
                    var dy:Number = ballA.y - ballB.y;
                    var dz:Number = ballA.z - ballB.z;
                    var dist:Number = Math.sqrt(dx*dx + dy*dy + dz*dz);
                    if(dist < radius * 2)
                    {
                        ballA.gotoAndStop(2);
                        ballB.gotoAndStop(2);
                    }
                }
            }
        }
```

The key part is in bold. The balls start out all red, and as they collide, they change color. Before long, all are blue.

Important formulas in this chapter

The important formulas in this chapter are those for 3D perspective, coordinate rotation, and distance.

Basic perspective:

```
scale = fl / (fl + z);
mc._xscale = mc._yscale = scale * 100;
mc._alpha = scale * 100;      // optional
mc._x = vanishingPointX + x * scale;
mc._y = vanishingPointY + y * scale;
mc.swapDepths(-z);      // optional
```

Coordinate rotation:

```
x1 = cos(angleZ) * x - sin(angleZ) * y;
y1 = cos(angleZ) * y + sin(angleZ) * x;

x1 = cos(angleY) * x - sin(angleY) * z;
z1 = cos(angleY) * z + sin(angleY) * x;

y1 = cos(angleX) * y - sin(angleX) * z;
z1 = cos(angleX) * z + sin(angleX) * y;
```

3D distance:

```
dist = Math.sqrt(dx * dx + dy * dy + dz * dz);
```

Summary

You now have the basics of 3D under your belt, and you've seen most of the basic motion code adapted for 3D. I have to say I kind of surprised myself by the number of times I was able to say, "This is the same as 2D, you just have to add a z variable . . . ," or something of the sort. I thought there would be more complex stuff to explain here, but most of it turned out to be rather simple.

You'll use a lot of what you learned here in the next chapter, where you actually begin to sculpt 3D forms with points and lines.

};shape.targetHeight = shape._height;
shape.onEnterFrame = function() {
var speed = 5;
this._width += (this.targetWidth - this._width)/speed;
this._height += (this.targetHeight - this._height)/speed;

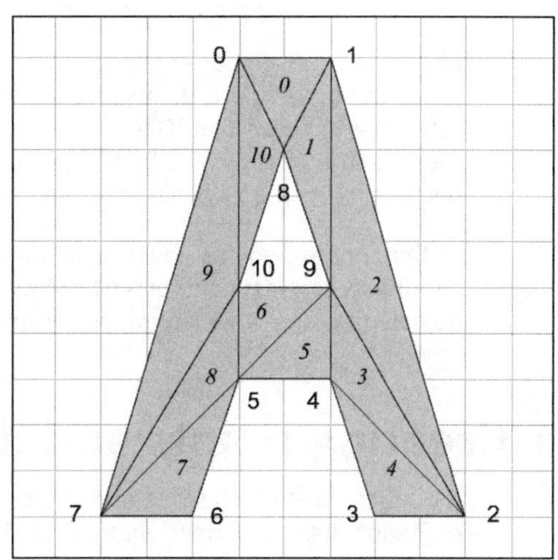

Chapter 16

3D LINES AND FILLS

What we'll cover in this chapter:

- Creating points and lines
- Making shapes
- Creating 3D fills
- Modeling 3D solids
- Moving 3D solids

Chapter 15 presented an introduction to 3D, but took you only as far as positioning objects in a 3D space and figuring out their size and screen position. The objects themselves were actually 2D. I made reference to those old 3D games where you could walk around an object or character and it would seem to turn to face you. That object or character was not actually turning—but it appeared that way because it was a 2D object, and that's the only view of it you had.

In this chapter, you're going to actually start doing 3D modeling in Flash. In particular, you'll learn about how to create and use 3D points, lines, fills, and solids. When you've finished this chapter, you'll be able to create a variety of shapes, move them, and rotate them, all in 3D.

Creating points and lines

It doesn't make much sense to make points in 3D without making some 3D lines, too. Since a point, by definition, has no dimension, it would be invisible. To start off with, though, you'll use movie clips as points, just so you can see where they are. From there, you simply need to draw some lines to connect the movie clips. Pretty easy. You've already done similar things, but now the movie clips will have perspective applied to them, to put them in a 3D space.

The point movie clip will contain a small black circle, say 10 pixels across. It will be exported with the name point. You'll attach a few of these points, rotate them based on the mouse position (as per some of the later examples in the previous chapter), and then draw some lines between them. The code itself is almost identical to that in the file `ch15_12.fla` from the last chapter. The main difference (other than the names of the clips) is the last part of the onEnterFrame, where you loop through drawing a line from the first point, through all the rest, to the last one. Here's the full code from `ch16_01.fla`; Figure 16-1 shows the result.

```
var numPoints:Number = 20;
var fl:Number = 250;
var vpX:Number = Stage.width / 2;
var vpY:Number = Stage.height / 2;

init();
function init() {
      for (var i:Number = 0; i<numPoints; i++) {
            var point:MovieClip = attachMovie("point",
                                              "point" + i, i);
            point.x = Math.random() * 200 - 100;
            point.y = Math.random() * 200 - 100;
            point.z = Math.random() * 200 - 100;
      }
}

function onEnterFrame():Void {
      var angleY:Number = (_xmouse - vpX) * .001;
      var cosY:Number = Math.cos(angleY);
      var sinY:Number = Math.sin(angleY);

      var angleX:Number = (_ymouse - vpY) * .001;
      var cosX:Number = Math.cos(angleX);
      var sinX:Number = Math.sin(angleX);
```

```
        for (var i:Number=0;i<numPoints;i++) {
            var point:MovieClip = this["point" + i];

            var x1:Number = point.x * cosY - point.z * sinY;
            var z1:Number = point.z * cosY + point.x * sinY;

            var y1:Number = point.y * cosX - z1 * sinX;
            var z2:Number = z1 * cosX + point.y * sinX;

            point.x = x1;
            point.y = y1;
            point.z = z2;

            if (point.z <= -fl) {
                point._visible = false;
            } else {
                point._visible = true;
                var scale:Number = fl / (fl + point.z);
                point._xscale = point._yscale = scale*100;
                point._x = vpX + point.x * scale;
                point._y = vpY + point.y * scale;
                point.swapDepths(-point.z);
            }
        }
        clear();
        lineStyle(1, 0, 100);
        moveTo(point0._x, point0._y);
        for (var i:Number=1;i<numPoints;i++) {
            var point:MovieClip = this["point" + i];
            lineTo(point._x, point._y);
        }
    }
```

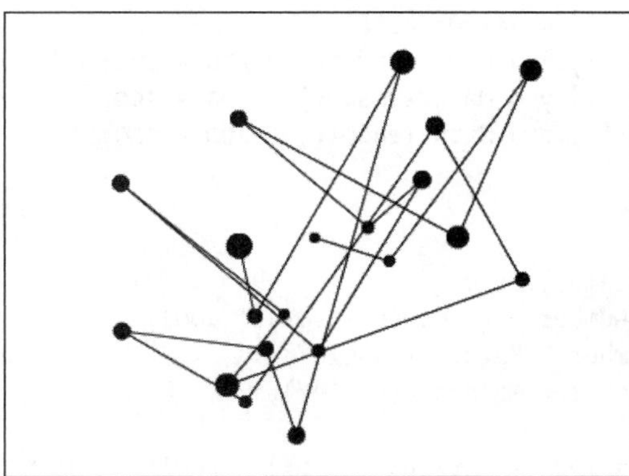

Figure 16-1. 3D points and lines

Now that's pretty cool. And there's not a whole lot to it, actually.

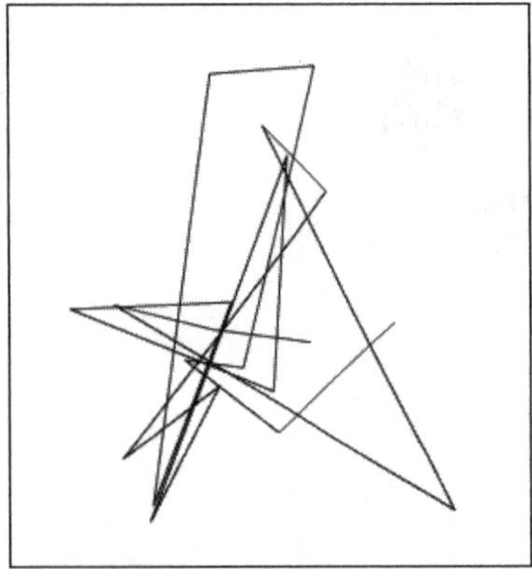

Figure 16-2. 3D lines with invisible points

If you're moving toward modeling 3D solids, you're going to want to eventually get rid of all those black dots. The first attempt at this is pretty basic. Just go into the point movie clip and delete the graphic of the black circle. That's it. You can see the result in `ch16_02.fla` and in Figure 16-2. The code is unchanged.

If you look at the earlier code listing, you'll see that some parts of it are now superfluous. The parts about `_xscale`, `_yscale`, swapDepths, and `_visible` are completely irrelevant for a movie clip with no graphics. There's nothing there to see or scale. You can follow this line of thought a little further and realize that this movie clip is currently being used only as a holder for five variables: x, y, z, _x, and _y. Using an entire movie clip for just that is overkill. A movie clip has many capabilities and uses up a fair number of resources. Using a movie clip in this way is like driving a tank down to the corner store to pick up a loaf of bread. If all you're doing is storing a few variables, a simple generic object will do the trick nicely and save on valuable memory.

The changes are surprisingly easy to make. The following listing is for `ch16_03.fla`, with the changes in bold. You should be able to follow it pretty easily.

```
var numPoints:Number = 20;
var points:Array = new Array();
var fl:Number = 250;
var vpX:Number = Stage.width / 2;
var vpY:Number = Stage.height / 2;

init();
function init() {
      for (var i:Number = 0; i<numPoints; i++) {
            points[i] = new Object();
            points[i].x = Math.random() * 200 - 100;
            points[i].y = Math.random() * 200 - 100;
            points[i].z = Math.random() * 200 - 100;
      }
}

function onEnterFrame():Void {
      var angleY:Number = (_xmouse - vpX) * .001;
      var cosY:Number = Math.cos(angleY);
      var sinY:Number = Math.sin(angleY);

      var angleX:Number = (_ymouse - vpY) * .001;
      var cosX:Number = Math.cos(angleX);
      var sinX:Number = Math.sin(angleX);
```

```
        for (var i:Number=0;i<numPoints;i++) {
            var point:MovieClip = points[i];

            var x1:Number = point.x * cosY - point.z * sinY;
            var z1:Number = point.z * cosY + point.x * sinY;

            var y1:Number = point.y * cosX - z1 * sinX;
            var z2:Number = z1 * cosX + point.y * sinX;

            point.x = x1;
            point.y = y1;
            point.z = z2;

            var scale:Number = fl / (fl + point.z);
            point.xPos = vpX + point.x * scale;
            point.yPos = vpY + point.y * scale;
        }
        clear();
        lineStyle(1, 0, 100);
        moveTo(points[0].xPos, points[0].yPos);
        for (var i:Number=1;i<numPoints;i++) {
            var point:MovieClip = points[i];
            lineTo(point.xPos, point.yPos);
        }
    }
```

Making shapes

Random lines are cool for demonstration purposes, but there's no reason you can't impose a bit of order on that mess. All it takes is getting rid of the initial loop that creates random x, y, and z's for those points and replacing it with some specific, predetermined values. For example, let's make a square. Figure 16-3 shows the square you'll draw and the 3D locations of its four corners.

Note that all the z values are the same. This is because a square lies on a plane. The easiest way to keep the square on the plane is to give all of its points the same measurement on one axis (here I chose the z axis) and define the square on the other two (x and y).

Here's the code that will replace the random point-creating loop:

```
points[0] = {x:-100, y:-100, z:100};
points[1] = {x: 100, y:-100, z:100};
points[2] = {x: 100, y: 100, z:100};
points[3] = {x:-100, y: 100, z:100};
```

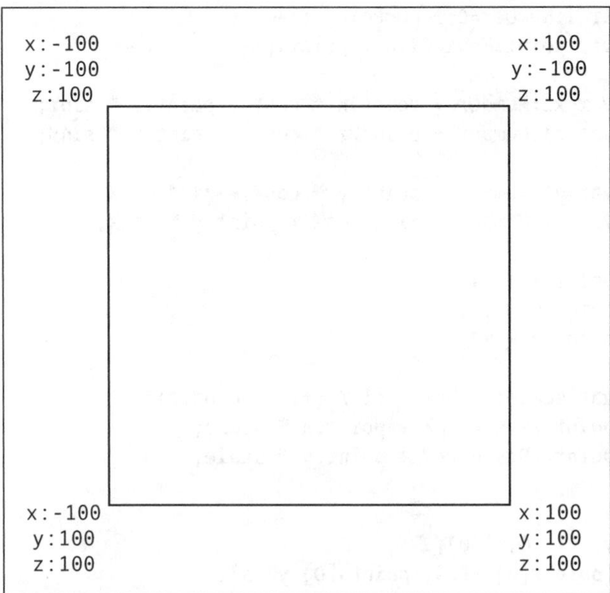

Figure 16-3. Coordinates of a square in 3D space

Also, since you're down to just four points now, you'll have to change numPoints to 4. The rest of the code should work just fine, but you'll make one addition: a line to connect the last point with the first, to close the shape. Here's the full code as seen in ch16_04.fla (Figure 16-4 shows the result):

```
var numPoints:Number = 4;
var points:Array = new Array();
var fl:Number = 250;
var vpX:Number = Stage.width / 2;
var vpY:Number = Stage.height / 2;

init();
function init() {
      points[0] = {x:-100, y:-100, z:100};
      points[1] = {x:100, y:-100, z:100};
      points[2] = {x:100, y:100, z:100};
      points[3] = {x:-100, y:100, z:100};
}

function onEnterFrame():Void {
      var angleY:Number = (_xmouse - vpX) * .001;
      var cosY:Number = Math.cos(angleY);
      var sinY:Number = Math.sin(angleY);

      var angleX:Number = (_ymouse - vpY) * .001;
      var cosX:Number = Math.cos(angleX);
      var sinX:Number = Math.sin(angleX);
```

```
        for (var i:Number=0;i<numPoints;i++) {
            var point:MovieClip = points[i];

            var x1:Number = point.x * cosY - point.z * sinY;
            var z1:Number = point.z * cosY + point.x * sinY;

            var y1:Number = point.y * cosX - z1 * sinX;
            var z2:Number = z1 * cosX + point.y * sinX;

            point.x = x1;
            point.y = y1;
            point.z = z2;

            var scale:Number = fl / (fl + point.z);
            point.xPos = vpX + point.x * scale;
            point.yPos = vpY + point.y * scale;
        }
        clear();
        lineStyle(1, 0, 100);
        moveTo(points[0].xPos, points[0].yPos);
        for (var i:Number=1;i<numPoints;i++) {
            var point:MovieClip = points[i];
            lineTo(point.xPos, point.yPos);
        }
        lineTo(points[0].xPos, points[0].yPos);
    }
```

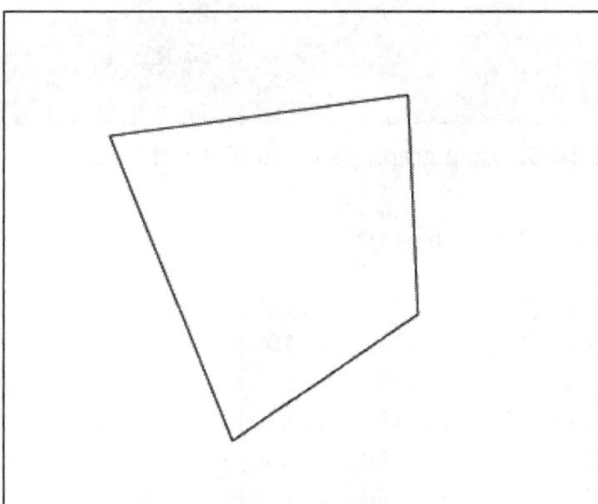

Figure 16-4. 3D spinning square

Fantastic—a spinning square! You should be able to create just about any flat shape now. I often plot out the points on a piece of graph paper beforehand (as shown in Figure 16-5) to help me out.

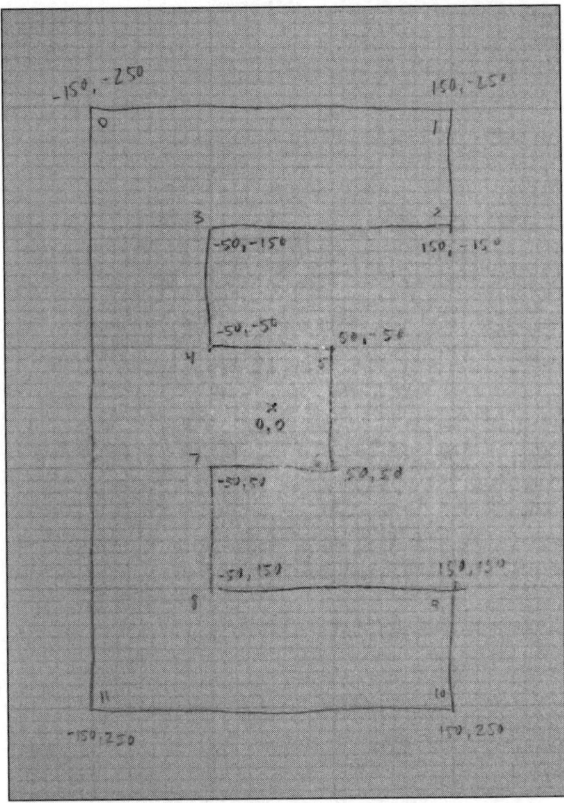

Figure 16-5. Using graph paper to plot out points

From this sketch, I can create my points like so:

```
points[0] =  {x:-150, y:-250, z:100};
points[1] =  {x: 150, y:-250, z:100};
points[2] =  {x: 150, y:-150, z:100};
points[3] =  {x: -50, y:-150, z:100};
points[4] =  {x: -50, y: -50, z:100};
points[5] =  {x:  50, y: -50, z:100};
points[6] =  {x:  50, y:  50, z:100};
points[7] =  {x: -50, y:  50, z:100};
points[8] =  {x: -50, y: 150, z:100};
points[9] =  {x: 150, y: 150, z:100};
points[10] = {x: 150, y: 250, z:100};
points[11] = {x:-150, y: 250, z:100};
```

and wind up with a spinning "E" as seen in ch16_05.fla and in Figure 16-6. Don't forget to change numPoints to 12 now. Later you'll make this value dynamic by using points.length.

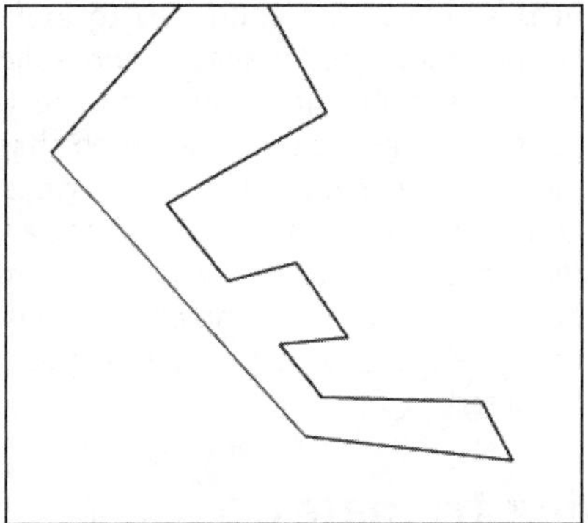

Figure 16-6. 3D spinning letter "E"

If you look at the code for this file, you'll see that I added one other little trick to it. I found that the shape was much too close to the viewpoint. I wanted to stick it off in the distance a ways. Your first thought might be to just increase the z value of all the points, but that would actually make the effect worse. For example, say I made z 500. As it rotated, z would go from 500 to –500, putting some of the points well behind the viewpoint and making a mess of things. Instead, I added a zOffset variable like so:

```
var zOffset:Number = 200;
```

I then added that in when figuring the scale:

```
var scale:Number = fl / (fl + point.z + zOffset);
```

This pushes the entire system, including the rotation of the system, out 200 pixels. The value for z will still be from 100 to –100, but the center of its rotation will be 200, so perspective will be calculated on values that wind up ranging from 300 to 100, well in front of the viewer. Try zOffset with other values and see how it works.

Creating 3D fills

As you might imagine, a large part of the work for fills has already been done. You've already created the points for a shape and connected them from one end to the other with a line. All you really need to do is add a beginFill and endFill to the drawing code. The code in the ch16_06.fla file does just that; see Figure 16-7 for the results. Here's the relevant section of code with the changes in bold:

```
clear();
lineStyle(1, 0, 100);
beginFill(0xffcccc, 100);
moveTo(points[0].xPos, points[0].yPos);
for (var i:Number=1;i<numPoints;i++) {
      var point:MovieClip = points[i];
      lineTo(point.xPos, point.yPos);
}
lineTo(points[0].xPos, points[0].yPos);
endFill();
```

This comes right at the end of the onEnterFrame function.

At this point, it's a good idea to look at how traditional 3D programs model shapes and solids. In the previous examples, both the square and the letter "E" are *polygons*. A polygon is simply a closed shape made of at least three line segments. Thus, a triangle is the simplest polygon. You'll find that in most, if not all, 3D modeling and rendering programs—even those that use patches, meshes, nurbs, and complex polygons—all 3D forms are finally reduced to a set of triangles just prior to being rendered.

Figure 16-7. First 3D fills

Using triangles

There are a number of advantages to using triangles—probably more than I know, but I'll cover a few here. First, with a triangle, you can be sure that all the points of the polygon are always on the same plane, since a triangle *defines* a plane. If you are still not sure why this is important, take the letter "E" example and randomly change around some of the z values of its points. While you may get some interesting results, they can also quickly become unexpected and unpredictable.

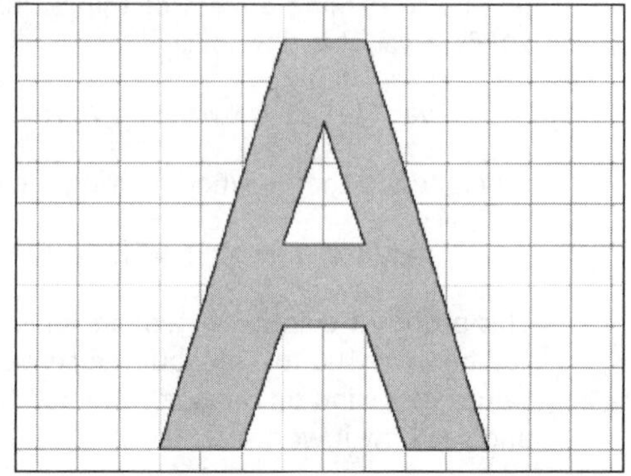

Figure 16-8. More complex 3D shape

Second, using triangles, it is sometimes easier to draw complex shapes. Consider Figure 16-8, for example.

This type of shape would be kind of tough to create with a single polygon. You'd have to double back on yourself at least once. You'd also get into the situation where every polygon you create would have a different number of points and require special handling. On the other hand, with triangles, you can model the "A" as shown in Figure 16-9.

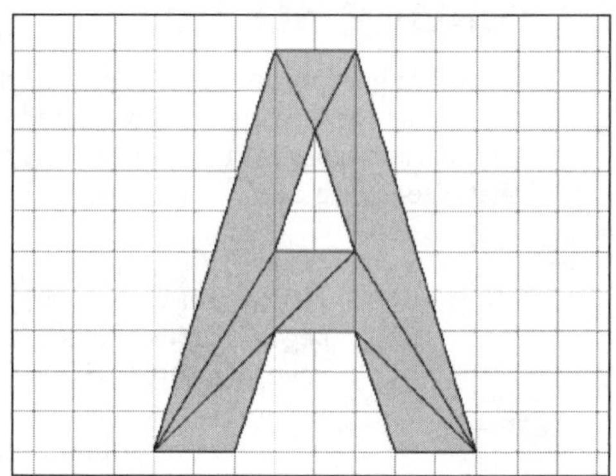

Figure 16-9. The same shape as in Figure 16-8, rendered with triangles

You can then set up a function that takes three points and renders a single triangle. You just need a list of points and then a list of triangles. One loop goes through the list of points, positions them, and applies perspective. Another loop goes through the triangle list and renders each one.

This isn't to say that you have to go with a triangle-only approach. You could make a function that dynamically renders a polygon of any number of sides. But to keep things simple and flexible here, you'll go with the triangles. Let's try it out with the letter "A" example. First, you need to define all of your points and triangles. As shown in Figure 16-10, I've laid out the shape, and numbered all of its points and each of its triangles.

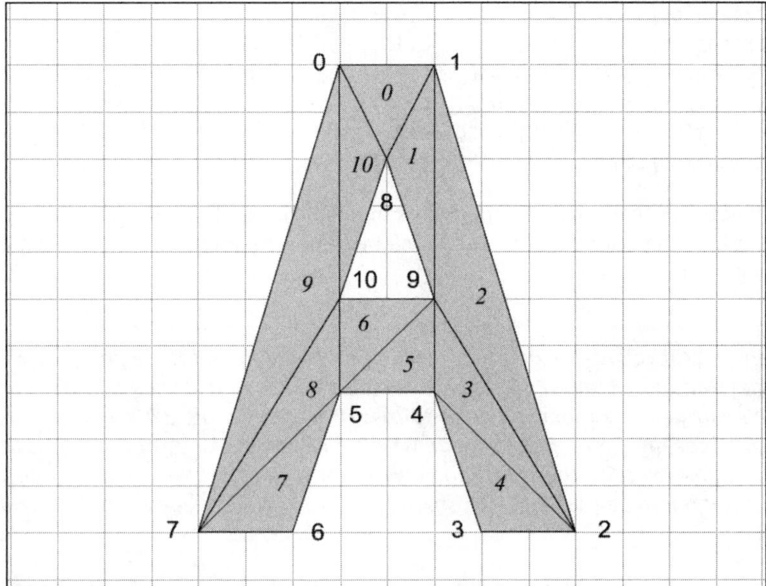

Figure 16-10. The points and polygons that make up this shape

When you graph out all the points, you get the following values:

```
points[0] =  {x: -50, y:-250, z:100};
points[1] =  {x:  50, y:-250, z:100};
points[2] =  {x: 200, y: 250, z:100};
points[3] =  {x: 100, y: 250, z:100};
points[4] =  {x:  50, y: 100, z:100};
points[5] =  {x: -50, y: 100, z:100};
points[6] =  {x:-100, y: 250, z:100};
points[7] =  {x:-200, y: 250, z:100};
points[8] =  {x:   0, y:-150, z:100};
points[9] =  {x:  50, y:   0, z:100};
points[10] = {x: -50, y:   0, z:100};
```

Next, you need to define the triangles. Each triangle is simply a list of three points; let's call them a, b, and c. You can make an object to hold each one and another array to hold the whole list. So, up top, you create the array:

```
var triangles:Array = new Array();
```

Then, in the init function, after defining all the points, you define the triangles:

```
triangles[0] =  {a:0, b:1,  c:8};
triangles[1] =  {a:1, b:9,  c:8};
triangles[2] =  {a:1, b:2,  c:9};
triangles[3] =  {a:2, b:4,  c:9};
triangles[4] =  {a:2, b:3,  c:4};
```

```
triangles[5] =  {a:4, b:5,  c:9};
triangles[6] =  {a:9, b:5,  c:10};
triangles[7] =  {a:5, b:6,  c:7};
triangles[8] =  {a:5, b:7,  c:10};
triangles[9] =  {a:0, b:10, c:7};
triangles[10] = {a:0, b:8,  c:10};
```

One thing you'll notice is that I ordered the points of each triangle to go in a clockwise direction. That isn't important at this stage of the game, but it will become very important in the next chapter, so it's a good habit to get into.

By the way, if you're thinking that plotting and entering all these points and triangles by hand is tedious, that's because it is tedious. And it's going to get worse when you get into modeling solid forms. That's why most 3D programs have visual modeling front ends to them, which give you all kinds of tools to create forms and extract all the points and polygons for you. Creating such a modeling front end might be possible in Flash, but it's well beyond the scope of this book!

Now, your rendering loop will look like this (don't worry, I'm going to give you the whole thing to look at in a bit):

```
clear();
var numTriangles:Number = triangles.length;
for(var i:Number =0;i<numTriangles;i++)
{
      renderTriangle(triangles[i]);
}
```

The last thing you need is a `renderTriangle` function that will draw a single triangle based on the three points given to it. That looks like this:

```
function renderTriangle(tri:Object):Void
{
      lineStyle(1, 0, 100);
      beginFill(0xffcccc, 100);
      moveTo(points[tri.a].xPos, points[tri.a].yPos);
      lineTo(points[tri.b].xPos, points[tri.b].yPos);
      lineTo(points[tri.c].xPos, points[tri.c].yPos);
      lineTo(points[tri.a].xPos, points[tri.a].yPos);
      endFill();
}
```

This code may look somewhat confusing, so let me explain it. The object passed in, `tri`, contains three values, a, b, and c. These are the points used to make up that particular triangle. But what are these numbers, actually? They're indexes to the `points` array. Let's take triangle 0. It's defined like so:

```
triangles[0] =  {a:0, b:1, c:8};
```

So, a, b, and c will equal 0, 1, and 8, respectively. Thus, the drawing code gets evaluated as such:

```
moveTo(points[0].xPos, points[0].yPos);
lineTo(points[1].xPos, points[1].yPos);
lineTo(points[8].xPos, points[8].yPos);
lineTo(points[0].xPos, points[0].yPos);
```

What you're doing is moving to point 0, and then drawing a line from there to point 1, to point 8, and back to point 0 again. That completes the triangle. This setup allows you to draw much more complex shapes, such as the "A" with a hole in it. When you run the code, you'll see something like Figure 16-11.

Figure 16-11. The "A" shape, rendered in 3D

Now at this point, these lines are too much, so you probably want to get rid of them by removing the lineStyle statement, leaving you with just the fills, as shown in Figure 16-12.

Figure 16-12. The "A" shape, with lines removed

And, just to keep you up-to-date on things, here's the code found in ch16_07.fla:

```
var points:Array = new Array();
var triangles:Array = new Array();
var fl:Number = 250;
var vpX:Number = Stage.width / 2;
var vpY:Number = Stage.height / 2;
var zOffset:Number = 200;

init();
function init() {
      points[0] = {x:-50, y:-250, z:100};
      points[1] = {x:50, y:-250, z:100};
      points[2] = {x:200, y:250, z:100};
      points[3] = {x:100, y:250, z:100};
```

```
        points[4] = {x:50, y:100, z:100};
        points[5] = {x:-50, y:100, z:100};
        points[6] = {x:-100, y:250, z:100};
        points[7] = {x:-200, y:250, z:100};
        points[8] = {x:0, y:-150, z:100};
        points[9] = {x:50, y:0, z:100};
        points[10] = {x:-50, y:0, z:100};

        triangles[0] =  {a:0, b:1,  c:8};
        triangles[1] =  {a:1, b:9,  c:8};
        triangles[2] =  {a:1, b:2,  c:9};
        triangles[3] =  {a:2, b:4,  c:9};
        triangles[4] =  {a:2, b:3,  c:4};
        triangles[5] =  {a:4, b:5,  c:9};
        triangles[6] =  {a:9, b:5,  c:10};
        triangles[7] =  {a:5, b:6,  c:7};
        triangles[8] =  {a:5, b:7,  c:10};
        triangles[9] =  {a:0, b:10, c:7};
        triangles[10] = {a:0, b:8,  c:10};
}

function onEnterFrame():Void {
        var angleY:Number = (_xmouse - vpX) * .001;
        var cosY:Number = Math.cos(angleY);
        var sinY:Number = Math.sin(angleY);

        var angleX:Number = (_ymouse - vpY) * .001;
        var cosX:Number = Math.cos(angleX);
        var sinX:Number = Math.sin(angleX);

        var numPoints:Number = points.length;
        for (var i:Number=0;i<numPoints;i++) {
                var point:MovieClip = points[i];

                var x1:Number = point.x * cosY - point.z * sinY;
                var z1:Number = point.z * cosY + point.x * sinY;

                var y1:Number = point.y * cosX - z1 * sinX;
                var z2:Number = z1 * cosX + point.y * sinX;

                point.x = x1;
                point.y = y1;
                point.z = z2;

                var scale:Number = fl / (fl + point.z + zOffset);
                point.xPos = vpX + point.x * scale;
                point.yPos = vpY + point.y * scale;
        }
        clear();
```

```
        var numTriangles:Number = triangles.length;
        for(var i:Number =0;i<numTriangles;i++)
        {
            renderTriangle(triangles[i]);
        }
    }

    function renderTriangle(tri:Object):Void
    {
        beginFill(0xffcccc, 100);
        moveTo(points[tri.a].xPos, points[tri.a].yPos);
        lineTo(points[tri.b].xPos, points[tri.b].yPos);
        lineTo(points[tri.c].xPos, points[tri.c].yPos);
        lineTo(points[tri.a].xPos, points[tri.a].yPos);
        endFill();
    }
```

Defining the triangles' colors

Now that you have everything functioning pretty well, let's go back and see if you can improve the code a bit. One thing that bugged me was the fact that the color for the fills was hard-coded in the renderTriangle function. That means that every triangle has to be the same color, unless you start making multiple functions, such as renderRedTriangle, renderBlueTriangle, and so forth, which would just be silly.

A better solution might be to pass in the color you want as a parameter, which would look like this:

```
function renderTriangle(tri:Object, col:Number):Void
{
    beginFill(col, 100);
    moveTo(points[tri.a].xPos, points[tri.a].yPos);
    lineTo(points[tri.b].xPos, points[tri.b].yPos);
    lineTo(points[tri.c].xPos, points[tri.c].yPos);
    lineTo(points[tri.a].xPos, points[tri.a].yPos);
    endFill();
}
```

Then you could pass in a color when you call the function. But that's really just moving the hard-coded value from one function to another one. Since that call to renderTriangle is in a for loop, all the triangles are still going to get the same color.

What you really want to do is have a color defined for each triangle. Well, why not just put that in the triangle object, along with the list of points? Then you can come up with something like this in the list of triangles:

```
triangles[0] = {a:0, b:1, c:8, col:0x6666cc};
triangles[1] = {a:1, b:9, c:8, col:0x66cc66};
triangles[2] = {a:1, b:2, c:9, col:0x66cccc};
triangles[3] = {a:2, b:4, c:9, col:0xcc6666};
triangles[4] = {a:2, b:3, c:4, col:0xcc66cc};
```

```
triangles[5] =  {a:4, b:5,  c:9,  col:0xcccc66};
triangles[6] =  {a:9, b:5,  c:10, col:0xcccccc};
triangles[7] =  {a:5, b:6,  c:7,  col:0x666666};
triangles[8] =  {a:5, b:7,  c:10, col:0x6666cc};
triangles[9] =  {a:0, b:10, c:7,  col:0x66cc66};
triangles[10] = {a:0, b:8,  c:10, col:0x66cccc};
```

Now each triangle has its own color. Since the renderTriangle function has a reference to each triangle object, it can easily use this color value in its beginFill call:

```
function renderTriangle(tri:Object):Void
{
	beginFill(tri.col, 100);
	moveTo(points[tri.a].xPos, points[tri.a].yPos);
	lineTo(points[tri.b].xPos, points[tri.b].yPos);
	lineTo(points[tri.c].xPos, points[tri.c].yPos);
	lineTo(points[tri.a].xPos, points[tri.a].yPos);
	endFill();
}
```

This is much cleaner and more portable, and it even opens up the idea of storing the point and triangle data in an external text or XML file, which could be loaded, parsed, and rendered at run time.

Figure 16-13 shows the result of ch16_08.fla. Not that you would necessarily want to color the triangles for a letter "A" like that, but it shows that you now have complete control over the color of each one, which will be useful when you start building more-complex models.

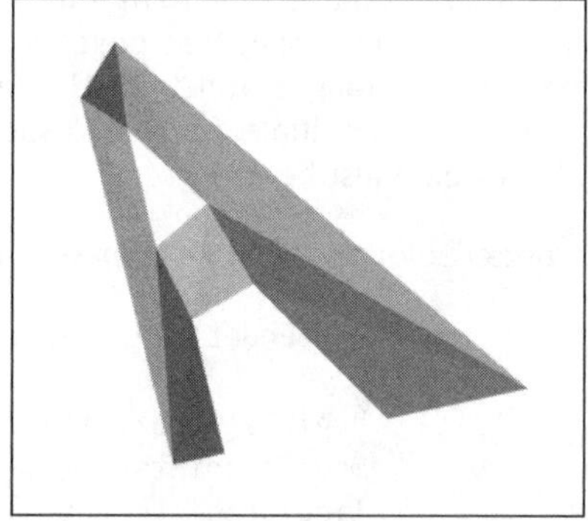

Figure 16-13. The "A" shape, with individually colored polygons

Modeling 3D solids

Well, we finally get down to where this chapter was originally headed: creating 3D solids in Flash!

In the computing world, the first example in any book or tutorial is almost always "Hello, World," a program that will in one way or another print those words to the screen. In programming 3D solids, the equivalent seems to be a spinning cube. Let's not break from tradition.

Modeling a spinning cube

First of all, you need eight points to define the eight corners of the cube. These are as shown in Figure 16-14.

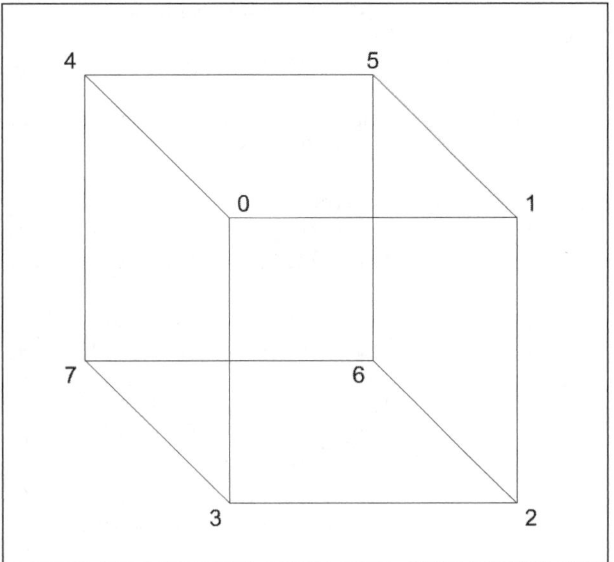

Figure 16-14. The points of a 3D cube

The points are defined like this in the code:

```
// front four corners
points[0] = {x:-100, y:-100, z:-100};
points[1] = {x:100, y:-100, z:-100};
points[2] = {x:100, y:100, z:-100};
points[3] = {x:-100, y:100, z:-100};
// back four corners
points[4] = {x:-100, y:-100, z:100};
points[5] = {x:100, y:-100, z:100};
points[6] = {x:100, y:100, z:100};
points[7] = {x:-100, y:100, z:100};
```

Then you need to define the triangles. Each face of the cube will consist of two triangles. There will be 12 triangles altogether—two each for the six faces. Again, I'm going to list the points for each triangle in a clockwise direction, as seen from the outer face of that triangle. It gets a little tricky, but try to rotate the cube in your mind so that the triangle you're defining is facing you, and then list the points in clockwise order from that viewpoint. For example, the front face is easy; Figure 16-15 shows the two triangles.

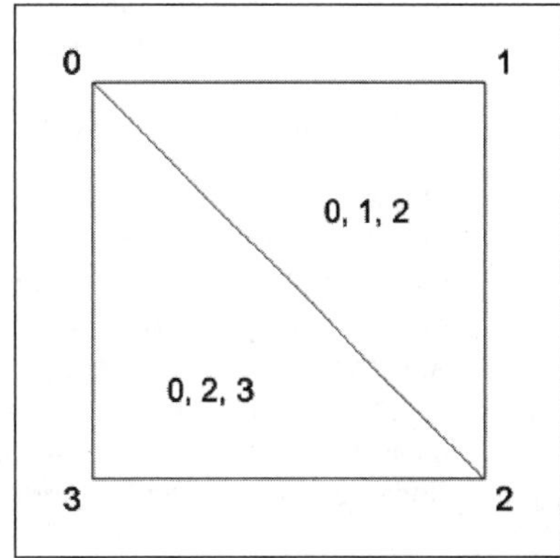

Figure 16-15. The front face of the cube

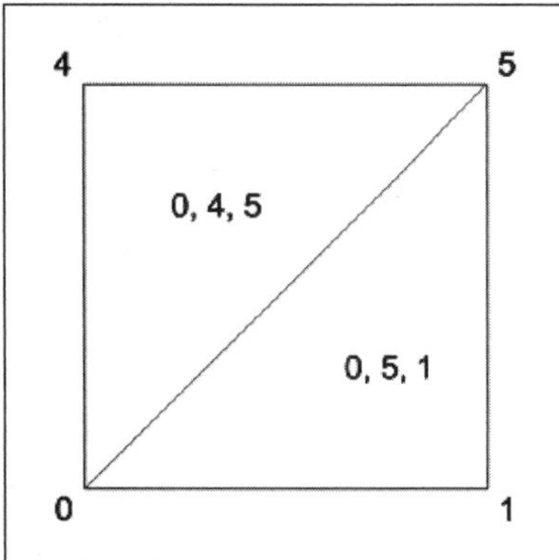

Figure 16-16. The top face of the cube

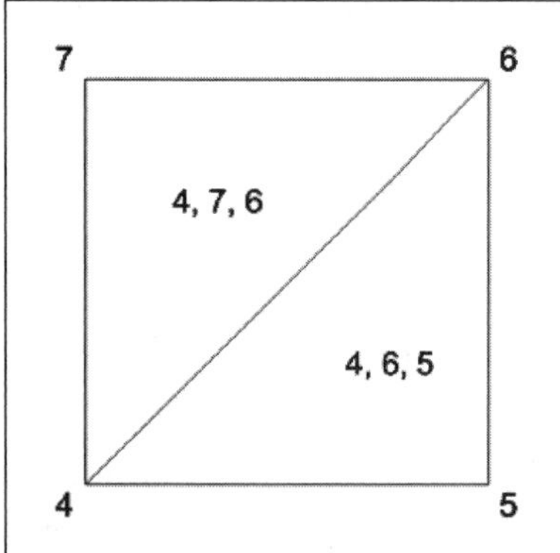

Figure 16-17. The back face of the cube

Figure 16-16 shows the top face.

And Figure 16-17 shows the back.

Continuing around with each face, you come up with the following triangle definitions:

```
// front
triangles[0] =  {a:0, b:1,  c:2, col:0x6666cc};
triangles[1] =  {a:0, b:2,  c:3, col:0x6666cc};
// top
triangles[2] =  {a:0, b:5,  c:1, col:0x66cc66};
triangles[3] =  {a:0, b:4,  c:5, col:0x66cc66};
//back
triangles[4] =  {a:4, b:6,  c:5, col:0xcc6666};
triangles[5] =  {a:4, b:7,  c:6, col:0xcc6666};
// bottom
triangles[6] =  {a:3, b:2,  c:6, col:0xcc66cc};
triangles[7] =  {a:3, b:6,  c:7, col:0xcc66cc};
// right
triangles[8] =  {a:1, b:5,  c:6, col:0x66cccc};
triangles[9] =  {a:1, b:6,  c:2, col:0x66cccc};
// left
triangles[10] =  {a:4, b:0,  c:3, col:0xcccc66};
triangles[11] =  {a:4, b:3,  c:7, col:0xcccc66};
```

Notice also that each face has a different color, as the two triangles that make up that face are the same color. Again, this clockwise orientation doesn't matter a whole lot right now, but in the next chapter, you'll use this for something called *backface culling*. This term refers to a way of determining which surfaces are facing you and which are facing away. You'll see why this is important in a moment.

The `ch16_09.fla` file is exactly the same as `ch16_08.fla`, with these new point and triangle definitions in the `init` function, and one other change. In the `renderTriangles` function, I changed the transparency of the fill from 100 to 50.

```
beginFill(tri.col, 50);
```

This allows you to see inside the cube and across to the opposite side. Why did I do this? Why not just have a solid cube? Well, go ahead and change 50 back to 100 and see what happens. Whoa—that's all messed up! You can see some of the back faces, some of the time. Other faces seem invisible all the time. What's going on? The faces on the back of the cube (the back faces) are always being drawn. And the triangles are being drawn in the same order, based on their position in the `triangles` array. So the faces at the bottom of the list always draw over the faces at the top of the list, and you get bizarre, unpredictable results like this. You need to *cull*, or weed out and get rid of, those back faces, since you don't need to render them.

Again, backface culling will be covered in detail in the next chapter, and you'll also learn how to apply some basic lighting on each surface, based on its angle. For the rest of this chapter, we'll just leave the transparency at 50 and live with it.

Figure 16-18 shows the finished 3D cube.

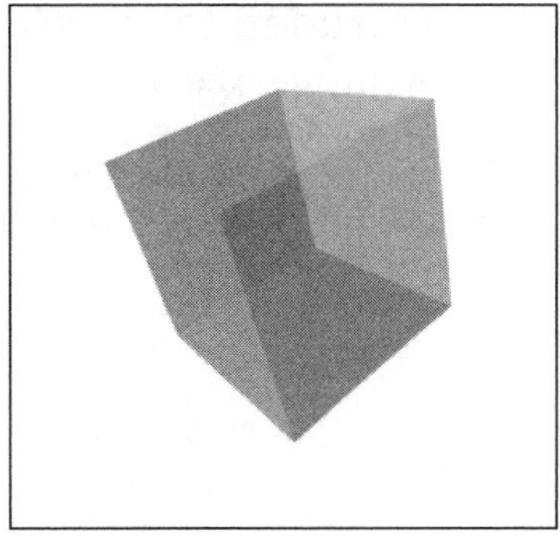

Figure 16-18. The resulting 3D cube

Modeling other shapes

Congratulations! You've mastered the spinning cube. Now you can move on to model all kinds of shapes. Just draw them out on a piece of graph paper, mark up the points and triangles, and put them into the arrays. It often helps to draw several views of the object, rotated so you can see each face and what points make up the triangles. This section offers a few to get you started.

Pyramid

Here's the code for a 3D pyramid (ch16_10.fla):

```
points[0] = {x:   0, y:-200, z:   0};
points[1] = {x: 200, y: 200, z:-200};
points[2] = {x:-200, y: 200, z:-200};
points[3] = {x:-200, y: 200, z: 200};
points[4] = {x: 200, y: 200, z: 200};

triangles[0] =  {a:0, b:1,  c:2, col:0x6666cc};
triangles[1] =  {a:0, b:2,  c:3, col:0x66cc66};
triangles[2] =  {a:0, b:3,  c:4, col:0xcc6666};
triangles[3] =  {a:0, b:4,  c:1, col:0x66cccc};
triangles[4] =  {a:1, b:3,  c:2, col:0xcc66cc};
triangles[5] =  {a:1, b:4,  c:3, col:0xcc66cc};
```

Figure 16-19 shows the result.

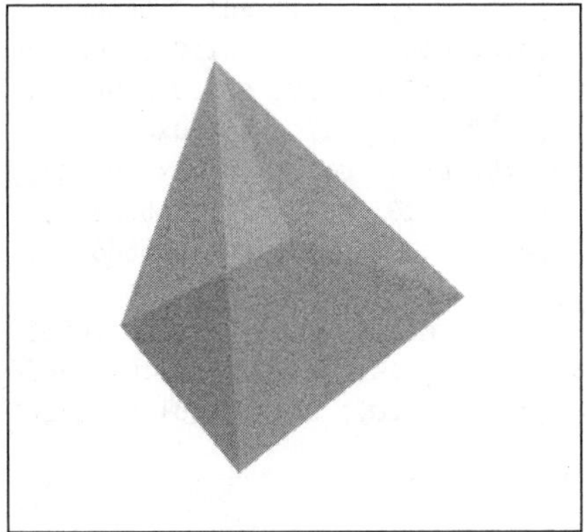

Figure 16-19. A 3D pyramid

Extruded letter "A"

In ch16_11.fla, I went all out and extruded the earlier letter "A" example. This meant copying the first 11 points, moving one set to a z of –50 and the other set to +50, then creating triangles for the second set (making sure they were still going clockwise as seen from the back), and finally making triangles to join the two sides. Tedious? You bet! But a nice effect when it was done:

```
points[0] =  {x: -50, y:-250, z:-50};
points[1] =  {x:  50, y:-250, z:-50};
points[2] =  {x: 200, y: 250, z:-50};
points[3] =  {x: 100, y: 250, z:-50};
points[4] =  {x:  50, y: 100, z:-50};
points[5] =  {x: -50, y: 100, z:-50};
points[6] =  {x:-100, y: 250, z:-50};
points[7] =  {x:-200, y: 250, z:-50};
points[8] =  {x:   0, y:-150, z:-50};
points[9] =  {x:  50, y:   0, z:-50};
points[10] = {x: -50, y:   0, z:-50};

points[11] = {x: -50, y:-250, z: 50};
points[12] = {x:  50, y:-250, z: 50};
points[13] = {x: 200, y: 250, z: 50};
points[14] = {x: 100, y: 250, z: 50};
points[15] = {x:  50, y: 100, z: 50};
points[16] = {x: -50, y: 100, z: 50};
points[17] = {x:-100, y: 250, z: 50};
points[18] = {x:-200, y: 250, z: 50};
points[19] = {x:   0, y:-150, z: 50};
points[20] = {x:  50, y:   0, z: 50};
points[21] = {x: -50, y:   0, z: 50};

triangles[0] =  {a:0, b:1,  c:8,  col:0x6666cc};
triangles[1] =  {a:1, b:9,  c:8,  col:0x6666cc};
triangles[2] =  {a:1, b:2,  c:9,  col:0x6666cc};
triangles[3] =  {a:2, b:4,  c:9,  col:0x6666cc};
triangles[4] =  {a:2, b:3,  c:4,  col:0x6666cc};
triangles[5] =  {a:4, b:5,  c:9,  col:0x6666cc};
triangles[6] =  {a:9, b:5,  c:10, col:0x6666cc};
triangles[7] =  {a:5, b:6,  c:7,  col:0x6666cc};
triangles[8] =  {a:5, b:7,  c:10, col:0x6666cc};
triangles[9] =  {a:0, b:10, c:7,  col:0x6666cc};
triangles[10] = {a:0, b:8,  c:10, col:0x6666cc};

triangles[11] = {a:11, b:19,  c:12,  col:0xcc6666};
triangles[12] = {a:12, b:19,  c:20,  col:0xcc6666};
triangles[13] = {a:12, b:20,  c:13,  col:0xcc6666};
```

```
triangles[14] = {a:13, b:20,  c:15,  col:0xcc6666};
triangles[15] = {a:13, b:15,  c:14,  col:0xcc6666};
triangles[16] = {a:15, b:20,  c:16,  col:0xcc6666};
triangles[17] = {a:20, b:21,  c:16,  col:0xcc6666};
triangles[18] = {a:16, b:18,  c:17,  col:0xcc6666};
triangles[19] = {a:16, b:21,  c:18,  col:0xcc6666};
triangles[20] = {a:11, b:18,  c:21,  col:0xcc6666};
triangles[21] = {a:11, b:21,  c:19,  col:0xcc6666};

triangles[22] = {a:0,  b:11, c:1,  col:0xcccc66};
triangles[23] = {a:11, b:12, c:1,  col:0xcccc66};
triangles[24] = {a:1,  b:12, c:2,  col:0xcccc66};
triangles[25] = {a:12, b:13, c:2,  col:0xcccc66};
triangles[26] = {a:3,  b:2,  c:14, col:0xcccc66};
triangles[27] = {a:2,  b:13, c:14, col:0xcccc66};
triangles[28] = {a:4,  b:3,  c:15, col:0xcccc66};
triangles[29] = {a:3,  b:14, c:15, col:0xcccc66};
triangles[30] = {a:5,  b:4,  c:16, col:0xcccc66};
triangles[31] = {a:4,  b:15, c:16, col:0xcccc66};
triangles[32] = {a:6,  b:5,  c:17, col:0xcccc66};
triangles[33] = {a:5,  b:16, c:17, col:0xcccc66};
triangles[34] = {a:7,  b:6,  c:18, col:0xcccc66};
triangles[35] = {a:6,  b:17, c:18, col:0xcccc66};
triangles[36] = {a:0,  b:7,  c:11, col:0xcccc66};
triangles[37] = {a:7,  b:18, c:11, col:0xcccc66};

triangles[38] = {a:8,  b:9,  c:19, col:0xcccc66};
triangles[39] = {a:9,  b:20, c:19, col:0xcccc66};
triangles[40] = {a:9,  b:10, c:20, col:0xcccc66};
triangles[41] = {a:10, b:21, c:20, col:0xcccc66};
triangles[42] = {a:10, b:8,  c:21, col:0xcccc66};
triangles[43] = {a:8,  b:19, c:21, col:0xcccc66};
```

Figure 16-20 shows the result.

As you can see, these things build up quickly. The original, flat "A" had 11 triangles. Extruding it somehow quadrupled that! This code still runs pretty smoothly on a half-decent computer, but you aren't going to get any massive 3D worlds with thousands of polygons in Flash. Still, you can do some pretty cool things, and the Flash Player improves in performance with each release, so who knows what the future holds?

Figure 16-20. An extruded letter "A"

Cylinder

One more shape example. This time I'm going to show you how you can create points and triangles with some math. The only thing I changed in ch16_12.fla was the init function (and I added a numFaces variable at the top). Instead of defining points and triangles by hand, I created an algorithm to do it for me and make a cylinder. Here's that init function:

```
var numFaces:Number = 20;

function init() {
	var index:Number = 0;
	for(var i:Number = 0;i<numFaces;i++)
	{
		var angle:Number = Math.PI * 2 / numFaces * i;
		var x:Number = Math.cos(angle) * 200;
		var y:Number = Math.sin(angle) * 200;
		points[index] = {x:x, y:y, z:-100};
		points[index + 1] = {x:x, y:y, z:100};
		index += 2;
	}

	index = 0;
	for(var i:Number = 0;i<numFaces-1;i++)
	{
		triangles[index] = {a:index,
		                    b:index + 3,
		                    c:index + 1,
		                    col:0x6666cc};
		triangles[index+1] = {a:index,
		                      b:index + 2,
		                      c:index + 3,
		                      col:0x6666cc};
		index += 2;
	}
	triangles[index] = {a:index,
	                    b:1,
	                    c:index + 1,
	                    col:0x6666cc};
	triangles[index+1] = {a:index,
	                      b:0,
	                      c:1,
	                      col:0x6666cc};
}
```

Now, I know this isn't the most lucid code, so let's go through it with some explanation and maybe a diagram or two.

You're going to loop around in a full circle and create points at certain intervals. For each loop, you first get an angle, which is the full circle, divided by the number of faces, times the particular segment you're working on.

You use that angle, with some trigonometry you should be well used to by now, to determine the x, y point for that point on the circle. You then make two points, one with a z of –100 and one with a z of +100. When this loop is done, you'll have two circles of dots, one close to you and one a bit farther away. Now you just need to connect them with triangles.

Again, you loop through for each face. This time, you create two triangles. Seen from the side, the first face looks like Figure 16-21.

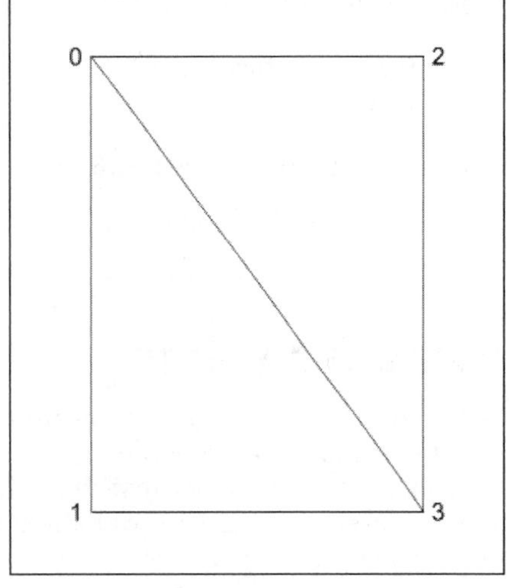

Figure 16-21. The first face of the cylinder

This makes the two triangles:

```
0, 3, 1
0, 2, 3
```

Since the `index` variable is 0, you can also define these like so:

```
index, index + 3, index + 1
index, index + 2, index + 3
```

which is exactly how you define the two triangles. You then increase `index` by 2 to handle the next face with points 2, 3, 4, and 5.

You do that up to the second-to-last face, and then connect the last one back to the first two points, 0 and 1, as shown in Figure 16-22.

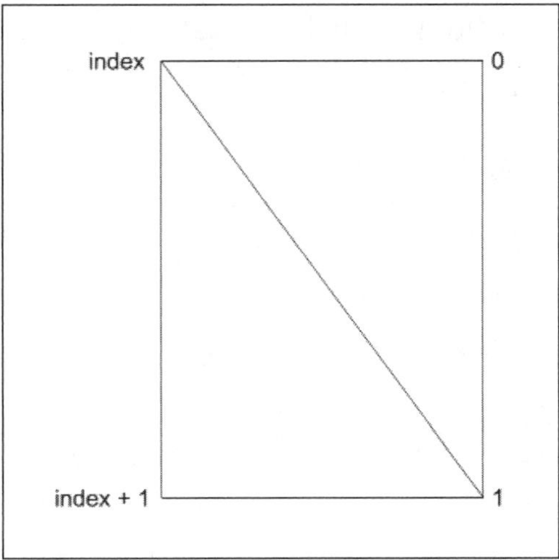

Figure 16-22. The last face of the cylinder

These wind up as follows:

```
index, 1, index + 1
index, 0, 1
```

with the result shown in Figure 16-23.

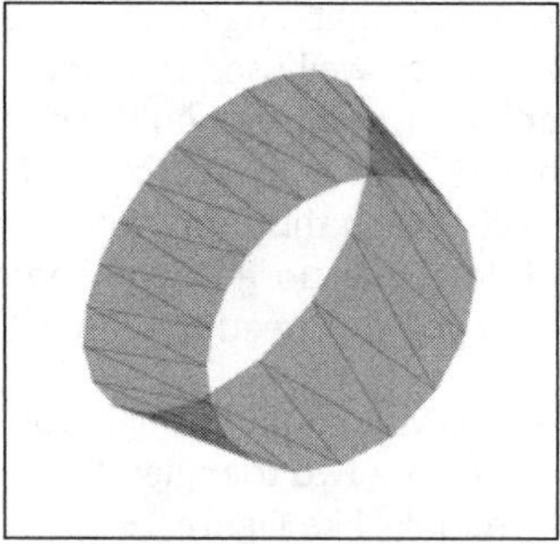

Figure 16-23. The resulting 3Dcylinder

Moving 3D solids

Moving one of the 3D solids you've created is really no different than moving a 3D movie clip around. You just need to change the center point that the form is based on. Originally, it will be placed at 0, 0, 0. You've already moved it on the z axis with the zOffset variable. Let's use the keyboard to dynamically change its position on the x and z axes.

First you'll add a variable for the xOffset:

```
var xOffset:Number = 0;
```

In the onEnterFrame function, you'll check for any of the cursor keys and adjust the xOffset or zOffset as needed:

```
        if(Key.isDown(Key.LEFT))
        {
              xOffset -= 10;
        }
        else if(Key.isDown(Key.RIGHT))
        {
              xOffset += 10;
        }
        if(Key.isDown(Key.UP))
        {
              zOffset += 10;
        }
        else if(Key.isDown(Key.DOWN))
        {
              zOffset -= 10;
        }
```

You've already dealt with the zOffset when determining scale:

```
var scale:Number = fl / (fl + point.z + zOffset);
```

Now you add xOffset to point.x, just before you calculate the screen position:

```
point.xPos = vpX + (point.x + xOffset) * scale;
```

Here's where you are with this, as seen in ch16_13.fla:

```
var points:Array = new Array();
var triangles:Array = new Array();
var fl:Number = 250;
var vpX:Number = Stage.width / 2;
var vpY:Number = Stage.height / 2;
var xOffset:Number = 0;
var zOffset:Number = 400;
var numFaces:Number = 20;

init();
function init() {
	var index:Number = 0;
	for(var i:Number = 0;i<numFaces;i++)
	{
		var angle:Number = Math.PI * 2 / numFaces * i;
		var x:Number = Math.cos(angle) * 200;
		var y:Number = Math.sin(angle) * 200;
		points[index] = {x:x, y:y, z:-100};
		points[index + 1] = {x:x, y:y, z:100};
		index += 2;
	}

	index = 0;
	for(var i:Number = 0;i<numFaces-1;i++)
	{
		triangles[index] = {a:index,
		                    b:index + 1,
		                    c:index + 3,
		                    col:0x6666cc};
		triangles[index+1] = {a:index,
		                      b:index + 3,
		                      c:index + 2,
		                      col:0x6666cc};
		index += 2;
	}
	triangles[index] = {a:index,
	                    b:index + 1,
	                    c:1,
	                    col:0x6666cc};
	triangles[index+1] = {a:index,
	                      b:1,
	                      c:0,
	                      col:0x6666cc};
}
```

```
function onEnterFrame():Void {
      if(Key.isDown(Key.LEFT))
      {
            xOffset -= 10;
      }
      else if(Key.isDown(Key.RIGHT))
      {
            xOffset += 10;
      }
      if(Key.isDown(Key.UP))
      {
            zOffset += 10;
      }
      else if(Key.isDown(Key.DOWN))
      {
            zOffset -= 10;
      }
      var angleY:Number = (_xmouse - vpX) * .001;
      var cosY:Number = Math.cos(angleY);
      var sinY:Number = Math.sin(angleY);

      var angleX:Number = (_ymouse - vpY) * .001;
      var cosX:Number = Math.cos(angleX);
      var sinX:Number = Math.sin(angleX);

      var numPoints:Number = points.length;
      for (var i:Number=0;i<numPoints;i++) {
            var point:MovieClip = points[i];

            var x1:Number = point.x * cosY - point.z * sinY;
            var z1:Number = point.z * cosY + point.x * sinY;

            var y1:Number = point.y * cosX - z1 * sinX;
            var z2:Number = z1 * cosX + point.y * sinX;

            point.x = x1;
            point.y = y1;
            point.z = z2;
```

```
            var scale:Number = fl / (fl + point.z + zOffset);
            point.xPos = vpX + (point.x + xOffset) * scale;
            point.yPos = vpY + point.y * scale;
        }
        clear();
        var numTriangles:Number = triangles.length;
        for(var i:Number =0;i<numTriangles;i++)
        {
            renderTriangle(triangles[i]);
        }
    }

    function renderTriangle(tri:Object):Void
    {
        beginFill(tri.col, 50);
        lineStyle(1, 0, 10);
        moveTo(points[tri.a].xPos, points[tri.a].yPos);
        lineTo(points[tri.b].xPos, points[tri.b].yPos);
        lineTo(points[tri.c].xPos, points[tri.c].yPos);
        lineTo(points[tri.a].xPos, points[tri.a].yPos);
        endFill();
    }
```

Summary

With what you've learned in this chapter, you should be well on your way to modeling your own 3D shapes in ActionScript and manipulating them in 3D space.

This chapter concentrated on the modeling aspect and on how to draw the lines and fills. In the next chapter, you'll explore how to create more solid-looking solids. All that material builds on the foundation of points, lines, and fills that you've covered here. So, when you're ready, let's move on!

};shape.targetHeight = shape._height;
shape.onEnterFrame = function() {
var speed = 5;

Chapter 17

BACKFACE CULLING AND 3D LIGHTING

What we'll cover in this chapter:

- Backface culling
- Depth sorting
- 3D lighting

In Chapter 16, I covered all the basics of modeling 3D solids: how to create the points, lines, and polygons that make up a form, even how to give each polygon a color. But if you recall, you just left that color with a 50% transparency, so you could see right through it. So while it was cool to be able to model complex 3D solids, you're still lacking a lot in terms of realism.

In this chapter, I'm going to remedy that by introducing you to backface culling (not drawing the polygons facing away from you), depth sorting (I covered this a bit in Chapter 15, but we'll take a new look at it in terms of polygons), and 3D lighting.

I think you will be amazed at the results on your 3D models once these three techniques are applied. After the first two, you will be able to create 3D solids that actually look solid. With 3D lighting, they will really come alive.

Before we begin, I want to give credit where it is due. Almost all of the code in this chapter was derived from techniques introduced by Todd Yard in Chapter 10 of *Macromedia Flash MX Studio* (friends of ED, 2002). (Todd is also the technical reviewer on this book, so it's not like I was going to sneak anything past him!) That particular chapter of *Macromedia Flash MX Studio* is probably the best single resource I've found anywhere on these subjects, and I've referred to it every time I've needed to apply any of these advanced 3D techniques. As that book is now more than three years old (ancient in terms of technical books) and two versions of Flash behind, I'm really happy to be able to pull the information forward and keep it available and current.

For the examples in this chapter, I am going to build on file `ch16_11.fla`, which, as you may recall, features a rotating, extruded, 3D letter "A." This serves as a sufficiently complex model that it will be pretty obvious if you do something wrong, and look pretty darn cool when you do everything right!

Backface culling

Backface culling was alluded to a couple of times in the last chapter, and now you are going to find out what it is all about and exactly how it works.

Remember that in the earlier models, you made all the fills semitransparent. The reason for this was that you were always drawing every polygon, and you had no control over what order they were drawn in. So a polygon on the back of the model might get drawn on top of one on the front of the model, creating some odd results. Giving them all an alpha value of 50% made them all relatively equal and let me put off this discussion while you concentrated on your modeling techniques. Now you are going to deal with it.

In principle, backface culling is pretty simple. You draw the polygons that are facing you, and you don't draw the ones that are facing away from you. The tricky part is determining which are which.

You should also remember that I was constantly reminding you to define the points of each polygon in a clockwise direction. Even though that is completely unnecessary for what you've been doing so far, you'll now see why this was so important, and why it was good to get into that habit from the start.

It's a neat little observation that if the points of a polygon are arranged in a clockwise fashion when that triangle is facing you, they will be counterclockwise when that polygon is facing away from you. You can see this demonstrated in Figure 17-1, which has a triangle facing you. (Since all the polygons you will be using will be triangles, I will occasionally mix the two terms. For the most part, I'll use "polygon" as a general term, and "triangle" to discuss a specific triangular polygon under discussion.)

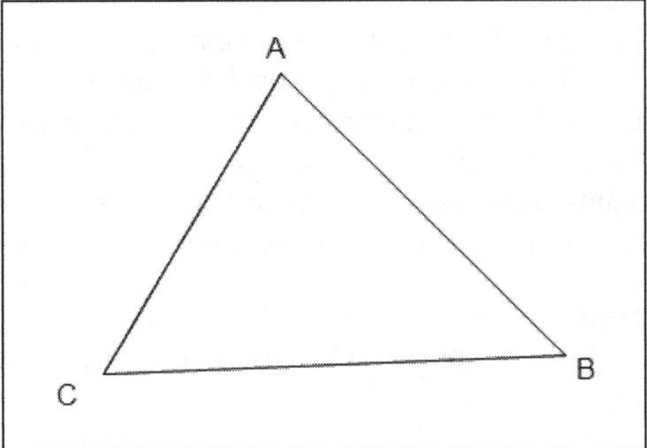

Figure 17-1. A triangle facing you has points in a clockwise direction.

And in Figure 17-2, I've rotated the triangle so it is facing in the opposite direction.

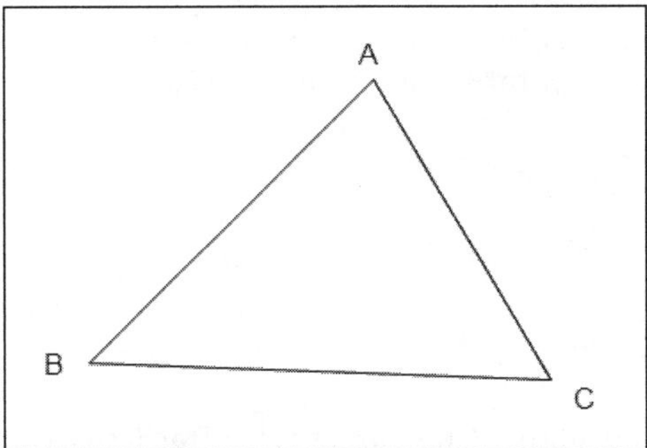

Figure 17-2. A triangle facing away from you has points in a counterclockwise direction.

Now you see that points go around in a counterclockwise direction.

There are a few points of clarification to make here. First of all, what do I mean when I say a polygon is "facing you"? I mean that the *exterior* side of the polygon is facing you. Although it's not obvious when I show a single triangle, remember that I'm talking about 3D solids here. In that case, each polygon has one exterior side and one interior side.

Another point is that when determining clockwise or counterclockwise, I'm talking about the *screen* positions of the points. Not the 3D x, y, and z positions, but the xPos, yPos position that is determined by applying perspective.

Finally, it should be noted that you could reverse the setup and make a system where counterclockwise polygons were the facing ones, and clockwise ones faced away. Either way works as long as you are consistent.

So again, we get back to the question, how do you determine if three points are arranged in a clockwise or counterclockwise direction? Think about it for a while. It's such an easy thing for your eyes to pick out, but when it comes down to putting it in code, it suddenly seems like a very abstract concept.

As I mentioned, the solution I'm going to give you here is based on the one given in *Macromedia Flash MX Studio*. But just to make sure I was providing the best method possible, I decided to see if I could come up with my own function to distinguish clockwise from counterclockwise. While I did manage to put something together that worked perfectly, it was twice as long as the existing solution and far more complex, involving coordinate rotation and lots of trig. Since I'm generally a nice guy, I decided to give you the simple one. And don't worry, it's just as accurate as my overly complex one!

What you're going to do is make a function called `isBackFace`. This will take three point objects as parameters, and return `true` if they are counterclockwise and `false` if they are clockwise. Here is that function:

```
function isBackFace(pointA:Object, pointB:Object, pointC:Object):Boolean
{
	// see http://www.jurjans.lv/flash/shape.html
	var cax:Number = pointC.xPos - pointA.xPos;
	var cay:Number = pointC.yPos - pointA.yPos;

	var bcx:Number = pointB.xPos - pointC.xPos;
	var bcy:Number = pointB.yPos - pointC.yPos;

	return cax * bcy > cay * bcx;
	{
		return true;
	}
	return false;
}
```

You see the link to the website, `http://www.jurjans.lv/flash/shape.html`. Todd Yard credited this site in *Macromedia Flash MX Studio*, so I'll pass it on. In addition to giving credit where it is due, the site has some excellent reference material and tutorials on many similar subjects.

For a quick explanation, the function calculates the lengths of two sides of the triangle, and with some sleight-of-hand multiplication and comparison, is able to tell which direction they are going. If you are interested in the specifics of why this works, see the site just mentioned, or do a search for "backface culling." I'm sure you'll find plenty of reading material. For now, though, I'm going to just say it is simple, quick, efficient, and 100% workable, and leave it at that!

So, how do you use this function? You'll call it in the `renderTriangle` function to see whether or not you actually do want to render said triangle or not.

```
function renderTriangle(tri:Object):Void
{
	var pointA:Object = points[tri.a];
	var pointB:Object = points[tri.b];
	var pointC:Object = points[tri.c];
```

```
        if(isBackFace(pointA, pointB, pointC))
        {
            return;
        }

        beginFill(tri.col, 100);
        moveTo(pointA.xPos, pointA.yPos);
        lineTo(pointB.xPos, pointB.yPos);
        lineTo(pointC.xPos, pointC.yPos);
        lineTo(pointA.xPos, pointA.yPos);
        endFill();
    }
```

Here you grab references to each of the three points and store them in pointA, pointB, and pointC. This helps to keep things clear. You then pass these three points to the isBackFace function, which returns true or false. If it returns true, you know the triangle is facing away from you and you don't need to render it. So at that point you call return, which exits the function. If isBackFace returns false, you need to render the triangle; go right ahead and do so. Notice also that the beginFill call is now using 100% alpha to make fully opaque fills rather than transparent ones.

As a reinforcement, here is the code for ch17_01.fla in its entirety, with the new parts in bold:

```
var points:Array = new Array();
var triangles:Array = new Array();
var fl:Number = 250;
var vpX:Number = Stage.width / 2;
var vpY:Number = Stage.height / 2;
var zOffset:Number = 400;

init();
function init() {
    points[0] =  {x: -50, y:-250, z:-50};
    points[1] =  {x:  50, y:-250, z:-50};
    points[2] =  {x: 200, y: 250, z:-50};
    points[3] =  {x: 100, y: 250, z:-50};
    points[4] =  {x:  50, y: 100, z:-50};
    points[5] =  {x: -50, y: 100, z:-50};
    points[6] =  {x:-100, y: 250, z:-50};
    points[7] =  {x:-200, y: 250, z:-50};
    points[8] =  {x:   0, y:-150, z:-50};
    points[9] =  {x:  50, y:   0, z:-50};
    points[10] = {x: -50, y:   0, z:-50};

    points[11] = {x: -50, y:-250, z: 50};
    points[12] = {x:  50, y:-250, z: 50};
    points[13] = {x: 200, y: 250, z: 50};
    points[14] = {x: 100, y: 250, z: 50};
    points[15] = {x:  50, y: 100, z: 50};
    points[16] = {x: -50, y: 100, z: 50};
    points[17] = {x:-100, y: 250, z: 50};
```

```
points[18] = {x:-200, y: 250, z: 50};
points[19] = {x:   0, y:-150, z: 50};
points[20] = {x:  50, y:   0, z: 50};
points[21] = {x: -50, y:   0, z: 50};

triangles[0] =  {a:0, b:1,  c:8,  col:0x6666cc};
triangles[1] =  {a:1, b:9,  c:8,  col:0x6666cc};
triangles[2] =  {a:1, b:2,  c:9,  col:0x6666cc};
triangles[3] =  {a:2, b:4,  c:9,  col:0x6666cc};
triangles[4] =  {a:2, b:3,  c:4,  col:0x6666cc};
triangles[5] =  {a:4, b:5,  c:9,  col:0x6666cc};
triangles[6] =  {a:9, b:5,  c:10, col:0x6666cc};
triangles[7] =  {a:5, b:6,  c:7,  col:0x6666cc};
triangles[8] =  {a:5, b:7,  c:10, col:0x6666cc};
triangles[9] =  {a:0, b:10, c:7,  col:0x6666cc};
triangles[10] = {a:0, b:8,  c:10, col:0x6666cc};

triangles[11] = {a:11, b:19,  c:12,  col:0xcc6666};
triangles[12] = {a:12, b:19,  c:20,  col:0xcc6666};
triangles[13] = {a:12, b:20,  c:13,  col:0xcc6666};
triangles[14] = {a:13, b:20,  c:15,  col:0xcc6666};
triangles[15] = {a:13, b:15,  c:14,  col:0xcc6666};
triangles[16] = {a:15, b:20,  c:16,  col:0xcc6666};
triangles[17] = {a:20, b:21,  c:16,  col:0xcc6666};
triangles[18] = {a:16, b:18,  c:17,  col:0xcc6666};
triangles[19] = {a:16, b:21,  c:18,  col:0xcc6666};
triangles[20] = {a:11, b:18,  c:21,  col:0xcc6666};
triangles[21] = {a:11, b:21,  c:19,  col:0xcc6666};

triangles[22] = {a:0,  b:11, c:1,  col:0xcccc66};
triangles[23] = {a:11, b:12, c:1,  col:0xcccc66};
triangles[24] = {a:1,  b:12, c:2,  col:0xcccc66};
triangles[25] = {a:12, b:13, c:2,  col:0xcccc66};
triangles[26] = {a:3,  b:2,  c:14, col:0xcccc66};
triangles[27] = {a:2,  b:13, c:14, col:0xcccc66};
triangles[28] = {a:4,  b:3,  c:15, col:0xcccc66};
triangles[29] = {a:3,  b:14, c:15, col:0xcccc66};
triangles[30] = {a:5,  b:4,  c:16, col:0xcccc66};
triangles[31] = {a:4,  b:15, c:16, col:0xcccc66};
triangles[32] = {a:6,  b:5,  c:17, col:0xcccc66};
triangles[33] = {a:5,  b:16, c:17, col:0xcccc66};
triangles[34] = {a:7,  b:6,  c:18, col:0xcccc66};
triangles[35] = {a:6,  b:17, c:18, col:0xcccc66};
triangles[36] = {a:0,  b:7,  c:11, col:0xcccc66};
triangles[37] = {a:7,  b:18, c:11, col:0xcccc66};
```

```
        triangles[38] = {a:8,  b:9,  c:19, col:0xcccc66};
        triangles[39] = {a:9,  b:20, c:19, col:0xcccc66};
        triangles[40] = {a:9,  b:10, c:20, col:0xcccc66};
        triangles[41] = {a:10, b:21, c:20, col:0xcccc66};
        triangles[42] = {a:10, b:8,  c:21, col:0xcccc66};
        triangles[43] 2= {a:8,  b:19, c:21, col:0xcccc66};
}

function onEnterFrame():Void {
        var numPoints:Number = points.length;
        for (var i:Number=0;i<numPoints;i++) {
                var point:MovieClip = points[i];

                var angleY:Number = (_xmouse - vpX) * .001;
                var cosY:Number = Math.cos(angleY);
                var sinY:Number = Math.sin(angleY);

                var angleX:Number = (_ymouse - vpY) * .001;
                var cosX:Number = Math.cos(angleX);
                var sinX:Number = Math.sin(angleX);

                var x1:Number = point.x * cosY - point.z * sinY;
                var z1:Number = point.z * cosY + point.x * sinY;

                var y1:Number = point.y * cosX - z1 * sinX;
                var z2:Number = z1 * cosX + point.y * sinX;

                point.x = x1;
                point.y = y1;
                point.z = z2;

                var scale:Number = fl / (fl + point.z + zOffset);
                point.xPos = vpX + point.x * scale;
                point.yPos = vpY + point.y * scale;
        }
        clear();
        var numTriangles:Number = triangles.length;
        for(var i:Number =0;i<numTriangles;i++)
        {
                renderTriangle(triangles[i]);
        }
}

function renderTriangle(tri:Object):Void
{
        var pointA:Object = points[tri.a];
        var pointB:Object = points[tri.b];
        var pointC:Object = points[tri.c];
```

```
            if(isBackFace(pointA, pointB, pointC))
            {
                  return;
            }

            beginFill(tri.col, 100);
            moveTo(pointA.xPos, pointA.yPos);
            lineTo(pointB.xPos, pointB.yPos);
            lineTo(pointC.xPos, pointC.yPos);
            lineTo(pointA.xPos, pointA.yPos);
            endFill();
      }

      function isBackFace(pointA:Object, pointB:Object, pointC:Object):Boolean
      {
            // see http://www.jurjans.lv/flash/shape.html
            var cax:Number = pointC.xPos - pointA.xPos;
            var cay:Number = pointC.yPos - pointA.yPos;

            var bcx:Number = pointB.xPos - pointC.xPos;
            var bcy:Number = pointB.yPos - pointC.yPos;

            return cax * bcy > cay * bcx;
      }
```

When you run that file, you'll get something that looks like what appears in Figure 17-3.

Figure 17-3. Backface culling in action

As you can see, you are a far cry better off than without the backface culling, and if you take a close look, you'll see that only the surfaces that are facing you are being rendered. But it still needs work. The problem now is that some of the faces that should be in back of others are showing up in front of them. If the term "depth sorting" comes to mind, you are truly on the ball. That is our next subject.

Depth sorting

Depth sorting, or z-sorting, is something we've already discussed in Chapter 15, when you were just applying perspective to movie clips. In that case, you took the negative of the z position and used that in swapDepths. Thus movie clips with a higher z (further away) were swapped to positions behind those with a lower z value (closer to the viewer).

At this point however, you are not dealing with multiple movie clips. All of the polygons are being drawn within the same movie clip (in this case the main timeline, or _root). Thus, whenever a particular polygon is drawn, it will be drawn on top of any that have been drawn earlier. So, rather than swapping anything's depth, you just need to determine which polygon gets drawn when. Specifically, you want to draw the ones that are farthest away first; then you draw the rest, working your way forward, so that the closest polygons are drawn last, covering anything they might be in front of.

So how do you do that? Well, you have all the polygons in an array called triangles. And when you draw the shape, you loop through triangles, drawing each triangle from zero through to the end. What you need to do is sort this array so that the triangle that is furthest away is in element zero of the array, and the one closest to the viewer is in the very last element.

For this, you will use the Array.sort method. This method actually has many different options. Used without any parameters, sort will try to sort the array alphabetically and/or numerically. You can also specify various options, such as to sort ascending or descending, with or without case sensitivity, etc. Of course, this simple sorting is only useful if the elements are strings and/or numbers.

There is also an Array.sortOn method, which is a little more useful. Say you had an array called employees, which was full of objects. Each object had a number of properties, such as name and age. You could sort this array based on the name property like so:

```
employees.sortOn("name");
```

Or on the age property like this:

```
employees.sortOn("age");
```

Unfortunately even this doesn't help you. Each element of your triangles array contains an object with a, b, and c properties, each of which are indexes to an element in the points array. You need to use these indexes to get the three point objects that make up the triangle. When you have the three points, you can then analyze their z values to get the overall depth of that particular triangle. That's what you eventually want to sort on. But that's quite a bit of logic. Obviously Flash doesn't come with a built-in method for such a thing! So how do you tell Flash to sort an array based on complex criteria like that?

Fortunately, there is one more way to use Array.sort. You can supply this method with the name of a sorting function, which you create. The function itself takes on a form like this:

```
function sortFunction(elementA, elementB):Number
{
      // return -1 if elementA should go before element B
      // return 1 if elementA should go after elementB
      // return 0 if no change should be made
}
```

The sorting function can then perform any kind of logic you want it to in comparing elementA and elementB, as long as it returns a –1, 0, or 1. To use this function to sort an array, you would call it like this:

```
myArray.sort(sortFunction);
```

That part of it is pretty simple. You just need to supply the function that contains that comparing logic.

For the purposes of this example, you'll make a method called triSort. It will look like this:

```
function triSort(triA:Object, triB:Object):Number
{
	var zA:Number = Math.min(points[triA.a].z, points[triA.b].z);
	zA = Math.min(zA, points[triA.c].z);

	var zB:Number = Math.min(points[triB.a].z, points[triB.b].z);
	zB = Math.min(zB, points[triB.c].z);

	if(zA < zB)
	{
		return 1;
	}
	else
	{
		return -1;
	}
}
```

Here, you are passed references to two triangles. For each triangle, you use Math.min to find the point with the lowest z value. In other words, the point that is closest to you. You store these in zA and zB. Then you compare these two values. If zA is less than zB, then triangleA is closer to you than triangleB, and should go later in the array, so it is drawn later. Thus you return 1. If the opposite is true, then you return –1. Theoretically, you could test to see if they are equal and if so return 0. But that is just an extra computation with no added benefit in this case.

So, when do you sort this array? Some time after you make all adjustments to the positions of the points, and just before you render the triangles. I've put it in the onEnterFrame function like so:

```
	clear();
	triangles.sort(triSort);
	var numTriangles:Number = triangles.length;
	for(var i:Number =0;i<numTriangles;i++)
	{
		renderTriangle(triangles[i]);
	}
```

Again, just to keep things current, here is the final code for ch17_02.fla:

```
var points:Array = new Array();
var triangles:Array = new Array();
var fl:Number = 250;
var vpX:Number = Stage.width / 2;
var vpY:Number = Stage.height / 2;
var zOffset:Number = 400;

init();
function init() {
```

```
points[0] =  {x: -50, y:-250, z:-50};
points[1] =  {x:  50, y:-250, z:-50};
points[2] =  {x: 200, y: 250, z:-50};
points[3] =  {x: 100, y: 250, z:-50};
points[4] =  {x:  50, y: 100, z:-50};
points[5] =  {x: -50, y: 100, z:-50};
points[6] =  {x:-100, y: 250, z:-50};
points[7] =  {x:-200, y: 250, z:-50};
points[8] =  {x:   0, y:-150, z:-50};
points[9] =  {x:  50, y:   0, z:-50};
points[10] = {x: -50, y:   0, z:-50};

points[11] = {x: -50, y:-250, z: 50};
points[12] = {x:  50, y:-250, z: 50};
points[13] = {x: 200, y: 250, z: 50};
points[14] = {x: 100, y: 250, z: 50};
points[15] = {x:  50, y: 100, z: 50};
points[16] = {x: -50, y: 100, z: 50};
points[17] = {x:-100, y: 250, z: 50};
points[18] = {x:-200, y: 250, z: 50};
points[19] = {x:   0, y:-150, z: 50};
points[20] = {x:  50, y:   0, z: 50};
points[21] = {x: -50, y:   0, z: 50};

triangles[0] =  {a:0, b:1,  c:8,  col:0x6666cc};
triangles[1] =  {a:1, b:9,  c:8,  col:0x6666cc};
triangles[2] =  {a:1, b:2,  c:9,  col:0x6666cc};
triangles[3] =  {a:2, b:4,  c:9,  col:0x6666cc};
triangles[4] =  {a:2, b:3,  c:4,  col:0x6666cc};
triangles[5] =  {a:4, b:5,  c:9,  col:0x6666cc};
triangles[6] =  {a:9, b:5,  c:10, col:0x6666cc};
triangles[7] =  {a:5, b:6,  c:7,  col:0x6666cc};
triangles[8] =  {a:5, b:7,  c:10, col:0x6666cc};
triangles[9] =  {a:0, b:10, c:7,  col:0x6666cc};
triangles[10] = {a:0, b:8,  c:10, col:0x6666cc};

triangles[11] = {a:11, b:19,  c:12,  col:0xcc6666};
triangles[12] = {a:12, b:19,  c:20,  col:0xcc6666};
triangles[13] = {a:12, b:20,  c:13,  col:0xcc6666};
triangles[14] = {a:13, b:20,  c:15,  col:0xcc6666};
triangles[15] = {a:13, b:15,  c:14,  col:0xcc6666};
triangles[16] = {a:15, b:20,  c:16,  col:0xcc6666};
triangles[17] = {a:20, b:21,  c:16,  col:0xcc6666};
triangles[18] = {a:16, b:18,  c:17,  col:0xcc6666};
triangles[19] = {a:16, b:21,  c:18,  col:0xcc6666};
triangles[20] = {a:11, b:18,  c:21,  col:0xcc6666};
triangles[21] = {a:11, b:21,  c:19,  col:0xcc6666};
```

```
        triangles[22] = {a:0,  b:11, c:1,  col:0xcccc66};
        triangles[23] = {a:11, b:12, c:1,  col:0xcccc66};
        triangles[24] = {a:1,  b:12, c:2,  col:0xcccc66};
        triangles[25] = {a:12, b:13, c:2,  col:0xcccc66};
        triangles[26] = {a:3,  b:2,  c:14, col:0xcccc66};
        triangles[27] = {a:2,  b:13, c:14, col:0xcccc66};
        triangles[28] = {a:4,  b:3,  c:15, col:0xcccc66};
        triangles[29] = {a:3,  b:14, c:15, col:0xcccc66};
        triangles[30] = {a:5,  b:4,  c:16, col:0xcccc66};
        triangles[31] = {a:4,  b:15, c:16, col:0xcccc66};
        triangles[32] = {a:6,  b:5,  c:17, col:0xcccc66};
        triangles[33] = {a:5,  b:16, c:17, col:0xcccc66};
        triangles[34] = {a:7,  b:6,  c:18, col:0xcccc66};
        triangles[35] = {a:6,  b:17, c:18, col:0xcccc66};
        triangles[36] = {a:0,  b:7,  c:11, col:0xcccc66};
        triangles[37] = {a:7,  b:18, c:11, col:0xcccc66};

        triangles[38] = {a:8,  b:9,  c:19, col:0xcccc66};
        triangles[39] = {a:9,  b:20, c:19, col:0xcccc66};
        triangles[40] = {a:9,  b:10, c:20, col:0xcccc66};
        triangles[41] = {a:10, b:21, c:20, col:0xcccc66};
        triangles[42] = {a:10, b:8,  c:21, col:0xcccc66};
        triangles[43] = {a:8,  b:19, c:21, col:0xcccc66};
}

function onEnterFrame():Void {
        var numPoints:Number = points.length;
        for (var i:Number=0;i<numPoints;i++) {
                var point:MovieClip = points[i];

                var angleY:Number = (_xmouse - vpX) * .001;
                var cosY:Number = Math.cos(angleY);
                var sinY:Number = Math.sin(angleY);

                var angleX:Number = (_ymouse - vpY) * .001;
                var cosX:Number = Math.cos(angleX);
                var sinX:Number = Math.sin(angleX);

                var x1:Number = point.x * cosY - point.z * sinY;
                var z1:Number = point.z * cosY + point.x * sinY;

                var y1:Number = point.y * cosX - z1 * sinX;
                var z2:Number = z1 * cosX + point.y * sinX;

                point.x = x1;
                point.y = y1;
                point.z = z2;
```

```
            var scale:Number = fl / (fl + point.z + zOffset);
            point.xPos = vpX + point.x * scale;
            point.yPos = vpY + point.y * scale;
        }
        clear();
        triangles.sort(triSort);
        var numTriangles:Number = triangles.length;
        for(var i:Number =0;i<numTriangles;i++)
        {
            renderTriangle(triangles[i]);
        }
}

function renderTriangle(tri:Object):Void
{
        var pointA:Object = points[tri.a];
        var pointB:Object = points[tri.b];
        var pointC:Object = points[tri.c];

        if(isBackFace(pointA, pointB, pointC))
        {
            return;
        }

        beginFill(tri.col, 100);
        moveTo(pointA.xPos, pointA.yPos);
        lineTo(pointB.xPos, pointB.yPos);
        lineTo(pointC.xPos, pointC.yPos);
        lineTo(pointA.xPos, pointA.yPos);
        endFill();
}

function isBackFace(pointA:Object, pointB:Object, pointC:Object):Boolean
{
        // see http://www.jurjans.lv/flash/shape.html
        var cax:Number = pointC.xPos - pointA.xPos;
        var cay:Number = pointC.yPos - pointA.yPos;

        var bcx:Number = pointB.xPos - pointC.xPos;
        var bcy:Number = pointB.yPos - pointC.yPos;

        return cax * bcy > cay * bcx;
}

function triSort(triA:Object, triB:Object):Number
{
        var zA:Number = Math.min(points[triA.a].z, points[triA.b].z);
        zA = Math.min(zA, points[triA.c].z);
```

```
        var zB:Number = Math.min(points[triB.a].z, points[triB.b].z);
        zB = Math.min(zB, points[triB.c].z);

        if(zA < zB)
        {
              return 1;
        }
        else
        {
              return -1;
        }
}
```

When you run this, you should have a perfectly rendered solid. You are really getting someplace now. The next step will boost you right over the top in terms of coolness!

Figure 17-4. Sorting the depths puts it all right!

3D lighting

While the last example is pretty close to perfect in terms of rendering, it still kind of lacks something. It's a bit flat. OK, OK, you already know where I'm heading with this, because it says so right in the section title, so let's add some 3D lighting.

Like backface culling, the specifics behind 3D lighting can get pretty complex and math intensive. I don't really have the space to get into a detailed discussion of all the finer points, but a quick web search will turn up more information on the subject than you could probably read in a lifetime. What I'm going to give you here are the basics, along with some functions you can use and adapt as needed.

First of all, you need a light source. A light source at its simplest has two properties: location and brightness. In more complex 3D systems, it may also be able to point in a certain direction, have a color of its own, have falloff rates, conical areas, etc. But all that is beyond the scope of what you are doing here.

First you'll create the light as a simple generic object:

```
var light:Object = new Object();
```

Then, in the init function, you'll position it and assign its brightness:

```
function init() {
      light.x = -200;
      light.y = -200;
      light.z = -200;
      light.brightness = 100;
      ...
```

Two things important to note here. One is that the position is used to calculate the angle of the light only. The strength of the light you are creating does not fall off with distance. Thus changing the x, y, and z to –2,000,000 or down to –20 would make no difference in terms of how brightly the object was lit. Only the `brightness` property will change that characteristic of the light. Also, brightness must be a number from 0 to 100. If you go outside of that range, you can wind up with some odd results. Later I'll show you how you can validate this value and make sure it is within range before using it.

Now, what the light source is going to do is change the brightness of the color of a polygon, based on the angle of the light that is falling on that polygon. So if the polygon is facing directly at the light, it will display the full value of its color. As it turns away from the light, it will get darker and darker. Finally, when it is facing completely away from the light source, it will be completely in shadow and colored black.

So, what you need is a function that will take a particular polygon, looks at the base color of that polygon and the angle and brightness of the light, and returns an adjusted color. Here is that function:

```
function getTriangleColor(tri:Object):Number
{
	var pointA:Object = points[tri.a];
	var pointB:Object = points[tri.b];
	var pointC:Object = points[tri.c];

	var lightFactor:Number = getLightFactor(pointA, pointB, pointC);

	var red:Number = tri.col >> 16;
	var green:Number = tri.col >> 8 & 0xff;
	var blue:Number = tri.col & 0xff;

	red *= lightFactor;
	green *= lightFactor;
	blue *= lightFactor;

	return red << 16 | green << 8 | blue;
}
```

This function gets passed a reference to a single triangle object. It then gets references to the three point objects that make up that triangle and passes them to another function, `getLightFactor`. You'll see that function in a moment. For now, you just need to know that it returns a number from 0.0 to 1.0. This is how much you need to alter the color of that particular triangle, 1.0 being full brightness, and 0.0 being black.

Now you can't just multiply the triangle's color by this `lightFactor`. That will give you a completely random color, not just a darker version of the original. What you need to do is separate out the red, green, and blue values of that color, multiply each one of *those* by the `lightFactor`, and then join them back together again.

Separating and joining color component values is fully covered in Chapter 4, and you use those exact techniques here to come up with a new color, which is returned by the function.

Now, how do you come up with this lightFactor? Let's look at the next function:

```
function getLightFactor(ptA:Object, ptB:Object, ptC:Object):Number
{
	var ab:Object = new Object();
	ab.x = ptA.x - ptB.x;
	ab.y = ptA.y - ptB.y;
	ab.z = ptA.z - ptB.z;

	var bc:Object = new Object();
	bc.x = ptB.x - ptC.x;
	bc.y = ptB.y - ptC.y;
	bc.z = ptB.z - ptC.z;

	var norm:Object = new Object();
	norm.x =   (ab.y * bc.z) - (ab.z * bc.y);
	norm.y = -((ab.x * bc.z) - (ab.z * bc.x));
	norm.z =   (ab.x * bc.y) - (ab.y * bc.x);

	var dotProd:Number = norm.x * light.x +
	                     norm.y * light.y +
	                     norm.z * light.z;

	var normMag:Number = Math.sqrt(norm.x * norm.x +
	                               norm.y * norm.y +
	                               norm.z * norm.z);

	var lightMag:Number = Math.sqrt(light.x * light.x +
	                                light.y * light.y +
	                                light.z * light.z);

	return (Math.acos(dotProd / (normMag * lightMag)) / Math.PI)
	        * light.brightness / 100;
}
```

Now, that is quite a function, huh? To *fully* understand all that's going on here, you'd have to have a good grasp on advanced vector math, but I'll try to walk through the bare basics of it.

First of all you need to find the *normal* of the triangle. This is a vector that is perpendicular to the surface of the triangle, as depicted in Figure 17-5. Imagine you had a triangular piece of wood and you put a nail through the back of it so it stuck out directly through the face. That nail would represent the normal of that surface. If you study anything about 3D rendering and lighting, you are going to see all kinds of references to normals.

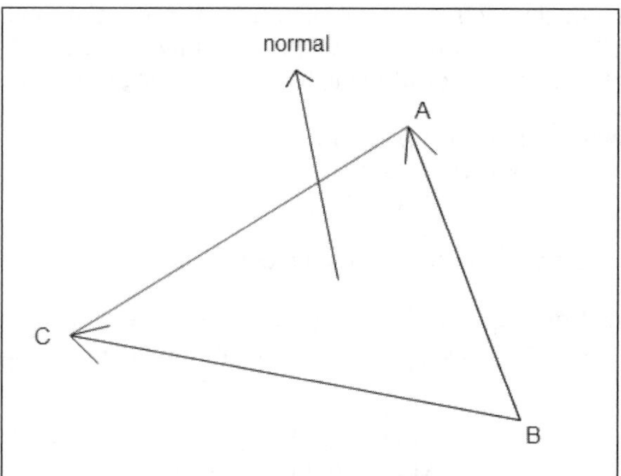

Figure 17-5. The normal is perpendicular to the surface of the triangle.

You can find the normal of a surface by taking two vectors that make up that surface and calculating their *cross product*. A cross product of two vectors is a new vector, which is perpendicular to those two. The two vectors you will use will be the lines between points A and B, and points B and C. Each vector will be held in an object with x, y, and z properties.

```
var ab:Object = new Object();
ab.x = ptA.x - ptB.x;
ab.y = ptA.y - ptB.y;
ab.z = ptA.z - ptB.z;

var bc:Object = new Object();
bc.x = ptB.x - ptC.x;
bc.y = ptB.y - ptC.y;
bc.z = ptB.z - ptC.z;
```

Then you calculate the normal, which is another vector. You'll call this object norm. The following code computes the cross product of the vectors ab and bc:

```
var norm:Object = new Object();
norm.x =   (ab.y * bc.z) - (ab.z * bc.y);
norm.y = -((ab.x * bc.z) - (ab.z * bc.x));
norm.z =   (ab.x * bc.y) - (ab.y * bc.x);
```

Again, I don't have the space to cover the details of why this is calculated this way, but this is the standard formula for calculating a cross product. If you are interested in how this is derived, you can check any decent reference on linear algebra.

Now you need to know how closely that normal aligns with the angle of the light. Another bit of vector math goodness is called the *dot product*, which is the difference between two vectors. You have the vector of the normal, and the vector of the light. The following calculates that dot product:

```
var dotProd:Number = norm.x * light.x +
                     norm.y * light.y +
                     norm.z * light.z;
```

As you can see, dot products are a bit simpler than cross products!

OK, you are almost there! Next, you calculate the magnitude of the normal, and the magnitude of the light, which you might recognize as the 3D version of the Pythagorean theorem:

```
var magN:Number = Math.sqrt(N[0] * N[0] +
                            N[1] * N[1] +
                            N[2] * N[2]);

var lightMag:Number = Math.sqrt(light.x * light.x +
                                light.y * light.y +
                                light.z * light.z);
```

Note that this `lightMag` variable is calculated every time a triangle is rendered, which allows for a moving light source. If you know that the light source is going to be fixed, you could create this variable at the beginning of the code and calculate it one time in the `init` function. This would add quite a bit of efficiency to the file. Finally, you take all these bits you've just calculated, and put them into the magic formula:

```
return (Math.acos(dotProd / (normMag * lightMag)) / Math.PI)
            * light.brightness / 100;
```

Basically, `dotProd` is one measurement and `normMag * lightMag` is another. Dividing these two gives you a ratio. Recall from our discussion in Chapter 3 that the cosine of an angle gives you a ratio, and the arccosine of a ratio gives you an angle. So using `Math.acos` here on this ratio of measurements gives you an angle. This is essentially the angle at which the light is striking the surface of the polygon. It will be in the range of 0 to `Math.PI` radians (0 to 180 degrees), meaning it's either hitting head on or completely from behind.

Dividing this angle by `Math.PI` gives you a percentage, and multiplying that by the percentage of brightness gives you your final light factor, which you use to alter the base color.

Remember I told you that the brightness of the light needs to be from 0 to 100. Here is where you can validate that if you are worried about someone setting it too high or low. Just before the `return` statement you could place lines like:

```
light.brightness = Math.min(light.brightness, 100);
light.brightness = Math.max(light.brightness, 0);
```

These will guarantee that the value stays in range.

OK, now all this was just to get a new color for the surface! Implementing it in your existing code is actually pretty easy. It goes right in the renderTriangle function. Where previously you were just using the base color of the triangle like so:

```
beginFill(tri.col, 100);
```

now you get the modified color and use that:

```
var col:Number = getTriangleColor(tri);
beginFill(col, 100);
```

To wrap things up, here is the full and final code for ch17_03.fla:

```
var points:Array = new Array();
var triangles:Array = new Array();
var fl:Number = 250;
var vpX:Number = Stage.width / 2;
var vpY:Number = Stage.height / 2;
var zOffset:Number = 400;
var light:Object = new Object();

init();
function init() {
      light.x = -200;
      light.y = -200;
      light.z = -200;
      light.brightness = 100;

      points[0] =  {x: -50, y:-250, z:-50};
      points[1] =  {x:  50, y:-250, z:-50};
      points[2] =  {x: 200, y: 250, z:-50};
      points[3] =  {x: 100, y: 250, z:-50};
      points[4] =  {x:  50, y: 100, z:-50};
      points[5] =  {x: -50, y: 100, z:-50};
      points[6] =  {x:-100, y: 250, z:-50};
      points[7] =  {x:-200, y: 250, z:-50};
      points[8] =  {x:   0, y:-150, z:-50};
      points[9] =  {x:  50, y:   0, z:-50};
      points[10] = {x: -50, y:   0, z:-50};

      points[11] = {x: -50, y:-250, z: 50};
      points[12] = {x:  50, y:-250, z: 50};
      points[13] = {x: 200, y: 250, z: 50};
      points[14] = {x: 100, y: 250, z: 50};
      points[15] = {x:  50, y: 100, z: 50};
      points[16] = {x: -50, y: 100, z: 50};
      points[17] = {x:-100, y: 250, z: 50};
      points[18] = {x:-200, y: 250, z: 50};
```

```
points[19] = {x:   0, y:-150, z: 50};
points[20] = {x:  50, y:   0, z: 50};
points[21] = {x: -50, y:   0, z: 50};

triangles[0] =  {a:0, b:1,  c:8,  col:0xffcccc};
triangles[1] =  {a:1, b:9,  c:8,  col:0xffcccc};
triangles[2] =  {a:1, b:2,  c:9,  col:0xffcccc};
triangles[3] =  {a:2, b:4,  c:9,  col:0xffcccc};
triangles[4] =  {a:2, b:3,  c:4,  col:0xffcccc};
triangles[5] =  {a:4, b:5,  c:9,  col:0xffcccc};
triangles[6] =  {a:9, b:5,  c:10, col:0xffcccc};
triangles[7] =  {a:5, b:6,  c:7,  col:0xffcccc};
triangles[8] =  {a:5, b:7,  c:10, col:0xffcccc};
triangles[9] =  {a:0, b:10, c:7,  col:0xffcccc};
triangles[10] = {a:0, b:8,  c:10, col:0xffcccc};

triangles[11] = {a:11, b:19,  c:12,  col:0xffcccc};
triangles[12] = {a:12, b:19,  c:20,  col:0xffcccc};
triangles[13] = {a:12, b:20,  c:13,  col:0xffcccc};
triangles[14] = {a:13, b:20,  c:15,  col:0xffcccc};
triangles[15] = {a:13, b:15,  c:14,  col:0xffcccc};
triangles[16] = {a:15, b:20,  c:16,  col:0xffcccc};
triangles[17] = {a:20, b:21,  c:16,  col:0xffcccc};
triangles[18] = {a:16, b:18,  c:17,  col:0xffcccc};
triangles[19] = {a:16, b:21,  c:18,  col:0xffcccc};
triangles[20] = {a:11, b:18,  c:21,  col:0xffcccc};
triangles[21] = {a:11, b:21,  c:19,  col:0xffcccc};

triangles[22] = {a:0,  b:11, c:1,  col:0xffcccc};
triangles[23] = {a:11, b:12, c:1,  col:0xffcccc};
triangles[24] = {a:1,  b:12, c:2,  col:0xffcccc};
triangles[25] = {a:12, b:13, c:2,  col:0xffcccc};
triangles[26] = {a:3,  b:2,  c:14, col:0xffcccc};
triangles[27] = {a:2,  b:13, c:14, col:0xffcccc};
triangles[28] = {a:4,  b:3,  c:15, col:0xffcccc};
triangles[29] = {a:3,  b:14, c:15, col:0xffcccc};
triangles[30] = {a:5,  b:4,  c:16, col:0xffcccc};
triangles[31] = {a:4,  b:15, c:16, col:0xffcccc};
triangles[32] = {a:6,  b:5,  c:17, col:0xffcccc};
triangles[33] = {a:5,  b:16, c:17, col:0xffcccc};
triangles[34] = {a:7,  b:6,  c:18, col:0xffcccc};
triangles[35] = {a:6,  b:17, c:18, col:0xffcccc};
triangles[36] = {a:0,  b:7,  c:11, col:0xffcccc};
triangles[37] = {a:7,  b:18, c:11, col:0xffcccc};
```

```
        triangles[38] = {a:8,  b:9,  c:19, col:0xffcccc};
        triangles[39] = {a:9,  b:20, c:19, col:0xffcccc};
        triangles[40] = {a:9,  b:10, c:20, col:0xffcccc};
        triangles[41] = {a:10, b:21, c:20, col:0xffcccc};
        triangles[42] = {a:10, b:8,  c:21, col:0xffcccc};
        triangles[43] = {a:8,  b:19, c:21, col:0xffcccc};
}

function onEnterFrame():Void {
        var numPoints:Number = points.length;
        for (var i:Number=0;i<numPoints;i++) {
                var point:MovieClip = points[i];

                var angleY:Number = (_xmouse - vpX) * .001;
                var cosY:Number = Math.cos(angleY);
                var sinY:Number = Math.sin(angleY);

                var angleX:Number = (_ymouse - vpY) * .001;
                var cosX:Number = Math.cos(angleX);
                var sinX:Number = Math.sin(angleX);

                var x1:Number = point.x * cosY - point.z * sinY;
                var z1:Number = point.z * cosY + point.x * sinY;

                var y1:Number = point.y * cosX - z1 * sinX;
                var z2:Number = z1 * cosX + point.y * sinX;

                point.x = x1;
                point.y = y1;
                point.z = z2;

                var scale:Number = fl / (fl + point.z + zOffset);
                point.xPos = vpX + point.x * scale;
                point.yPos = vpY + point.y * scale;
        }
        clear();
        triangles.sort(triSort);
        var numTriangles:Number = triangles.length;
        for(var i:Number =0;i<numTriangles;i++)
        {
                renderTriangle(triangles[i]);
        }
}
```

```
function renderTriangle(tri:Object):Void
{
      var pointA:Object = points[tri.a];
      var pointB:Object = points[tri.b];
      var pointC:Object = points[tri.c];

      if(isBackFace(pointA, pointB, pointC))
      {
            return;
      }

      var col:Number = getTriangleColor(tri);
      beginFill(col, 100);
      moveTo(pointA.xPos, pointA.yPos);
      lineTo(pointB.xPos, pointB.yPos);
      lineTo(pointC.xPos, pointC.yPos);
      lineTo(pointA.xPos, pointA.yPos);
      endFill();
}

function isBackFace(pointA:Object, pointB:Object, pointC:Object):Boolean
{
      // see http://www.jurjans.lv/flash/shape.html
      var cax:Number = pointC.xPos - pointA.xPos;
      var cay:Number = pointC.yPos - pointA.yPos;

      var bcx:Number = pointB.xPos - pointC.xPos;
      var bcy:Number = pointB.yPos - pointC.yPos;

      return cax * bcy > cay * bcx;
}

function triSort(triA:Object, triB:Object):Number
{
      var zA:Number = Math.min(points[triA.a].z, points[triA.b].z);
      zA = Math.min(zA, points[triA.c].z);

      var zB:Number = Math.min(points[triB.a].z, points[triB.b].z);
      zB = Math.min(zB, points[triB.c].z);

      if(zA < zB)
      {
            return 1;
      }
      else
```

```
        {
            return -1;
        }
    }

    function getTriangleColor(tri:Object):Number
    {
        var pointA:Object = points[tri.a];
        var pointB:Object = points[tri.b];
        var pointC:Object = points[tri.c];

        var lightFactor:Number = getLightFactor(pointA, pointB, pointC);

        var red:Number = tri.col >> 16;
        var green:Number = tri.col >> 8 & 0xff;
        var blue:Number = tri.col & 0xff;

        red *= lightFactor;
        green *= lightFactor;
        blue *= lightFactor;

        return red << 16 | green << 8 | blue;
    }

    function getLightFactor(ptA:Object, ptB:Object, ptC:Object):Number
    {
        var ab:Object = new Object();
2       ab.x = ptA.x - ptB.x;
        ab.y = ptA.y - ptB.y;
        ab.z = ptA.z - ptB.z;

        var bc:Object = new Object();
        bc.x = ptB.x - ptC.x;
        bc.y = ptB.y - ptC.y;
        bc.z = ptB.z - ptC.z;

        var norm:Object = new Object();
        norm.x =   (ab.y * bc.z) - (ab.z * bc.y);
        norm.y = -((ab.x * bc.z) - (ab.z * bc.x));
        norm.z =   (ab.x * bc.y) - (ab.y * bc.x);

        var dotProd:Number = norm.x * light.x +
                             norm.y * light.y +
                             norm.z * light.z;
```

```
        var normMag:Number = Math.sqrt(norm.x * norm.x +
                                       norm.y * norm.y +
                                       norm.z * norm.z);

        var lightMag:Number = Math.sqrt(light.x * light.x +
                                        light.y * light.y +
                                        light.z * light.z);

        return (Math.acos(dotProd / (normMag * lightMag)) / Math.PI)
                * light.brightness / 100;
    }
```

In addition to the new functions and other changes I mentioned, I also made all the triangles the same color, as you see in Figure 17-6, as I think it shows off the effect of the lighting much better.

Figure 17-6. 3D solid with backface culling, depth sorting, and 3D lighting

Summary

Wow! That was a lot of work for just three examples! But I think the results are well worth it. You now have the tools to make some pretty stunning 3D movies. And it goes without saying that there are a lot of variations you can throw in here. For instance, in the last example, the light is stationary and the object moves. Try moving the light around instead. (It's just a matter of altering its x, y, and/or z positions.) In fact, as a bonus, you can check out `ch17_04.fla`, where I have the light controlled by the mouse. You might want to try to get the light orbiting around a stationary object.

That about wraps up our main discussion of 3D. In the next chapter, you'll be looking at matrix math, which is often used as an alternative to some of the scaling and rotation methods you've been using so far, and thus is something you'll often see in 3D programming.

Part Five

ADDITIONAL TECHNIQUES

};shape.targetHeight = shape._height;
shape.onEnterFrame = function() {
var speed =5;
this._height += (this.targetHeight - this._height)/speed;
};

Chapter 18

MATRIX MATH

What we'll cover in this chapter:

- Matrix basics
- Matrix operations
- The Matrix class in Flash 8

In this chapter, I'm not necessarily going to introduce any new types of motion or physics or methods of rendering graphics. What I am going to do is give you an introduction to *matrices*, which provide an alternative way of doing a lot of the things you've already been doing.

Matrices are used quite often in 3D systems for rotating, scaling, and translating (moving) 3D points. They are also used quite a bit in various 2D graphics transformations. You might recall that the `beginGradientFill` movie clip method uses a matrix to position, size, and rotate the gradient. Flash 8 makes more frequent use of matrices in many of its new functions.

In this chapter, you'll see how to create a system of 3D matrices to manipulate movie clips in 3D and look into several built-in uses of matrices in Flash. Oh, and I'm quite proud of myself for not having made a single corny reference to any Keanu Reeves movie yet. Let's see how long I can restrain myself.

Matrix basics

A matrix, by simplest definition, is a grid of numbers. It can have one or more horizontal rows and one or more vertical columns. Figure 18-1 shows some matrices.

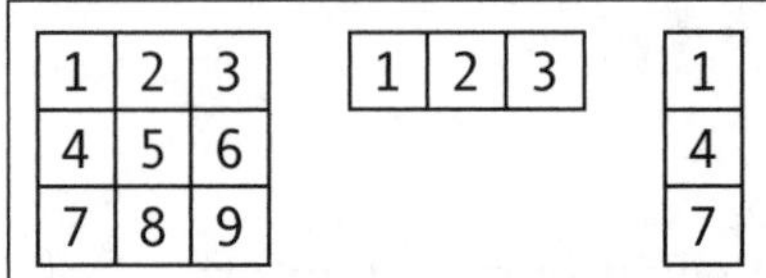

Figure 18-1. A 3×3 matrix, a 1×3 matrix, and a 3×1 matrix

Any particular matrix is usually represented by some variable, such as `M`. To refer to a specific cell in a matrix, you use the variable name with the row and column number in subscript. For example, if the 3X3 matrix in Figure 18-1 is called `M`, then `M2,3` is equal to 6, as it refers to the second row, third column.

The cells of a matrix can contain not only simple numbers, but also formulas and variables. If you've ever used a spreadsheet, that is basically one big matrix. You can have one cell hold the sum of a column, and another cell multiplies that sum by some fraction that's held in another cell, and so forth. So you see that matrices can be pretty useful.

Matrix operations

Now, where a spreadsheet is kind of a free-form matrix, the matrices we'll be dealing with are a lot more structured, and have all kinds of rules associated with them for what we can do with them and how to do it.

Most instructional material on matrix math that I've seen takes one of two approaches. The first school describes how to do the operations in detail, using matrices full of seemingly random numbers. You learn the rules, but you have no idea why you are doing certain things or what the result means. It's like playing a game where you arrange the numbers in a pretty pattern.

The second approach is to describe the contents of the matrices in detail and skim over the operation, with vague instructions such as "and then you just multiply these two matrices together and get this...," leaving the reader with no idea how this multiplication is done.

To ensure you understand how matrices work, I've chosen to walk the line between these two methods, starting with presenting some matrices containing meaningful values, and then describing how to manipulate them.

Matrix addition

One of the more common uses of matrices is manipulating 3D points. A 3D point contains a value for x, y, and z positions. We can easily view this as a one by three matrix like so:

```
x  y  z
```

Now say you want to move this point in space, also called *translating* the point. What you need to know is how far to move it on each axis. You can put this in a *translation matrix*. This is another 1×3 matrix that looks something like this:

```
dx  dy  dz
```

Here, dx, dy, and dz are the distances to move on each axis. Now you need to somehow apply the transformation matrix to the point matrix. This is done with matrix addition, which is pretty simple. You just add each corresponding cell together to make a new matrix containing the sum of each cell. Obviously, to add two matrices, they need to be the same size. For translation, you do this:

```
x  y  z  +  dx  dy  dz  = (x + dx)  (y + dy)  (z + dz)
```

Here, the resulting matrix could be called x1, y1, z1, and contains the new position of the point after it has been translated. Let's try it with some actual numbers. Say your point was at 100, 50, 75 on x, y, z, and you wanted to move it -10, 20, -35. Here's how that would look:

```
100  50  75  +  -10  20  -35  =  (100 - 10)  (50 + 20)  (75 - 35)
```

Thus, when you perform the addition, you get 90, 70, 40 as the point's new position. Pretty simple, right? You probably already noticed the correlation to velocity, where the velocity on each axis is added to the position on that axis. Same deal here. We're just looking at it a bit differently.

If you had a larger matrix, you would still carry on the same way, matching up the cells. We won't be dealing with matrix addition for anything larger than three by one matrices here, but I'll give you an abstract example:

```
a  b  c      j  k  l      (a + j)  (b + k)  (c + l)
d  e  f  +   m  n  o  =   (d + m)  (e + n)  (f + o)
g  h  i      p  q  r      (g + p)  (h + q)  (i + r)
```

And that's about all you need to know about matrix addition. After I cover matrix multiplication, I'll show you how to put together some actual functions to use in a matrix-based 3D engine.

Matrix multiplication

Much more common for doing 3D transformations is *matrix multiplication*, which is usually used for scaling and rotating. We won't actually be using 3D scaling in this book, as the examples cover using either points, which can't be scaled, or movie clips, which do not have any 3D "thickness" and are therefore only scaled in two dimensions. Of course, you could build a more complex engine that could scale an entire 3D solid. You'd then need to write additional functions that would alter the 3D points making up the solid based on the new size. That's beyond the scope of what we're doing here, but since scaling is a very simple and clear demonstration of matrix multiplication, I'll run you through an example.

Scaling with a matrix

First you'll need to know an object's existing width, height, and depth—in other words, its measurement of size on each of the three axes. This of course creates a 3X1 matrix:

```
w  h  d
```

As you probably realize, w, h, and d stand for width, height, and depth. Next you need a scaling matrix like the following:

```
sx   0   0
 0  sy   0
 0   0  sz
```

Here, sx, sy, and sz are the percentages to scale on that particular axis. These would be in terms of a fraction, so that 1.0 is 100%, 2.0 is 200%, 0.5 is 50%, etc. You'll see why the matrix is laid out this way in a minute.

One thing you need to know about matrix multiplication is that in order to multiply two matrices, the first matrix must have the same number of *columns* as the second one has *rows*. The first one can have any number of rows, and the second can have any number of columns, as long as these criteria have been met. In this case, you are fine, as the first matrix has three columns (w, h, d), and the scaling matrix has three rows.

So, how do you multiply these things? Let me just go ahead and do it and see if you can see the pattern:

```
                 sx   0   0
w  h  d    *      0  sy   0
                  0   0  sz
```

This produces the following matrix as a result:

```
(w*sx + h*0  + d*0)  (w*0  + h*sy + d*0)  (w*0  + h*0  + d*sz)
```

When you get rid of all the zeros, it winds up as this:

```
(w*sx)  (h*sy)  (d*sz)
```

This is pretty logical, as you are multiplying the width (x axis measurement) by the x scaling factor, the height by the y scaling factor, and the depth by the z scaling factor. But, what exactly did we do there? All those zeros are kind of occluding things, so let's abstract it a bit so the pattern is clearer.

```
                a  b  c
u  v  w    *    d  e  f
                g  h  i
```

Now you can see the pattern emerge in this result:

```
(u*a + v*d  + w*g)  (u*b  + v*e + w*h)  (u*c  + v*f  + w*i)
```

You can see that you move across the first row of the first matrix (u, v, w) and multiply by each first element in each row of the second (a, d, g). Adding those together gives you the first element for the first row of the result. Doing the same with the second column of the second matrix (b, e, h) gives you the second column result.

If you have more than one row in the first matrix, you then repeat the actions with that second row, which gives you the second row of the result:

```
u  v  w         a  b  c
x  y  z    *    d  e  f
                g  h  i
```

which gives you this 3X2 matrix as a result:

```
(u*a + v*d  + w*g)  (u*b  + v*e + w*h)  (u*c  + v*f  + w*i)
(x*a + y*d  + z*g)  (x*b  + y*e + z*h)  (x*c  + y*f  + z*i)
```

Now let's see some matrix multiplication in something that you will actually use—coordinate rotation. Hopefully the scaling example will make it more clear what we're doing.

Coordinate rotation with a matrix

First of all, you need to dig up your 3D point matrix:

```
x  y  z
```

This will hold the coordinates of the point you want to rotate. Now of course, you need a rotation matrix. As you know, you can rotate on any one of three axes. You'll create each of these types of rotation as separate matrices. Let's start with x axis rotation matrix:

```
1    0    0
0   cos  sin
0  -sin  cos
```

Now you have some sines and cosines in there, and the obvious question might be, "The sine or cosine of what?" Well, it's the sine or cosine of whatever angle you're rotating by. If you're rotating that point by 45 degrees, it would be the sine and cosine of 45 degrees. (Of course, in code, you'd use radians.)

Now, let's perform matrix multiplication with this and a 3D point matrix and see what results you get.

```
                  1    0    0
x  y  z    *      0   cos  sin
                  0  -sin  cos
```

For that, you get

```
(x*1 + y*0  + z*0)  (x*0  + y*cos - z*sin)  (x*0  + y*sin  + z*cos)
```

Cleaning that up gives you

```
(x)  (y*cos - z*sin)  (z*cos + y*sin)
```

This translates roughly to the following in ActionScript:

```
x = x;
y = Math.cos(angle) * y - Math.sin(angle) * z;
z = Math.cos(angle) * z + Math.sin(angle) * y;
```

Now, if you think back to Chapter 10, where I discussed coordinate rotation, you'll see this is exactly how you were accomplishing x axis rotation. This isn't a big surprise, as matrix math is just a different way of looking at and organizing various formulas and equations.

From here, you can easily create a matrix for y axis rotation:

```
 cos  0  sin
  0   1   0
-sin  0  cos
```

And finally, one for rotation on the z axis:

```
 cos  sin  0
-sin  cos  0
  0    0   1
```

It would be good practice to go ahead and multiply each of these by an x, y, z matrix and verify that you get the same formulas you used for coordinate rotation on those two axes in Chapter 10.

Coding with matrices

OK, you know enough of the basics to start putting this stuff into code. You'll be re-creating a file similar to ch15_12.fla from Chapter 15, so you might want to have that file open as a reference. Actually, you can reuse quite a bit from that file. In ch18_01.fla, I kept the same ball movie clip in the library, exported with the linkage name ball, and then just stripped out the rotation code from ch15_12.fla's code. I replaced that code with a couple of function calls to rotateX and rotateY. Of course, your next step will be to create those functions, but here is your starting point:

```
var numBalls:Number = 50;
var fl:Number = 250;
var vpX:Number = Stage.width / 2;
var vpY:Number = Stage.height / 2;
```

```
init();
function init() {
      for (var i:Number = 0; i<numBalls; i++) {
            var ball:MovieClip = attachMovie("ball", "ball" + i, i);
            ball.x = Math.random() * 200 - 100;
            ball.y = Math.random() * 200 - 100;
            ball.z = Math.random() * 200 - 100;
      }
}

function onEnterFrame():Void {
      for (var i:Number=0;i<numBalls;i++) {
            var ball:MovieClip = this["ball" + i];

            var angleY:Number = (_xmouse - vpX) * .001;
            rotateX(ball, angleX);

            var angleX:Number = (_ymouse - vpY) * .001;
            rotateY(ball, angleY);

            if (ball.z <= -fl) {
                  ball._visible = false;
            } else {
                  ball._visible = true;
                  var scale:Number = fl / (fl + ball.z);
                  ball._xscale = ball._yscale = scale*100;
                  ball._x = vpX + ball.x * scale;
                  ball._y = vpY + ball.y * scale;
                  ball.swapDepths(-ball.z);
            }
      }
}
```

First create the rotateX function. This will take the ball's x, y, z coordinates, put these in a 1×3 matrix, and then create an x rotation matrix based on the given angle. These matrices will be in the form of arrays. Finally, it will multiply these two matrices together using the matrixMultiply function, which you also need to create! The result of the multiplication will be another array, so you have to assign those values back to the ball's x, y, and z coordinates.

```
function rotateX(ball:MovieClip, angle:Number):Void
{
      var position:Array = [ball.x, ball.y, ball.z];

      var sin:Number = Math.sin(angle);
      var cos:Number = Math.cos(angle);
      var xRotMatrix:Array = new Array();
      xRotMatrix[0] = [1,   0,    0 ];
      xRotMatrix[1] = [0,  cos, sin];
      xRotMatrix[2] = [0, -sin, cos]
```

```
        var result:Array = matrixMultiply(position, xRotMatrix);
        ball.x = result[0];
        ball.y = result[1];
        ball.z = result[2];
}
```

And here is the matrix multiplication function:

```
function matrixMultiply(matrixA:Array, matrixB:Array):Array
{
        var result:Array = new Array();
        result[0] = matrixA[0] * matrixB[0][0] +
                    matrixA[1] * matrixB[1][0] +
                    matrixA[2] * matrixB[2][0];

        result[1] = matrixA[0] * matrixB[0][1] +
                    matrixA[1] * matrixB[1][1] +
                    matrixA[2] * matrixB[2][1];

        result[2] = matrixA[0] * matrixB[0][2] +
                    matrixA[1] * matrixB[1][2] +
                    matrixA[2] * matrixB[2][2];
        return result;
}
```

Now this particular matrix multiplication function is hard-coded to multiply a 3×1 matrix by a 3×3 matrix, since that's what you'll be doing in each case. You could use `for` loops to make a more dynamic function that could handle any sized matrices, but let's keep things simple here.

Finally, create your `rotateY` function. If you understand the `rotateX` function, this one should look pretty obvious. You just create a y rotation matrix instead of an x rotation matrix.

```
function rotateY(ball:MovieClip, angle:Number):Void
{
        var position:Array = [ball.x, ball.y, ball.z];

        var sin:Number = Math.sin(angle);
        var cos:Number = Math.cos(angle);
        var yRotMatrix:Array = new Array();
        yRotMatrix[0] = [ cos, 0, sin];
        yRotMatrix[1] = [  0,  1,  0 ];
        yRotMatrix[2] = [-sin, 0, cos]

        var result:Array = matrixMultiply(position, yRotMatrix);
        ball.x = result[0];
        ball.y = result[1];
        ball.z = result[2];
}
```

And there you have it. You could also create a `rotateZ` function if you want. Since we don't actually need that for this example, I'll leave it as an exercise for you to do on your own.

Now if you run `ch18_01.fla` and compare it to `ch15_12.fla`, I think you'll find that the original from Chapter 15 runs a lot smoother. The one using matrix math may have a bit of noticeable choppiness on your computer, as it does on mine. The reason for this is that you're already performing quite extensive math for the 3D rotations, scaling, etc. When you get into matrix math, you wind up doing a whole lot of extra calculations. When you start multiplying the matrices, you're actually doing four multiply-times-zero operations, and adding the four results to other numbers. That's eight math operations that essentially do nothing at all. Multiply that times 50 objects, and two rotations per frame, and you get 800 superfluous calculations per frame! I guess that explains the choppiness.

What I'm trying to say is that the use of matrices of 3D in Flash is not very efficient for large numbers of objects at this time. Some people still prefer to use matrices for 3D though, and it works fine for a small number of objects.

Even if you don't use matrices for 3D, you'll still find them useful for other purposes, and I'll cover these next. Use of matrices in 3D provides a nice introduction, as you can see how they relate to formulas you already know. Also, matrices are used extensively for 3D in other languages that are far more efficient than ActionScript currently. In these languages, you can afford to spend a few CPU cycles in order to gain the neat organization that matrices can offer your code. If you wind up attempting 3D animation in anything other than Flash, you are bound to run into matrices again. And, who knows where the Flash player will be in a few years? There may come a day when these techniques are perfectly suitable for Flash.

The Matrix class in Flash 8

As mentioned, one good reason for knowing about matrices is that Flash 8 ActionScript embraces them so much. In fact, there's even a built-in `Matrix` class in Flash now. If you take a look at the Flash help files, for the `flash.display.Matrix` class, you'll find that they are quite clear and informative. If you've understood everything up to now in this chapter, you should have no problem grasping that material. Since it is so well written, I won't waste space rehashing it all, but I will give a quick summary and a couple of examples.

A matrix is used mainly to transform (rotate, scale, and translate) a movie clip. Any movie clip now has a property called `transform`. This is an object that contains another property called `matrix`. If you create an instance of the `Matrix` class and assign it to this `movieclip.transform.matrix` property, it will alter the form, size, or position of that movie clip. You'll see some concrete examples very shortly.

Basically, the matrix in the `Matrix` class is a 3×3 matrix set up like so:

```
a  b  tx
c  d  ty
u  v  w
```

The u, v, and w are set to 0, 0, and 1 automatically and are used internally. They are unchangeable, so you don't have to worry about them. (More explanation on what they actually are and do appears in the help files.) You can create a new Matrix with the following syntax:

```
import flash.display.Matrix;
var myMatrix:Matrix = new Matrix(a, b, c, d, tx, ty);
```

So what do all these letters mean? Well, tx and ty are pretty easy. These control the position of the movie clips by translating it on the x and y axis. The a, b, c, and d are a little trickier because they are so dependent on each other. If you set b and c to 0, you can use a and d to scale the movie clip on the x and y axes. If you set a and d to 1, you can use b and c to skew the movie clip on the y and x axes, respectively. Finally, you can use a, b, c, and d together in a way that I'm sure you'll find very familiar. In this case, they would be laid out like this:

```
 cos  sin  tx
-sin  cos  ty
  u    v   w
```

Of course, you can see that this contains a rotation matrix, and it will indeed rotate the movie clip. Naturally, cos and sin in this example refer to the cosine and sine of a particular angle (in radians) that you wish to rotate the movie clip by. Let's try that one out.

File ch18_02.fla contains a movie clip on stage, with an instance name clip. You can put any content in it that you want. I put a small photo of a flower in mine. Here is the code to go on frame 1 of the timeline:

```
import flash.geom.Matrix;

var angle:Number = 0;
onEnterFrame = function()
{
      angle += .05;
      var cos:Number = Math.cos(angle);
      var sin:Number = Math.sin(angle);
      clip.transform.matrix = new Matrix(cos, sin,
                                         -sin, cos,
                                          270, 200);
}
```

Here you have an angle variable that increases on each frame. The code finds the sine and cosine of that angle and feeds them into a new Matrix object, in the way specified for rotation. I've also applied a 270, 200 translation, which centers the clip. (I hard-coded these to the dimensions of my movie for clarity, but in a finished project, you probably want to use fractions of Stage.width and Stage.height.) The new matrix is assigned to the transform.matrix property of the clip. Test this and you have a spinning picture, which Figure 18-2 gives you some idea of.

Figure 18-2. Rotation with a matrix

Now, you may be wondering why you don't just change the _rotation property of the clip. It's true that in this simple case, that would be a much simpler solution. But there may be many cases where you are dealing with a lot of angles and radians and sines and cosines, and it will actually be much easier to just assign a matrix like this, rather than converting everything back to degrees and changing the _rotation.

But for another, far more practical demonstration, let's try skewing. *Skewing* means stretching something out on one axis so that one part goes one way and the other part goes the other way. *Italic letters* are an example of a skew. The top part of the letters goes to the right and the bottom part to the left. This is something that has always been notoriously tricky in Flash, but is incredibly easy with the Matrix class. As I said earlier, you set a and d of the matrix to 1. The b property is the amount to skew on the y axis, and the c controls the skew on the x axis. Let's try an x skew first. In ch18_03.fla, I replaced the clip contents with a dynamic text field with a bunch of text in it, set the font to Arial and embedded the font, as depicted in Figure 18-3.

It's important to embed the font if you are doing any kind of transformation on text; otherwise, the text will disappear when it is rotated, scaled, etc.

Then I put this code on frame 1:

```
import flash.geom.Matrix;

onEnterFrame = function()
{
      var skewX:Number = (_xmouse - 270) * .01;
      flower.transform.matrix = new Matrix(1, 0, skewX, 1, 270, 200);
}
```

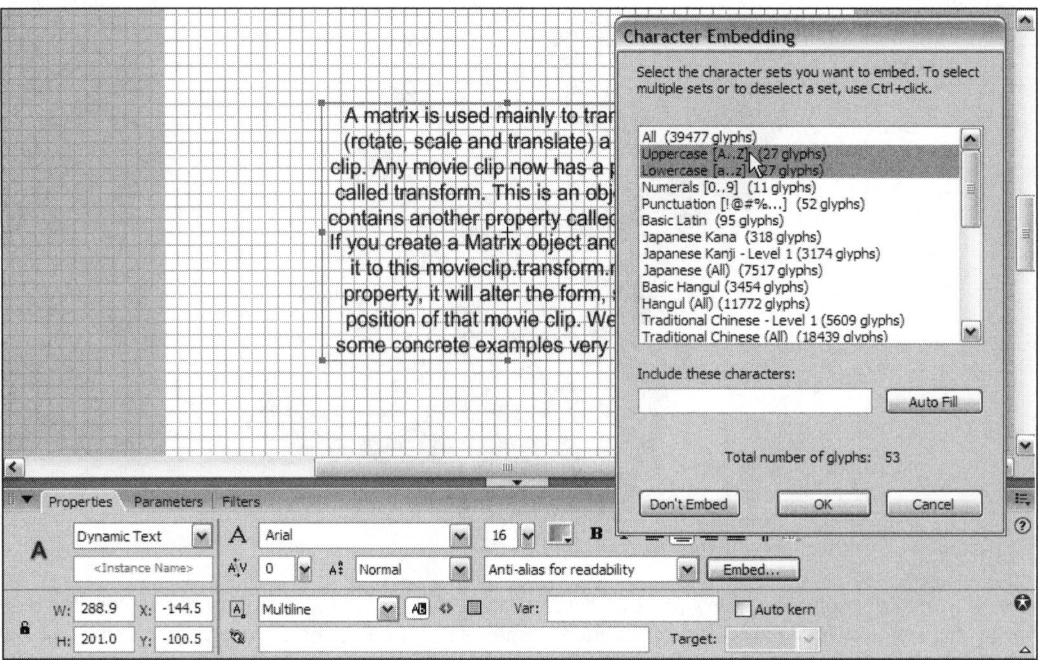

Figure 18-3. Embedding the fonts before transforming a text field

Here I made the skewX variable relative to the mouse's x position, offset from the center of the stage. I then multiplied that by .01 to keep the skew in a manageable range, and fed that into the matrix.

Now when you test this movie, you will see how you can skew an entire movie clip, including text, as you see in Figure 18-4. While this was possible before the Matrix class, if you know anyone who has tried it, show them the preceding code, and watch them start drooling! Or, if you tried it yourself, then you already know what I mean.

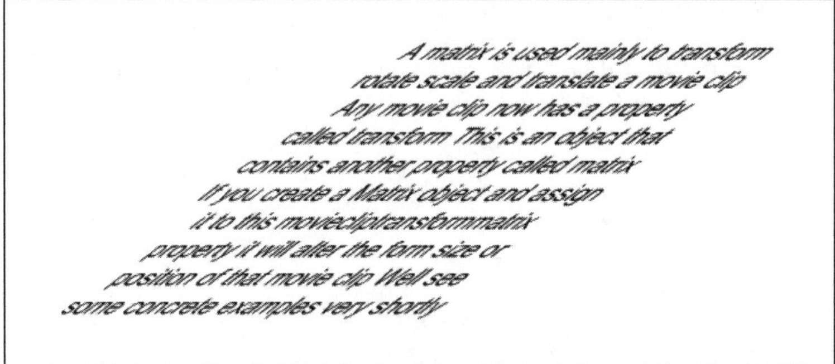

Figure 18-4. Movie clip with text, skewed on the x axis

In ch18_04.fla, I did the same thing with the y axis:

```
import flash.geom.Matrix;

onEnterFrame = function()
{
      var skewX:Number = (_xmouse - 270) * .01;
      var skewY:Number = (_ymouse - 200) * .01;
      flower.transform.matrix = new Matrix(1, skewY, skewX, 1, 270, 200);
}
```

Figure 18-5 gives you a feel for how skewing a movie on two axes turns out.

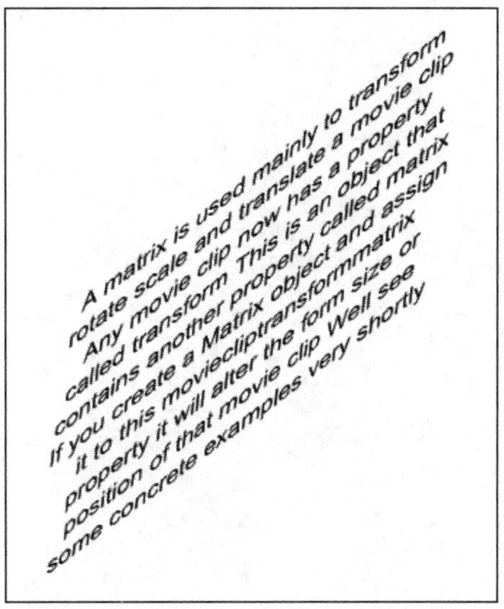

Figure 18-5. Movie clip with text, skewed on both axes

It's pretty amazing to be able to do this kind of effect so easily. If you aren't sure where you would use this kind of effect, I'll tell you that movie clip skewing is used quite often for pseudo-3D. As you move your mouse around in the last example, you can probably already see how it appears to have some perspective, as if the text was leaning over and spinning around. It's not particularly accurate 3D, as the letters that appear to be far away from you are actually the same size as those close to you. But it can be used for some pretty convincing effects. There are a few tutorials out there on the Web that show you how to accomplish this kind of pseudo-3D with skewing. Use of the Matrix class will probably cut the code in those examples in half.

Again, be sure to check out the help files for the Matrix class, as there are a *lot* of other goodies in there. Also, realize that that is not the only place Flash 8 utilizes matrices. You might want to take a look at ColorMatrixFilter, ConvolutionFilter, the various MovieClip fill and gradient methods, and the flash.geom.Transform class. Matrices galore in there!

Summary

I've covered the basics of what matrices are, how to use them and combine them, and created some pretty cool effects with them in this chapter. Now that you have the concepts in your head, you're ready to take advantage of the power that matrices can offer, and hopefully won't shy away from using them when you encounter them in the built-in methods of Flash 8, as you surely will.

};shape.targetHeight = shape._height;
shape.onEnterFrame = function() {
var speed = 5;
this._width += (this.targetWidth - this._width)/speed;
this._height += (this.targetHeight - this._height)/speed;

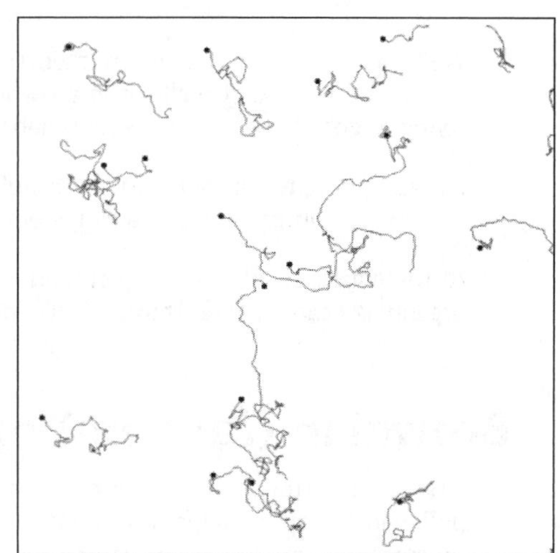

Chapter 19

TIPS AND TRICKS

What we'll cover in this chapter:

- Brownian (random) motion
- Random distribution
- Interval- and timer-based animation
- Collisions between same-mass objects
- Integrating sound
- Useful formulas

Well, you made it to the last chapter. This one I set aside for all the little things I really wanted to tell you about, but didn't really fit in anywhere else, or would have distracted from the main points I was trying to get across in some other chapter.

I'm also going to regroup all the formulas we've been coming up with and listing at the end of each chapter, so this can serve as a single point of reference for them.

As these various subjects are just random bits and pieces (albeit useful bits), there's not a whole lot of organizing I can do here. Thus each section will be a standalone unit. So, without further ado, here we go.

Brownian (random) motion

First some history. One day, a botanist named Robert Brown was trying to look at some grains of pollen in a drop of water and found that they were randomly moving around. Even though there was no current or motion in the water, those little grains just never settled down. He found the same thing happened with dust particles, so it wasn't like the pollen was swimming. Even though he hadn't the slightest idea why they did this, and neither he or anyone else really offered an explanation for several decades, he somehow got the phenomenon named after him—just for noticing it!

The way Brownian motion is explained these days is that the zillions of water molecules in a drop of water are in constant motion, even if the water appears to be still. These molecules collide with the pollen or dust particle, and in doing so, transfer some of their momentum to it. Since even a speck of dust is a million times heavier than a single water molecule, each collision doesn't do much. But when you have so many millions of collisions per second, it starts to add up.

Now some of the molecules might be hitting on one side, and some on the other. Overall, they are going to generally average out. But over time, you are going to see fluctuations, where more are hitting, say, on the left side, and it's enough to start the particle moving a bit to the right. Then more might hit on the bottom, and the particle starts to move upwards. Again, these eventually average out, so it doesn't usually result in much momentum in any one direction. You get this random floating-around action.

You can easily simulate this in Flash. On each frame, you just calculate random numbers to add to the x and y velocity of a moving object. The random numbers should be calculated to be either positive or negative, and usually quite small, say in a range from –0.1 to +0.1. You can do that like so:

```
vx += Math.random() * 0.2 - 0.1;
vy += Math.random() * 0.2 - 0.1;
```

Multiplying the random decimal by 0.2 gives you a number from 0.0 to 0.2. Subtracting 0.1 makes it –0.1 to 0.1. It's important to add some friction into this, otherwise the velocities tend to build up, and things start zipping around unnaturally. In `ch19_01.fla`, I've created 50 particles and have them floating around with Brownian motion. The particle is a movie clip with a small black circle in it named dot and exported with that name. Here is the code:

```
var numDots:Number = 50;
var friction:Number = 0.95;

init();
function init():Void
{
	for(var i:Number = 0;i<numDots;i++)
	{
		var dot:MovieClip = attachMovie("dot", "dot" + i, i);
		dot._x = Math.random() * Stage.width;
		dot._y = Math.random() * Stage.height;
		dot.vx = 0;
		dot.vy = 0;
	}
}

function onEnterFrame():Void
{
	for(var i:Number = 0;i<numDots;i++)
	{
		var dot:MovieClip = this["dot" + i];
		dot.vx += Math.random() * 0.2 - 0.1;
		dot.vy += Math.random() * 0.2 - 0.1;
		dot._x += dot.vx;
		dot._y += dot.vy;
		dot.vx *= friction;
		dot.vy *= friction;

		if(dot._x > Stage.width)
		{
			dot._x = 0;
		}
		else if(dot._x < 0)
		{
			dot._x = Stage.width;
		}
		if(dot._y > Stage.height)
		{
			dot._y = 0;
		}
		else if(dot._y < 0)
		{
			dot._y = Stage.height;
		}
	}
}
```

Most of this is old news to you, so I've put the relevant bits in bold.

Figure 19-1 shows how running this code appears on screen.

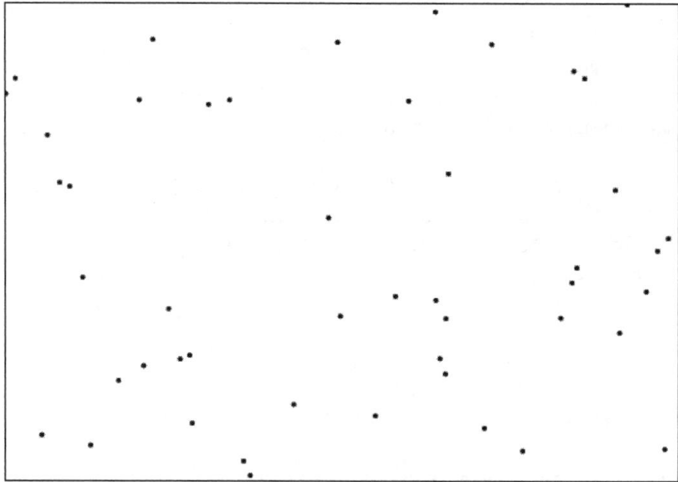

Figure 19-1. Brownian motion

In ch19_02.fla, I reduced the number of dots to 20. I then added the line

```
lineStyle(1, 0, 50);
```

to the init function, and changed the first part of onEnterFrame to include some drawing code.

```
function onEnterFrame():Void
{
	for(var i:Number = 0;i<numDots;i++)
	{
		var dot:MovieClip = this["dot" + i];
		moveTo(dot._x, dot._y);
		dot.vx += Math.random() * 0.2 - 0.1;
		dot.vy += Math.random() * 0.2 - 0.1;
		dot._x += dot.vx;
		dot._y += dot.vy;
		lineTo(dot._x, dot._y);
		dot.vx *= friction;
		dot.vy *= friction;
```

This draws a line from where each dot is before it moves, to where it is after it moves. So it draws its own path, as shown in Figure 19-2. You'll often see these kinds of diagrams if you look up the term Brownian motion.

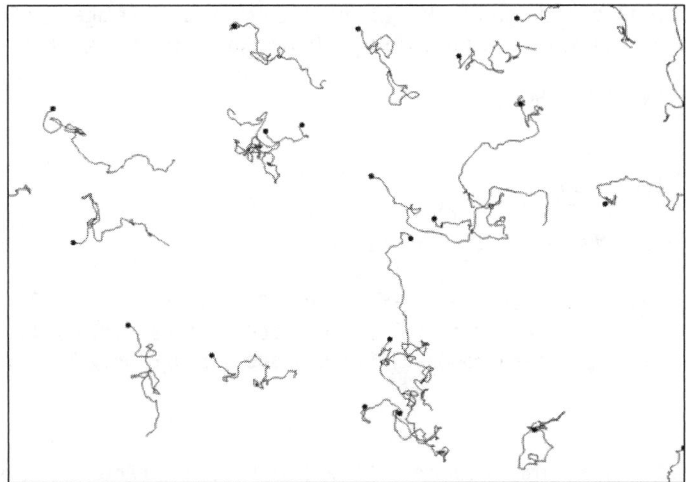

Figure 19-2. Brownian motion with trails

Brownian motion is useful any time you want something to be moving around as if it was floating with no volition of its own, with no forces really acting on it. You can also add it to a movie clip that has some other motion applied to it, to give it a sense of randomness. An example would be a fly or bee that's buzzing around. You might have it moving along in some path, but adding in some random motion could make it look much more lifelike.

Random distribution

From time to time, you may want to create a bunch of objects and place them at random positions. You've seen how this is done many times throughout the book. Here we'll look at a few different methods of doing this, and the different results that they will give you.

Square distribution

If you want the objects to randomly cover the entire stage, that's pretty simple. Just choose a random number up to the stage's width for x, and a random number up to its height for y. In fact, you did just that in the preceding section:

```
for(var i:Number = 0;i<numDots;i++)
{
	var dot:MovieClip = attachMovie("dot", "dot" + i, i);
	dot._x = Math.random() * Stage.width;
	dot._y = Math.random() * Stage.height;
	...
```

But say you wanted to kind of clump the dots in near the center of the stage, say 100 pixels to either side, top or bottom of the center. You could do something like the following, which is in `ch19_03.fla`:

```
var numDots:Number = 50;

init();
function init():Void
{
	for(var i:Number = 0;i<numDots;i++)
	{
		var dot:MovieClip = attachMovie("dot", "dot" + i, i);
		dot._x = Math.random() * 200 - 100 + Stage.width / 2;
		dot._y = Math.random() * 200 - 100 + Stage.height / 2;
	}
}
```

This creates a random number from –100 to +100 and adds it to the center point of the stage, so all of the dots will be no farther than 100 pixels on either axis from the center. Figure 19-3 shows what that gives you.

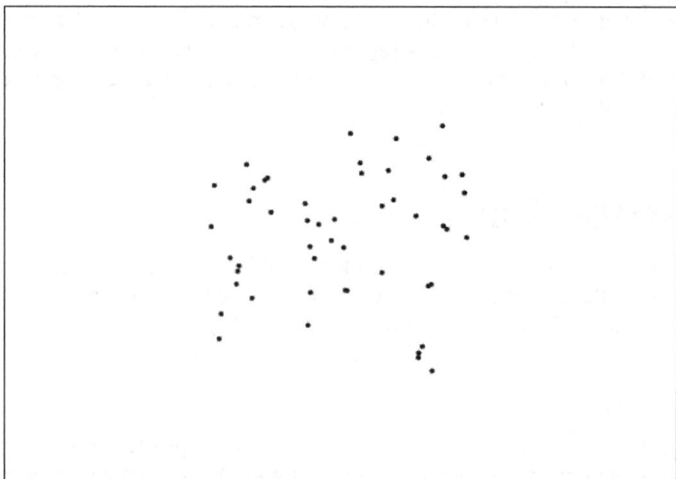

Figure 19-3. Randomly placed dots

Not too bad. But if you crowd them in a bit more by making a lot more dots (300) and reducing the area to 100 by 100, you'll notice something odd starting to happen. Here's the code from `ch19_04.fla`:

```
var numDots:Number = 300;

init();
function init():Void
{
	for(var i:Number = 0;i<numDots;i++)
	{
```

```
            var dot:MovieClip = attachMovie("dot", "dot" + i, i);
            dot._x = Math.random() * 100 - 50 + Stage.width / 2;
            dot._y = Math.random() * 100 - 50 + Stage.height / 2;
        }
    }
```

And Figure 19-4 shows what you get.

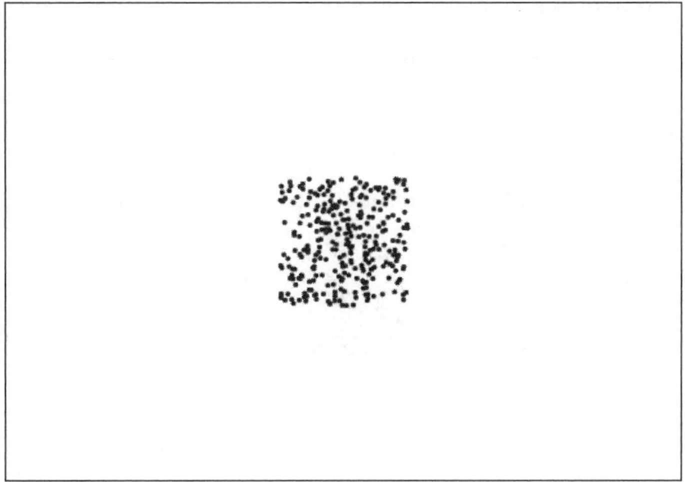

Figure 19-4. This method starts to form a square. Not so random looking anymore.

As you see, the dots are starting to form a square. Maybe that's OK, but if you are trying to make some kind of explosion or star system or something of the sort, a square doesn't look too natural. If a square distribution is not exactly what you are looking for, try moving on to the next technique.

Circular distribution

While slightly more complex than a square distribution, circular distribution really isn't too hard to do. First you need to know the radius of your circle. Let's keep it at 50, to match the last example. This will be the maximum radius that a dot can be placed from the center. You'll take a random number from zero to that number to use as the radius for each dot. Then you'll choose a random angle from 0 to PI * 2 radians (360 degrees), and use a quick bit of trig to find the x and y position of the dot. Here's the code from ch19_05.fla:

```
var numDots:Number = 300;
var maxRadius:Number = 50;

init();
function init():Void
{
    for(var i:Number = 0;i<numDots;i++)
    {
```

```
            var dot:MovieClip = attachMovie("dot", "dot" + i, i);
            var radius:Number = Math.random() * maxRadius;
            var angle:Number = Math.random() * (Math.PI * 2);
            dot._x = Math.cos(angle) * radius + Stage.width / 2;
            dot._y = Math.sin(angle) * radius + Stage.height / 2;
      }
}
```

And that gives you a picture like the one in Figure 19-5.

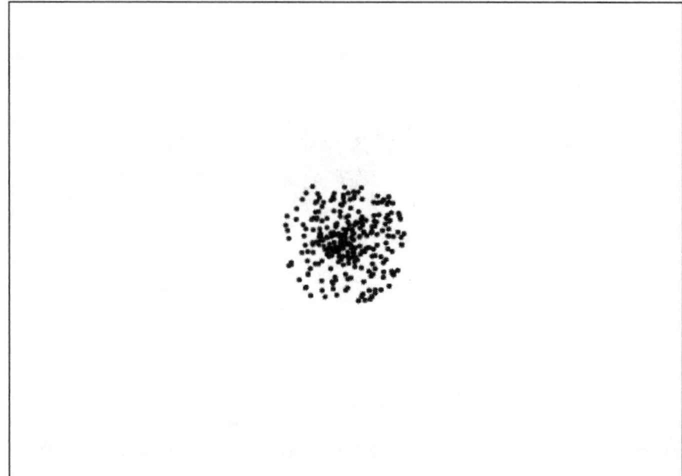

Figure 19-5. Circular random distribution

This is much more natural for most of the types of applications I mentioned earlier. However, you might notice that the dots seem to be even more clumped around the center of the circle. This is because an even distribution exists along the radius, meaning there are as many dots in the center as near the edge. But because the center has less space, they are more crowded.

Again, this may be fine for some applications, but Sean O'Shell (`http://www.pixelwit.com`) once challenged me to come up with a way of making the dots appear more uniformly distributed throughout the circle. I have to admit I was stumped, and the solutions I tried were pretty complex. Finally, he gave me a very simple solution, as you can see in `ch19_06.fla`:

```
var numDots:Number = 300;
var maxRadius:Number = 50;

init();
function init():Void
{
      for(var i:Number = 0;i<numDots;i++)
      {
            var dot:MovieClip = attachMovie("dot", "dot" + i, i);
```

```
            var radius:Number = Math.sqrt(Math.random()) * maxRadius;
            var angle:Number = Math.random() * (Math.PI * 2);
            dot._x = Math.cos(angle) * radius + Stage.width / 2;
            dot._y = Math.sin(angle) * radius + Stage.height / 2;
        }
}
```

By taking the square root of the random number, it has a bias towards 1 and away from 0, which is just enough to smooth out the distribution. You can see the result in Figure 19-6. Nice one, Sean!

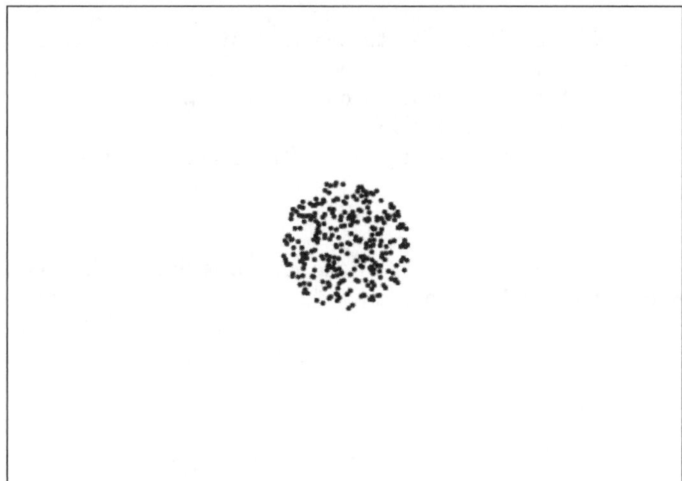

Figure 19-6. A smoother distribution

Biased distribution

Finally, you may want to give the random objects free range over the entire stage, but have them tend to show up in the middle area. You'd find some out on the edges, but the closer to the center you got, the more there would be. This would be somewhat like the first circular example, but applied to a rectangular area.

You do this by generating multiple random numbers for each position, and then averaging them to get the final value. For example, say the stage is 500 pixels wide. If you generate an x position for each object with just one random number, then each object has an equal chance of being anywhere in that range. But if you generate two random numbers from 0 to 500, and take the average, there's a bit higher chance that it will be somewhere in the middle rather than out towards the edges.

Let's look at that in a little more depth. There is some chance that both numbers might be in a "high" range, say from 300 to 500. There's about the same chance that both might be in a low range, from 0 to 200. But there's a higher chance that one will be high and one low, or one middle and one high or low, or even both in the middle. All of these possibilities will average out to place the dot closer to the middle.

OK, let's see it in code. As usual, you'll start on one dimension. Using the same dot movie clip as the previous examples, here's the code (ch19_07.fla):

```
var numDots:Number = 300;
var maxRadius:Number = 50;

init();
function init():Void
{
      for(var i:Number = 0;i<numDots;i++)
      {
            var dot:MovieClip = attachMovie("dot", "dot" + i, i);
            var x1:Number = Math.random() * Stage.width;
            var x2:Number = Math.random() * Stage.width;
            dot._x = (x1 + x2) / 2;
            dot._y = Stage.height / 2 + Math.random() * 50 - 25;
      }
}
```

Here you are generating two random numbers, x1 and x2, and setting the dot's x position to the average of them. The y position is simply randomly near the center. This gives you something like this:

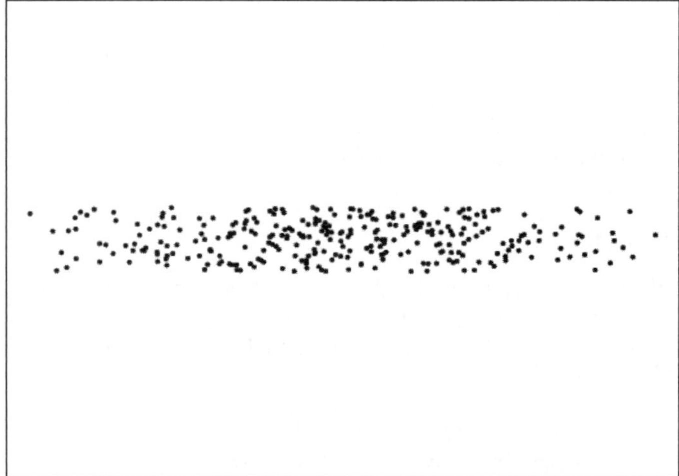

Figure 19-7. Biased distribution with one iteration

The effect isn't too pronounced here, but you can see that there is a bit more clumping in the center, and more space at the edges. Creating more random numbers and averaging them will make it more obvious. You'll move this into a for loop to make it dynamic (ch19_08.fla):

```
var numDots:Number = 300;
var maxRadius:Number = 50;
var iterations:Number = 6;
```

```
init();
function init():Void
{
      for(var i:Number = 0;i<numDots;i++)
      {
            var dot:MovieClip = attachMovie("dot", "dot" + i, i);
            var x:Number = 0;
            for(var j:Number = 0;j<iterations;j++)
            {
                  x += Math.random() * Stage.width;
            }
            dot._x = x / iterations;
            dot._y = Stage.height / 2 + Math.random() * 50 - 25;
      }
}
```

Here the iterations variable controls how many numbers you will average. You start out with the variable x equal to zero, and add each random number to it. Finally, you divide that by the number of iterations for the final value. This gives you a picture like the one in Figure 19-8.

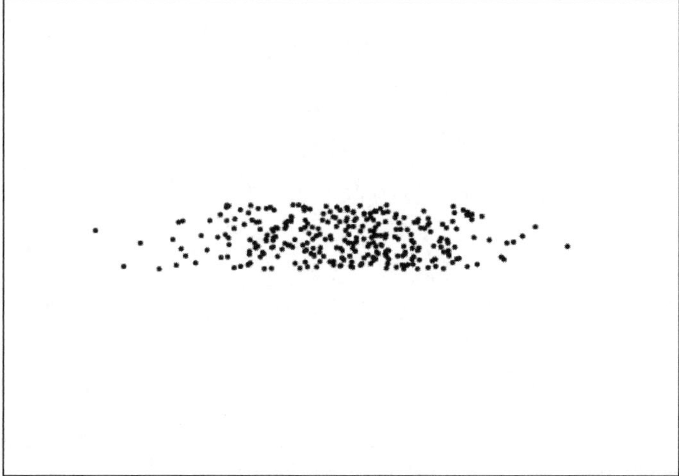

Figure 19-8. Biased distribution with six iterations

It is now easy to do the same thing for the y axis, and in `ch19_09.fla`, you do just that:

```
var numDots:Number = 300;
var maxRadius:Number = 50;
var iterations:Number = 6;

init();
function init():Void
{
      for(var i:Number = 0;i<numDots;i++)
      {
```

```
                var dot:MovieClip = attachMovie("dot", "dot" + i, i);
                var x:Number = 0;
                for(var j:Number = 0;j<iterations;j++)
                {
                        x += Math.random() * Stage.width;
                }
                dot._x = x / iterations;

                var y:Number = 0;
                for(var j:Number = 0;j<iterations;j++)
                {
                        y += Math.random() * Stage.height;
                }
                dot._y = y / iterations;
        }
}
```

This gives you a distribution like the one in Figure 19-9.

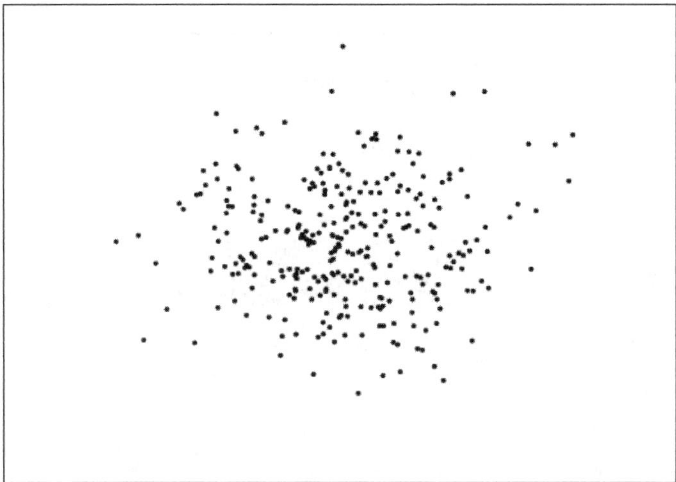

Figure 19-9. Two-dimensional biased distribution.

To me, this is the most random, explosive, star-system-like distribution of them all, though it is also the most intensive to generate. At any rate, you now have at least four ways to generate random positions.

Interval- and timer-based animation

In all the examples in the book so far, animation has been done by placing motion code inside an `onEnterFrame` function. I've always found this to be the simplest method, as the concept of frames is so deeply ingrained in Flash, and it's sitting right there ready for you to use.

However, a lot of people, particularly those coming from non-Flash programming environments, are not so comfortable with this model. To them, an interval-based animation model (using the setInterval function) seems to offer more precise control over the speed of the animation. So we'll take a look at that.

Then we'll look at timer-based animation, a technique that can be used with either frames or intervals.

Interval-based animation

The key methods for interval-based animation are setInterval and clearInterval. You'll also need some other function, analogous to onEnterFrame, that will contain your motion code. Here is the basic syntax for setInterval and clearInterval:

```
var id:Number = setInterval(myFunction, milliseconds);
clearInterval(id);
```

As you can see, setInterval takes two parameters. (There is also a three-parameter version, which you'll find especially useful for class-based code. See the Flash help files for the syntax.) The first is a reference to a function, and the second is how often to run that function, in terms of milliseconds. For example, you could say

```
var id:Number = setInterval(move, 50);
```

As soon as you call this, Flash waits 50 milliseconds, and calls the move function. It calls it again 50 milliseconds later, and again, continuously, until you say

```
clearInterval(id);
```

This ends the execution of that interval. If you are absolutely sure that you never want to stop the interval from running, you don't need to capture its ID. But if you don't, realize that there is no easy way to stop that function from executing.

So, theoretically, setInterval gives you millisecond-level control over the speed of your animation—a vast improvement over frames, which are notoriously inaccurate. However, I say "theoretically," because there are several things to be aware of.

Let's see how to create the first example. File ch19_10.fla is an almost complete copy of ch6_04.fla, which has a ball that moves around the stage and bounces off the edges. All I did was rename the onEnterFrame function to move, and set an interval to run it every 20 milliseconds. I also decreased the frames per second of the movie down to 1, since intervals supposedly have nothing to do with frame rate, right?

```
init();
function init()
{
      top = 0;
      left = 0;
      bottom = Stage.height;
      right = Stage.width;
      ball = attachMovie("ball", "ball", 0);
      ball._x = Stage.width / 2;
```

```
        ball._y = Stage.height / 2;
        vx = Math.random() * 10 - 5;
        vy = Math.random() * 10 - 5;
        id = setInterval(move, 20);
}
function move(Void):Void
{
        ball._x += vx;
        ball._y += vy;
        if (ball._x + ball._width / 2 > right)
        {
                ball._x = right - ball._width / 2;
                vx *= -1;
        }
        else if (ball._x - ball._width / 2 < left)
        {
                ball._x = left + ball._width / 2;
                vx *= -1;
        }
        if (ball._y + ball._height / 2 > bottom)
        {
                ball._y = bottom - ball._height / 2;
                vy *= -1;
        }
        else if (ball._y - ball._height / 2 < top)
        {
                ball._y = top + ball._height / 2;
                vy *= -1;
        }
}
```

This should wind up calling the move function about 50 times per second (1,000 milliseconds divided by 20), which should be sufficient to move the ball around the screen quite smoothly. But, when you run this, you get something entirely unexpected (at least I didn't expect it the first time I saw it). The ball is jumping across the stage at a rate of about one jump per second—which is the frame rate. But each jump is much more than 5 pixels, which is the maximum it could move in any direction per jump (per the random vx and vy assigned). What's going on?

Well, if you think back to Chapters 1 and 2, where I talked about basic animation, you may remember that the model needs to be updated, and then the screen needs to be refreshed based on the new model. Here, the interval function is reliably updating the model and moving the ball 5 pixels every time it runs, but still the screen is only being refreshed when Flash enters a new frame. Simply running a function does not force Flash to redraw.

Fortunately, the good people at Macromedia saw this coming and gave you another little tool to use: updateAfterEvent. This is a function you can call from within certain other functions to force Flash to refresh the screen, even if it is not a scheduled frame redraw.

The updateAfterEvent function can't just be called any time from any old function. As its name implies, it *updates* the screen *after* an *event*. It can be used within onClipEvent blocks and event handler functions for most mouse and key events. And fortunately, it can also be used in a function specified in setInterval. OK, so you fix up the example to add the line

```
updateAfterEvent();
```

as the last statement in the move function (ch19_11.fla).

Now things are definitely better. Much smoother. But if you realize that the ball should be updated 50 times per second, you are basically looking at what should be a 50 fps movie. This means that the ball should be moving quite a bit faster than the original movie from Chapter 4, which was coded at 31 fps. But it's actually moving more slowly.

The problem, it turns out, is that setInterval *is* actually somewhat tied to frame rate. Supposedly, Flash is able to run about ten intervals in any given frame. Since your frame rate is 1 fps, you are actually maxing out at about 10 updates per second. So, if you change the frame rate to 5, you should be able to get the equivalent of 50 fps. On my PC, that still looks pretty jumpy, but if I go up to about 10 fps, it starts looking good.

There is something more should you know about how setInterval works, as it affects how accurate the timing will be. What actually happens is that as soon as the setInterval function is called, Flash waits the specified amount of time and then calls the named function. Only when that function is finished executing does the count for the next interval begin. As an example, say you have set the interval to run every 20 milliseconds. But say there is so much code in that function, that it takes 30 milliseconds to execute it all. In this case, your function will actually run about every 50 milliseconds. As there is no way to accurately determine how fast code will run on the end user's machine, in many cases, interval-based animation winds up being no more accurate than frame-based animation.

If you really need accuracy, timer-based animation is the way to go.

Timer-based animation

Timer-based animation is the method to use if the speed of objects in your movie needs to be constant. This might be the case in many types of games. As you've seen, neither frame- nor interval-based animation can be counted on for a specific rate of playback. A complex movie on an older, slower computer may run at a third or less of the speed it was designed for. As you'll see shortly, when you use a timer, you'll get speed you can count on, no matter what frame rate the final movie ends up running at.

The first thing you need to do is change the way you think about velocity. Up to now, when I said, for example, vx = 5, the units you were using were *pixels per frame*. In other words, the object would move 5 pixels on the x-axis each time a new frame was encountered. In interval-based animation, of course, it would be 5 pixels per interval.

For timer-based animation, you'll actually start using real measurements of time, like seconds. Since you are dealing with a whole second, rather than a small fraction of one, the value needs to be much higher. If you had something moving at 10 pixels per frame at 31 frames per second, that is very roughly 300 pixels per second. Again, I hijacked the bouncing ball movie from Chapter 6, changing the init function to the following (ch19_12.fla):

```
function init()
{
	top = 0;
	left = 0;
	bottom = Stage.height;
	right = Stage.width;
	ball = attachMovie("ball", "ball", 0);
	ball._x = Stage.width / 2;
	ball._y = Stage.height / 2;
	vx = 300;
	vy = 300;
	start = getTimer();
}
```

I bumped up the velocities, as described previously, and left them at hard-coded values, rather than randomly determined. I then created a variable called start, and set it to the result of the function getTimer. The getTimer function is often misunderstood, but is actually quite simple. It returns the number of milliseconds the movie has been running—that's all it does. There is no way to clear it, reset it, change it, or anything else. It's just a counter.

Now, that might seem rather useless, but if you call getTimer once and store its value, and then call it again later and subtract the two values, you will know exactly—down to the millisecond—how much time elapsed between the two.

So here is the strategy: you call getTimer at the beginning of each frame and see how many milliseconds elapsed since the last frame. If you divide that by 1,000, you'll have what fraction of a second elapsed. Since your vx and vy are now in terms of pixels per second, you can multiply them by this fraction and know how much to move the object. Also, don't forget to reset the value of the start variable so you can measure the next frame. Here is the onEnterFrame function of ch19_12.fla:

```
function onEnterFrame(Void):Void
{
	var elapsed:Number = getTimer() - start;
	start = getTimer();
	ball._x += vx * elapsed / 1000;
	ball._y += vy * elapsed / 1000;
	if (ball._x + ball._width / 2 > right)
	{
		ball._x = right - ball._width / 2;
		vx *= -1;
	}
	else if (ball._x - ball._width / 2 < left)
	{
		ball._x = left + ball._width / 2;
		vx *= -1;
	}
	if (ball._y + ball._height / 2 > bottom)
```

```
        {
            ball._y = bottom - ball._height / 2;
            vy *= -1;
        }
        else if (ball._y - ball._height / 2 < top)
        {
            ball._y = top + ball._height / 2;
            vy *= -1;
        }
    }
```

Test that out and you'll see that the ball moves at about the same speed as the original. But the really amazing thing is that you can publish the movie at any frame rate you want, and it will still move at the same speed! Try as high as 120 fps, or as low as 12 fps, and you'll see that the speed of the ball is the same. Of course, the higher rates make for a much smoother movie, and the lower ones are quite jumpy, but the velocity itself should be consistent.

You can apply this technique to any example in the book that contains velocity. In doing so, you'll also need to apply a similar technique to any acceleration or repeated forces, such as gravity, as these are also time based. Values for acceleration actually have to be much larger when converted to this type of animation, because acceleration is defined as distance-per-time interval, per time interval. For example, gravity is approximately 32 feet per second, per second.

So where gravity might be something like 0.5 in a frame-based movie of around 30 fps, it would have to be more like 450 here. That's 0.5 * 30 * 30. Then you would apply it like so:

```
vy += gravity * elapsed / 1000;
```

Go ahead and try gravity applied like this to the last example, with a value of 450. You should find it just about equal to the same frame-based movie with a gravity of 0.5.

One tactic with this kind of technique is to set the movie's frame rate to something very high, like 60. Although nobody's machine will likely meet that actual frame rate, it will guarantee that anybody viewing the movie will see it at the smoothest possible playback possible.

Collisions between same-mass objects

Remember good old Chapter 11 and conservation of momentum? That was some pretty serious code. It happens you can make it a little bit simpler when two objects of the same mass collide. Basically, along the line of collision, such objects simply swap their velocities. While you still have coordinate rotation to determine that line of collision, as well as the object's velocities on it, this wipes out the complex conservation of momentum stuff. To see how it works, let's go back to file `ch11_06.fla`, which we'll use as the base for the next example, `ch19_13.fla`. I'm not going to list all of the code from the original here, as it's quite a big file. But let's take a look at the `for` loop that created all the balls:

```
for(var i:Number = 0;i<numBalls;i++)
{
    var ball:MovieClip = attachMovie("ball", "ball" + i, i);
    ball._x = Math.random() * Stage.width;
```

```
        ball._y = Math.random() * Stage.height;
        ball.vx = Math.random() * 10 - 5;
        ball.vy = Math.random() * 10 - 5;
        ball._xscale = ball._yscale = ball.mass = Math.random() * 250 + 20;
    }
```

For the new file, you'll start by removing that last line, shown in bold. This will make all the balls the same size and remove the notion of mass, effectively giving them all the same mass.

Next you want to go down to the checkCollision function. Find the section that reads like this:

```
// rotate ball0's velocity
var vel0:Object = rotate(ball0.vx, ball0.vy, sine, cosine, true);

// rotate ball1's velocity
var vel1:Object = rotate(ball1.vx, ball1.vy, sine, cosine, true);

// collision reaction
var vxTotal:Number = vel0.x - vel1.x;
vel0.x = ((ball0.mass - ball1.mass) *
          vel0.x + 2 * ball1.mass * vel1.x) /
         (ball0.mass + ball1.mass);
vel1.x = vxTotal + vel0.x;
```

This is the part that finds the velocities along the line of collision, and, along with their masses, figures out the result of the collision. The part labeled "collision reaction" is the part that factors in the conservation of momentum, and this is the part you can get rid of. You can replace that portion with code that simply swaps vel0 and vel1. This makes the whole section just shown look like this:

```
// rotate ball0's velocity
var vel0:Object = rotate(ball0.vx, ball0.vy, sine, cosine, true);

// rotate ball1's velocity
var vel1:Object = rotate(ball1.vx, ball1.vy, sine, cosine, true);

// swap the two velocities
var temp:Object = vel0;
vel0 = vel1;
vel1 = temp;
```

This could be even further optimized, but I'll leave it like this for clarity's sake. Here you've gotten rid of a good bit of math, and if you test the file before and after, you should be seeing the same thing.

Integrating sound

One thing that has been conspicuously absent from this book has been the use of sound. While sound is not directly a part of animation, well-done sound effects can go a long way to making a Flash movie more immersive and realistic.

You can use sound in Flash in different ways. You could add a musical or environmental background track that just plays while your movie is running. In this case, you simply set up the sound to start playing when the movie starts. The easiest way to do that would be to import the music file into the library (by selecting File ➤ Import ➤ Import to Library). Then, open the library and drag the new sound item onto the stage in frame 1. Now the sound will play as soon as your movie starts.

If it is a long song, it might be OK that it just plays once, but if it is a shorter sound, you probably want it to loop. To do this, select the frame that the sound is on, and then look at the Properties panel. You'll see a drop-down list displaying the option Repeat, and next to that a text field with the number 1 in it. You can enter another number to have the sound file play multiple times, or just change the Repeat to Loop, and it will play indefinitely.

But far more relevant to animation would be sounds that play when a certain event happens in a movie. The most obvious would be a collision. A ball hits a wall or another ball, and you hear "bang" or "boing" or "splat" or whatever. For this, a simple timeline-based sound won't do. You need the ability to start the sound via ActionScript.

For this example, I'm again going back to `ch06_04.fla`, with the ball bouncing off the walls. Each time it hits a wall, I want it to make a sound. The new file is saved as `ch19_14.fla`.

First, you are going to need a sound effect to use. There are many sources of free sound effects on the web. One of the most popular sites for sound for Flash is good old FlashKit. In addition to their loops section, which are musical files, they have a sound effect library at `http://www.flashkit.com/soundfx/`. The effects are organized by categories such as Cartoon, Interfaces, Mechanical, etc., and the site has well over 6,000 sound effect files to date, so you should be able to find something there to suit your needs. You can preview the effects right on the page, and when you find one you like, download it. Either wav or mp3 format will be fine. Save it to your hard disk and then import it to your library as demonstrated previously.

After I import a file sound, I usually double-click it and change its name to something more concise. Flash uses the full file name, along with the extension, as a library item name, which is usually a bit much to type in code. For this example, I downloaded a "boing" sound, so I just renamed it `boing`.

Now, to make a sound available to your code, you have to export it for ActionScript. This is done in exactly the same way as exporting a movie clip symbol for ActionScript, as covered in Chapter 2. I chose the default linkage name, `boing`. Now the sound is ready for use.

To use sounds in ActionScript, you need to create a Sound object. This is as simple as saying something like

```
mySound = new Sound();
```

Sound objects are always tied to a particular movie clip instance. If you create it as shown previously, it will be tied to the main timeline, or `_root`. That is fine for this simple example, but if you have multiple sounds and want to control things like their volumes and panning independently (we won't be getting into that here), you'll want to assign them to different movie clips, like so:

```
sound1 = new Sound(mc1);
sound2 = new Sound(mc2);
```

Now that you have a Sound object, you need to tell it what sound file to play. There are different options here, such as loading an external mp3 file, or even streaming an mp3 from a server. But for the purposes of this example, you want it to play the sound you just imported into the library. You do that with attachSound, giving it the linkage name of the sound you want to play.

```
mySound.attachSound("boing");
```

Now your sound is ready to play at your command. All you have to do is say

```
mySound.start();
```

at any point and the sound effect will play. There are optional parameters to start, such as the seconds to offset the sound, and how many times to play the sound, but the default use as shown will play the sound once from the beginning, which usually serves the purpose. Here is the full code for ch19_14.fla, showing the creation of the Sound object, and you can see that whenever the ball hits a wall, it plays that sound.

```
init();
function init()
{
      top = 0;
      left = 0;
      bottom = Stage.height;
      right = Stage.width;
      ball = attachMovie("ball", "ball", 0);
      ball._x = Stage.width / 2;
      ball._y = Stage.height / 2;
      vx = Math.random() * 10 - 5;
      vy = Math.random() * 10 - 5;
      boing = new Sound();
      boing.attachSound("boing");
}
function onEnterFrame(Void):Void
{
      ball._x += vx;
      ball._y += vy;
      if (ball._x + ball._width / 2 > right)
      {
            boing.start();
            ball._x = right - ball._width / 2;
            vx *= -1;
      }
      else if (ball._x - ball._width / 2 < left)
      {
            boing.start();
            ball._x = left + ball._width / 2;
            vx *= -1;
      }
      if (ball._y + ball._height / 2 > bottom)
      {
```

```
            boing.start();
            ball._y = bottom - ball._height / 2;
            vy *= -1;
        }
        else if (ball._y - ball._height / 2 < top)
        {
            boing.start();
            ball._y = top + ball._height / 2;
            vy *= -1;
        }
    }
```

Test the movie and see . . . hear the difference that sound can make. Of course, finding the *right* sounds to use in the right circumstances, and not overdoing it, is an art in itself.

Useful formulas

Throughout the book, I've presented various formulas relating to the different motion and effects you've been creating. I've tried to distill the most useful, and most used, formulas, equations, and code snippets, and list these at the end of each chapter. I also thought it would be useful to have these all in one place, so I've gathered them all together here as a one-shot reference to those things I think you'll need to use the most. I know that I, for one, will have a bookmark on this page.

Chapter 3

Basic trigonometric functions:

```
sine of angle = opposite / hypotenuse
cosine of angle = adjacent / hypotenuse
tangent of angle = opposite / adjacent
```

Radian/degree conversion:

```
radians = degrees * Math.PI / 180
degrees = radians * 180 / Math.PI
```

Rotating to the mouse (or any point):

```
// substitute _xmouse, _ymouse with the x, y point to rotate to
var dx = _xmouse - movieclip._x;
var dy = _ymouse - movieclip._y;
movieclip._rotation = Math.atan2(dy, dx) * 180 / Math.PI;
```

Waves:

```
// assign value to _x, _y or other property of movie clip,
// use as drawing coordinates, etc.
// note: angle does not have to be zero,
// but must be defined as something prior to adding speed
angle = 0;
```

```
onEnterFrame = function(){
   value = center + Math.sin(angle) * range;
   angle += speed;
}
```

Circles:

```
// assign position to _x and _y of movie clip,
// use as drawing coordinates, etc.
onEnterFrame = function(){
   xposition = centerX + Math.cos(angle) * radius;
   yposition = centerY + Math.sin(angle) * radius;
   angle += speed;
}
```

Ovals:

```
// assign position to _x and _y of movie clip,
// use as drawing coordinates, etc.
onEnterFrame = function(){
   xposition = centerX + Math.cos(angle) * radiusX;
   yposition = centerY + Math.sin(angle) * radiusY;
   angle += speed;
}
```

Distance between two points:

```
// points are x1,y1 and x2,y2
// can be movie clip positions, mouse coordinates, etc.
dx = x2 - x1;
dy = y2 - y1;
dist = Math.sqrt(dx*dx + dy*dy);
```

Chapter 4

Converting hex to decimal:

```
trace(hexValue);
```

Converting decimal to hex:

```
trace(decimalValue.toString(16));
```

Combining component colors:

```
color24 = red << 16 | green << 8 | blue;
```

Extracting component colors:

```
red = color24 >> 16;
green = color24 >> 8 & 0xFF;
blue = color24 & 0xFF;
```

Drawing a curve through a point:

```
// xt, yt is the point you want to draw through
// x0, y0 and x2, y2 are the end points of the curve
x1 = xt * 2 - (x0 + x2) / 2;
y1 = yt * 2 - (y0 + y2) / 2;
moveTo(x0, y0);
curveTo(x1, y1, x2, y2);
```

Chapter 5

Convert angular velocity to x, y velocity:

```
vx = speed * Math.cos(angle);
vy = speed * Math.sin(angle);
```

Convert angular acceleration (any force acting on an object) to x, y acceleration:

```
ax = force * Math.cos(angle);
ay = force * Math.sin(angle);
```

Add acceleration to velocity:

```
vx += ax;
vy += ay;
```

Add velocity to position:

```
movieclip._x += vx;
movieclip._y += vy;
```

Chapter 6

Remove an out-of-bounds object:

```
if(mc._x - mc._width / 2 > right ||
   mc._x + mc._width / 2 < left ||
   mc._y - mc._height / 2 > bottom ||
   mc._y + mc._height / 2 < top)
{
      mc.removeMovieClip();
}
```

Regenerate an out-of-bounds object:

```
if(mc._x - mc._width / 2 > right ||
   mc._x + mc._width / 2 < left ||
   mc._y - mc._height / 2 > bottom ||
   mc._y + mc._height / 2 < top)
{
      // reset mc position and velocity.
}
```

Screen wrapping for an out-of-bounds object:

```
if(mc._x - mc._width / 2 > right)
{
   mc._x = left - mc._width / 2;
}
else if(mc._x + mc._width / 2 < left)
{
   mc._x = right + mc._width / 2;
}
if(mc._y - mc._height / 2 > bottom)
{
   mc._y = top - mc._height / 2;
}
else if(mc._y + mc._height / 2 < top)
{
   mc._y = bottom + mc._height / 2;
}
```

Apply friction (the correct way):

```
speed = Math.sqrt(vx * vx + vy * vy);
angle = Math.atan2(vy, vx);
if(speed > friction)
{
   speed -= friction;
}
else
{
   speed = 0;
}
vx = Math.cos(angle) * speed;
vy = Math.sin(angle) * speed;
```

Apply friction (the easy way):

```
vx *= friction;
vy *= friction;
```

Chapter 8

Simple easing, long form:

```
var dx:Number = targetX - movieclip._x;
var dy:Number = targetY - movieclip._y;
vx = dx * easing;
vy = dy * easing;
movieclip._x += vx;
movieclip._y += vy;
```

Simple easing, abbreviated form:

```
vx = (targetX - movieclip._x) * easing;
vy = (targetY - movieclip._y) * easing;
movieclip._x += vx;
movieclip._y += vy;
```

Simple easing, short form:

```
movieclip._x += (targetX - movieclip._x) * easing;
movieclip._y += (targetY - movieclip._y) * easing;
```

Simple spring, long form:

```
var ax:Number = (targetX - movieclip._x) * spring;
var ay:Number = (targetY - movieclip._y) * spring;
vx += ax;
vy += ay;
vx *= friction;
vy *= friction;
movieclip._x += vx;
movieclip._y += vy;
```

Simple spring, abbreviated form:

```
vx += (targetX - movieclip._x) * spring;
vy += (targetY - movieclip._y) * spring;
vx *= friction;
vy *= friction;
movieclip._x += vx;
movieclip._y += vy;
```

Simple spring, short form:

```
vx += (targetX - movieclip._x) * spring;
vy += (targetY - movieclip._y) * spring;
movieclip._x += (vx *= friction);
movieclip._y += (vy *= friction);
```

Offset spring:

```
var dx:Number = movieclip._x - fixedX;
var dy:Number = movieclip._y - fixedY;
var angle:Number = Math.atan2(dy, dx);
var targetX:Number = fixedX + Math.cos(angle) * springLength;
var targetY:Number = fixedX + Math.sin(angle) * springLength;
// spring to targetX, targetY as above
```

Chapter 9

Distance-based collision detection:

```
// starting with mcA and mcB
var dx:Number = mcB._x - mcA._x;
var dy:Number = mcB._y - mcA._y;
var dist:Number = Math.sqrt(dx*dx+dy*dy);
if(dist < mcA._width / 2 + mcB._width / 2)
{
        // handle collision
}
```

Multiple object collision detection:

```
var numObjects:Number = 10; // for example
for(var i:Number = 0; i<numObjects-1; i++)
{
        // evaluate reference using variable i. For example:
        var objectA = this["object" + i];
        for(var j:Number = i+1; j<numObjects;j++)
        {
                // evaluate reference using j. For example:
                var objectB = this["object" + j];

                // perform collision detection
                // between objectA and objectB
        }
}
```

Chapter 10

Coordinate rotation:

```
x1 = Math.cos(angle) * x - Math.sin(angle) * y;
y1 = Math.cos(angle) * y + Math.sin(angle) * x;
```

Reverse coordinate rotation:

```
x1 = Math.cos(angle) * x + Math.sin(angle) * y;
y1 = Math.cos(angle) * y - Math.sin(angle) * x;
```

Chapter 11

Of course, the big one is the formula for conservation of momentum. In straight mathematical terms:

```
           (m0 - m1) * v0 + 2 * m1 * v1
v0Final = ----------------------------
                   m0 + m1

           (m1 - m0) * v1 + 2 * m0 * v0
v1Final = ----------------------------
                   m0 + m1
```

And in ActionScript, with a shortcut:

```
var vxTotal:Number = vx0 - vx1;
vx0 = ((ball0.mass - ball1.mass) * vx0
      + 2 * ball1.mass * vx1) / (ball0.mass + ball1.mass);
vx1 = vxTotal + vx0;
```

Chapter 12

Basic formula for gravity:

$$force = G * m1 * m2 / distance^2$$

ActionScript-friendly implementation in full:

```
function gravitate(partA:MovieClip, partB:MovieClip):Void
{
      var dx:Number = partB._x - partA._x;
      var dy:Number = partB._y - partA._y;
      var distSQ:Number = dx*dx + dy*dy;
      var dist:Number = Math.sqrt(distSQ);
      var force:Number = partA.mass * partB.mass / distSQ;
      var ax:Number = force * dx / dist;
      var ay:Number = force * dy / dist;
      partA.vx += ax / partA.mass;
      partA.vy += ay / partA.mass;
      partB.vx -= ax / partB.mass;
      partB.vy -= ay / partB.mass;
}
```

Chapter 14

Law of Cosines:

$$a^2 = b^2 + c^2 - 2 * b * c * \cos A$$
$$b^2 = a^2 + c^2 - 2 * a * c * \cos B$$
$$c^2 = a^2 + b^2 - 2 * a * b * \cos C$$

And in ActionScript:

```
A = Math.acos((b * b + c * c - a * a) / (2 * b * c));
B = Math.acos((a * a + c * c - b * b) / (2 * a * c));
C = Math.acos((a * a + b * b - c * c) / (2 * a * b));
```

Chapter 15

Basic perspective:

```
scale = fl / (fl + z);
mc._xscale = mc._yscale = scale * 100;
mc._alpha = scale * 100;      // optional
mc._x = vanishingPointX + x * scale;
mc._y = vanishingPointY + y * scale;
mc.swapDepths(-z);            // optional
```

Coordinate rotation:

```
x1 = cos(angleZ) * x - sin(angleZ) * y;
y1 = cos(angleZ) * y + sin(angleZ) * x;

x1 = cos(angleY) * x - sin(angleY) * z;
z1 = cos(angleY) * z + sin(angleY) * x;

y1 = cos(angleX) * y - sin(angleX) * z;
z1 = cos(angleX) * z + sin(angleX) * y;
```

3D distance:

```
dist = Math.sqrt(dx * dx + dy * dy + dz * dz);
```

};shape.targetHeight = shape._height;
shape.onEnterFrame= function() {
var speed = 5;
this._width += (this.targetWidth - this._width)/speed;
this._height += (this.targetHeight - this._height)/speed;
};

INDEX

Numbers

A

D

E

F

G

H

M

S

T

U

V

W

X

Y

Z